Praise for the previous edition

'This book supports the approaches that the Humanities module advocates in a very accessible way. It gives key messages to the trainees on the importance of considering children's learning as a whole and not in individual boxes. The case studies link the theory and practice together and provide thoughtful reflective experiences for the reader. An excellent book.'
Mrs Marion Hobbs, Edge Hill University

'This book is recommended as essential reading for the module undertaken by our students in year 2. It is clearly written and provides a sound background as well as offering a good range of examples.'
Mr Julian Kranz, Sunderland University

'A timely and eminently readable comprehensive resource for student teachers and practising teachers alike. It explores many practical examples of how to provide cross-curricular learning across a wide age range, effectively supported by clear theoretical underpinning.'
Michael Lansley, Chichester University

'Very useful text with a wide range of practical and well-informed ideas for classroom practice.'
Ms Ingrid Spencer, University of Leicester

'A fantastic overview of cross-curricular approaches to learning – well grounded in theory.'
Miss Elizabeth Taylor, Liverpool John Moores University

SAGE was founded in 1965 by Sara Miller McCune to support the dissemination of usable knowledge by publishing innovative and high-quality research and teaching content. Today, we publish more than 750 journals, including those of more than 300 learned societies, more than 800 new books per year, and a growing range of library products including archives, data, case studies, reports, conference highlights, and video. SAGE remains majority-owned by our founder, and after Sara's lifetime will become owned by a charitable trust that secures our continued independence.

Los Angeles | London | Washington DC | New Delhi | Singapore

CROSS-CURRICULAR LEARNING 3-14

Los Angeles | London | New Delhi
Singapore | Washington DC

SAGE Publications Ltd
1 Oliver's Yard
55 City Road
London EC1Y 1SP

SAGE Publications Inc.
2455 Teller Road
Thousand Oaks, California 91320

SAGE Publications India Pvt Ltd
B 1/I 1 Mohan Cooperative Industrial Area
Mathura Road
New Delhi 110 044

SAGE Publications Asia-Pacific Pte Ltd
3 Church Street
#10-04 Samsung Hub
Singapore 049483

Editor: James Clark
Assistant editor: Rachael Plant
Production editor: Tom Bedford
Copyeditor: Elaine Leek
Proofreader: Caroline Stock
Indexer: Anne Solamito
Marketing manager: Dilhara Attygalle
Cover design: Naomi Robinson
Typeset by: C&M Digitals (P) Ltd, Chennai, India
Printed and bound by
CPI Group (UK) Ltd, Croydon, CR0 4YY

© Jonathan Barnes 2015

First edition published 2007
Reprinted in 2008 and 2009

Second edition published 2011
Reprinted 2011

This third edition published 2015

Library of Congress Control Number: 2014946302

British Library Cataloguing in Publication data

A catalogue record for this book is available from the British Library

ISBN 978-1-4462-9703-2
ISBN 978-1-4462-9704-9 (pbk)

At SAGE we take sustainability seriously. Most of our products are printed in the UK using FSC papers and boards. When we print overseas we ensure sustainable papers are used as measured by the Egmont grading system. We undertake an annual audit to monitor our sustainability.

CROSS-CURRICULAR LEARNING 3-14

JONATHAN BARNES

THIRD
EDITION

Los Angeles | London | New Delhi
Singapore | Washington DC

*'… just help them find where they can be creative
and fulfilment will follow.'*

To Gerry Tewfik who said these words and inspired many of the
principles which underpin this book and to Kay and Bill Barnes, my
parents, to my wife, Cherry, my dear sister, Jane, and Jacob, Esther,
Naomi and Ben who have patiently encouraged me towards clarity of
values and personal creativity.

CONTENTS

About the Author   xi
Preface to the Third Edition   xiii
Acknowledgements   xv

Introduction   1

 1 What Should Schooling in the Twenty-first Century
    Look Like?   19
 2 Cross-Curricular Policy and Practice   49
 3 What Does Good Cross-Curricular Practice Look Like?   84
 4 Social Perspectives on Learning   110
 5 What Does Neuroscience Tell Us About Cross-Curricular
    Learning?   128
 6 Psychology and Cross-Curricular Learning   158
 7 The Pedagogy of Cross-Curricular Learning   184
 8 What Values Should We Apply?   206
 9 What Themes Are Suitable for Cross-Curricular Learning?   228
10 How Can We Assess Cross-Curricular and Creative Learning?   245
11 How Should We Plan for Cross-Curricular Activity?   266
12 Key Issues for Debate   301

References   323
Websites   339
Index   344

ABOUT THE AUTHOR

Jonathan Barnes is senior lecturer in Education at Canterbury Christ Church University. He has lifelong interests in music, geography, history, religion and art. These cross-curricular leanings led him first to teach history and geography and the history of art in two Kent secondary schools in the 1970s, then to become a primary class teacher for most of the 1980s. His passion for relevance and engagement in learning led him to devise a ground-breaking interdisciplinary curriculum based wholly on the school locality in the Kent school of which he was head throughout the 1990s.

Since 2000, as a teacher educator Jonathan has researched links between the 'science of learning', cross-curricular and creative approaches and the well-being of teachers and children. He has taught both children and teachers for extended periods in India, Germany, Kenya and Malaysia, instituting innovative curriculum projects. In the UK he has worked with national organizations such as English Heritage, Engaging Places, the Victoria and Albert and Maritime Museums in London as well as being a popular speaker on creative and cross-curricular approaches to teaching. He brought together his wide and disparate experience in a ground-breaking autobiographical PhD entitled, 'What sustains a life in education?' He continues to be involved in teacher education and research involving the links between Arts and well-being at Canterbury Christ Church's Sidney De Haan Research Centre.

PREFACE TO THE THIRD EDITION

In the year that the second edition of this book was published our youngest son died of leukaemia. He was a sparkling, talented, humorous, friendly and confident individual, happy in his skin. He loved his education. In his primary schooling he identified that music and the piano was what he loved best. His family, friends, teachers and subsequent secondary school hugely encouraged that love. Though he succeeded easily at other subjects, it was music and music-making that really made his eyes light up. By the end of secondary schooling, with three excellent A levels, confidence, energy, loads of friends and the world ahead of him he was accepted at the Royal Academy of Music for piano studies. He finished his first year with a bunch of credits and prizes. He was never able to return.

The profound agony of his loss will never leave us. We, his parents, brother and sisters, have our every thought and action coloured by 2011. So as I re-write this book three years after his death and in the light of major policy changes in education, my personal experience colours every rewritten sentence, every new reference. For Jacob, education was all he had outside of friends, family and music. When I read policy documents about education *preparing* children for university, their role in society, adulthood, their role in the economy or even *for life* – I feel anger. My wife taught children with profound special needs most of her life and many of them only lived long enough to go to school. So our views on the meaning of education have become clear, sharp and less compromising because of an experience we would not wish on anyone, but find we have shared with many.

Education should be about learning *now*. The experience of childhood itself should be a rich, exciting and fulfilling one. The experience of school should be one in which every child finds their passion and is able to choose from a colourful palette of different ways of understanding and loving the world. Every child's happiness and well-being should be the *raison d'être* for schooling. Its curriculum and pedagogy should be the vehicles for assuring the child's personal, physical, social, moral and intellectual health. This cannot be assured unless teachers and teaching assistants themselves feel in a similarly high state of well-being.

Well-being *in the present* can become an aim of education. Well-being can be found in activity, through intellectual stimulation in every subject available. It can be discovered in relationships encountered. Well-being should be nurtured by a healthy and sustainable physical environment and found in the clarity of a moral landscape shared. Well-being is created in the discovery of the passions that will make our eyes sparkle for the rest of our lives.

Thankfully most don't die young. An education that pays attention to building a fascinating and stimulating present, however, is the surest way to provoke the motivation and staying power that creates a happy and habitual lifelong learner. For me, that view has not changed in 42 years of teaching, but it now feels a million million times more important.

Jonathan Barnes
September 2014

ACKNOWLEDGEMENTS

There is no doubt that monumental thanks go to my wife, Cherry, who has loved, sustained, inspired and encouraged me throughout a difficult year so crammed with important family events that writing a book seemed impossible. Similarly, my children Ben, Naomi, Esther and Jacob have contributed in ways they are not always fully aware of. They have tolerated my divided attention and listened, always with love and patience, to my overexcited conversation on the topics raised in this book.

Many friends and colleagues have been generous with their time and attention. Stephen Scoffham, particularly, has courageously read chapters and generously commented in fine, informed and intelligent detail. But I must also thank Vanessa Young, Linden West, David Wheway, William Stow, Glen Sharp, Jane Stamps (my inspiring sister), Paul Thompson, Ian Shirley, Robert McCrea, Ken and Matt Miles, Andrew Lambirth, Robert Jarvis, Bryan Hawkins, Grenville Hancox, William Stow, Teresa Cremin, Tony Booth and Judy Baker who met my fervour for curriculum reform with enthusiasm and added their own wisdom to my thinking. I owe a great deal to them.

I have attempted not to identify individual schools who have helped, because the messages they give can apply across schools in many different locations and settings. The following schools, without their town or county, will know who they are when I thank them for accommodating me on my research. I admire them all for their immense energy, inspiration and hope: Astor Arts College, Bethersden Primary School, Bodsham C of E Primary School, Brockhill Performing Arts College, Brompton Westbrook School, Goodwill Primary School, Grange Primary School, Hythe Community Infants School, Nightingale Primary School, Ospringe Primary School, St Nicholas School, St Peter's Methodist School, St Stephen's Junior School, The Churchill School, The Coram School, The Priory School, West Rise Junior School and Woolmore Primary School.

Organizations and individuals have also helped in many ways and I have been grateful for moral support and photographic materials from the Scottish Children's Parliament, Room 13, Future Creative, Kent, the HEARTS project, Siemens, Canterbury Christ Church University, Jane Heyes, Tony Ling, Dorothee Thyssen and Priory Sue.

Finally, I thank SAGE Publications for their patient and wise editorial and organizational support.

Publisher's Acknowledgements

SAGE would like to thank the following people whose reviews of the book helped to shape the new edition:

Anthony Barlow, University of Roehampton

Marion Hobbs, Edge Hill University

Dennis Howlett, University of Cumbria

Kate Hudson, University of Bedfordshire

Louise Wormwell, Newman University

INTRODUCTION

Curriculum freedom is high on the political agenda. I write this book to make a twenty-first-century case for placing cross-curricular experience at the heart of the school curriculum. It attempts to steer a path between the heavy emphasis on separate 'core' and 'foundation' subject disciplines which has characterized primary and secondary education since 1990 and the over-generalizing and usually adult-led tendencies of 1970s-style 'topic work'. The book is intended for head teachers and coordinating teachers planning a securely based, cross-curricular approach to children's learning, teacher education students, educationalists and education tutors. It is also for policy-makers wishing to understand the research behind the 'child-centred' and 'progressive' methods that are so often maligned in press and public statements. I offer a guiding rationale for cross-curricular teaching and learning, practical suggestions, planning formats, carefully chosen case studies, research evidence and issues for debate.

Innocence and experience

And Priests in black gowns, were walking their rounds,

And binding with briars, my joys and desires. (Blake, 1789 [1967])

Our experience of the world is cross-curricular. Everything that surrounds us in the physical world can be seen and understood from multiple perspectives. As adults we tend to perceive each aspect of the perceptible and imagined universe from a variety of more or less 'experienced' viewpoints. The 'innocent' eyes of the child have probably always seen a different world to that of their parents and elders. When, as experienced adults, we look at the tree or bramble outside our window, depending on our education and experience we will each 'see' it in slightly different ways; we may 'know' something of its biology or its geographical implications – the part it plays in reducing the impact of pollution or releasing oxygen. We may, like Blake, think of the poetic or symbolic resonances of our bramble, its potential as an art object or the way it enhances or spoils a view. Perhaps a child is more likely to know the same tree as a quiet place for talking, a hiding place, a threat, a magical mine of fascinating moving things, a den, magic or just one side of a goal. Perhaps the bramble will represent an uncomfortable memory of scratches, a threat or a source of tasty blackberries – the possible associations are endless.

Children may need liberating from an adult-dominated curriculum. Perhaps a 'relentless focus on the basics' (Gov.UK, 2010a, website) is not the best way to include and enthuse all children in the aim to build a learning society. One of the threads that bind this book will be the suggestion that it is important for the child to enjoy being a child, to enjoy learning *now* for its own sake and not primarily for some future role they may or may not take on in the adult world. This emphasis on the child's 'here' and 'now' will involve the examination of various research and curricular attempts to discover what is important to children in today's school classes. The concentration on making connections between curriculum and children's lives will result in considering how we as teachers might help to use children's distinctly different viewpoints, as motivation, method and model for their learning. It seems from all we know about children learning, that motivation, self-esteem, personal relevance, authentic challenge and a sense of achievement are all crucial. So too is *time* to reflect and dream, time to finish what seems important and time to choose. Current research on emotional well-being and children strongly suggests that inner feelings of personal happiness including a sense of control over aspects of life, is not just a key motivator for now, but also central to future good health and security. Enjoying that same sense of well-being is just as important for their teachers and needs to be addressed centrally in staff development practices and teacher education. What experiences, attitudes and resources can we weave into our curricula that make the generation of positive feelings more likely for each child and teacher?

Research

This book is underpinned by a range of research projects involving teachers, student teachers and children aged 3–14. My own research was conducted in six recent projects:

- the Higher Education Arts and Schools (HEARTS) projects funded jointly by the Esmee Fairbairne Trust and the Gulbenkian Foundation (Barnes and Shirley, 2005, 2007)
- the Creative Teaching for Tomorrow (CTFT) project funded by Creative Partnerships and Future Creative (Cremin et al., 2009)
- the TRACK project, where primary school children tracked the development of creativity within their own schools (Powell and Barnes, 2008)
- a series of observations in case study schools between July 2005 and May 2014, followed up by email and telephone interviews with key members of staff
- two research studies on arts and children's well-being (Barnes, 2013b, 2014a, 2014b)
- my own PhD thesis on values and resilience in successful teachers (Barnes, 2013a, 2013b).

In addition to this empirically grounded work which I draw upon throughout the text, I include themed reviews of recent research by others, from which I draw tentative conclusions relevant to the classroom. The research has employed mixed methods, in particular interviews, observations and field notes, and *autoethnography* – thinking about the influence of my own history and character in the development of the values and educational practice I propose.

Interviews

I interviewed school heads and/or heads of curriculum in six of the case study schools about their views on curricula in general and their own school curriculum in detail. In each semi-structured interview, I asked about principles, views on creativity, cross-curricular links and the organization of principles into a curriculum. I also held a series of group interviews with children engaged in cross-curricular activity. Some children were given cameras, and in two cases a video, to capture key moments in their work at school. These images were used to guide conversations that were recorded and transcribed. I also made dated research notes on informal interviews or informal comments from children whilst engaged in cross-curricular activities in school. I interviewed teachers in 10 different schools, teaching 3–14-year-olds in cross-curricular settings. Some of these interviews were fully transcribed and analysed as part of a research study for Future Creative, Kent (Cremin et al., 2009) and in field notes in my research journal. These schools are acknowledged at the beginning of this book.

Many interviews were followed up with email conversations and enquiries, which also formed part of the evidence base for this book.

Observations

I have had the privilege of observing many lessons in many different indoor and outdoor settings (Barnes, 1994, 2014a, 2014b; Barnes and Hancox, 2004; Dismore et al., 2008; Engaging Places website, 2009; Powell and Barnes, 2008). Observations were, with permission, supplemented by photographs, many of which you will see in the text. Notes taken in observations were again analysed for themes and salient examples, which illustrated theoretical positions.

Autoethnography

The interpretations and viewpoints taken are my own. I come from a particular and unique history, like all of us. Take, for example, one moment in my life:

> I am in St Paul's Cathedral, an 11-year-old school choirboy temporarily covering the services for the 'real' choir. Standing at the foot of the odd and fascinating monument to John Donne, I am waiting to process into the choir of the vast cathedral. The light is streaming in through gold-coloured windows to my right and the overpowering organ music of Olivier Messiaen is crashing and echoing around the colourfully mosaic-ed walls. I am fully aware and proud that minutes later I am to be altering the environment by my sounds and my presence in a daily ceremony once central to my culture.

The experience of joy was so positive, affirming, overpowering, almost transcendental that I have struggled ever since to re-create it in other forms for myself and the children I work with. That moment and many others profoundly influenced my attitude to the combining of subjects in interpreting experience.

Equally powerful was my experience 40 years later as a head teacher:

> I am in a meeting with a school inspector who tells me that our creative and cross-curricular ideas are 'too risky' and I should only consider continuing them after the Standard Assessment Tests (SATs) results have achieved well above the expectations for our particular school. This painful and unnerving experience galvanized me to action. I decided I was in the wrong job and moved to teacher education.

I cannot fail to keep both (and many, many more) stories in mind as I examine the curricula of schools, and read prospectuses, learned papers and government proposals. The stories in my life profoundly influence the views I take. The views I take have been shaped by the very mind that holds those views. My mind is also part of a culture, indeed many cultures, part of a profession and part of a team of professionals and friends who deeply impact upon my thinking. In writing several versions of my own autobiography for my doctoral thesis, I have become very aware of such layers of influence. Reflexive study has shown that this book is an attempt to make sense of the aspects of my own life that might have a bearing on the curriculum. In research terms, therefore, I have used my fully written-out autobiographies as a further source of research data. These data have been used to maintain an awareness of the sources of my assumptions and sometimes to challenge or seek corroboration of them.

The chapters

Chapter 1 briefly explores some relevant aspects of the twenty-first-century world into which our children have been born. These aspects are highly selective, but chosen because of their implications for education and, particularly, potential plans for the curriculum that children will follow. There can be no escape from the fact that, currently, adults make the decisions, produce the plans and control the direction of learning. That this is as things should be does not seem unreasonable. The experienced adult perhaps might have the advantage of a wiser, longer and wider perspective. But the second thread running through this book is the proposition that adults in school should be easy with a more complex set of roles than simply planner, imparter and assessor of knowledge and 'standards'. Perhaps a key distinction between a trainer and a teacher is that the teacher allows space for individual learners to be different from one another; indeed, such individual differences could be seen as the chief resource of the teacher. There may be times when power relationships in a class are more appropriately shifted towards the children. In a cross-curricular setting, conscious of the child's cultural, spiritual, social, physical, personal and intellectual needs, the teacher may at different times be follower, co-learner, instructor, coach, observer, adviser, assistant, mentor, conscience, Master of Ceremonies (MC), servant or inspiration.

Chapter 2 discusses recent education policy with regard to cross-curricular and creative learning. Chapter 3 examines a fairly detailed set of case studies in ordinary schools, which show some of the variety and range of cross-curricular approaches. Chapters 4, 5, 6 and 7 consider the classroom implications of social, neuroscientific, psychological and pedagogical research.

The remainder of the book is devoted to practical guides on implementing a cross-curriculum in your school. The issue of the role of the individual subject disciplines must be discussed, however, before we begin to address the idea of teaching across them.

Discipline or not?

Howard Gardner, educationalist, psychologist and neurologist, and argued by some to be amongst the most influential of Western thinkers on education, once argued that the 'scholarly disciplines' were the most significant invention of the last two millennia. The subject disciplines represent for Gardner, 'the most advanced and best ways to think about issues consequential to human beings' (Gardner, 2004: 138). Yet it is clear from other areas of his writing and research that he also believes 'any topic of significance can, and should, be represented in a number of different ways in the mind' (Gardner, 2004: 141). Gardner, like Hirsch, his critic (Hirsch, 1999, 2007), is a great defender of subject skills and subject knowledge but sees twenty-first-century education as providing 'the basis for enhanced understanding of our several worlds – the physical world, the biological world, the world of human beings, the world of human artefacts and the world of the self' (Gardner, 1999b: 158). He follows this by a revealing statement about the relative importance of disciplined knowledge and skills:

> the acquisition of literacy, the learning of basic facts, the cultivation of basic skills, or the mastery of the ways of thinking of the disciplines ... should be seen as means, not ends in themselves ... literacies, skills and disciplines ought to be pursued as tools that allow us to enhance our understanding of important questions, topics and themes. (Gardner, 1999b: 159)

British writers (for example, Alexander, 2010; Lucas et al., 2013; Robinson, 2001; Robinson and Aronica, 2010; Wrigley et al., 2012) argue with equal passion for the breakdown of subject boundaries. Some argue for a competencies-based curriculum to 'open minds' (RSA Opening Minds Curriculum, website), some the development of a curriculum that engenders 'a creative and critical orientation towards experience' (Abbs, 2003: 15), a curriculum that makes sense to pupils rather than teachers (Halpin, 2003: 113), more opportunities for play (Goouch and Powell, 2013), less curricular prescription (Alexander, 2010), a stronger values base (Booth and Ainscow, 2011) or an emotionally literate curriculum (Morris and Scott, 2002). The sum of educational advice grows daily.

There are principles, however, which may well reach beyond specific cultural and institutional contexts, and these are examined in Chapter 8. There is no shortage of educational research and general advice on how to enhance the learning experience of a child, but few publications offer usable models within which the ideals of cross-curricular and creative learning may be realized in practice. This book hopes to address such a need in Chapters 9, 10 and 11.

Organization

You will read here an argument for a balance between the unique skills, knowledge and attitudes of each 'traditional' subject and the uniquely motivating effects of cross-curricular and child-centred learning. This book is written now because with new primary and secondary national curricula and many new self-governing schools, free schools and academies there is a massive opportunity to rethink the curriculum. The rapidly growing interest in thematic and cross-curricular approaches in primary schools has spread increasingly to Year 7 and 8 classes in secondary school. This interest was growing before the publication of the abandoned reports on primary and secondary education by Sir Jim Rose (2008, 2009), but more sustainably in the ongoing influence of Robin Alexander's Cambridge Primary Review (Alexander, 2010; CPR, 2014). A practical guide for the leaders of academies and academy chains, schools consortia, education, training and teacher development organizations, teachers in service and student teachers seems necessary because of concerns that guiding principles should be debated and established and direct guidance offered. I believe that the curriculum should be packed with opportunities for each child to find his or her strengths and activities which provide genuine challenge and multiple prospects for individual achievement. It is hoped that you will find workable examples of how such activities and experiences can be successfully planned and delivered.

The book is divided into chapters with clear foci. You do not have to read the chapters in any particular sequence, but can read them in order of their relevance to you. Each chapter is headed by a question or broadly descriptive title that indicates the theme:

Chapter 1: What should schooling in the twenty-first century look like?
Chapter 2: Cross-curricular policy and practice
Chapter 3: What does good cross-curricular practice look like?

Chapter 4: Social perspectives on learning
Chapter 5: What does neuroscience tell us about cross-curricular learning?
Chapter 6: Psychology and cross-curricular learning
Chapter 7: The pedagogy of cross-curricular learning
Chapter 8: What values should we apply?
Chapter 9: What themes are suitable for cross-curricular learning?
Chapter 10: How can we assess cross-curricular and creative learning?
Chapter 11: How should we plan for cross-curricular activity?
Chapter 12: Key issues for debate

There are summaries at the beginning and end of each chapter. Key questions continue the debate at the end of each chapter and there are full lists of references and websites at the end of the book.

You may already have noticed that this book is well illustrated. Most illustrations come from the schools consulted and researched in writing this book. If information, principles, examples and issues are shown visually as well as in text, a different, perhaps deeper and more personal, level of understanding may be gained. There seems little doubt that visual images form an increasingly important part in the world of communication and knowledge, and every advertiser knows that images and objects have a powerful effect upon our minds and imaginations. I argue that we also learn through the feelings and associations that images generate in us. I believe we vastly underestimate the power of the visual in our teaching and learning. By more fully exploiting our species' ability to make fine and wide-ranging visual discriminations, we access areas of knowing beyond words. Each chapter is therefore illustrated with examples of children's work and children working in a variety of contexts. Photographs and diagrams are used as models too, but names of individuals are changed and schools are identified only by their region.

Definitions

It is fairly easy to define the unique qualities of each National Curriculum subject; the National Curriculum document (DfEE/QCA, 1999) provides a clear lead on this for each of the nine subjects of the curriculum, Information and Communications Technology, and (later) Citizenship, Personal, Social and Health Education and Modern Foreign Languages. The various Special Advisory Councils on Religious Education in Schools (SACREs) in each education authority have made their own definitions of Religious Education. However, definitions of the terminology used in discussions on cross-curricular approaches are often vague and used interchangeably. In this book, the following definitions apply.

The curriculum

The narrow definition is the subjects, topics and emphases chosen (usually by adults) to be the focus of learning in a school. In the context of this book, however, a broader definition, which also includes the 'hidden curriculum' of attitudes, assumptions, environments, relationships and school ethos, is used.

A discipline

The generally accepted skills, knowledge, language and attitudes that characterize a traditional area of learning within a culture. A discipline differs from a subject in that the term 'subject' is generally confined to the knowledge belonging to a particular area of learning. The word discipline or subject-discipline suggests something more demanding – the 'rules', skills, thought processes, values and typical activities that distinguish one domain of learning from another. A discipline is both a broader and more active concept than a subject. Disciplinary learning concentrates upon aspects that are applied in the real world, often in combination with other disciplines. Each discipline is presided over by past luminaries and 'policed' by a field of experts, located in 'subject associations', academies, universities or colleges who judge where the discipline is moving and what constitutes knowledge and standards within it.

For progress within a discipline, traditionally creative advances have needed to be accepted by what Csikszentmihalyi (1997) calls 'the field', the groups of experts culturally accepted as the gatekeepers of the discipline. In this internet era, exclusive concepts like 'expert' and 'field' are under-challenge, but at present and in education the dominant and conservative view is that there is an established body of knowledge and skills for each discipline and there are arbiters of good practice within them. Disciplinary understanding is shown when students are able to use the knowledge and 'ways of thinking of a particular subject discipline, appropriately in novel situations' (Boix-Mansilla et al., 2000).

Various subject associations fight tirelessly and effectively for the maintenance of a disciplinary approach to teaching and learning in both secondary and primary schooling. The current emphasis on clear objectives and the carefully planned progression of skills and knowledge in the disciplines, championed by the subject associations, has significantly contributed to best teaching and learning in schools.

Meaningful experiences

A meaningful, or what some schools call a 'wow', experience (Ofsted, 2010a) is an encounter that emotionally engages and drives a child or children to want to understand and know more. This kind of experience is highly motivating for the recipient. A meaningful experience does not need to be a high-profile event, resource-heavy and weeks in the planning. Effective single-subject teachers daily utilize a wide variety of engaging techniques to motivate, enhance, illustrate and summarize learning. Some of these experiences are so powerful that for a time they fully engage the whole class – they are clearly meaningful. A meaningful experience is simply one that grasps learners' attention at emotional, physical, sensory, social and/or intellectual levels. A story well read, an interesting visitor from the community, a visit to the school pond or the high street may be made personally meaningful, usually by fully engaging for a while the emotions or the senses.

Teaching

Teaching is the transmission of knowledge, skills and understandings from one source to another. In schools, we imagine that most teaching is done by teachers and other adults, though closer examination might show that sources like technology, environments, peers, accidental experience and personal interests teach as much. Those influencing teacher education (Abbs, 2003; Arthur and Cremin, 2010; Halpin, 2003; Lucas et al., 2013; Pollard, 2008; Wrigley et al., 2012) frequently remind us that didactic teaching does not automatically result in learning. Children have to 'agree' to enter into the learning their teacher wants them to achieve and therefore much teaching must involve motivating the child to want to learn.

Thinking

Thinking is the mental representation of ideas. Good thinking can be considered as the process in which people are mentally engaged in attempts to solve a difficult or challenging task and which results in improvement in a person's intellectual power (Shayer and Adey, 2002).

Learning

Learning is the mental and physical internalization of knowledge, skills, language and attitudes. These learned features may then be transferred and used in new contexts and combined with others to solve problems and understand issues. The learning of many life skills may not be related to any discipline, but be part of growing up into a particular set of cultures and communities. Learning arises, perhaps chiefly, from the everyday accidents and incidents of life, but schools specialize in passing on the learning of past generations in a planned and disciplined way. I have proposed that the real world is best understood through the lenses of a number of disciplines and that cross-curricular learning should be a significant part of the curriculum of every school, but there are several different ways of promoting learning across the curriculum.

Cross-curricular learning

When the skills, knowledge and attitudes of a number of different disciplines are applied to a single experience, problem, question, theme or idea, we are working in a cross-curricular way. The experience of learning is considered on a macro level and with the *curriculum* as focus.

Topic-based, project or thematic curriculum

These terms are used interchangeably to mean a curriculum where at least part of the week is devoted to the study of a particular theme or topic (like water, our school/village/community/marsh/forest/beach, 'beauty', India or the microscopic life in the school pond) through the eyes of several curriculum subjects. The *stimulus* becomes the focus for learning.

Creativity

The ability in all humans imaginatively or practically to connect two or more ideas together to make a valued new idea.

Creative teaching

Teaching that uses the teacher's own inherent and learned creativity to make learning accessible.

Teaching for creativity

The intention of the teacher is to stimulate and develop the creativity inherent in every child in any subject or experiential context.

Assumptions

It is impossible to write a book on aspects of the school curriculum without making many assumptions. You will become aware of many as you read this book and should apply a critical mind to them. Certain assumptions must be brought into the open from the outset, however. The previous definitions make it clear that, along with many other educationalists, I believe *all children and teachers are potentially creative in some aspect* (see Barnes, 2010, 2013a, 2013b; Craft, 2000, 2005; Craft et al., 2008; Csikszentmihalyi, 1997; Perkins, 1992; Sternberg, 1997b, 2008). This is an important assumption because cross-curricular work is often seen as a way of stimulating and nurturing creative thinking. I also believe that *creativity is best stimulated in cross-curricular and authentic contexts.*

It is assumed that *generating thinking is an important role of education.* Professor David Perkins summarized 20 years of research into children's learning in the following memorable phrase: 'Learning is a consequence of thinking' (Perkins, 1992: 34). Although this statement can sound blindingly obvious, when reflected upon in the light of much current practice, it provokes a number of key questions: do schools generally put children's *thinking* at the centre of the learning experience? Is there a difference between politely sitting, listening and following instructions (or not!) and thinking? Are trainee teachers taught to generate thinking in their classes or to pass on a body of knowledge and skills?

This book also assumes that *intelligence is not a single and measurable entity*, that in different times, cultures and settings different behaviours seem to be intelligent. Each psychologist and educationalist will have a slightly or dramatically varying view of intelligence, but few today hold the early twentieth-century view that it is something measured in intelligence tests alone. However we see intelligence – a combined working of several mental processors, our intellectual faculties, our natural mental and physical dispositions, a combination of memory, inherited 'g' factor and individualized creative, practical and analytical strengths – it is only a meaningful concept when it is applied in a relevant cultural setting. We use it when we attend, engage, think or act.

It is assumed that *not all children respond positively to the same style of teaching or the same stimulus*; it is therefore understood that cross-curricular approaches will not suit all children. The good teacher hopes to engage all children, but in Sternberg's words, 'he or she needs the flexibility to teach to different styles of thinking, which means varying teaching style to suit different styles of [student] thought' (Sternberg, 1997a: 115). Engagement *may*, for some individuals, be gained in setting up periods of solitary, academic, convergent and purely cerebral activity, but experience and research (Abbs, 2003; Bandura, 1994; Barnes and Shirley, 2007; Csikszentmihalyi, 2002; Lucas et al., 2013) suggest it comes more often from a mix of social, practical, personally relevant and creative activity.

The final assumption is more contentious – it is that *education is at least partly about helping children appreciate, enjoy and understand their lives and worlds now*. Geographer Simon Catling has written persuasively of the 'marginalization' of children in both their school environments and their neighbourhoods, and he sees a 'discontinuity between their real lives and the school curriculum' (Catling, 2005: 325). A child's world is clearly very different from an adult's. A Western child's world, which might well include an *iPod*, *Raspberry Pi*, which allows children to make their own computer, 'blue tooth' connections, satellite television, the internet, video and computer games, social networking sites, mobile phones and digital versatile discs (DVDs), is technologically and geographically more sophisticated than that of many adults that surround them. There are other worlds of the child too: of play, fantasy, playground morality, safe and unsafe places, people or products, unarticulated barriers, taboos, fashion, fast food, loud music, cheap drugs and earlier sexual maturity. These worlds are little seen or understood by many of the adults surrounding them. Indeed, such worlds of children may not even be acknowledged in some primary classrooms. This book is written to suggest ways in which adults can adjust the curriculum so that children's worlds are represented and widened, and their views, concerns and interests allowed for, celebrated and developed. It is suggested that a major route towards a more child-centred education is through creative and cross-curricular responses to real experience.

The history

Cross-curricular learning has a long pedigree. Educators since the beginnings of formal education have been conscious that combined perspectives were required in order to understand aspects of the physical, social or personal world. More than two millennia ago, Plato promoted a mix of story, physical education and music in an early version of Personal, Social and Health Education (PSHE) and citizenship. In his curriculum, Plato combined subjects to serve a higher goal than simple disciplinary instruction: 'Anyone who can produce the best blend of the physical and intellectual sides of education and apply them to the training of character is producing harmony in a far more important sense than any mere musician' (Plato, *The Republic*, 1955: 155).

Cross-curricular pedagogies infer a particular set of values and attitudes. These are often liberal, inclusive, constructivist and perhaps more recently also relativist and intercultural. Plato, who despite many elitist and exclusive ideas on education, called it 'the initial acquisition of virtue by the child, when the feelings of pleasure and affection, pain and hatred that well up in his soul are channeled in the right courses before he can understand the reason why' (Plato, *The Laws*, 1970: 653b).

Seventeenth- and eighteenth-century pioneers: nature and meaning

Unlike Plato, the seventeenth-century Czech philosopher Jan Comenius believed that education was for *all* people and that nature was herself the great teacher. Comenius was an early champion of physical and outdoor education, and saw physical education, playing with ideas, artefacts and materials, and learning by easy stages as essential foundations for education. Sometimes known as the 'father of modern education', he was probably the first to illustrate children's textbooks. But his views on internationalism in education, his belief that teachers should understand the developing mind of the child and his insistence on teaching 'with the greatest enjoyment' and *thoroughly*, put him at the forefront of influences on modern educational thought in Europe. His eloquent and humane approach to learning is captured by the following paragraph from his book *The Great Didactic*, published in 1649:

> The proper education of the young does not consist in stuffing their heads with a mass of words, sentences, and ideas dragged together out of various authors, but in opening up their understanding to the outer world, so that a living stream may flow from their own minds, just as leaves, flowers, and fruit spring from the bud on a tree. (Comenius, 1967: 82)

Jean Jacques Rousseau (1712–78) was also deeply inspired by the natural world. The eighteenth-century 'Enlightenment' brought forth, and to an extent rested upon, powerful and romantic philosophies like his. Rousseau was a believer in the inborn good of humanity and was the originator of the idea of 'the noble savage'. Typical of the intellectuals and artists of his time, he was awed and fascinated by nature. He believed that education was needed in order to learn how to live and that the best learning was accomplished very near to the natural world. Rousseau felt that experience was the starting point for learning. He used very physical and sensory images throughout his writing: for example, the metaphor of education as plunging into the cold waters of the Styx, or feeling the warts on the back of the toad to illustrate natural learning. He saw education as a meeting of the natural, the practical and the cultural; as he put it in his education treatise *Émile ou de l'éducation*, of 1762:

> This education comes from nature, from men or from things. The inner growth of our organs and faculties is the education of nature, the use we learn to make of our growth is the education of men, what we gain by our experience of our surroundings is the education of things. (Rousseau, 1762, website)

> We are each taught by three masters. If their teaching conflicts, the scholar is ill-educated and will never be at peace with himself; if their teaching agrees, he goes straight to his goal, he lives at peace with himself, he is well educated. (1762, website)

First by using the senses, then by making and using artefacts and, finally, by seeking truth in arts, science and religion, Rousseau expressed a progression which was much later taken up by Piaget. But he also had strong views about the adult domination of the curriculum: 'We never know how to put ourselves in the place of children; we do not enter into their ideas; we lend them ours, and, always following our own reasonings, with chains of truths we heap up only follies and error in their heads' (1762, website).

Comenius and Rousseau among many thinkers of the seventeenth and eighteenth centuries suggested that education was lifelong, aligned with nature and, by implication, cross-curricular because it relied upon helping the child interpret and understand their day-to-day *experience* of the world. They argued that children should be allowed to be children before they were 'men' and accepted philosopher Locke's view that children were rational beings. Such thoughts on the meaning and purpose of education still underpin many of the arguments of those who defend cross-curricular, experiential and child-centred approaches to learning.

Nineteenth-century pedagogues: play, purpose and perfection

As formal and eventually state-run education developed throughout the Western world in the nineteenth century, Rousseau's educational philosophies were added to by thinkers and teachers such as Johann Pestalozzi (1746–1827) and Friedrich Froebel (1782–1852). Pestalozzi wanted children to learn through activity and arrive at their own answers. The personality was all important and each child needed to be taught with love in the context of direct concrete experience and observation. Froebel's major contribution was the foundation of the 'kindergarten' and his powerful arguments for the importance of play. These early nineteenth-century progressives advocated primary education through practical activity, objects, 'natural' interest and spontaneity. Contemporary traditionalists, on the other hand, encouraged the pragmatic and efficient mass education techniques of textbook and rote learning required by religiously conservative and rapidly industrializing countries. In line with the times, however, even the radical pioneers maintained a religious justification for their ideas:

> I wish to wrest education from the outworn order of doddering old teaching hacks as well as from the new-fangled order of cheap, artificial teaching tricks, and entrust it to the eternal powers of nature herself, to the light which God has kindled and kept alive in the hearts of fathers and mothers, to the interests of parents who desire their children grow up in favour with God and with men. (Pestalozzi, quoted in Silber, 1965: 134)

> The purpose of education is to encourage and guide man as a conscious, thinking and perceiving being in such a way that he becomes a pure and perfect representation of that divine inner law through his own personal choice; education must show him the ways and meanings of attaining that goal. (Froebel, 1826: 2)

Twentieth-century child-centred education

Much modern education theory is still underpinned by the work of Jean Piaget. He and his followers suggested, from the 1920s, that humans go through distinct stages of learning (Piaget, 1954). Passing through periods of sensory-motor exercise and reflex actions, to exploratory activity consisting of either pre-conceptual or intuitive experimentation with tangible things, humans finally arrive at a state of 'formal operations', which relies upon reason, imagination and abstract thinking. At each stage, the child is said to be learning through *accommodation* and *assimilation* – essentially through making and understanding errors. Piaget likened the developing child to a scientist constantly making, testing and revising hypotheses. Piaget's theories still underpin much of our educational and curriculum decision making, though many have recognized that the developmental stages he described need not be tightly ascribed to particular ages but apparently need to be passed through in sequence at *any* age if a new concept is to be fully learned.

Lev Vygotsky's (1962, 1978) and, later, Jerome Bruner's work on the centrality of social intercourse in helping children make sense of the world has also had profound impacts upon schools and curricular organization (Bruner, 1968, 1996). Under their influence, many school sessions have introduced forms of 'scaffolded learning', where 'more knowledgeable others' support the concept formation of the rest. Learning is seen by these psychologists as primarily a social activity: 'making sense is a social process; it is an activity that is always situated in a cultural and historical context' (Bruner and Haste, 1987: 4).

The current context

It has become almost a truism of educational criticism that in these times of perhaps unprecedented change we need to develop a flexible and learning society. The lifelong learning lobby is well accepted and strong, and organizations such as the Campaign for Learning (website) have much support from a broad spectrum including education, politics and industry. However, *what* is to be learned is very much more debatable. Homespun American philosopher Eric Hoffer noted in the middle of the twentieth century that current education may not be relevant: *'In times of change learners inherit the earth, while the learned find themselves beautifully equipped to deal with a world that no longer exists'* (Hoffer, website). But late in the same century, some of Britain's educated elite applauded heartily when Sir Roy Strong argued for a distinctly narrow and culturally exclusive definition of the curriculum:

> It is more important for a young person to be made to wonder at the architecture of something like the Palace of Versailles or glimpse what underlies … a single scene in a Mozart opera than to paint another bad picture or bang a drum in the false interests of self expression. (SCAA, 1997)

This debate rumbles on against a background of massive social, political and technological change, as you will read in Chapters 1 and 2, but it is an essential debate. What we teach, what we require children to know and understand, will without doubt significantly change the minds of the generations that will shape the twenty-first century.

How we teach is equally important. Governments have became newly concerned with individual well-being, partly as a result of alarming statistics on depression (Children's Society, 2014, website; Layard, 2006; Layard and Dunn, 2009; UNICEF, 2013, website; WHO, 2012, website). The new interest in well-being has sparked a number of initiatives directed at a more holistic view of health. Education is now seen to play a key role in the physical and mental health of children and the curricular implications are wide.

The curriculum in today's schools is increasingly complex. It is set to become more diverse and less centralized. Those responsible for schools have to respond to concerns about falling standards in 'basic' as well as 'general' knowledge. Teachers feel they should address public and political perceptions of declines in behaviour and morality. At the same time, parents have become empowered to demand individualized solutions for the barriers their children face. Yet schools often feel starved of the resources, training, support and recognition that would help them meet such demands. As governments have increasingly involved themselves in the minutiae of educational practice, they have been expected to provide general solutions to these challenges – Chapters 2 and 3 discuss the progress of government intervention as well as providing guidance for those in academies and 'free schools' seeking curricular freedom.

CHAPTER 1

WHAT SHOULD SCHOOLING IN THE TWENTY-FIRST CENTURY LOOK LIKE?

Chapter aims

This chapter will discuss global, technological, social, economic and personal change and reflect upon some implications for schools and schooling. It suggests that children's development, priorities and rights should be taken seriously in any decisions about the curriculum. The chapter also shows how the issues relevant to children are cross-curricular in nature. By the end of this chapter you will have been introduced to the values that underpin this book under the following headings:

- education about and for the future
- learning that maximizes children's interest in technologies
- a curriculum that recognizes global inter-relationships
- a curriculum that recognizes the importance of personal relationships
- a curriculum to support the development of character and positive identity.

What you think a school should be like depends on the values you hold. What a school *is* like results from the values of those who dominate it. Values – the fundamental beliefs that guide all levels of action – are particularly reflected in the curriculum a school offers. *Curriculum*, as used throughout this book, is defined broadly to include not just the subjects taught, but also the choices made within those subjects, the styles and means chosen to teach them, the activities, attitudes, environments, relationships and beliefs that pervade a school. Successful school communities work hard to clarify their fundamental beliefs before considering their curriculum. This book explores cross-curricular and creative developments in primary and secondary curricula because of my experience that connection-making and creativity are essential to a morally and intellectually good education.

We are constantly reminded of the unprecedented rates of change we experience as we travel through the twenty-first century (for example, Greenfield, 2010; Robinson and Aronica, 2010; Hicks, 2014). Illustrations of the exponential growth of knowledge, the development of technology, nanotechnology, micro-biology, robotics, artificial intelligence and the rest, pepper most writing and thinking about the future. This is not the place to comment on predictions, but it is safe to say that the world the children of today will inherit will be very, very different from our present one. Our children will have to face the results of climate change, rising sea levels, pandemics, human cloning, increased population pressures, global terrorism, economic instability and rapidly changing job markets. Forecasters predict water, oil and food shortages, mass migrations and ensuing warfare. Taking a more optimistic view, whilst climate change is inevitable our children may witness more concerted international cooperation to address it. They may also experience just government, longer, healthier lives, a more equitable sharing of the earth's resources and the global development of sciences and technologies to address new and old challenges. Either way, today's children live in times of rapid and global

Illustration 1.1   Teachers can have a major influence on children's futures. School children from a village in south India

transformation that will quite literally change human minds and societies. The well-being of a significant minority in the UK and US seems to be in decline. Since 2009, measures of well-being measured by the Children's Society have fallen steadily so that in its latest report some 20% of children aged 8–15 describe their well-being as below the mid-point of two standardized scales and 10% place themselves as 'low' (Children's Society, 2014, website). What curriculum can do to address the uncertainties and unhappinesses of children is the subject of this book. How we can empower children with values, hope, meaning and confidence in addition to knowledge, are the underlying themes.

Preparing for an uncertain future

The future has always been uncertain. Rapid advances in technology and global communications have made us hyper-sensitive to the speed and unpredictability of change. The education we currently offer our children may not be good enough to help them thrive in, and live fulfilling lives through the twenty-first century (see Beetham and Sharpe, 2013). Aside from Computing, Modern Foreign Languages (MFL), Citizenship and PSHE, the 2014 National Curriculum for England (DfE, 2013a) contains the same subject requirements as an early twentieth-century primary school. By contrast, the curricula of Scotland and Northern Ireland, the abandoned Rose recommendations (2009) and the Cambridge Primary Review (Alexander, 2010) all claim that cross-curricular themes or groupings more properly address our changing times and uncertain future. Whilst legislating for increased emphasis on separate subjects and a stronger focus on English, Mathematics and Science for English local authority schools, the coalition government of 2010 stressed that a percentage of curriculum time (up to 30%) could be seen as the 'school curriculum'. Academies, free schools and independent schools are given more freedom to decide on their curricula though inspection and the continued use of 'league tables' will ensure that subjects are not treated equally.

Schools are guided towards making more partnerships with the community. As schools and their communities become more involved with each other, the issues and concerns that dominate lived experience should be reflected in the curricula and pedagogies they develop. To be understood fully each question or problem inevitably requires insights and skills of several subject disciplines. As education becomes less centralized and teacher education more centred on schools via Schools Direct, Teaching Schools and Teach First, teachers at the chalkface will need more guidance on how to link subject learning authentically to the real world.

Meaningful and effective schooling outlives temporary curriculum change. Successful teachers have always been able to make restrictive curricula relevant to children. Schools have, for example, taken the opportunity offered by Citizenship and PSHE to propose curricula that address the personal, local (and now global) futures that young people have always cared about (Alexander, 2010; Alexander and Potter, 2005; Hicks, 2014; Layard and Dunn, 2009; Ofsted, 2010b). Those interested in 'futures education' (the study of views about probable, possible and preferable futures) have championed curricula aimed at helping children think more critically and creatively about the future (for example, Catling and Willey, 2009; Hicks, 2006; Scoffham, 2010). Motivated by the desire to involve and empower children, schools have championed ecologically, socially or culturally sensitive issues relevant to their communities. Other schools have revitalized the experience of children through working with local arts and creativity organizations or national bodies like: Creative and Cultural Education (CCE), CapeUK, the Royal Society of Arts (RSA) and the Curriculum Foundation (website).

Today's young people differ in some ways from those of the past. Youngsters contemplating the future in this century seem to expect a less utopian prospect than the 'baby boomers' of the 1950s. Research amongst children in the USA, UK, Sweden and Canada shows children to be both serious and worried about the future (Catling, 2010). They are pessimistic about societal health, equality, wealth, security, poverty and relationships but, paradoxically, remain generally hopeful about their *own* futures. Children appear to be gloomy about the world's future and especially worried about issues currently headlined in the news. This shift away from perceptions of general optimism of the 1990s (see Bentley, 2006) is evidenced as public policy is increasingly targeted on well-being, health, sustainability, conservation, safety and security.

Contrary to youthful optimism for their personal future, Hicks (2006) showed that boys' views about the *world's* future tend towards the gender-stereotypically violent and destructive, dominated by wars, terrorism, natural disasters and disease. It seems that girls more often imagine a generalized peaceful and idealistic future, but continue to be worried about disease and pollution. These contrasts may be driven by popular culture as much as genetics.

Economy and culture encourage us to live life in the present. Children and adults alike are aware that today's consumerist public policy will deeply and negatively impact upon our futures but such knowledge scarcely affects our behaviour. Fewer and fewer people vote or play an active role in local or national democracy, yet more know about its importance. Bentley confronts these paradoxes in expressing radical aims for education. He argues:

we are searching for means through which individuals can transform themselves through a process of internal discovery and self-actualization, by participating in the reshaping of the shared context in which they live out their individual lives. (Bentley, 2006)

Confidence and fulfilment are important aims of education. Opportunities for self-actualization (Maslow, 1943) or the development of self-efficacy (Bandura, 1994) seem rare for many children and often peripheral to school decisions. Neither liberation of the unique attributes of every child nor the notion of social intelligence (Gardner, 1993; Goleman, 2006) have been systematically addressed across UK schools. Few schools are as values-driven as Makiguchi's *Soka* schools in Japan, which attempt to live out values like justice, fairness and peacemaking in their curriculum and relationships with the local and world community (Sharma, 2008). Values and purposes evident in education philosophies and aims for millennia, have in many cases been squeezed out of the curriculum. Reference to the twin aims of nurturing individuality and fostering better social and global relationships are therefore important among the themes running through this book.

In addition to their keen interest in aspects of the future, a number of topics have become pressingly relevant to the twenty-first-century child. National and international studies (for example Office for National Statistics, 2012, website; WHO, 2012, website) suggest the following pre-occupations of young people:

- information and communications technology
- global politics/issues
- relationships
- individualism and the sense of self.

These powerfully motivating interests form the starting point of the suggestions about curricula that are the subject of this book.

Harnessing children's interest in information and communications technology

Nowhere are the rapid changes in the developed and developing world more evident than in the area of ICT. Growing numbers of people in all societies have access to powerful and sophisticated technologies that two decades ago were the stuff of science fiction. In 2013, 75% of 5–16-year-old children reported having at least one computer at home

Illustration 1.2 A Year 2 boy's view of the future: guns, army, bang bang, bullets, dried up river, dried up stones

In the USA the figures are higher. Of those children who do not have a home computer, the overwhelming majority are poor, adding further disadvantage in homework and access to knowledge.

Home computers and the internet are heavily used by children aged 9–16. Twice as many boys as girls used the internet to get information in all 35 countries studied by the World Health Organization (WHO, 2012, website). Yet one survey showed that 40% of 15-year-old girls considered the social networking site *Facebook* more important to them than family (Techeye, 2010, website); it was used by 73% of 12–17-year-olds in 2014 (Pew website). The internet has rapidly become a preferred source of

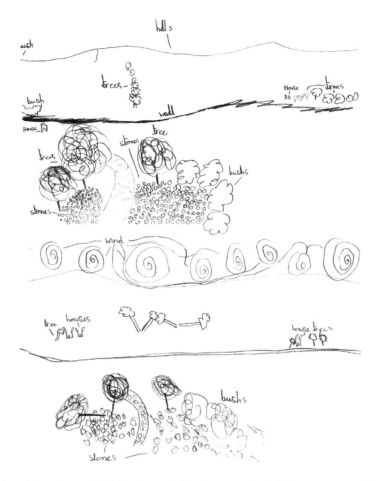

Illustration 1.3   A Year 2 girl's view of the future: wind, fallen trees and bushes, shattered houses

information for the young and e-reading devices owned by about 50% of adults are becoming more frequently used by young people. As parents become increasingly technology-literate themselves they talk to their children more about the dangers of the internet and place privacy controls on their computers. Large numbers of children regularly play internet-based games and use social networking sites to contact and make friends. Increasingly *Pintrest*, *Instagram*, *YouTube* and other special interest facilities are used too. Young people see such technologies as very influential on their lives (BBC News, 2010, website). Some of the worst implications of these easy, anonymous and sometimes unpoliced contacts are well known.

Illustration 1.4   Children gather enthusiastically around a computer in a village school in south India

   Case study 1   A cyberworld fairy story

Year 11 pupils at a Dover school were given a free choice of fairy story to update and perform within a single session. They chose to rewrite *Little Red Riding Hood*. After starting their play at the end, but in the traditional manner with Red Riding Hood quizzing a wolf disguised as grandma about her big teeth and hairy arms, the students did a 'time warp' sequence and the audience was catapulted to the beginning of the story. The scene was the chilling context of a twenty-first-century Red Riding Hood sitting alone at her bedroom computer. She was in an internet chat room talking to a paedophile 'wolf' pretending to be her grandmother. (McCrea, 2005)

Currently around 90% of British children between 11 and 16 (CBBC Newsround, website) have a mobile phone (cell phone). To children, the advantages of mobile phones over other ICT are privacy and control. Children report that for their mobiles, they need no permission, have little supervision and they appreciate the possibilities of constant communication (Childnet International, website). Some estimates suggest teenagers average up to four hours a week text-messaging their friends.

Children today say they like the internet and mobiles because these give them the greatest independence over what they see and find out.

Children like the ways ICT helps them discover and connect to friends, and they appreciate the way it can help them create and communicate visually and in sound; about 90% of those above the age of 12 in the USA have posted their picture on *Facebook* or other social network. Around 40% of 11-year-old and 60% of 13-year-old boys in Britain use the internet or mobiles to communicate with friends *every day* (WHO, 2012, website). Through the internet and mobile technology, children have access to music, sports and world news, advertising and powerful new games; can communicate with television and film stars; vote out an unpopular *Big Brother* resident or catapult an unknown to *X Factor* stardom. Children are also increasingly aware of the dangers of new technologies. Most have dealt with text bullies, unwanted pornography, salespeople and crackpots well before their parents find out about it. Sadly, some do not have the personal resources to cope with such onslaughts and the ghastly results of the abuses of ICT are all too evident from news reports and investigative journalism. There are, however, interesting and positive uses of mobile phone technology which suggest it is a grossly underused feature in our current school curricula.

The monitor screen also continues its major influence on children's lives. About 62% of English children at age 11 watch TV more than 2 hours a day, many of them alone in their bedrooms (Public Health England, 2013, website). In the USA 71% of 8–18-year-olds have a TV in their bedroom (University of Michigan, website). As direct watching decreases, the selection of particular programmes through *iPlayer* and other customer-controlled internet technologies increases. Most estimates place the average US or British child as watching up to 4 hours of television per day – significantly less time than most spend with family. Evidence of large numbers of children alone in their room using televisions, games consoles, computer monitors and videos for more than 28 hours a week conjures up a rather lonely image. Susan Greenfield has suggested we may already have reached the point where, for some families, many of the traditional parental roles – imparting culture, providing a model, resolving conflict, telling stories, sharing knowledge, passing on morals, sayings, advice and wisdom – have been unintentionally delegated to the monitor screen (Greenfield, 2010). Attachment and social health may be affected by this trend.

A Romanian study once attempted to capture the influence of TV. By far, the chief role models of school-aged children were film stars and television personalities (Popenici, 2006). A stirring judgement on our profession was that teachers were amongst the least likely adults to be considered as role models, scoring lower than 'terrorists'. There are reasons

Illustration 1.5   Teacher introducing the video camera to 8-year-olds in a class project on the future of the local school environment

for national variations in such figures but teachers and parents are often less important, in the short term, to children than they think.

Even the subject of children's toys is not without its implications for education. Aside from the plethora of toys linked to video, television and computer game characters, the new generation of interactive cyber toys respond 'intelligently' to particular types of treatment or 'grow' or change with time or display 'real' facial expressions. The toy *RoboSapien* is sold as 'truly a fusion of technology and personality'. Such toys may be argued to create new kinds of moral and ethical dilemmas. Do they and their descendants teach particular values and attitudes to children? Do they come with 'hidden agendas'? If so, what are they and who decides?

Any web search will deliver large numbers of statistics and studies about ICT use amongst children and young people. Some findings should be interpreted with care because of the social/political agendas of their sponsors. But a thorough reading of research in these areas tells a consistent story of large numbers of children spending significantly more hours with ICT than they do at school. The fact that much of this activity may well be solitary or unsupervised is an issue largely for parents, but there are serious implications for schools too.

Schools use ICT too little. Currently, and perhaps understandably, mobile phones are rarely welcome in the classroom. Internet use – particularly the use of interactive and user-centred sites – is less developed in schools than at home despite the ubiquity of interactive whiteboards. The class digital camera, recorder or video may remain little used for lack of time. Television and film is less used now in school than 25 years ago, but *Wii* technology and other Web 2.0 possibilities have not yet become common features of classroom experience. Such technologies are very much part of the child's world and perhaps schools should systematically consider their use as motivators and means in formal educational settings (Riddle, 2009).

Signs of change are already apparent. ICT is argued to deepen understanding and promote new learning more effectively than traditional methods. The use of newer technologies like *Raspberry Pi*, small drones tablets and micro computers give children more control over what and how they learn. As a result, many schools and academies make the provision of laptops or 'tablets' a priority. Teachers plan from packaged lessons on the internet, 'Virtual' curricula and internet links are available for almost any theme or age group. The ethical and practical implications of easy and cheap 3-D printing are already with some schools (Beetham and Sharpe, 2013). Even the power of the mobile phone can be well utilized for educational purposes – texting a précis description, utilizing the camera or recording applications, contacting another school following a similar theme, permission to 'phone a friend' in the playground for help in a class quiz or voting for a school council member by text message might all be used to enliven school learning.

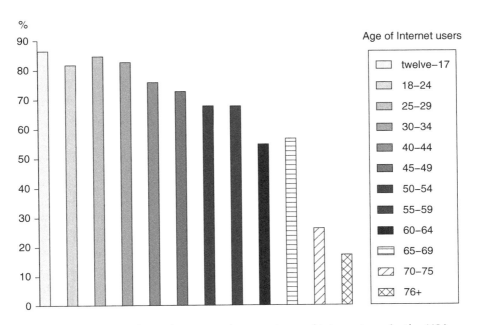

Figure 1.1   Graph to show the age and percentage of internet use in the USA

Case study 2   Using the mobile phone in school

A rural primary school in Suffolk asked groups of six children on field-work near the school to cooperate in using a mobile phone to text succinct (they could send only a 150 character message) descriptions concerning a range of contrasting environments near their school to a central group back in the classroom 'headquarters'. The 'HQ team' plotted the incoming summaries against appropriate locations on a base map so that the descriptive journey was already recorded as the 'environmental' teams returned to class.

In considering the power of ICT to influence the lives and thinking of children, we are confronted with questions of value:

- How can we use these technologies in accordance with our agreed values?
- How do we develop good and wholesome attitudes through ICT?
- How do we decide what good and wholesome is?
- *Should* schools be extending the time children spend with ICT?

Supporting children's interest in global themes

Schools have never been immune from political debate. Easily available and global communications should have made the possibilities for engagement with big issues even stronger. We have almost instant awareness of major events anywhere in the world. Dramatic, violent or tense international situations, threats, images and moral issues can appear daily in our homes and communities. In the past, such trauma would confront an unlucky individual only a few times in a lifetime. Despite the disturbing and challenging nature of many images open to children, there are surprisingly few guidelines or exemplars on how to address current events within the curriculum. Timetables in many schools have become inflexible. Tightly packed daily schedules rarely allow time for discussion or questions on real issues from the local, national or international news. Few British schools found the time or courage to follow the example of an international school in Dar es Salaam which organized a series of civilized and informed debates between children of all faiths and none, within a few days of the attacks of 11 September 2001 in the USA. Yet most schools found plenty of curriculum time to focus on the Football World Cup in Brazil 2014. If our curricula have become too crowded to debate more serious world events, international issues and global or local politics, perhaps we are causing the very apathy many teachers complain about in their children.

Bruner (1968) reminds us that no issues are too complex for children. Emotive subjects like terrorism, war, poverty, HIV/AIDS, pollution, social inequality, disasters or peace treaties, are important to children as well as adults. Despite falling numbers of live TV viewers, current events programmes like the Children's British Broadcasting Corporation's (CBBC) daily *Newsround* and its associated website continue to attract audiences of 200,000 children and still around 34% of 6–12-year-olds watch it. Whilst research (Pew website) shows a decline in young people's news reading, the rapid rise in *Facebook* and *Twitter* means that world news can come to them even faster. Increasing viewer figures and donations show that TV/internet campaigns like *Make Poverty History*, the ONE campaign, *Comic Relief* and *Sport Relief* have significantly raised young people's consciousness of and participation in addressing world poverty.

Illustration 1.6   Children interviewing a local Member of the European Parliament and the Scottish Children's Commissioner on matters of global importance (Courtesy of Scottish Children's Parliament)

Such initiatives catch the imagination of schools and children perhaps because they demonstrate that ordinary voices can influence seemingly impersonal trends in the global economy.

Young people are at ease with digital media. Many have automatic functions on their mobile phones informing them instantly of key cricket or football scores or 'breaking news'. Video, internet and television channel facilities on mobiles, Mp3s and *iPods* are accessible to many children in the rapidly developing countries of Asia and South America too. Each new technology brings the world closer to the child's life, but perhaps in ways that make the events they portray seem less real.

Children frequently express an interest in 'green issues'. Topics such as poverty, pollution, deforestation and climate change are regularly highlighted in films, children's TV and curriculum initiatives (e.g. Eco-Schools, see website). TV and internet campaigns supporting water, rainforest and developing world anti-pollution projects regularly reach ambitious targets from school and individual donations. The David Puttnam documentary *'We are the people we've been waiting for'* (Puttnam, 2009, website) was used in many secondary schools to direct young people's existing commitment towards global issues and their place in their education now. Individual schools and clusters have been instrumental in raising awareness of environmental issues nearer home too.

The apparent interest in global issues is not straightforward however. Children's connection with the wider world seems dependent upon what has been highlighted by the television and tabloid news editors. Very few American children knew where Ukraine, Iraq or Afghanistan were before the wars there, and the word 'tsunami' meant little to most children before December 2004. For British children, Haiti and the Mississippi Delta were unknown before the 2010 tragedies of earthquake and oil spill and Rio de Janeiro was unheard of before the World Cup of 2014. Whilst global communications have successfully raised consciousness, place and general geographical knowledge is often poor. A study of world 'place knowledge' amongst 18–20-year-old prospective teachers on a UK teacher education course showed a serious ignorance about the location of many foreign countries outside Western Europe (Catling, 2004). The same lack of knowledge can apply to environmental or development issues. Unless a child attends a school that has followed up leads such as the United Nations' (UN's) millennium development goals (UN, website) or the Eco-Schools programme, or an individual teacher has shared an interest in a particular concern, then children's exposure to crucial aspects of their changing world remains a lottery.

Illustration 1.7   Shared endeavour often promotes improved relationships

It is not difficult to fire children's interest in the environment. They experience signs of environmental ill-health all around them in dying trees, polluted rivers, fly-tipping, disappearing countryside and asthma. Concerns about the future of environments also arise from children's apparently generic interest in nature, life forms and the outdoors. Students of teaching frequently remark on the good behaviour of children engaged in well-planned fieldwork. Schools with a clear environmental focus to their curriculum capitalize on this interest and use it to generate the feeling that individuals can do something to change the probable future of damaged or threatened environments. The Eco-Schools programme is a good example of a well-supported initiative providing guidance and resources to feed these interests. Suggested and potentially engaging topics, such as litter, waste, energy, water, transport, healthy living and school grounds, however, require a range of very specific subject skills and knowledge to bring them alive for children. Sustainability is a values theme that runs through many of the case studies and recommendations of this book.

Recognizing the importance of relationships

The popularity of *Facebook*, *Twitter* and other social networking sites among young people arises naturally from their interest in relationships.

Websites and magazines devoted to personal, beauty and relationship problems of young people have also grown in recent years. Relationships are important to all, but for the developing psyche of the child they may dominate everything. The Children's Society shows that family relationships are fundamentally important to children and that these relationships are best when children perceive they are granted a degree of autonomy (Children's Society, 2014, website). The numbers of children who contact the charity *ChildLine* either by phone or online continues to grow. This UK charity gives support to children who are abused, fearful or worried. In 2013 the charity, now run by the National Society for the Prevention of Cruelty to Children (NSPCC), was contacted 1.5 million times and supported over 290,000 children (NSPCC, website). The vast majority of clients were between 5 and 15 years old and about a third of cases concerned bullying and interpersonal relationship problems. Concerns about family, peers, friendships, who they can trust and who is caring towards them are central to children's lives (see Illustration 1.7). Still the large majority (the Children's Society suggests four-fifths) of children are flourishing in relationships and material terms, but those suffering poor relationships often demand a disproportionate degree of attention.

The family into which a child is born provides the first and most powerful model of relationships. Attachments form rapidly in the first hours of life and we recognize that the interrelationships within family go on influencing the trajectory of our lives well beyond childhood. We know too that deprivation and poverty begins negatively to affect the progress of the child along every line of development from very early on in their lives (Marmot, 2010, website). Family emotional and environmental support is key to a child's learning and development within school. Family members are often the most important role models. Despite the obvious importance of families there may be a mutual suspicion between schools and families, and few schools currently place family centrally in their curriculum and practice. The establishment of multi-agency children's centres, Sure Start and various extensions of the school day have, however, had a positive effect on school, family and community links. There are several aspects of twenty-first-century life, however, where mistrust may be growing.

Recent reports show a growing atmosphere of suspicion. One large-scale study involving 160,000 children shows, for example, that only 65% of English children aged 11–15 (53% in the USA) could agree with the statement, 'I find my peers kind and helpful'. By contrast, 84% in Macedonia or 82% in Sweden agreed with the same statement (WHO, 2012, website). UNICEF places the UK bottom of a 21-nation league in 'family and peer relationships' (UNICEF, 2013, website). Distrust may be evidence of social polarization and increasing suspicion between generations, sub-cultures and communities. The gap between the educational achievement of rich and poor children continues to widen in the UK outside London (*Guardian*, 2014, website).

Polarization is likely to be increased by schools if they do not recognize and address the gulf between their aims and values and those of their children. Popenici found that in Romania most secondary-aged children saw school as simply instrumental to getting a good job, and that a school's interest in altruism, goodness, education and sincerity was somewhat irrelevant to their lives (Popenici, 2006). If a school community is given genuine opportunity to discuss and agree their values, however, they will most often arrive at similar caring and community values (Booth and Ainscow, 2011).

Intercultural and cross-community understanding is clearly crucial to national and international peace and progress in the twenty-first century. Schools can play their part in making the world a better place, through respect for each other and their attitude to ability and disability, gender, those of other religions and none, ethnic minorities, travellers, new or transient families, or those of different sexual orientation or family arrangement. Relationships between cultures and sub-cultures have been subject to a number of UK government-sponsored initiatives, especially since the Stephen Lawrence Inquiry of 1999 (Stephen Lawrence Inquiry, website) and the subsequent Race Relations Act 2000 (Ajegbo, 2007).

Wholesome relationships are, of course, important to personal well-being and inclusion in any community. Children need them to feel secure if they are to learn. We give little formal attention to building, maintaining and understanding the environment of relationships in our curricula and yet – as Daniel Goleman (1996, 1999, 2006) remind us – 'emotional intelligence' can be more important than other kinds of intelligence. By emotional intelligence, Goleman means the ability to understand and handle one's own emotions (the subject of the next section) and relationships, and how to understand and deal with those of others. Emotional literacy programmes have been very successfully introduced in a number of schools seriously approaching the PSHE and Citizenship curriculum. The danger is that these non-compulsory and constantly threatened aspects of the primary curriculum are left to chance and pressure on timetables means that such themes are often dealt with in a cursory and unplanned manner.

Helping develop a positive sense of self

As far as we know, our sense of self is a defining human characteristic. Self-consciousness is argued to have massive survival and evolutionary advantages (Damasio, 2010; Dawkins, 2003; Morris, 2004) and with it comes awareness of good and bad about our world. The concept of 'self' is, as Damasio puts it: 'the critical biological function that allows us to know sorrow or know joy, to know suffering or know pleasure, to sense embarrassment or pride, to grieve for lost love or lost life' (Damasio, 2000: 4). Deutscher (2006) calls language 'the invention that invented us', in that self-talk or thought shapes both consciousness and identity.

The twenty-first century has seen increasing interest in cultural and personal identities. Philosophy for children in schools (for example Fisher, 2008; P4C website) is part of this development. Damasio has devoted his career to research in the area of self-consciousness and describes two identifiable selves in our minds: a *core self* and an *autobiographical self*. The core self is that sense of consciousness where objects, sounds and senses around us are not only perceived but understood within our mind to be being perceived at that moment by ourselves. Core consciousness is consciousness in the moment, here and now, 'ceaselessly recreated for each and every object with which the brain interacts' (Damasio, 2000: 17). The autobiographical self consists of a set of memories of situations that bear centrally and usually invariably upon an individual's life: 'who you were born to, where and when, your likes and dislikes, the way you usually react to a problem or conflict, your name … your anticipated future' (p. 17). Significant to education, Damasio draws three key conclusions from his work on selfhood. He suggests first that both the core and autobiographical self are interrelated; secondly, that consciousness is inseparable from emotion; and finally, that the sense of self exists to maintain or promote the healthy equilibrium of the body. Deutscher (2010) and Greenfield (2009, 2010) remind us of the crucial impact of culture and language on that self.

Four questions of central educational importance emerge from research into identity:

1. If core consciousness is so totally dependent upon the senses and society, what do we do in our curriculum positively to introduce, develop and enhance experience across all the senses and social groups?
2. If the fully developed sense of self includes a clear sense of autobiographical self, what help are we giving children in school to identify their own *individualized* and special sense of identity confidence and belonging? How are we adding to their own *positive* memories, responses, talents and opinions? (Illustration 1.8)
3. If emotion is so closely linked with consciousness, are we spending enough time and effort in our teacher education on understanding emotion? In the education of children, are we planning for the positive engagement and enhancement of their *feelings*?

4. If self-awareness has developed from language and from nature as a way of promoting, assessing and fine-tuning our health, what are we doing in our curricula *holistically* and positively to involve both mind, body and relationships in the learning process?

The word 'positive' appears in each of the four key educational implications of current thinking on self. Many writers attempt to place their scientific conclusions outside any values framework, but teachers and the curriculum can have no such luxury. Almost everything teachers do is interpreted in some way as support or denial of some value or another. Each facet of the child's world described so far has implied questions of value. Moral choices are at the heart of what society has required of its teachers and this fact can be used to generate vital discussion and decisions in schools. If we agree, for example, on a desire to work to make the world 'a better place', common sense might suggest that we agree on

Illustration 1.8   A 12-year-old introducing David Miliband (UK ex-government minister) to a group presentation on identity

what better might mean. We might, for example, start by establishing a culture in which a positive sense of self, behaviour, feelings, relationships and environment are more likely than negative ones. The theme of promoting well-being through the educational choices we make runs through every chapter in this book.

Well-being is as important to our learning as it is to our relationships. A wide body of research (see Chapters 4, 5 and 6) suggests that the inner and underlying sense of what we simply call 'happiness' is the most common foundation for the transferable and lifelong learning we aim for in schools. Happiness is not always easy to come by. After basic needs are catered for, increased wealth does not seem to increase happiness (Layard, 2005, 2006; Young Foundation, 2010). The USA and the UK are amongst the richest countries in the world, but can manage only 26th and 28th rankings in a 35-nation survey of life satisfaction in 11-year-olds. The Marmot Review reminded us that one in four of UK children live in poverty, significantly more than the rest of northern Europe (Marmot, 2010, website). Figures and unfavourable comparisons have concentrated government attention on child well-being (e.g. ONS, 2012, website; UNICEF, 2013, website).

Not everyone sees happiness as an appropriate aim for education. Children's personal happiness may be seen as the sole responsibility of the family. Teachers' happiness is perhaps the job of management and not curriculum. Critics of the happiness debate cite numerous examples of great but unhappy people, like Van Gogh, Schumann or Sylvia Plath. Clearly some well-known and painful paths to success suggest that effective learning does not always come from 'being happy'. These examples do not negate the value of aiming at a default position of well-being. Neither does aiming at well-being throughout the school setting deny the importance of supporting children and teachers as they live through life's inevitable periods of suffering, difficulty and pain.

The famous bipolar creators rarely created anything in their times of deep depression, but rather used periods of more positive emotion to express, process and make sense of their negative experiences. Few would suggest that we deliberately make children depressed in order that they become more creative. Neither is the depressed state typical of the mind at its most creative (see Csikszentmihalyi, 1997; Layard, 2005). Lasting learning often and rightly involves difficulty and stress, but unless these pressures are experienced *against a background* of deeper personal security, learning is likely to be associated with negative feelings. A preponderance of negative life experiences seems more likely to result in a relative lack of resilience and self-efficacy (Bandura, 1994; Fredrickson and Tugade, 2004; Layard and Clark, 2014).

Personal happiness is generally and deeply important to us. There is clearly something universally recognizable in the happy face (Ekman, 2004), positively interpreted even by children with neurological barriers to emotion such as severe autism (Howard-Jones and Pickering, 2005). Even very young babies respond positively to a smiling face from any cultural source. Several strands of current research now suggest that feelings of positive emotion generate high-level, transferable and creative learning at social, physical and intellectual levels. Placing emphasis on positive aspects of the child's self, and supporting all to feel included, may not simply be a more efficient way of teaching – it seems to contribute to general health too. Damasio (2003) suggests that positive emotion, particularly the feeling of joy, signifies a biological state of: 'optimal physiological coordination and smooth running of the operations of life ... [Joy is] not only conducive to survival, but survival with well-being' (p. 137). In other words, when we are happy our minds and bodies are in their best state. Our brains respond to positive states by releasing the neurotransmitters that signal satisfaction and security probably in order to help us maintain the state of positivity. Damasio describes an unbroken loop between body and mind – the happy/ healthy body promotes a more happy/efficiently working mind and vice versa. If this is the case, then seeking curricular opportunities to create the sense of joy in as many children as possible must be considered a desirable way for them to be and to learn. Teaching with *enjoyment* as a major aim seems to have the potential to serve mind and body, here and now, and also to create in children a positive sense of self that will benefit them well into the future.

These findings mirror those by 'positive psychologists' like Csikszentmihalyi (2002), Fredrickson (2003, 2009) and Seligman (2004), who also propose that positive emotional states are the optimum mental conditions for learning, social and intellectual connection-making, discovery, creativity and invention. A particularly accessible hypothesis in this regard is Fredrickson's 'broaden and build' theory of positive emotions. This is examined in Chapter 4.

There also seem to be strong links between happiness and creativity (Csikszentmihalyi, 1997). Veteran 'people watcher' Desmond Morris has suggested that our feeling of happiness relates to 'the degree to which we find ourselves able to exercise the particularly human skills of creativity, the use of symbols including symbolic language, and family relationships' (Morris, 2004). A recurring theme of this book is the relationship between the self involved in creative activity and the sense of contentment, achievement, fascination, engagement and joy we often call happiness.

Illustration 1.9   Enjoyment is not always shown in the smile, but shows itself here in intricacy, concentration and application (Courtesy Gifted and Talented Summer Academy, Canterbury)

The developing self of the child is also prey to a powerful set of negative influences. Notions of rampant materialism, excessive wealth, risky behaviour, violence, fame and narrow concepts of physical beauty are all too easily assimilated (Greenfield, 2010). These features of young life are constantly reinforced by toys, advertising, television, film, computer, internet and video images. Human young are probably genetically predisposed to finding joy in these things, but it is also commonly held that such simple pleasures do not bring particularly long-lasting satisfaction. Indeed, studies of lottery winners throughout the world have demonstrated the short-lived nature of happiness from material wealth. Left to their own devices without ICT to distract them, children quickly find enjoyment in physical and social activities. Physical play clearly engages the vast majority of young mammals. A casual observation of children during games sessions and at playtime shows most exhibiting wide grins, sparkling eyes, relaxed faces and joyful conversation – the key signals of happiness. It seems particularly disastrous that school sports and PE are so constrained by time, especially since negative body image and obesity are growing issues in developed societies like the UK and the USA (WHO, 2012, website; Young Foundation, 2010).

Schools of the twenty-first century are right to be thinking hard about what implicit and explicit values they wish to teach their pupils. Perhaps the call for more complex and challenging activities in the curriculum results from a feeling that it is in creative, often symbolic, physical activity that lasting human satisfaction is to be found (Morris, 2004). Political demands on schools have sometimes resulted in significant conflicts of values in this regard. In the context of 'back to basics' demands on US education (Hirsch, 1999), Csikszentmihalyi castigated schools and parents for:

> making serious tasks dull and hard and frivolous ones exciting and easy. Schools generally fail to teach how exciting, how mesmeris-ingly beautiful science or mathematics can be; they teach the rou-tine of literature or history rather than the adventure. (1997: 125)

Csikszentmihalyi provides evidence from his own research which sug-gests that creative individuals in all walks of life go beyond the limita-tions of genetic or cultural programming to live 'exemplary lives ... [which] show how joyful and interesting complex symbolic activity is'. Attitudes to the self – how I learn best, what I find fascinating, satisfying, pleasure-giving, helpful – can be developed through education, but it is essential that we consider carefully what kind of 'selves' we are helping to create in our classrooms.

How can we know what it is like to be a child in the twenty-first century?

Life is hard for many children in the first quarter of the twenty-first cen-tury. Children suffer disproportionately according to a range of measures. In the developing world, five-sixths of the world's children have the least access to scarce resources and around 25,000 of them die each day because of poverty; 150 million under 14 have to work for their and their family's survival (UNICEF, 2010, website). On the evidence of researchers and current media headlines, many young people in the resource-rich and developed world live a pretty sad and lonely existence too. Poverty of all kinds singles children out for special problems. The gap between rich and poor continues to widens but so too does the gap between rich and poor within the USA and the UK. Health inequalities, a current focus of international and UK studies (WHO, 2012, website; Young Foundation, 2010), show, for example that life expectancy and restricting illnesses correlate closely with levels of deprivation. Children born in the UK into low-status, low-income families have a higher death rate in infancy,

Illustrations 1.10, 1.11, 1.12   Seek out the facial manifestations of happiness, the smile, the shining eyes, the raised cheekbones and the un-furrowed brow (Photos: Cherry Tewfik)

lower birth weights, are smaller, more prone to psychological problems and have higher levels of stress and illness than their richer neighbours (Marmot, 2010, website; Rees et al., 2012).

Wealth too has brought its problems. Young people in some advanced economies are reported to be increasingly involved in risky behaviour. Several studies demonstrate the rapid growth in behavioural and emotional difficulties amongst the young, and rising rates of teenage alcoholism, early smoking, depression, self-harm and suicide (Collishaw et al., 2004; Layard and Dunn, 2009). Indeed, Collishaw's report recorded that in the UK behavioural and emotional problems among teenagers had risen by over 70% in the past 25 years. The UNICEF and WHO reports (UNICEF, 2013, website; WHO, 2012, website), graphically present many of the possible causes of such trends: family breakdown, bullying, loss of trust, lack of success or pleasure in school, stress, loneliness and subjective health problems. Within many categories of health-related behaviour, young people in England (not necessarily in the UK as a whole) and the USA were shown to be amongst the least happy in the Western world. Eighty-five per cent of British children continue to report high levels of life satisfaction but it is difficult to argue with the well-established research methodologies and comparative figures of international bodies.

The most important way of finding out about what concerns children is by asking them. The pupil voice movement is still in its infancy in the UK and USA but increasingly schools are listening. In *The School I'd Like*, Catherine Burke and Ian Grosvenor asked children their views on school (Burke and Grosvenor, 2003) and life in general (Davey et al., 2010). The collected children's statements plead for a very different school environment to the one that many adults may *think* children would like. Here are a few provocative suggestions for the schools of the future:

- Children will learn more about the future than the past.
- Adults will listen to them and not dismiss their opinions.
- Children will be free to be children.
- Children will not be 'treated as herds of identical animals wanting to be civilized before we are let loose upon the world. It will be recognized that it's our world too.'
- Playgrounds would have 'something to play with'.
- 'Power will be evenly spread throughout the school.'
- 'More time should be devoted to art, design and technology.'
- The curriculum will be 'concerned with fulfilment'.

Several case studies from this book will outline projects where children have taken the lead in successfully defining and achieving what they

Illustrations 1.13, 1.14, 1.15   Each child shows engagement in a different way, but it is recognizable across time and culture (Photos: Cherry Tewfik)

wanted to learn and make in environments where the 'locus of control' was passed to them. These may still seem radical more than 200 years after Rousseau's idealized, and naturally good, 'noble savage' approach to the education of the child (see Introduction).

The reconstruction of children's services under the *Every Child Matters* initiative (DfES, 2004, website), was based upon 'five outcomes' arising from consultations with children about their hopes and needs. The basic needs to be healthy, stay safe, enjoy and achieve, make a positive contribution and achieve economic well-being formed a guide to education, social and health policy until 2010. Since May 2010, requirements for schools to report on the well-being of children were relaxed, but government continued to see itself as enabling children

> to overcome disadvantage and deprivation so they can fulfil their innate talents and take control of their own destiny … [and affirming a] belief in the power of human agency to give meaning, structure and hope to every life. (Gove, 2009)

Since the United Nations Convention on the Rights of the Child (UNICEF, 1989, website) national education systems across the world are charged not just with the education and socialization of children, but also the active promotion of their personal/emotional security, health and well-being. Schools are the only agencies in a position to enact such policies and philosophies amongst all children. In the next chapter we examine some schools' attempts to address the central issues for children of the twenty-first century.

Summary

The twenty-first century has challenges like every other century. Aside from the obvious implications of overpopulation, there are three major differences to the challenges of this century: the much more rapid *pace* of change (Figure 1.2), their perceived often *negative* character in the minds of modern children and their *global* characteristics.

The changes and challenges in our world, and consequently our minds, cannot be kept local; our global economy, instant communications and global pollution have meant that whatever happens in one place quickly affects every other. If they want, ordinary people, particularly teachers and children, are now in a position to exert some influence over the interrelated future of this world, but to do so effectively we need to be very clear about what we value most. The answers to questions of value

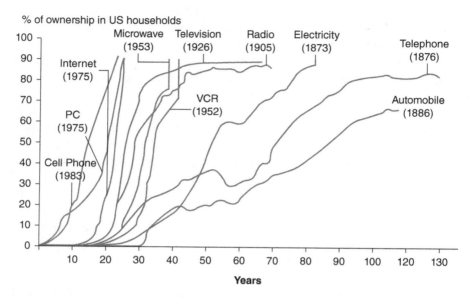

Figure 1.2 How long it takes new technologies to reach a mass market. Where cell phones, internet and personal computers penetrated 20% of the US market in less than 20 years, it took the car and the telephone 50 years to achieve the same take-up

should underpin all our education decisions. So far, we have selected and examined five key areas of special interest to children:

- the future (which is taken to include environmental as well as personal concerns)
- ICT
- global politics
- relationships
- the self.

Research and experience in these areas point to the needs for a curriculum that liberates children from the combined threats of materialism, fear, exclusion and lack of confidence and fulfilment. Each of the following statements suggest arguments for a more cross-curricular, creative, meaningful and child-centred approach:

1. *Security about the future is an essential prerequisite for the happy child.* A curriculum that addresses children's anxiety about the personal and global future (as well as insecurities about the self and

relationships) is crucial if we agree that school activities should be relevant to their lives.

2. *A sense of personal control over aspects of their daily life is central to children's motivation for learning.* A concentration on developing emotional literacy, the constructive use of ICT and establishment of personally meaningful, curricular experiences to interpret and examine is more likely to generate personal engagement among children.

3. *It is possible for ordinary individuals to make a positive impact upon global and environmental issues.* It is suggested that cross-curricular themes that touch upon children's culturally or genetically determined interests in any area are more likely to generate involvement.

4. *Opportunities to build and deepen positive relationships with others are embraced by children.* We should seek a curriculum, teaching methods, community links and classroom organization that offer a range of activities to promote and utilize such relationships.

5. *The child's positive self-image is fundamental to a healthy mind and body.* Education should therefore be physically active and individualized as far as possible and aim to promote a personal sense of achievement and resilience and to discover the strengths of each individual.

Research and professional opinion across health education and social care is united in focusing on mental and social health, the sense of security, feelings of autonomy and choice. Each of these concepts and each area of special interest to children is dependent upon judgements of value. Every school should work to identify, agree *and live* its guiding values and establish a values-led curriculum designed to improve the lives and daily experience of all children. I believe such decisions and actions would significantly and positively impact on the character of twenty-first-century life.

Key questions for discussion

- Do you think that we are living in pessimistic times?
- What do you think schools can do about integrating family learning into the curriculum and structures of the school?
- What can the playground tell us about children's learning? How could this be integrated into the curriculum?
- What are the pluses and minuses of ICT in the lives of children?

(Continued)

(Continued)

- How can we make relationships a more central part of our curriculum?
- How can we ensure times of happiness and positivity for every child?
- What can the school do about the health of the child?

Further reading

Greenfield, S. (2003) *Tomorrow's People*. Harmondsworth: Penguin.

Hicks, D. (2014) *Educating for Hope in Troubled Times: Climate Change and the Transition to a Post Carbon Future.* Stoke on Trent: Trentham Books.

Robinson, K. and Aronica, L. (2010) *The Element: How Finding Your Passion Changes Everything.* Harmondsworth: Penguin.

CHAPTER 2

CROSS-CURRICULAR POLICY AND PRACTICE

Chapter aims

This chapter summarizes the history of cross-curricular approaches and the development of more recent policy and practice in British education. It aims to demonstrate the philosophical and educational background to the ideas presented in this book. It introduces an original and research-based taxonomy of seven different styles and purposes of cross-curricular learning. By the end of this chapter you will have considered:

- some philosophical and psychological influences on cross-curricular practice
- government reports sympathetic to cross-curricular approaches
- the development and demise of cross-curricular approaches in the National Curriculum
- current contributions to the cross-curricular debate, including the Cambridge Primary Review
- the approach to cross-curricular teaching and learning used in this book
- an original and research-based taxonomy of cross-curricular styles.

Cross-curricular approaches to teaching and learning have a long history. Linkages between the language and skills of more than one discipline are implicit in ancient Greek and medieval Chinese views of education. In both traditions drama, music, philosophy and literature, with their distinctive skills, vocabularies and histories, were expected to be combined. The amalgamation of different subject approaches is often seen in the work of influential teachers and communicators. Polymaths like Aristotle, the Persian astronomer Avicenna, composer/ philosopher Hildegard of Bingen, Leonardo Da Vinci or the Indian poet and reformer Tagore, each fused personal expertise in several subjects to make important contributions to global knowledge. On a different scale some cultures unite subjects considered separate domains in Western traditions. For example many societies in south and west Africa call dance and music by the same name (Blacking, 1974). Experiences, understood through the eyes of a number of different subject disciplines, exemplify the educational philosophies and recommendations of seventeenth-, eighteenth- and early nineteenth-century philosopher/ educationalists like Comenius, Rousseau, Pestalozzi and Froebel. Thinking and learning across disciplinary traditions is far from a 'progressive' or modern idea.

Twentieth-century cross-curricular thinking

Connecting across a *curriculum* – the educational experiences offered by an institution – may be seen as a twentieth-century contribution. The concept of a 'child-centred' curriculum spread via early twentieth-century educational thinkers like John Dewey (1859–1952) in the USA and Rudolf Steiner (1861–1925) in Europe. Dewey's 'democratic' approach was founded on ideas of freedom and the provisional, negotiated nature of knowledge. He argued that children should be deeply and personally involved in the creation of knowledge through problem solving and experiment, and that community would be enriched by individuals whose personal experience had been enlarged through education. Education in Dewey's eyes was rarely an individualistic activity; in his writing and lectures, he was at pains to stress the importance of the group. In the gendered language of the time he wrote:

> I believe that the only true education comes through the stimulation of the child's powers by the demands of the social situations in which he finds himself. Through these demands he is stimulated to act as a member of a unity, to emerge from his original narrowness of action and feeling, and to conceive of himself from the standpoint of the welfare of the group to which he belongs. Through the responses which others make to his own activities he comes to know what these mean in social terms. The value which they have is reflected back into them (Dewey, 1897: 77–80).

Steiner's ideas were more spiritual and personal – like Rousseau he believed in the innate wisdom of human beings. In proposals for his 'Waldorf schools', Steiner (1919) gave a detailed outline of a developmentally based curriculum strongly infused with the arts. The Waldorf curriculum is both subject-based and thematic – the overarching theme is the development of selfhood. It is designed to mirror and guide the child's unfolding dexterity, consciousness, creativity and imagination. Its classical aims – to cultivate responsibility for the earth and other people and prepare children for the challenges of the future – are met through a curriculum designed to be personally engaging, spiritually conscious, experience-based and responsive to the physical world of nature. A Steiner curriculum often uses separated subjects, but also provides regular opportunities to put subject learning into cross-subject contexts like plays (that can take up curriculum time in a wide range of subjects for a whole term), building projects, exhibitions, displays, walks in the countryside and seasonal celebrations.

The 1931 Hadow Report took up Dewey's ideas in the UK. Even in its time, its proposals were considered radical. Hadow reflected 'progressive' child-centred philosophies in suggesting that learning, especially in the primary school, should be seen in terms of 'activity and experience rather than knowledge to be acquired and facts to be stored' (UK Board of Education, 1931: para. 75). *Knowing* and *doing* were in some ways seen as synonymous with each other, and purposeful activity suited to the child's specific environment needed to be planned in accordance with the varying nature of children. Unfortunately, as Alexander (2010) reminds us, Hadow's emphasis on activity resulted in the unintended and unhelpful polarization between experience and knowledge which has clouded the debate over cross-curricular learning ever since.

Although the Hadow Report was hailed as a triumph for progressive, constructivist education, in the UK the spirit of its recommendations was not fully advanced until the Plowden Report (DES, 1967). This influential and well-researched report compiled evidence from professional, academic and interest groups to argue that:

> Rigid division of the curriculum into subjects tends to interrupt children's trains of thought and of interest and to hinder them from realizing the common elements in problem solving … some work at least, should cut across subject divisions at all stages of the primary school. (DES, 1967: para. 535, p. 197)

In its chapter on 'Children learning in school' (DES, 1967: para. 202, p. 189), Plowden cited a roll-call of eighteenth-, nineteenth- and twentieth-century progressives to bolster its case. In addition to the educationalists already mentioned, Maria Montessori, Rachel Macmillan, Susan Isaacs, Jean Piaget and Jerome Bruner – names that still feature in the education debate today – were called upon to defend 'active learning' – experience-led, 'discovery' approaches in primary education and beyond.

Much of the discovery approach was underpinned by the work of psychologist Jean Piaget (1954), discussed in Chapter 6. Piaget's influence on US and Western European education, to an extent, fed individualistic interpretations of child development, whereas the (then) newly translated research of a Russian, Lev Vygotsky, highlighted the social aspects of learning. Whilst Piaget's stages of development envisaged what Bruner called a 'lone scientist', Vygotsky was clear that the social context was fundamental to language, concept formation and learning (Vygotsky, 1962). Vygotsky observed that learning occurred in similar playful, genuinely exploratory contexts to those observed by Piaget, but Vygotsky believed concepts were more easily formed and understood and that learning was more permanent when the learner thought, spoke and discovered with others. Much educational thought in the 1960s and 1970s therefore linked group work, mixed ability, even mixed ages with cross-curricular activity. In truth, few schools of the 1960s or 1970s ventured very far down the Plowden path and most primary pedagogy remained steadfastly didactic (Alexander et al., 1992: paras 19 and 20).

Only nine years after Lady Plowden's recommendations, British Prime Minister James Callaghan made his 'Ruskin College' speech (Callaghan, 1976, website) calling for a 'Great Debate' on education and expressing the unease felt by parents and employers regarding 'the new informal methods of teaching, which seem to produce excellent results when they are in well-qualified hands but are much more dubious when they are not'. This was a concern already expressed by Plowden in considering the implications of her recommendations. Callaghan's speech and rapid progress towards a national curriculum effectively stifled the development of cross-curricular teaching and learning in all but the most confident British schools. Rather than spreading the 'excellent results' of those well-qualified teachers, the impact of 'dubious' teaching became the focus of education policy.

The 1988 Education Reform Act significantly added to the power of the Secretary of State to legislate some of the fine detail of schooling, and for the first time introduced a legal entitlement to a set of separated subjects taught to a statutory programme called the National Curriculum.

The National Curriculum 1989–2010

The early versions of the English National Curriculum (DES, 1989; DfEE, 1999) subdivided primary children's learning into 10 subjects (11 with Religious Education (RE) and 12 after 2010 when Modern Foreign Language was added). These subjects were divided into a 'core' of English, Mathematics and Science, and 'foundation' (Art, Design/Technology, Geography, History, Information and Communications Technology (ICT), Music, Physical Education plus RE). Sex education, Citizenship and Personal, Social and Health Education (PSHE) were also added by 2009 but remained outside the foundation category and their nature depended upon the children's age and school policy. At all times, the core was to be given privileged status in terms of time, inspection, public reporting, statutory tests and school league tables to report results. Most schools quickly settled into a routine of English and Maths every morning and the other subjects distributed across the week with Science given a little more time than the other subjects.

The first National Curriculum for England and Wales proved cumbersome and difficult to implement. Reviews introduced a slimmer and more open version maintaining the emphasis on Mathematics, English and Science. Cross-curricular links were included in these revisions for Key Stages 1–3 in the mid 1990s, but presented in tiny, grey print in the margins of the pure subject orders. Increased time was given to Mathematics and English after 1997 when the National Literacy Strategy (NLS) and the National Numeracy Strategy (NNS) were introduced into primary schools. Extra time was made available for the strategies to become established, by relaxing legal requirements to report on the 'Foundation Subjects' (Ofsted, 1998). NLS and NNS were not statutory, but league tables and a punitive inspection regime ensured that very few schools dared disregard the detailed interference in pedagogy these strategies represented. Though they were later subsumed in the Primary National Strategy, these strategies had an almost immediate and negative effect upon the teaching of the foundation subjects and Science, in terms of ever-diminishing local authority support, rapidly declining quality of teaching and shortened time for learning in them. (This decline in confidence and standards within the foundation subjects was further consolidated by local authority cutbacks after the economic downturn of 2008.) Cross-curricular teaching almost disappeared in many schools between 1997 and 2003, partly as a result of attempts to help teachers manage a still dense programme of learning.

The Qualifications and Curriculum Agency (QCA, 1998a) seemed to bolster subject divisions through detailed schemes of work for Key Stage 1, 2 and 3 for each of 12 subjects. Intended only as guidance, the QCA schemes became seen as part of the National Curriculum for many English schools between 1997 and 2010. Public and political pressure continued to ensure that, through the UK, Mathematics and English remained dominant in time allocation, status, inspection and training. Only the Curriculum Guidance for the Foundation Stage (CGFS) for 3–5-year-olds retained a cross-curricular rationale (DfEE, 1999).

The word 'enjoyment' entered the official education vocabulary in 2003 in the context of government attempts to free-up a rapidly narrowing curriculum. *Excellence and Enjoyment* (DfES, 2003a) summarized advice to schools on creating a motivating and yet rigorous curricular atmosphere in schools. It reminded schools that rigid subject boundaries were not statutory and that the curriculum could successfully be organized in ways that made connections between subjects and between school learning and authentic experience. Continuing Ofsted and league table focus on the core subjects meant that only the most secure schools tended to follow this advice.

Other countries within the UK were more structurally committed to cross-curricular thinking. In Northern Ireland's Common Curriculum 1991 the themes 'The Environment and Society' and 'Creative and Expressive Studies' were used as contexts within which to apply separate subject learning (Northern Ireland Curriculum, website). Later and as a constructive result of the troubles, 'Cultural Heritage' and 'Education for Mutual Understanding' became required cross-curricular themes for both primary and secondary pupils. Across the UK, broad amalgamations of subjects and experience-led learning remained alive, partly under the influence of Storyline® (Storyline, website) and the Scottish 5–14 curriculum where History, Geography and Modern Studies were combined under the heading of the 'Social Subjects' (SOED, 1993). Each subject shared the same skills descriptors. Cross-curricular approaches occupied an even more central position in Scotland's *Curriculum for Excellence* (Scottish Executive, 2004).

In England, threats to arts education after 1997 prompted a nationally and internationally influential report. The National Advisory Council on Creative and Cultural Education (NACCCE, 1999) responded to the inequality of subject provision in England by recommending parity of *all* subjects in the curriculum. Whilst this report was influential on educationalists and creative and cultural organizations it did not significantly affect the curriculum. Another revised and further slimmed down National Curriculum (DfEE, 1999) included 'cross-curricular thinking skills', but the

NACCCE's recommendation of subject parity was ignored. Indeed, the term 'foundation subjects' was replaced in some official documents by the somewhat demeaning term 'non-core' in 2000. From 1999 onwards, Physical Education (PE) hours were reduced, school fields were sold, field trips, school concerts and plays became less frequent and the arts continued to disappear from school and teacher education curricula (Rogers, 1999, 2003). The 'Standards' for Qualified Teacher Status (QTS) from this period require trainee teachers only to 'have *sufficient* understanding of a *range* of work' *across* History *or* Geography, Art/Design *or* Design/ Technology and the *performing* arts (Teacher Training Agency (TTA), 2003). This directive surreptitiously replaced music and other individual arts disciplines as a requirement for QTS, and relegated Geography, History and Design/Technology too. As a result, local authority foundation subject in-service training and advice declined, subject advisers lost their jobs or combined subject roles and Advanced Skills Teachers often with heavy class responsibilities, carried out the bulk of subject support. Out-of-school visits, swimming, concerts, school productions and other 'extra curricular' activities dwindled (Barnes, 2001; Bell, 2004; Rogers, 2003). Opportunities for quality cross-curricular work were progressively squeezed out of the English curriculum for lack of time and declining subject training and expertise.

New official roles for schools had the potential to affect the curriculum young children received. As social and political pressures pushed schools to take on functions traditionally met by families, social and health services (HMG, 2004), the curriculum became more complex. Interest in the non-statutory Citizenship and PSHE rose as international comparisons rated the UK low on child happiness, and physical, social and mental health scales (see WHO, 2012, website). Inspections and education authority advice devoted more space to the National Curriculum's cross-curricular thinking skills, like creative thinking (see DfES, 2006a, website). In England, Ofsted required inspection reports and school self-assessments on child well-being for the first time in this period and detailed advice was given to schools on the Social, Emotional Aspects of Learning (DfES, 2005, website; SEAL, 2006, website). Reports and advice from Ofsted often linked child emotional, intellectual and social well-being with creative and cross-curricular approaches to the curriculum (see Ofsted, 2002, 2009a, 2009b, 2010b). Connections between the cross-curriculum and children's sustained engagement were also made by the Department of Health's 'Healthy Schools' campaign (DoH/DfES, 2005) and the Department for Culture, Media and Sport's support for Creative Partnerships (a pre-Coalition government initiative encouraging long-term links between schools and creative practitioners in the community).

Developments in human rights policy affected curricula on an international scale too. The United Nations Convention on the Rights of the Child (UNICEF, 1989, website), of which the UK was an early signatory, has major educational implications. After 1990 academic writing, reports, commissions, surveys and evaluations on schools and schooling, included children's views, sometimes for the first time. A message supporting a more open, flexible experience and child-relevant curriculum was commonly conveyed by such consultations (for example, Burke and Grosvenor, 2003; Layard and Dunn, 2009; Powell and Barnes, 2008). Pupil voice became a feature of school organization and young people's opinions on curriculum and pedagogy is now taken seriously in many schools (Ruddock and MacIntyre, 2007). In almost every consultation, pressures for both curriculum simplification and increased relevance came from both children and their teachers.

The UK Labour government reviewed the secondary and then the primary curriculum (Rose, 2009) in attempts to rationalize and reduce this overcrowded and complex curriculum. Key Stage 3 curricula remained subject-based but teachers were given considerably more flexibility over curriculum content and coverage. For primary schools, Rose tackled perceived overload by suggesting the thematic approach. The Rose Review, though barred from examining assessment and league tables, was set up as a rival to the independent Cambridge Primary Review (CPR). The CPR funded by the Esmee Fairbairn Foundation from 2006 onwards, published its report four years later (Alexander, 2010) and has had significant impacts upon Initial Teacher Education programmes and many school curricula.

Reviews of education and a new National Curriculum 2013

The problem of an overcrowded yet narrowed primary curriculum was a starting point for two major reviews published in 2009/10. Jim Rose represented the views of many when he stated:

> The availability of time and its management will continue to pose considerable problems unless a better fit of curriculum content to the capacity of primary schools can be achieved. The National Curriculum ... is overcrowded, leaving teachers with insufficient time to enable children to engage adequately with every subject required by law. (Rose, 2009: para. 2.3)

At the same time, Rose reported the concerns of many of its respondents who saw the primary curriculum as:

narrowed by the Key Stage 2 National Curriculum tests, the focus of Ofsted inspections and the National Strategies … [and that] as a result of these external pressures the principle of an entitlement to a broad and balanced curriculum is, in effect, denied to many children. (Rose, 2009: para. 2.4)

The following points gathered from wide-ranging consultations directed Rose's decisions on curriculum:

- a reduction in content with greater flexibility and less prescription
- a clear set of culturally derived aims and values
- the securing of high achievement in literacy, numeracy and ICT
- explicit opportunities for children to benefit from subject teaching and cross-curricular studies that cover the principal areas of our history, culture and achievement and the wider world
- explicit opportunities throughout to foster children's personal development and good attitudes to learning. (Rose, 2009: para. 2.12)

The Rose Interim and Final Reports (Rose, 2008, 2009) proposed both increased subject rigour and thematic approaches. These reports suggested that effective learning could occur between subjects and in mixtures of subjects but also that standards in the individual subjects must be improved through being separately taught. At the time Rose's recommendations were in line with Ofsted (2010a), which simultaneously confirmed that raising standards in individual subjects was in no way compromised by good-quality creative and cross-curricular work. In a sample of good and outstanding schools covering four key stages, Ofsted stated that teachers:

> felt confident in encouraging pupils to make connections across traditional boundaries, speculate constructively, maintain an open mind while exploring a wide range of options, and reflect critically on ideas and outcomes. This [Ofsted comments] had a perceptible and positive impact on pupils' personal development, and their preparation for life beyond school. (Ofsted, 2010a: 4)

Ofsted confirmed that in successful schools applying cross-curricular initiatives, 'the distinctiveness of individual subjects was not diminished' (Ofsted, 2010a: 11).

Rose proposed that this mix of subject rigour and motivating cross-curricular approaches could be organized under six 'areas of learning':

- understanding the arts
- understanding English, communication and languages
- scientific and technological understanding
- understanding mathematics
- understanding physical development, health and well-being
- historical, geographical and social understanding.

The hastily published, distributed, then abandoned *National Curriculum Primary Handbook*, based on Rose's review (DCSF/QCDA, 2010), picked out 'cross-curricular studies' as a strand in its common format for all programmes of learning. The UK Coalition government of May 2010 rejected Rose's recommendations and returned primary schools to the national curriculum of 1999 awaiting the new Department for Education's (DfE) curriculum revision, to be effective from September 2014 (DfE, 2013a). The Coalition refocused teachers' attention on 'traditional subjects', avoided mention of creativity or cross-curricular approaches. Replacing these 'woolly' approaches with 'relentless focus on the basics', didactic methods, subject-based teaching and a single approach to the teaching of reading – somewhat contradicting its rhetoric of 'flexibility' (Gov.UK, 2010a, website). The work of the Assessment Reform Group was also terminated at this time.

The Coalition government placed flexible and community-based curricula, improved access to the poorest children, and subject or theme-based academies and free schools at the core of their education policy. Having ditched the Rose Review, the Education Department turned to what it called the 'best work' from the Alexander Review (*TES*, 2010, website), without specifically indicating what the best work was.

A balance of disciplinary skills and cross-curricular themes, however, characterized the more nuanced, widely consultative and research-based Cambridge Primary Review (CPR) chaired by Robin Alexander (Alexander, 2010). The CPR addressed the contradictions evident in Coalition policy by tracing the roots of public policy on curriculum and identifying the main problems facing primary and early secondary schooling today. Considerable emphasis is placed on the aims and values of education and curriculum, the dangers of politicization, loss of professional and local autonomy and the 'pernicious dichotomy' (Alexander, 2010: 243) between a broad and balanced curriculum and high standards in the basics. It combines aims of education and domains of learning to propose a curriculum flexible enough to serve a wide variety of communities and localities.

Alexander's eight domains are not far from Rose's 'areas of learning' or the 'curriculum areas' in Scotland's Curriculum for Excellence. The addition of faith/belief and ethics/citizenship introduces an important values component to the curriculum itself. The omission of computing and personal development emphasizes their cross-curricular nature over the sense that they are 'subjects' in their own right. The cross-curricular tone of Alexander's proposals are clear. Domains like 'place and time' and 'arts and creativity' clearly expect connections between Geography and History and Art, Music and Drama (and significantly, creativity across the range of non-artistic subjects). But equally, the headings, physical/emotional health, language, oracy and literacy, citizenship and ethics and science/technology also imply approaches that cut across traditional subject boundaries – oracy, emotional health and citizenship may be explored in any context and across contexts. All categories involve English language as applying across the whole curriculum.

The CPR stresses that schools and communities should decide upon the interpretation and application of aims and the ways the domains are taught. A 'community curriculum' devoted to locally significant issues should, according to Alexander, take 30% of teaching time. Schools in turn should decide upon the programmes of study they follow in applying the 70% devoted to the National Curriculum.

Aims of education (working towards ...)		Domains of learning
personal well-being		Arts and creativity
personal engagement		Citizenship/ethics
personal empowerment		
personal autonomy		Faith and belief
respect and reciprocity for others		Language, oracy and literacy
interdependence and sustainability		
local, national and global citizenship		Mathematics
participation in culture and community		Physical/emotional health
knowing, understanding, making sense		
fostering skill		Place and time
exciting the imagination		Science/technology
enacting dialogue		

Figure 2.1 Aims and domain of the curriculum according to Alexander, 2010

In stressing what a domain *is not*, Alexander highlights the problems inherent in cross-curricular pedagogies of the past. The domains his report proposes are not:

- a slot in the school's weekly timetable
- an invitation to low-grade topic work in which thematic serendipity counts for more than knowledge and skill. (Alexander, 2010: 265–6)

In stating what domains *are*, Alexander also helps build a case for revisiting (with caution) cross-curricular approaches. Domains are professional, pedagogical, categories that teachers should apply where appropriate to enhance, explain and extend children's experience The collections of concepts chosen to represent domains have 'an identifiable and essential core of knowledge and skill', the capacity to fulfil one or more educational aims, and can be justified as serving the social, personal, spiritual, moral, physical, intellectual and cultural needs of the child. In the CPR proposals all subjects have equal weight and in recent work with the subject associations this principle has been reiterated (CPR, 2014).

The Tickell Review concentrated on the Early Years Foundation Stage (DfE, 2011, website). It called for more and better training for nursery, playgroup and children's centre staff and reiterated the fundamental importance of play, exploration and activity in the development of young children. It also made significant recommendations regarding creative practice by including play, exploration and activity in the Early Years 'Profile'. The review recommended approaches that should run through all Early Years education, including: 'finding out and exploring', 'being involved and concentrating', 'keeping on trying', 'having their own ideas' and 'choosing ways to do thing and finding new ways'. This steer ensured that the UK Coalition government of 2010 retained cross-curricular and creative approaches for the education of children in their early years (0–5 years). In the Statutory Framework for the Early Years Foundation Stage (EYFS) 'areas of learning' include 'understanding the world' and 'expressive arts and design'. Educational programmes must also involve experiences for children in 'communication and language', 'physical development' and 'personal, social and emotional development' (DfE, 2012). The introduction stresses the equality and inter-connectedness of the areas of learning (DfE, 2012: 4) and links with subjects that appear in the National Curriculum followed by those above 5 years. It is a pity that in the National Curriculum the links between subject perspectives, the creative and exploratory approach and the importance of practical activity are not highlighted in the same way.

The Coalition government of 2010–2015 significantly added to the number of powers vested in the Secretary of State for Education. In 1976 the Secretary of State had only the direct power to open and close schools, manage the number of teachers and remove air-raid shelters from school playgrounds. By 2012 some 2000 new powers had been granted, significantly affecting the choices open to schools, parents and teachers (Twigg, 2012). Teacher education has changed for many too. School-centred initial teacher training (SKITT), Teach First, 'Troops to Teachers' and Schools Direct (DfE, 2014c, website) offer significantly more influence to schools and academy chains – often to the detriment of well-thought-out cross-curricular approaches. The push to open academies and free schools has resulted in local authority administered schools being in the minority by 2015. The hasty transfer of many schools from local authority to state-funded independence has not always had the positive effect envisaged by the advocates of free schooling. Regional Schools Commissioners have had to be appointed to deal with complaints and take on many other roles formerly handled on a more local level.

The speed of change has affected teachers' health. The steady increase in external influence on the curriculum between 1976 and 2015 has had many unintended effects, including a significant rise in teacher self-reported stress levels and absences due to stress. Seventy-six per cent of teachers report stress levels that are affecting their health and over 50% say their teaching would be better if they were less stressed (Teacher's Assurance, 2013, website). This is why teacher well-being is such an important consideration in staff development programmes – retention, recruitment, teacher excellence and efficiency are all negatively affected by poor well-being.

The revised and re-issued primary National Curriculum for England (DfE, 2013) makes no mention of cross-curricular approaches. The curriculum for Key Stage 3 (11–14-year-olds) includes the Personal Learning and Thinking Skills (PLTS) which are to be applied across the whole curriculum and does give schools the freedom to make links between subjects and subject programmes. For primary schools the 2014 curriculum deliberately omits guidance on educational approaches in an effort to give schools and teachers more sense of control. We have seen how this omission is *not* made in the Scottish, Northern Irish and Welsh curricula but the abandonment of cross-curricular links also runs counter to curriculum advice elsewhere in the English-speaking world. The Australian curriculum highlights 'cross-curricular priorities' which include: Sustainability, Civics and Citizenship, Health and PE, the Arts and Economics and Business (Australian Curriculum Assessment and Reporting Authority, 2013, website). British Columbia's (BC) New

Curriculum proposes personal and social, thinking and communication competencies, claiming that:

> In a world of growing diversity and challenge, schools must do more than help students master the sets of knowledge and skills acquired through the standard subject areas. They must prepare students fully for their lives as individuals and as members of society, with the capacity to achieve their goals, contribute to their communities and continue learning throughout their lives. (British Columbia Ministry of Education, 2013, website)

Cross-curricular subjects like Citizenship and ICT (replaced by 'Computing), are omitted from the 2014 Primary Curriculum. Cross-curricular approaches, however, continue to be valued by both primary and secondary schools. Cross-curricular methods have been perceived to have motivating, inclusive, sensitizing, enriching and uniting effects (Faultley and Savage, 2012). For their school-based curriculum, many intend to use the 30% available time *outside* the National Curriculum for cross-curricular approaches. Teachers have noticed, however, that there is not just one type of cross-curricular learning. There are many styles and types and each may have a different purpose. As schools plan to implement the new educational freedoms offered by the new National Curriculum, they are asking for guidance on how to organize an integrated curriculum that is effective, challenging and supports relevant, deep learning. The subject associations and expert teams have provided this but there remains little advice that crosses the whole curriculum. This book offers such advice in the light of experience and the research and recommendations of a range of educationalists and practitioners.

What is good cross-curricular teaching and learning?

Cross-curricular learning occurs when the skills, knowledge and attitudes of a number of different disciplines are applied to a single theme, problem, idea or experience. The term cross-curricular applied to both teaching and learning suggests considering education at a macro level, with the *curriculum* as the focus, but cross-curricular approaches may also have micro implications involving the style of pedagogy, classroom organization, environment and individual interactions. Cross-curricular methods can be effective in teaching and reaching ethical solutions, building individual and group motivation, sustaining interest and raising standards – this I see as good practice. Cross-curricular approaches can equally be made ineffective by trivializing, confusing, misleading, constructing new misconceptions and also by failing to provide a moral context for learning – this I would call poor practice.

As well as detailed discussion of values, Alexander recommends 'ethics' to be part of the curriculum, calling education 'a fundamentally moral affair' (Alexander, 2010: 16). Aims, values and purposes may differ between communities served by a curriculum, but the curriculum must stand on agreed, clear, values-based foundations if it is to be considered 'good' in a moral sense. It must also be good in a professional sense.

A base of separate subject knowledge is vitally important. If teachers want, in the words of the CPR, to 'excite the imagination, provoke dialogue, foster skills and encourage the child to explore, understand and make sense' (2010: 257–8), they must value subject knowledge. This does not mean that teachers should know everything about each of the traditional subjects – rather, that they should be familiar with the distinctive lens each subject provides on the same reality. The detail of the unique and specialized language, skill set, disposition and core knowledge of each subject should be well understood by at least one staff member in every school. Teachers must expect to be comfortable with regularly sharing that knowledge with their colleagues.

Good cross-curricular pedagogy should also be relevant. Relevance involves the teachers' increasing interaction with the world of their children. This knowledge of children's 'here and now' can be built into every lesson to motivate participation and engagement and involvement. The local community, its concerns and environments are another source of relevant issues and contexts. Schools should incorporate local visits, partnerships and community groups in their programmes of personal and professional development. Curriculum decisions must also be professionally relevant – conscious of research, subject priorities and in line with the aims of education. In short, teachers should 'be able to give a coherent justification citing evidence, pedagogical principle [and] educational aim for all their choices in school' (Alexander, 2010: 308).

Detailed advice on how to be a good cross-curricular teacher comes from Andrew Pollard (2010). Effective practice requires excellence in the science, art and craft of teaching. Cross-curricular approaches must also be research-informed, which is why Chapters 4, 5, 6 and 7 in this book are devoted to the evidence from psychological, social scientific, neuroscientific and pedagogical enquiry. Working between and across subject boundaries also requires what Pollard (2010: 5) sees as a 'responsive, creative, and intuitive' approach able to maximize on the unexpected reactions of children encountering real problems and using the skills and knowledge of several subjects to solve them. All teaching requires the 'mastery of a full repertoire of pedagogical skills and practices' (p. 5), but cross-curricular teaching specifically requires high levels of ability to work with Pollard's skills list A:

Pedagogical skills list A

- Construct or use scenarios that require the perspectives of several subjects
- Value and use diversity of response and insight
- Follow children's lead
- Find entry points to learning to match the individual
- Link ideas from different subject areas
- Be a co-learner

Well used, the pedagogical skills in list A will generate motivation, creative thinking and sustain interest, but may not on their own raise standards in individual subjects. To create the challenge necessary to build new knowledge and skills, the good cross-curricular teacher also needs to use several of the skills in skills list B:

Pedagogical skills list B

- Direct children's enthusiasm towards the acquisition of pre-planned, *whole-class subject goals* in two or more subjects
- Direct children's enthusiasm towards *individual subject progression goals* in two or more subjects
- Plan shared meaningful multi-sensory experiences to generate *focused* enquiry and challenge
- Teach *specific* skills and knowledge across a range of subjects as required by children
- Teach *specific* skills and knowledge across a range of subjects
- Empower children to use newly learned skills and knowledge to solve problems, address issues or understand cross-curricular themes
- Plan integral assessment opportunities within each unit of work

List B is a demanding skill set that usually requires more than one mind, so the final pedagogical skills in list C involve interactions with others:

> **Pedagogical skills list C**
>
> - Work in teams with other teachers to promote progression in children's learning
> - Work with practitioners from the community outside school to promote progression in children's learning
> - Work with children to generate plans, ideas and solutions

Poor cross-curricular teaching results in fragile, temporary, untransferable and difficult-to-articulate learning. If our aim is to generate both enjoyment *and* excellence in terms that can be assessed and, to a degree, measured, then combinations of skills from each of lists A, B and C are needed. Too much cross-curricular teaching in the past concentrated only on list A. List B is of equal importance – the teacher should *teach* as well as promote learning in all cross-curricular contexts. Practically speaking and because learning for both teachers and children is a social affair, list C reminds us that schools should be collegiate institutions working with the widest community.

Cross-curricular learning varies in its aims and pedagogies. I have identified through observation and research a number of contrasting cross-curricular contexts that may be useful in planning and assessing classroom activity that connects several subjects.

A cross-curricular taxonomy

The best cross-curricular projects combine the promotion of creative thinking with the maintenance of disciplinary rigour and challenge. It needs to be stressed from the outset that whilst 12 different subject disciplines *may* be applied to a single theme, research suggests that subject progression and integrity is best ensured by limiting the subjects involved in cross-curricular work to two or three (Barnes and Shirley, 2007; Jacobs, 2004; Roth, 2000). In offering a classification of cross-curricular approaches, I recognize a range of differing aims and purposes. I use data from a series of recorded lesson observations made over five years and my own continuing teaching experience, and from this analysis I have identified eight distinct types of cross-curricular teaching and learning. The types often overlap and sometimes projects involve several styles, but the types of cross-curricular learning can be described as:

- tokenistic
- hierarchical
- single transferable subject
- theme-based
- multi-disciplinary
- inter-disciplinary
- opportunistic
- double-focus.

Each contrasting mode of cross-curricular learning can be applied within thematic, project or topic-based approaches to the curriculum, but may also arise from planned whole class experiences or events.

Tokenistic cross-curricular approaches

Tokenistic cross-curricular approaches are only cross-curricular in name. It may look like there are two or more subjects involved in an activity but genuine connections are not made between subjects; there is no particular aim for the second subject and learning is only increased in the main subject. For example, a song, perhaps *Greensleeves*, might be used to introduce a history topic, but if the song is already known, nothing is made of it or added to it and little is done to enhance music learning, the only extra aim is to bring some extra interest to a history theme.

Hierarchical cross-curricular teaching and learning

Hierarchical cross-curricular methods aim at achieving progress in one discipline by also teaching aspects of another. This is probably the most common context in which cross-curricular thinking and learning takes place. Again a teacher may be planning to use *Greensleeves* to introduce the Tudors, but this time the children are to learn to play the tune on the recorder and improvise a simple metallophone and tambour accompaniment as part of a session on Tudor court life. Equally, a lesson on the detailed painting of a portrait might be conducted in French, extending Modern Languages vocabulary and grammar. A six-figure grid reference lesson in Geography might be used to help children understand and apply the idea of coordinates in Mathematics. In each case, learning a skill in one subject is used to support learning in another, perhaps higher-status subject. Effective and lasting learning in one subject is often provoked by calling upon another, as many of us who learned times tables by chanting or rapping remember. However, in hierarchical cross-curricular teaching and learning, knowledge, skills and understanding in the 'inferior' may be only slightly improved. The danger is that in thematic curricula some disciplines like Music, Art, Dance, Geography, Design/Technology and drama may become cast forever in this subservient, serendipitous and submissive role.

Arts subjects are often used in hierarchical contexts. Traditionally, the arts involve participation on emotional and physical as well as intellectual levels and are often argued to generate a sense of belonging, motivation and satisfaction (see Evans and Philpott, 2009; Roberts, 2006). Used in hierarchically weaker contexts, new arts skills, knowledge and attitudes may not be learned, though wider elements like communication, emotional literacy, motivation and enjoyment may actually be enhanced.

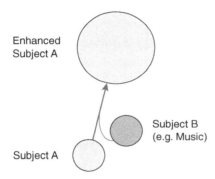

Enhanced
Subject A

Subject B
(e.g. Music)

Subject A

Figure 2.2   Hierarchical cross-curricular learning. Learning in the 'superior' subject (Subject A, for example English) is enhanced with help from an 'inferior' subject (in this case Music), which is not necessarily developed by its combination

Many would argue that using a subject as an inferior partner in a learning hierarchy is the easiest way to make sure it appears *at all* in an overcrowded curriculum. Those who feel insecure in their ability to teach the fundamental modes of thought of a particular discipline may find it less threatening to place their 'weaker' subjects in this position, but hierarchical methods can also be highly motivating and extend learning to more pupils. If Music, Art, PE or Geography is used as the 'way in' to language, Mathematics, Science or ICT for a particular group of children, then hierarchical approaches may be seen as more inclusive and motivating than 'straight' subject teaching. Similarly, the application of new 'core subject' knowledge in the context of a foundation subject project can make literacy or numeracy more meaningful and relevant to children. Often, however, little progress is made in the 'inferior' subject.

Illustration 2.1   Technology (in this case the use of class digital cameras) used to enhance skills in language

---

   Case study 1   'Head, shoulders, knees and toes'

Three British student teachers visiting a class in a rural school in India used the song 'Heads, Shoulders, Knees and Toes' to teach Tamil children the English terms for parts of the body. The children then translated the song into Tamil. The lesson ended with the three students singing 'Heads, Shoulders ...' to the class in Tamil.

Single transferable subject learning across the curriculum

Single transferable subject approaches aim to improve learning in a single subject (especially: English, Mathematics, Citizenship (Key Stage 3) or PSHE) by deliberately applying its perspective to a range of other curriculum areas. In single transferable subject approaches, the focus is on the subject itself and not on a motivating experience. This happens to English automatically because speaking, listening and usually writing is involved in learning across all other subjects. In subject-specific weeks or 'discovery days' a teacher might plan to apply a mathematical, PSHE or citizenship understanding to a wide range of other curriculum areas. But any subject could share the stage across the standard curriculum to enrich another. There are musical or scientific ways of interpreting and deepening the study of Art, Citizenship, Design/Technology English, History, Geography, Mathematics, Modern Languages, PE, PSHE, Science, RE, just as there are English ways. As with other modes of cross-curricular learning, teachers' planning should clarify the specific new learning aims for the transferable subject as well as those for its partner subject. This approach to cross-curricular learning may provoke particularly original insights and new perspectives because of the unexpected juxtaposition of subjects.

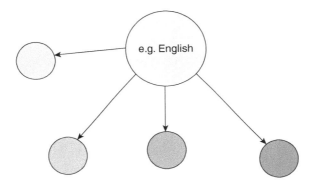

Figure 2.3   Single transferable subject learning across the curriculum

Theme-based cross-curricular approaches

Theme-based approaches use a theme to generate exploration through the eyes of several different subjects. The topics and projects of the 1960s to 1980s attempted to use themes to unify teaching and learning across the curriculum. When these themes were in the hands of confident and knowledgeable teachers they worked well to inform and motivate children. Often, however, tenuous links and unclear aims limited the learning. The failures of the past do not necessarily mean that the thematic methods are intrinsically wrong. Teachers must however consider their themes carefully. Choose themes that are:

- authentic (i.e. are generated by a genuinely shared interest)
- related in some way to the rich resources of the community
- capable of being sustained and resourced throughout a term or allotted period
- well-planned (i.e. have specific and valued subject targets, outcomes and purposes)

- well-assessed (i.e. assessments link with the targets and promote further learning)
- serviced only by subjects that genuinely add to understanding.

A relevant and authentic theme may be used to generate learning in a wide variety of subjects – far more than the two or three generally recommended in cross-curricular work – but no subject should be included unless it is essential to deepening understanding of the theme and unless itself it can be better understood through application to the theme.

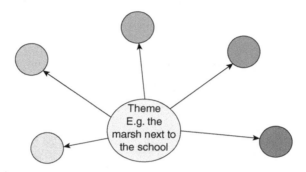

Figure 2.4   Theme-based leaning across the curriculum

Multi-disciplinary cross-curricular teaching and learning

Multi-disciplinary cross-curricular approaches aim at using a single experience or theme to develop higher levels of understanding and performance in two or more disciplines. The most effective multi-disciplinary projects arise from powerful and emotionally significant experiences that are shared by both children and teachers (Barnes and Hancox, 2004; Barnes and Shirley, 2005, 2007; Scoffham, 2013). In multi-disciplinary approaches, two or maybe three subjects are applied to a single shared experience. The disciplines are introduced and developed separately to throw light on a happening, event, issue, problem or question. Whilst the single meaningful experience and subsequent subject learning may be shared, in multi-disciplinary teaching and learning the teacher will have no intention of combining them. Student teachers find linking separate subject learning to events in this way (more fully developed in the Scottish Curriculum for Excellence – see website) is manageable for them and enjoyable for their children. Multi-disciplinary approaches can also treat all disciplines as equal. However, the most effective multi-disciplinary work in schools depends upon high degrees of planning, confidence and teacher knowledge (see Ofsted, 2010a; Roth, 2000). This approach is seen by many as the most appropriate cross-curricular approach for novice teachers since it does not involve the planning of complex interrelationships between the disciplines. It is also easier to assess and ensure progression.

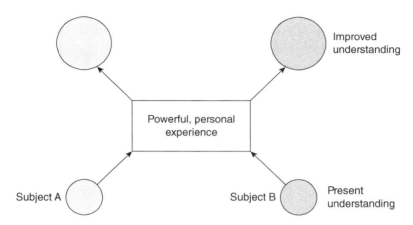

Figure 2.5   Multi-disciplinary cross-curricular learning. Discrete learning in two or three subjects is enhanced by arising from a shared meaningful experience

📂 Case study 2   A journey in dance

In an east London primary school, Year 4 pupils took a short journey through a nature reserve with a 'journey stick' (a 15cm strip of card with a band of double-sided sticky tape attached). Children were directed to collect six tiny objects that caught their eye on their journey. Returning to class, each child made a sketch map of their journey, using recently taught geographical skills in map-making. They used keys and symbols to represent where they found each of their objects. Their maps were discussed and displayed in the classroom.

   Separately, the children were given a PE challenge. In groups of five, they gathered ideas for a shape to represent each of six different places. On site, each group was asked to construct those shapes with their bodies and record them using the class camera. Back at school, the groups used printouts of their photographs to discuss and refine their shapes and eventually reconstruct them for the rest of the class. The teacher advised on stability, contrast and safety. Pairs of groups were

(Continued)

(Continued)

then asked to copy each other's shapes and work out ways of morphing one shape into the next. The teacher then taught a range of simple linking movements so that the groups could transform one shape into the next. Finally, the six groups were placed around the school field and the class performed the progress of their journey in the medium of dance.

Children's geographical learning was founded upon previously taught skills of map-making and their dance learning on structure and transformation was part of an ongoing programme of PE. Teachers reported that the experience took children to higher standards than expected in both subjects.

(www.engagingplaces.org.uk/teaching%20resources/art69235)

Illustration 2.2   Physical and social skills at the beach

Inter-disciplinary cross-curricular teaching and learning

Inter-disciplinary cross-curricular methods aim at progression in two or more subjects, and the promotion of creative thinking and connection-making

between *the subjects involved.* The prefix 'inter-' indicates joining, sharing or combining. Inter-disciplinary learning occurs when disciplines are combined to explain, understand or express a particular experience or idea or to solve a problem. Different disciplines offer differing interpretations of the same event or problem just as each individual brings their own individual insights to them. Inter-disciplinary approaches often result in some kind of collaborative response – a presentation, or group solution, performance or product. Student teachers report that this method of cross-curricular teaching generates particularly creative responses among children and encourages imaginative approaches to teaching.

The fusion of knowledge and skills between disciplines is common in the arts and advertising. New music, for example, pervades popular culture – TV, film, video games, promotional or advertising videos, websites and DVDs. Though music may provide background, it is composed in highly sophisticated ways, fully exploiting the established skills and knowledge of the discipline, so as to satisfy, stimulate or influence the intended listener. But film music composers need to know a great deal about human responses to images. They use musical structures and clichés to enhance the emotional power of pictures and words crafted by experts. The music is less comprehensible without the image and the images less affecting without the music; both have equal and complementary status. In schools examples of such combinations of disciplines grew with the work of Creative Partnerships (CP) (2002–2011) (Creativity, Culture and Education, 2012, website).

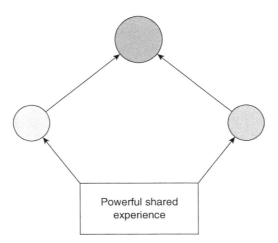

Figure 2.6   Inter-disciplinary learning. Learning in two subjects is taken forward as a result of a shared learning experience and then creatively connected in a presentation using the skills and knowledge of both subjects more-or-less equally

Illustration 2.3   Teachers perform their haiku on a staff development day combining drama and music skills and knowledge

Combining subjects in an inter-disciplinary mode can be more challenging than multi-disciplinary teaching. This approach requires not only confidence in both disciplines used but also a speculative, flexible, highly inclusive and bold teaching style, very much like the 'signature pedagogies' identified by Pat Thomson and her team who studied the CP archive (Thomson et al., 2012). In a successful project, the combination of several sets of disciplinary skills builds upon an initial meaningful experience and constructs something entirely new. Thus, an exhibition, a museum collection, event, procession, game, play, dance, composition, map, poster, debate or film might result from the fusion of two perspectives. Ideally, knowledge and understanding in the separate subjects increases as a result of the new insights generated by the combination. We know from research that this is not always the case. Studies (Barnes and Shirley, 2005, 2007; Roth, 2000; Willingham, 2013) have shown that applying two, three or four subjects to the same experience can produce a 'bland broth' of half-understood ideas and fresh misconceptions. Inter-disciplinary teaching and learning can easily result in less clarity about what a subject entails, therefore the cross-curricular teacher needs to be confident in subject knowledge, clear about learning intentions and plan genuine challenges for each subject to be successful in taking learning forward. As Ofsted observed in its survey of creative schools:

Occasionally, teachers failed to grasp that creative learning was not simply a question of allowing pupils to follow their interests; careful planning was needed for enquiry, debate, speculation, experimentation, review and presentation to be productive ... Lack of confidence ... sometimes growing from insecure subject knowledge, led to a more didactic approach ... which then encouraged greater dependency from pupils. (Ofsted, 2010a: 26)

 Case study 3   Movement haikus

Each student in a Year 7/8 group in Canterbury, Kent, wrote their own haiku [a Japanese poetry form consisting at its simplest of three lines: five syllables, seven syllables and five syllables) arising from a trip to the cathedral. In groups of five or six, they shared their haikus and chose one which they agreed could best be transformed into a series of tableaux. The group then used their bodies to construct three still scenes, each expressing a line in the chosen haiku. They then worked on improvising movement links between the three freeze-frames. They performed their haikus in silence as the rest of the class observed and wrote peer evaluations.

Planned learning intentions linked to and extending previous learning in both English and PE were clearly understood by all children. The authentic challenge of non-verbally expressing their experience in the cathedral led them to achieve at levels well above their own and their teacher's expectations.

Opportunistic cross-curricular teaching

Opportunistic cross-curricular teaching allows children to dictate the depth and direction of learning in subject categories arising from a shared theme or experience. The world beyond the classroom is cross-curricular. Every made object is the product of connections between subjects like Mathematics, Science, History, English, MFL and Geography. All environments, situations, ideas and concepts can be looked at from numerous points of view. Learning can therefore arise from any open and enquiring interaction with the world. The experienced and creative early years specialist is relaxed about building upon chance happenings in class and generating deep and transferable learning in any subject (see Austin, 2007; Cremin et al., 2009). Opportunistic approaches to promoting cross-curricular learning are child-led. They cannot easily be planned, they are unpredictable and include an element of risk. This does not mean that the teacher is a mere facilitator or observer – direct teaching often underpins the best opportunistic learning.

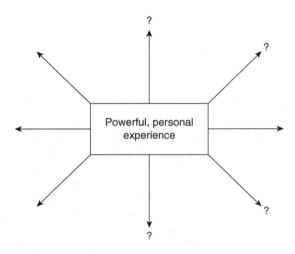

Figure 2.7 Opportunistic cross-curricular teaching. The teacher exploits unpredictable and child-led learning opportunities arising from a powerful and shared experience

Children's genuine responses come unplanned and unexpected. Confident teachers capture these moments and build them into opportunities to develop understanding. On the other hand, the teacher may carefully design a series of 'focusing exercises' – small-scale activities that support the child or children in having a 'present tense' and sensory interaction with a place, object or person(s) – and watch to see how children respond and what questions arise. Teachers clearly require good subject knowledge to be able to exploit the unexpected in this way. They must also feel empowered to follow the lead given by children, knowing that they have the support of colleagues and school leaders. In the current 'high accountability' structures, it may not be easy for teachers to feel this degree of professional trust.

Opportunistic cross-curricular learning, however, was a successful feature of many projects sponsored by CP (see Creativity, Culture and Education, 2010; House of Commons Education and Skills Committee, 2007; Roberts, 2006), and continues in some of the projects run by the independent arts education agencies that succeeded Creative Partnerships. Partly as a result of the United Nations Convention on the Rights of the Child (UNICEF, 1989, website), the child's voice has become more prominent in planning the curriculum – opportunistic methods are thus discussed more often (see Bragg, 2010). But whilst the pupil voice movement gathers pace, restrictive and over-assessed curricula appear even more dominant (see Alexander, 2010). In the UK, non-specialist primary teachers are trained in specific approaches to the teaching of reading and mathematics but their preparation for the teaching of other subjects is patchy (Rogers, 2003). In Teaching Schools and Schools Direct, where much professional learning happens *in situ,* the lack of good foundation subject expertise has implications for both teacher education and opportunistic methods of teaching. Novice teachers need opportunities to play with ideas in the disciplines themselves before generating genuine and personally relevant questions within the disciplines. Only through personally experiencing the framing of core questions and answering real questions within a discipline can a teacher successfully plan progression in a child's learning in that subject. This argues for a broad and balanced education for both primary and secondary teachers, where they can develop confidence in a range of subjects in order to be able to build upon children's responses to real experience.

Illustration 2.4   Nursery children visit the local park (see case study 5, Chapter 3)

Illustration 2.5   Nursery children in south India play with materials and pattern

   Case study 4   Engaging Places

A whole primary school community was taken to a modern financial centre in London. After a series of focus exercises where they were helped to become sensorially aware of the place through smell, touch, sight, sound and feelings, they were left in groups to collect ideas about the place to present to the rest of the school. Groups decided on a wide range of inventive and unusual presentations that were shared with the school in following weeks. Presentations included huge cane and paper sculptures, recorded sound trails, 'smell maps', an art exhibition, a taste lesson – none of which were planned but all of which were supported by teachers and assistants.
(www.engagingplaces.org.uk/network/art66179)

Double-focus cross-curricular teaching

Double-focus cross-curricular teaching attempts to promote a balance between experience-based and disciplinary opportunities for learning. A curriculum consisting of both separate subject teaching and regular opportunities to put that subject teaching into combined action needs two pedagogical foci. This mode of curriculum organization centres equally upon teaching and learner and involves the total curriculum of a school.

In my definition of double-focus teaching, each discipline is of equal importance. Where a curriculum offers all disciplines equally, the chances of every child finding a route into learning that suits them increases dramatically. Traditionally, we have valued some subjects so highly that failure in them signifies failure in education generally. In the USA and Europe, children might be first-class musicians, map readers, sportspeople, naturalists, peacemakers, artists or aesthetes, but if they find serious difficulties in the national language and mathematics they are said to have Special Educational Needs. In the UK, all too often such children lose their precious music, geography, PE, science or art lessons to English or maths booster classes. A double-focus approach suggests the belief that improvements in the core subjects are better secured when the child feels a sense of achievement and progress in any subject that can be developed into a personal strength or passion (see Robinson and Aronica, 2010). The good teacher works to ensure progression at the appropriate level in each subject for each child, but curriculum planning also provides regular chances for the creative application of newly learned subject skills.

The second focus in a double-focus curriculum is on a regular series of cross-curricular events. Each year-group shares at least six meaningful experiences each year. These events are intended to provide short,

Illustration 2.6   Creativity generates a sense of achievement

planned opportunities to put learning in two or three subjects into action in an authentic and challenging situation. Children may learn through hierarchical, multi-disciplinary, inter-disciplinary or opportunistic methods of teaching. The events or challenges are followed up with focused subject teaching related to the experience but also to give opportunities for assessment.

When children apply new learning to new situations, they expose the degree of their understanding. In applying learning and planning solutions using the skills in computing, geography, languages, D/T, PE, RE, languages, history, art, music, maths, PSHE and citizenship or science, children inevitably and richly use language. Cross-curricular working generates persuasive and technical language, the shaping of language into reports, plays, poems, stories or labels and the extension of language in arguments, debates, presentations and supporting others. Equally, the ease with which children use modern technology means that, given the resources, cross-curricular presentations will imaginatively use cameras, websites, synthesized and recorded sound and a range of visual presentation packages. English and Computing are well served by all cross-curricular approaches.

Cross-curricular approaches are not confined to planned themes, events or activities. Cross-curricular, experimental and creative references can be and often are made during the normal course of separate subject teaching.

 Case study 5   Room 13

A primary school linked to a Room 13 (see website) project in East-bourne, Sussex, visited a retirement home near the school. A group of children drew portraits of some of the residents whilst the older people draw their portraits. Many stories arose from the conversations stimulated by this activity. Brian Stent's story was one of them that linked to the children's local history study and so the children asked to make their own video of the story. Combining skills in acting, animation, film-making and historical enquiry the children from Year 5 made a beautiful film of their findings (West Rise Junior School, *YouTube* 2010, website). The experience, the story and the filming led children to research much more deeply into the history of World War II in their town and in Europe.

In this school the standard curriculum continues throughout the year and uses exciting and principled methods to teach it. When children finish their work or can persuade their teacher, they are given a ticket to go to 'Room 13'. Here a professional film-maker and artist helps the children (in groups and singly) to follow various interests they have developed. Typical experiences outside the classroom include building, exploring, visiting, sailing and looking after a farm and farm animals and these provoke a wide variety of responses. In Room 13, children are encouraged to think philosophically about these powerful experiences and then apply new or developing skills and ideas to authentic communal artwork, films and animations.

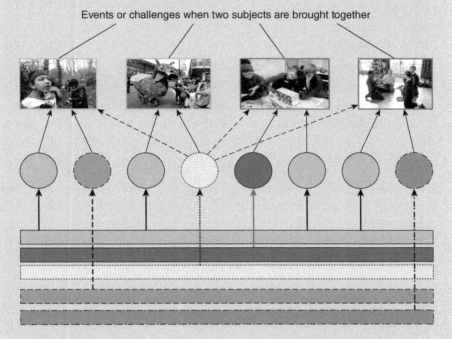

Figure 2.8   Double-focus cross-curricular learning. Learning in each curriculum subject continues separately throughout the year but is regularly joined with one or two others and applied to a shared experience

Summary

Cross-curricular approaches have been part of education for millennia. In recent centuries, they have become associated with progressive education, perhaps because of the protective attitudes of those who police the individual subject disciplines, perhaps in England because of a puritan sense that having fun whilst learning is somewhat suspect. As we face a future of exponential and unpredictable change, we need cross-curricular methods that encourage group solutions, collaborative learning, creative combinations and the development of independent learners. The generation of confident, imaginative and adaptable children may be the best route towards the happy population and flexible workforce that analysts suggest we need.

Apart from tokenistic approaches, there are at least seven different ways of organizing cross-curricular teaching and learning:

- hierarchical
- single transferable subject
- theme-based
- multi-disciplinary
- inter-disciplinary
- opportunistic
- double-focus.

They may overlap and different projects may use several of them at a time. Each approach, however, has different aims and strengths, but to be effective means of learning all cross-curricular learning should rest on the following principles:

1. Use powerful and meaningful sensory experiences to motivate learning.
2. Use only two or three subjects to interpret or build upon such experiences.
3. Expect English and Computing to be integral parts of all cross-curricular teaching and learning.
4. Plan specific and progressive learning targets in each subject represented.
5. Assess the success of learning by arranging for children to apply their learning to real situations.
6. Work hard at all times to increase teacher subject knowledge.

Key questions for discussion

- What topics have you seen operating successfully in a cross-curricular way?
- What kind of cross-curricular teaching and learning have you observed in schools? Give examples.
- How can we adequately assess two or three subjects within a cross-curricular module?
- What are the advantages of cross-curricular learning?
- Should subjects like Music be justified in the curriculum only because they have 'a hugely positive effect on numeracy and language skills'? (Gov.UK, 2010b, website)

Further reading

Alexander, R. (2010) *Children, Their World, Their Education: The Report of the Cambridge Primary Review*. London: Routledge.

Robinson, K. and Aronica, L. (2010) *The Element: How Finding Your Passion Changes Everything*. Harmondsworth: Penguin.

Savage, J. (2012–14) *Cross-Curricular Teaching and Learning in the Secondary School*, series (The Arts, English, Foreign Languages, Humanities, Computing and Mathematics). London: Routledge.

CHAPTER 3

WHAT DOES GOOD CROSS-CURRICULAR PRACTICE LOOK LIKE?

Chapter aims

This chapter will use real examples to demonstrate different styles of cross-curricular work in primary and secondary schools. After discussing the relationships between cross-curricular learning and what some schools have called a 'creative curriculum' the chapter illustrates contrasting approaches. By the end of the chapter you will have been introduced to case studies illustrating the following cross-curricular styles:

- topic or thematic
- experiential
- cross-phase
- innovative national/international
- short-term
- child-led.

Our differences are a joy to individuals and surely humankind's greatest resource. Individual uniqueness does not apply simply to our DNA, irises or fingerprints, but to the almost infinite range of potential links making up each human's history, intelligence and personality. There are an immeasurable number of possible connections between the neurons (or brain cells) controlling our sensory, physical and emotional faculties. These in turn interact in every person with the neurons that construct and hold our unique memories and prompt us to make conscious, unconscious, rational, irrational, intellectual, intuitive, imaginative or reflex responses. Such a wealth of possibilities suggests that we each experience the world around us in subtly (and not so subtly) different ways. I believe that effective cross-curricular approaches mirror and maximize on this valuable diversity.

How can we educate if we are all so different? In the context of human variability it would be foolish to suggest that there could be a finite range of answers to the question, 'What does good cross-curricular practice look like?' Good practice in curriculum arrangement and approach is likely to be as diverse as any other aspect of human organization.

It is a wonder that humans can communicate so effectively. Considering the potential for some of the billions of neural connections to misfire, it seems little short of miraculous that we ever establish shared perceptions. The teacher's job is to build shared understandings – mutually acceptable views of aspects of our world. School curricula are designed to support teachers in shaping children's minds by providing the intellectual, narrative and social settings for learning.

Curricula are bound to vary in their effectiveness. In the context of this book, recommendations and examples are guided by values like love, hope, community, positive relationships, inclusion, sustainability and health outlined in Chapter 1. A curriculum that energizes, motivates, provokes and sustains high-quality learning within a clear values set is doing a good job, regardless of whether or not it requires children to work across subjects. This book is *not* written to suggest that all teaching and learning should be cross-curricular. I claim rather that cross-curricular methods are highly motivating and for most children and provide a learning context that can easily be made relevant. Cross-curricular learning is also predisposed to the application and promotion of fundamental values because of its inherent need for connection-making.

The case studies

I have chosen seven case studies to illustrate a range of successful cross-curricular learning opportunities. Each case study sits within a set of identified values. Each arose from collaborative and detailed planning, depended upon meaningful and shared experience and resulted from the focused application of subject knowledge, real and relevant activity, and frequent formative assessment. The case studies include examples of single transferable subject, thematic, multi-disciplinary, inter-disciplinary and opportunistic modes of learning and double-focus approaches to the school curriculum. They involve long and short units and cover:

- a music and PSHE project in a 0–3 children's centre (inter-disciplinary)
- a multi-subject marshland project in a 7–11 junior school (thematic)
- a whole school values project (single transferable subject)
- a two-term project on the school locality in a 3–11 school (double-focus)
- a cross-phase language and languages day with Years 6 and 7 (multi-disciplinary)
- an RSA *Area-Based Curriculum* project covering three main subjects (multi-disciplinary)
- four Eco-School projects using different cross-curricular styles.

Human ingenuity means that new examples of cross-curricular learning appear all the time. *Whenever* teachers and children apply learning in more than one subject, cross-curricular practice is happening. When deep, transferable, useful learning occurs in more than one subject as a result, *effective* cross-curricular practice is happening.

Illustration 3.1   Effective cross-curricular learning happens through generating conditions that involve the child

In each example, cross-curricular and creative thinking did not just 'happen' – it was the result of thought, planning and usually of secure teacher knowledge. Objectives were met because teachers and other adults were constantly aware of them during planning and whilst children were working. Many case study schools brought in outside experts to take learning forward. The use of expert visitors from the community can make a significant difference to children's learning. Teachers often note that children are more able cheerfully to accept pinpointed criticism and stretching targets from non-teacher experts than themselves (see Brice Heath and Wolf, 2005; Thomson et al., 2012). The case studies confirm that partnership with members of the local community is not simply good for citizenship education but has much wider learning benefits (Ofsted, 2010b). Whether the expert was a carer, the mayor, an imam, nurse, artist, beekeeper, town planner or a great-grandmother, his or her knowledge helped raise standards of achievement, promoted the sense of belonging to a living, changing community and provided authoritative, rigorous alternatives to standardized assessments.

Creative curricula

Many schools employ what they call 'a creative curriculum'. There is no generally accepted definition or guide to such a curriculum, but very usually it is linked with cross-curricular activity. Craft (2000) helpfully calls creativity, 'possibility thinking'. Any curriculum designed to help children see different possibilities or make new connections in order to find answers to real questions is likely to promote creativity. Indeed, curricula like the International Primary Curriculum (IPC, website) and the RSA's *Opening Minds* (RSA, 2003) specifically intended to promote a range of connections. Arthur Koestler's (1964) insight that creativity is a result of 'bisociation' seems relevant here. Bisociation means the (usually unexpected) meeting of two distinctly different planes of thought. Sternberg (2003) picked up this idea as one of nine types of creativity and calling the bisociative type 'integration', where creative input integrates two formerly diverse ways of thinking. We may, for example, be analysing in some detail the decorative markings on a Victorian teapot while carrying out an investigation in History, and something makes us think of the markings as reminiscent of music. This unpredicted link between applied pattern and music may result in an imaginative, original and valued musical composition. The chances of making unusual juxtapositions of ideas, approaches and knowledge are high but appropriately unpredictable, in a curriculum where different viewpoints exist side by side and unexpected links are expected (see Ofsted, 2002).

Connections can be encouraged by curriculum choices. The case studies are designed to illustrate some different ways of connecting subjects, themes, individuals and learning styles across and outside the statutory curriculum.

Case study 1   The Haringey Lullabies Project: music promoting the development of language and communication with emotional and social health

The Haringey Lullabies project was designed to address a range of needs in both children's centres and community. It was funded by *Youth Music* (website) in line with their express aim is to 'transform lives through music'. Three children's centres serving an area of high economic deprivation and a community hosting many ethnic minorities, combined to employ a singer/songwriter to work with their children over a two-year period. The aims were to improve standards of music delivery in the centres, to positively affect personal, social and emotional development in children at risk of delay, improve English language and to develop closer dialogues between parents and children's centres. In terms of cross-curricular models the project employs a version of an interdisciplinary approach.

The singer Angeline meets with individual parents or primary carers and discusses the things their child loves doing, the funny things they say, their favourite pets, toys and relatives and any particular messages their carer wishes to have included in a bespoke song or lullaby. This information is openly collected and during the process the singer begins to try out culturally sensitive tunes and rhythms to carry the words. After the relaxed, often joyful conversation, the singer goes away to form the whole dialogue into catchy and highly individualized lyrics and completes tune and accompaniment. The following week a prototype lullaby is sung through to the parent/carer with guitar accompaniment and corrections are made to pronunciations and details of the lyrics. The completed song is then sung to the child and close relatives at the children's centre and CD copies are made – one for the family and one for the centre. These songs are then played at home, in the car, in the children's centres, whenever the child wants to hear it. The other children in the children's centre learn the choruses quickly and join in. The child subject of the lullaby quickly recognizes the song as 'their' song, and dances, smiles, gestures or sings along in response. Each time the song is played at the centre or at home parents and teachers report that the child becomes more confident and positively responsive to it. Eighty lullabies of this kind were created within a single year of part-time association with these families. Teachers and parents have noted the following benefits for participating children and families:

- Musical skills like singing, improvising and rhythm have begun to transfer to the children's centre staff.
- Focus children generally show increased signs of well-being, including greater involvement, stronger confidence, more resilience and better relationships.

- Children listened very carefully for repeated phrases and key words and responded increasingly enthusiastically to the songs. Many sang the words of the songs and spoke enthusiastically about the unique stories held in them.
- All centres noted a closer dialogue between home and centre in parents/carers who had been involved in the project.

Illustration 3.2   Angeline composing a lullaby with a parent

 Case study 2   An example of theme-based cross-curricular learning: West Rise Junior school's marsh project

A junior school in Eastbourne, Sussex, uses its unique location and a range of related themes to unite its curriculum. Its head teacher explains the background:

> As luck would have it, our school is located on land where the second largest Bronze Age settlement in Europe was once situated – many of the artefacts that have been found within the peat are on display at the British Museum in London. Being on a major archaeological site is an exciting educational opportunity … we have embraced the Bronze Age in a big way.

(Continued)

(Continued)

> Next to the main school site is an area of marshland owned by the local authority ... we asked the authority if we could lease the 120 acres of land, including two vast lakes, as part of our school grounds. We wanted the land to be the environment for a living history project. The authority agreed a 10-year tenancy ... this was followed by annual funding from Natural England for us to maintain the area and buy a tractor and quad bikes for farming.
>
> (Mike Fairclough, personal communication)

Thus started a curriculum project able to link every subject to the ongoing experience of looking after a Site of Special Scientific Interest, five water buffalo, establishing a replica Bronze Age village and learning a range of country skills. The school currently runs the following projects involving its children and teachers working together:

- **Forest School**: with local members of the RSBP
- **Archaeology**: investigations with Eastbourne Museum
- **Bronze Age Roundhouse**: building a roundhouse for school and community use
- **British Black Bee Sanctuary**: children help tend almost a million honey bees, located in the marsh
- **Boating**: Children learn to row real coracles and canoe on the lake
- **Countryside Sports**: clay shooting event, gun dogs and fly fishing
- **Water Buffalo**: tending the school's herds of water buffalo and sheep
- **Bronze Age Vision for the Marsh**: working towards a reconstructed Bronze Age village on the marsh.

In this project the theme(s) are so strong and so authentic that they sustain a whole year's worth of highly focused learning involving every subject. The experiences are so powerful in generating engagement that subject knowledge and skills across the curriculum are learned at a high level, alongside the personal, social and emotional skills involved in genuine team work. Though some of the activities are unusual for such young children, governors and parents are supportive and an Ofsted inspection in 2013 rated the school 'outstanding' for the behaviour and safety of pupils. They also commented that the pupils were 'exceptionally keen to learn and listen avidly to what their teachers and their classmates have to say in a mature and self-disciplined way' and that 'pupils achieve

Illustration 3.3   A primary child helping feed the school's buffalo (Photo: Mike Fairclough)

well throughout the school and in a wide variety of subjects', they 'are are very keen to tell visitors about its special features and how much they benefit from them' (Ofsted, 2013, website).

Illustration 3.4   Beehive with a welcome message for the bees from Year 4 (Photo: Mike Fairclough)

A theme-based curriculum has its learning dangers. Children may be unsure which subject they are learning when involved in activities such as beekeeping, building a wooden causeway or paddling a coracle. The teacher's role in every case is to build on the real experience and examine with the children exactly how it links to established and progressive disciplinary knowledge and skills. In these Eastbourne examples children leaned from highly personal perspectives, the science of the life cycle and ecological importance of bees, how to design and construct safe and sustainable structures, the historical significance of the coracle and about the physical aspects of manoeuvring of a boat. It seems obvious that learning in such contexts will be memorable, deep, transferable and transformative for very many children. Authentic and relevant projects like this always present real challenges to be overcome. By their very nature real world contexts provoke aspiration and supply their own exacting assessment criteria.

Illustration 3.5   The half-completed Bronze Age roundhouse (Photo: M. Fairclough)

 Case study 3   A cross-curricular term covering the entire curriculum for a 4–11 primary school – a second example of a theme-based approach

A Norfolk primary school for children 7–11 takes its values very seriously. It worked with Norfolk County Council and the *Index for Inclusion*

(Booth and Ainscow, 2011) on raising expectations, clarifying school values and responding to these priorities in curriculum and teaching. The school chose a cross-curricular approach and 'respect' as its key value. There are displays *'respect yourself'*, *'respect others'*, *'respect belongings'*, *'respect the environment'* around the hall and corridors of the school. The curriculum throughout the week refers to the core values in the context of each subject. At the beginning of the school year the children consider what respecting themselves and others actually means in their life. They write and draw about their perceptions of respecting belongings and the environment and these are shared around the school. These early understandings are then developed through the subject curriculum:

- What does respecting the environment look like in the context of an Egyptian irrigation scheme on the Nile?
- Where in this area are there good examples of respect for the environment?
- How can we show respect for the environment by making improvements to the school grounds that take account of climate change?
- How can I express respect for the environment through the arts?
- How does the idea of respecting belongings apply to archaeology or a museum display in the school?
- How does war and conflict work against the idea of respect for belongings?
- 'Who is my neighbour?' – discussed in a Religious Education context and demonstrated in the school's charitable activities.
- How should I respect myself through the food and drink I eat?
- How does science help me understand how to respect myself?
- In what ways can number help me understand respect for the environment?
- Which historical characters have helped us understand what respecting others looks and feels like?
- How can I use words and gestures to communicate my beliefs about respecting others?

Questions like those above have an existential quality for children as well as adults. Within the school curriculum they have become overarching questions that hold together units of work in Science, Mathematics, Geography, History, RE, Citizenship or PSHE. In relating learning in the subject disciplines to fundamental values, the school has found that it expresses one of its core aims – to be a values-creating school.

Illustration 3.6   Children planning their presentation

   Case study 4   An inner-city London school uses a double-focus cross-curricular approach for two terms

This 3–11 school works with children from nursery through to the end of Key Stage 2. It serves a busy and heavily built-up part of east London with a diverse community. It chose the local environment as the linking context for its curriculum and planned three 'whole school experiences' to motivate engagement and learning. The visits were to:

- the streets around the school
- a nature reserve
- Canary Wharf.

In addition to closely following the school's health and safety and child protection policies, the following guidelines for each visit were agreed by the school staff and parent/governor helpers:

- All (adults and children) should see themselves as learners.
- Children should be paired in differing age groups (nursery children were paired with Year 6 children, Reception with Year 5 and so on).
- Learning would occur in groups consisting of three pairs of children and an adult.
- The same 'Focus exercises' (see pp 97–100) would be used at each site.

- Adults should participate in the exercises alongside children.
- Adults would use the words 'us' and 'we' throughout the visits.
- Adults were to stress the 'present tense' experiential nature of all activities.
- The visits would go ahead whatever the weather.

The school made the visits at roughly six-week intervals. Each outdoor experience lasted a morning and ended with a picnic. During the visit the mixed-aged groups talked animatedly, made decisions, took photos, made maps, collected words, sounds, smells, feelings and images, drew pictures, rubbed and felt surfaces, counted, estimated, recorded sounds and imagined links. Each activity kept the learners in the present; there was no talk about the future uses of the information collected via the focus exercises and little conversation about learning itself. In a school of more than 300 pupils with 50 adult co-learners there were no reports of behaviour problems during any of the trips.

On returning to school, children went back to their usual age-group classes and teachers picked up aspects of the trip to develop through the curriculum. For example, after the Canary Wharf visit the Year 1 classes developed information from the sound maps, 'spatialization' and photo frame exercises into extended musical compositions where their detailed sound maps and personal sound records were combined to make a graphic score. The music was performed in two school assemblies and on a parents evening. Year 3 changed their smell trail into a 'taste trail', first of all being taught about the science of taste and then using blind-fold sampling of Stilton cheese, mango, lime, coffee, 'raw' chocolate and other strong-tasting foods to consolidate their learning. Later, they constructed a mapped treasure hunt based on taste identification and challenged another class to find their way to the treasure (chocolate of course!). A Year 4 teacher also used a map created by one group to make a large classroom display where each landmark on a beautifully presented map was represented by a series of poetic descriptions arising from the 'fridge magnet' exercise. After the nature reserve visit, the Year 5 class mounted a public art exhibition where framed paintings, prints and photographs arising from the visit were sold in order to fund the creation of their own mini nature trail in the school grounds.

The example above provides examples of both multi- and inter-disciplinary cross-curricular responses – classes responded in different subject ways to the same experience. Whilst subject-based activities related to the visits continued to occupy each class for three or four weeks, the remainder of the curriculum time was devoted to an unrelated programme of learning in the remaining subjects.

Illustration 3.7   Intense faces and focused body language often characterize collaborative projects (Photo: Ian Bottle)

Illustration 3.8   A 'wow' moment at Canary Wharf

'Wow' experiences and focus exercises

The meaningful encounters generate deep involvement. Shared experience can easily be transformed to a 'wow' experience in unusual locations, with contrasting approaches and unexpected groupings. The places visited in case study 4, though very near the school, were unfamiliar to well over half the pupils. The teachers and children had never experienced a whole-school outing before and it was very unusual for the Year 6 class to spend extended time with those in the nursery. The initial impact of each environment was strong, children expressed this in 'wow's and excited talk, but interest was sustained and deepened by the series of focus exercises.

Focus exercises are sensory activities intended to be fully inclusive and help all learners experience aspects of a place, theme, object or person in fine detail. In each place, focused listening, careful looking, sensitive smelling or touching and accurate looking were encouraged through these open-ended exercises (see below for a sample of these exercises). They were open-ended because there was no initial objective other than to fully experience the sight, sound, touch, smell or view of usually unnoticed features. Children and adults in their unfamiliar groupings entered into these exercises with gusto and real involvement. The social and sensory aspects of the learning process were fully explored but also generated questions, thoughts and conversations which went well beyond the exercises themselves.

Outside-school focus exercises

1. Word frame photo

Everyone is given a viewfinder with a different key word written on it (e.g. red, sad, lonely, awesome, dangerous, etc.). Using your viewfinder to frame it, look around for details (small ones are usually best) which illustrate that key word. Capture your decision in a photo and also include the key word on your viewfinder in the photo. Use the same viewer to frame five representations of the same word. (Thanks to Catherine Greig)

(Continued)

(Continued)

2. Spatialization

Draw a circle to represent a bird's-eye view of your head, put some ears at 3 o'clock and 9 o'clock and a nose at 12. Listen carefully for sounds around you. Decide the location of the separate sounds and the direction of movement if the sound is moving (like an aeroplane or a car). Mark the location of each sound in the appropriate area around the diagram of your head.

3. Big picture

On a large sheet of paper (A1 or A2), each of four people draws a big impression of the skyline in front of them. One person should draw the skyline looking north, one east, one south and one west. You should use bold, colourful felt-tip pens. The four team members should then join their drawings to make a continuous collaborative image of 360° of the skyline.

4. Texture rubbing and words

Find a place where two different materials and/or textures meet. Feel the join between them and then talk about the different textures which meet there. Make a rubbing of the join and a little of each material and annotate the rubbing with words describing the two textures.

5. Colour match

Use coloured paint swatches to find natural and made matches in the environment. Peel off the double-sided sticky tape and attach as many examples of each colour to its corresponding paint colour as possible.

6. Mapping

Make a map of a little journey you have taken showing significant landmarks (buildings, plants, shadows, furniture and unexpected things which strike you as important). Use your map in one of the following ways:

(a) emotional maps: how do you feel in each place? Mark the emotions you feel in different places on your map using words or colours. For example, which place makes you feel small, lonely, excited, frightened, cold, happy, sad, ill, etc.?

(b) sound maps: what are the dominant sounds in different areas of your map? Draw symbols or write words that capture the locations of different sounds in the environment.

(c) smell maps: what smells can you identify in this place? Mark on the boundaries between different dominating smells. For example, where is there a more natural woody, vegetation smell?

Where can you smell coffee or cakes? How are the smells near the water different?

7. Fridge magnet poems

Fold a piece of plain A4 paper into 16 rectangles by folding in half four times.

Walk around a chosen place and just write in each rectangle random words that pop into your head as you walk. Stop when you have one word per rectangle. Back in class tear out the rectangles and rearrange them into meaningful sentences or phrases. You can add in up to eight short words like: the, a, but, or prepositions, you can discard up to eight words and you can change word endings if you need to.

8. Object links

Each group of four or five picks up two random objects from an object collection in class. They take their object to a place of their choice. At the place they invent links between the object and the place. Each member of the group has a turn to make two interesting, unexpected, funny or quirky links. Back in class the group is given two contrasting characters and each child has to combine characters, objects and place into the **middle** part of a story (they do not have to introduce characters, scenes etc. or resolve any crisis.).

9. A sense of touch

Each member of the group is to go into their own space and sit or stand alone. Feel walls, pebbles, plants, fences, etc. nearest you. Jot down fragments of sentences that describe the fine detail of the physical sensations in the fingers as you feel the immediate environment.

10. Haiku

Each person in the group is to write a three-line haiku (five syllables, then seven, then five syllables only) that captures the essence of a tiny detail of the place they are in. A haiku often starts with a sensitive description in the first two lines and in the last-five syllable line, the thoughts 'flip' to a 'higher' or more profound association.

11. Snapshot view

Divide into pairs. In each pair, one of the partners closes their eyes and is led very carefully by their open-eyed partner. When the open-eyed partner sees an unusual or interesting image, they position their friend in the optimum viewing position and then squeeze the hand of their partner. The partner then opens their eyes for the length of the hand squeeze. Do this five times and then swap roles.

(Continued)

(Continued)

12. One shot only

Each member of the group is allowed one still photograph only (so it has to be a good one). Discuss shots with the whole group but each individual must take a photograph.

13. A dramatic happening

Plan a dramatic modern (or future) event that could only have happened in your place. Act it out. Summarize the story in three freeze-frame montages. Discuss and draw/plan/note what you would absolutely *have* to construct on your school stage if you wanted to act the scene out back at school. For example, would the light need to be coming from a certain side? Would there have to be a step here, an arch there? Would the arch have to be low/pointed/stone/crumbly? Etc.

14. Say it in one

Each group has to produce five 'one-shot movies' lasting one minute. Each person will have the opportunity to make a movie. It should be a planned and continuous shot taken by one member but the shot should be discussed by the whole group.

(With thanks to Robert Jarvis for ideas for 2, 11, 12 and 14)

	Canary Wharf	Nature trail	Tour of streets around the school
Nursery			
Reception	Words: labelled photographs: 30 dark things, 20 red things, 45 cold things, 12 scary things, etc.	Collections – made and natural, colours	
Year 1	Musical journey – composition project		Shapes project – graphs of the most common mathematical shapes found in the locality
Year 2		Art gallery project – paintings of the woodland canopy and close-ups of natural detail collected in drawings and digital images	Designing and making 'Snow world' environments and learning about the history of the seventeenth-century winter markets on the Thames

Year 3	Taste trail – science of taste and geography plan-making project		
Year 4		Growth and decay – a science project on the life cycle of the minibeasts collected on the nature trail and the science of decay	
Year 5			Illustrated stories to be read to Reception children, based upon five personally collected items from the streets and gardens around the school
Year 6		Emotional mapping – geography mapping skills and knowledge, direction	
Gifted and talented cross-phase group	A geometric 'made' environment using forms, patterns and textures found in Canary Wharf – applying design/ technology skills and mathematical knowledge		

Figure 3.1   A sample of class follow-up sessions for each year group after their three visits in the school locality

Illustration 3.9   Using word frames

Case study 5   A cross-curricular module with a cross-phase group of Year 6/7 children

The transition between Year 6 and Year 7 is a difficult one for children. Primary education practice and the pedagogies and curricula of secondary level are often seen, even by teachers, as very different from each other. Two schools belonging to the same academy chain in northwest England wanted to work to break down these barriers. A cross-curricular language project was devised to launch their new relationship. Both schools had enthusiastic languages teachers who worked together to gather a team of history and English specialists. The cross-curricular group devised a short multi-disciplinary module intended to break down barriers between the schools through the creative combination of subjects with classes where Year 6 and 7 children were mixed. Their work was to be shared with and responded to by two parallel schools in France.

There was no large-scale 'wow' experience to set the module going. Instead a series of focus exercises was chosen to engage children and give them reason to express themselves in another language. The school included some interesting eighteenth-century buildings and large grounds. The first 'word frame' exercise was intended to help the children find English words to describe the detail and unique and historical qualities of their school environment. Adjectives like 'classical', 'decorative', 'patterned', 'symmetrical', 'peaceful', 'circular' and 'funny' were used. In a subsequent lesson the same exercise was repeated in French, using nouns like *mur, porte, fenêtre, jardin, champs* and *arbre*. These exercises were done inside and outside the school.

Other exercises followed using the fridge magnet idea first in English and then again using nouns in French. English words were assembled into poetic sentences and phrases and French words used to construct simple descriptive sentences using given adjectives. These language-based focus exercises stimulated a great deal of agitated and enthusiastic talk. The teachers found that setting time limits – 10 minutes for the key words and the poems – helped focus minds more productively. Opportunities to work alone back in the classroom, as in the poem exercise, were particularly valued by some children. Many Year 7 children reported that they felt very motivated by these activities: 'It was great to get out and do real stuff', said one. 'I can't explain it, but when we were doing the exercises I felt really excited and wanted to do much more of it. I 'specially liked it when we were in pairs on the key words, we kept sparking off new ideas from each other,' said another.

Following up

The focus exercises used in case study 5 provided motivation and a series of small-scale shared experiences for the children in both classes. When questioned, the vast majority of the class said they felt 'excited', 'energetic', 'happy', 'enthusiastic', 'interested' and 'questioning'. Teachers confirmed pupils' high levels of engagement by applying the Ferre Laevers Leuven Involvement Scale (see Chapter 6). Children's enthusiasm carried through the follow-up sessions, which used history or geography skills hierarchically to take learning in French forward.

The pupils in Year 7 were given a degree of freedom in deciding on the relevance of the focus exercises for their learning in French. Several groups used the words to make a PowerPoint presentation illustrating the meaning of their French words. Other groups used the fridge magnet idea to make English poems from their collections of 16 words and placed them beside their simple French sentences relating to the same places around school. Motivation to complete and improve the follow-up activities was provided by the teacher introducing the class to a class in Boulogne via a Skype® link up. Some French children introduced themselves and then asked the English children to send them information about their school via email. Richly illustrated French poems and PowerPoints about their school were sent by email towards the end of the course. The Year 6 class constructed a series of 'I like …' poems about their school and illustrated them in their own PowerPoint presentations with inserted musical background using the *Madpad* app.

Illustration 3.10   Arranging found words into a poem

Case study 6 A primary school following the Royal Society of Arts (RSA) Area Based Curriculum in Peterborough using a multi-disciplinary approach

The school is located very near to Peterborough Cathedral, though few children have been there except on RE visits. It has a high percentage of newly arrived families and serves a community of many faiths. The cathedral is very keen to make living contacts with the local community and a strong outreach programme designed to work with people of all faiths and none. The RSA Area Based Curriculum supported schools in Peterborough to work with community partners to build in children a greater attachment to their community, to embed schools more deeply into the community and to motivate engaging, more lasting learning. The first project jointly designed by cathedral and school was to mount a 'Question Time' event at the cathedral with Year 4 and 5 children. Children were supported beforehand in asking searching questions on faith and community, arguing their point and listening carefully to others. The cathedral was keen to hear the views and deepen their relationships with the school and was particularly anxious through deepened contact with the school to develop its inter-faith stance in the community. A very successful Question Time where children asked profound questions about diversity, and tolerance, and 'why people from different religions can't live together all over the world' has led to many further collaborations. The school now visits the cathedral regularly to initiate maths investigations (the building's west front is an essay in Euclidian geometry) and learn about the science of forces, as well as extending its local history study. The cathedral has used the contact to build more and to explore 'its role as a faith institution in an increasingly diverse city' (RSA Peterborough Project, website).

 Case study 7 Cross-curricular projects linked to the Eco-Schools scheme, illustrating a range of cross-curricular approaches

Chapter 1 stressed the importance of the sustainability agenda for the 21st century. The children we teach now will live their adulthoods in a rapidly changing environment dramatically affected by climate change, rising sea levels, water shortages and shortages of resources.

Any school that ignores this issue is missing a significant opportunity to make a positive difference to the way children live their lives. The Eco-Schools programme is huge and international and 'guides schools in their sustainable journey', towards meaningful Education for Sustainable Development (ESD) (see Eco-Schools, website). Over 11,000 English schools have an award from them and 17,000 schools are registered with them. In Scotland 98% of local authority schools are linked with the Eco-Schools project, under *Keep Scotland Beautiful.* Wales and Northern Ireland have wide memberships amongst their primary and secondary schools. The nine key topics of Eco-Schools – energy, water, biodiversity, school grounds, healthy living, transport, litter, waste and global citizenship – focus children on what they can do to change themselves and the environment in more sustainable ways. These subjects obviously link to Geography and Science but can be powerfully addressed through every other curriculum area. The following case studies illustrate a range of cross-curricular manifestations of the sustainability agenda.

7(a) *A carbon reduction scheme in a secondary school in Cornwall (thematic)*

Penair School worked with the local authority and the Carbon Trust to reduce its energy consumption by 10%. This involved both behaviour change on the part of staff and children and also technological changes to the school plant such as the installation of solar panels and the purchasing of energy efficient equipment. For the children it resulted in a series of whole school events like assemblies and themed weeks on aspects of sustainability. The annual 'Turn Off Fortnight' allow pupils an opportunity to monitor the energy consumption. Using *Energy View*, the online facility to help businesses save energy, pupils were able to monitor highs and lows in consumption and the effect of their annual 'Turn Off Fortnight'. The Eco team also uses its maths skills to publish the school's energy data each week and to see the impact of the new solar panels. Pupils decided to issue congratulations to teachers who turned class lights off at lunch and break times and gentle reminders to those who forgot. From this start the school has developed a range of other eco-friendly practices they hope will change behaviour at home and school.

7(b) *Classroom waste into eco-bricks project in a middle school (multi-disciplinary)*

Downsbrook Middle School is also interested in the recycling of waste. Each class was issued with a briquette-making machine, a building

(Continued)

(Continued)

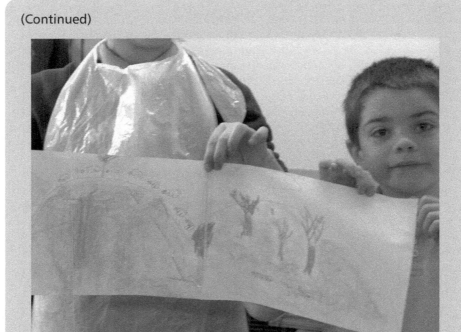

Illustration 3.11   Six-year-olds sharing thoughts about the possible changes in the view from a classroom window in 50 years' time. (Left hand side, present; right hand side, future)

mortar tray and two buckets. Children collected all waste paper and in the buckets turned it back into pulp. They forced the soggy pulp into their briquette machine that squeezed out excess water and dried the resulting bricks in the sun. Classes competed with each other as to who could produce the most bricks. After a term 1,000 bricks had been produced, enough to build an earthquake-proof house in the grounds of the school (linking the recycling to another project). The school planned these activities carefully to meet targets in both the Design/Technology and the Geography curriculum. The bricks are now sold as fuel for open fires and wood burning stoves and children tell us they have a high calorific value.

7(c) *Scotland's schools reducing their carbon footprint (opportunistic)*

Lawthorn Primary School in North Ayrshire is serious about reducing its carbon footprint. The school understands its global responsibilities and has identified six target areas to work on: buildings, energy, water, food, transport and waste. Each can be approached using any curriculum subject. Around its buildings it has planted 180 new trees and made a willow classroom to provide shade and outdoor learning in the summer. Using an energy monitor scheme run by the children it has reduced energy consumption by 43% by keeping a close eye on its use of lights and radiators. It has saved water by placing 'hippo bags' in each toilet cistern. The school grows its own vegetables and fruit and this activity plus the curriculum reminds children of the problems of food production around the world. Through their campaign to get to school in greener ways children have persuaded parents to share cars, walk to school more often and encourage the use of safe routes and bicycles. There has been a reduction of 60% in car use on the school run. The kitchens produce both breakfasts and lunches and the schools eco-campaign aims to reduce food waste by 80% .

For other examples of Scottish Eco-Schools projects see Education Scotland (Educationscotland, website).

A school's values will show in its curriculum. Those with a serious concern for the future of the planet and their children often have specific policies for Education for Sustainable Development (ESD). One purpose-built Eco-School recognizing that 'education impacts on society today and in the future' states: 'Our curriculum reflects values in society that promote the development of equality of opportunity, economic well-being, a healthy just democracy and a sustainable future.' Indeed ESD could and probably should be the guiding principle that unites all curriculum areas. Some schools have tried do this, one states:

> Sustainable living and learning is at the heart of the curriculum and everything we do at Ashley, with all our half-termly topics directly linked to an element of sustainable living. We look to develop energy and environmentally conscious individuals who care about the world around them and understand what is required to sustain individual, team and global well-being. (see Ashley Primary School, website)

Cross-curricular education is highly motivating. Whether we tie powerful experiences to a few traditional subjects or to major themes like ESD, inclusion, global rights or global citizenship, the result of authentic experience is true engagement. Once engaged, children can be supported to sustain their interest by well-planned teaching, fair, committed, respectful and compassionate attitudes and a focus on the joy and beauty of the world around them. Teaching children of any age to love their environment, enjoy the moment, have the courage to stand up for what is right and true, trust each other and to hope for the future are sustainable and moral aims for education. My experience tells me that cross-curricular learning most easily enables this approach.

Summary of major points arising from the case studies

- Each study illustrates different ways to build local and child-centred relevance.
- There is no optimum timescale for good cross-curricular practice; a day, a week, a term, two terms and a whole-school curriculum are each represented.
- The fewer the curriculum subjects represented within a single theme, the more teachers are able to help raise subject standards and ensure curriculum progression and coverage.
- Each study relied upon and promoted maximum physical and emotional involvement in an authentic setting.
- Each study generated creative links to subjects across the curriculum.
- Each study integrated working adults as experts and partners from the wider community.
- Activities and themes held equal fascination for both the adults and children involved.
- Each activity required and was founded upon detailed and lengthy planning in order to ensure progression and curriculum coverage.
- Every study was reported by teachers to have generated a high degree of focus, motivation and exemplary behaviour on the part of the children (and adults).
- Some cross-curricular themes like Education for Sustainable Development (ESD), Inclusion and Global Citizenship go beyond subjects to influence the way we think and are.

Key questions for discussion

- Can you identify the difference between inter-disciplinary and multi-disciplinary cross-curricular activities?
- What kind of teacher do you think would be most at home with opportunistic methods of cross-curricular teaching?
- Are the kind of activities outlined in the case studies and focus exercises feasible for novice teachers? Give your reasons.

Further reading

Faultley, M. and Savage, J. (2012) *Cross-Curricular Teaching and Learning in the Secondary School: The Arts*. London: Routledge.

Hosack Janes, K. (2013) *Using the Visual Arts for Cross-Curricular Teaching and Learning: Imaginative Ideas for the Primary School*. London: Routledge.

Wilson, A. (ed.) (2005) *Creativity in the Primary Classroom*. Exeter: Learning Matters.

Wyse, D. and Rowson, P. (2008) *The Really Useful Creativity Book*. London: Routledge.

CHAPTER 4

SOCIAL PERSPECTIVES ON LEARNING

Chapter aims

This chapter outlines sociological and social psychological perspectives that argue the communal benefits of cross-curricular learning. It introduces some key thinkers and contexts on social learning. The chapter discusses the role of friendships, learning groups, community relationships and social values like kindness, fairness and inclusion. By the end of this chapter you will have thought about the education significance of:

- friendships
- group learning
- community
- culture
- socio-political concepts like equality, fairness and inclusion
- the role of places: locality, visits, school, classroom
- the special role of objects.

Humans are social creatures. Family, friendships, communities, cultures and, relatively recently, language (Mithen, 2005) evolved out of human sociability. Even before the development of language archaeology shows that *homo sapiens* demonstrated exceptional ability to bond and form cohesive social groups. With the development of language between 100,000 and 60,000 years ago, humans found powerful new ways to communicate within and between their groupings, progressing from nouns and verbs (probably rapidly), to description, metaphor, memory and analogy (Dunbar, 1998, website). From the archaeological record we can trace a history of creative connections between ideas, things, materials, places and people (Mithen, 1996). Most human communities use some kind of schooling to pass these connections on to future generations and extend the present possibilities of ideas. In the West and for more than a century, social scientists, archaeologists and anthropologists have studied human groups and the social nature of creativity, discovery and invention, sometimes comparing them to our closest primate relatives.

Understandings of social learning are highly influenced by values. Vygotsky's influential views (1962, 1978) arose from a Marxist ideology that saw the social as the all-powerful force for good or evil. Education for Vygotsky was the route through which social reconstruction would happen, and therefore research into the social nature of learning was essential. In translation, Vygotsky's ideas had a new impact within Western, capitalist and hierarchical societies. His theories about how children learned were taken up by educationalists like Bruner (1968) and Wood (2001), whose prosaic term 'scaffolding' replaced Vygotsky's 'Zone of Proximal Development' to describe the way in which more experienced others support our learning. In the more individualistic and competitive West, psychologist Bandura (1994) developed his social learning theory showing that those modelling learning behaviours on observation of others were more successful in retaining and transferring knowledge. Lave and Wenger (1991) emphasized the influence of the place where learning happens and Bourdieu (1984) the culture within which it takes place, whilst Bernstein (1971, 1996) showed the power of language to include or exclude the learner. Vygotskian ideas were taken into the current century by Vera John-Steiner, whose work on interactionist approaches (2006; John-Steiner et al., 2008) helped us understand the social nature of creativity. More broadly, writers like Alexander (2010), Bawden (2006, website), Dunbar (2003), Goleman (2006), Noddings (2003), Pollard (1996, 2008) and Rogoff (2003) have highlighted the essential role of others in all learning. Neuroscientists have more recently joined the debate. Usha Goswami, for example, stated that the social nature of learning can now be 'safely concluded' (Goswami and Bryant, 2007).

If the observations of this cross-disciplinary range of scientists and thinkers are accurate, then as teachers we should reflect carefully on the social as well as physical environments we construct and influence. Whilst we cannot plan for each child's unique experience of others, the generalized environment teachers *do* control can be constructed so that interactions we would call positive are more likely than negative ones.

Children can make choices too. Pinker's (2002) view of children as 'partners in human relationships' and not 'lumps of putty to be shaped', reminds us of the importance of developing less hierarchical social relationships and listening to the child's voice. If 'positive', 'constructive' or 'good' experiences for children are to outweigh negative ones, then social values like collaboration, sharing, fairness and kindness must be championed in schools. Noddings (2003) reminds us, however, that without the support of safe, relevant, nourishing surroundings, respectful systems, positive curricula and personal friendships, such values are difficult to sustain. Schools, education administrators and novice teachers miss a vital ingredient of successful learning if they fail to address the issue of social learning.

Social learning

Bruner (1960) proposed that curricula and classrooms should be arranged to maximize on children's tendency to learn socially. He also noted that language shared between learners is essential to the extension and consolidation of learning. These observations led him to devise a curriculum and rearrange classrooms in ways that challenged more traditional arrangements in schools in the USA and UK. Bruner's curriculum, *Man: a Course of Study* (see MACOS, 2010, website), rested upon three big questions – each holding an implied social element:

- What is uniquely human about human beings?
- How did they get that way?
- How could they be made more so? (MACOS, 2010, website)

Bruner also proposed the intriguing idea of the 'spiral curriculum'. Its underlying principle is that children should 'revisit … basic ideas repeatedly, building upon them until they grasp the full formal apparatus that goes with them' (Bruner, 1960: 13). He suggested that children in collaborative groups could handle 'difficult' questions related to values, philosophy and science, given appropriate language, structure, motivation, opportunity for intuition and others to scaffold the learning. This proposition was expressed succinctly:

> We begin with the hypothesis that any subject can be taught effectively in some intellectually honest form to any child at any stage of development. (p. 33)

Relevance and activity were considered crucial to learning, and that often such relevance is defined and sustained by peer group and contagious enthusiasm. Bruner put it this way:

motives for learning must be kept from going passive ... they must be based as much as possible upon the arousal of interest in what there is to be learned, and they must be kept broad and diverse in expression. (p. 80)

Education, creativity and cultural initiatives have often been driven by beliefs in the social nature of learning, for example, *Sing up*, *Youth Music, Forest Schools* (websites) and the *Learning Outside the Classroom* manifesto (DfES, 2006b, website). Schools remain cautious of such advice, however. Teachers are highly conscious of the parallel and undiminished development of target-driven and compliance cultures. Competition between schools and a relentless drive to improve test results and league table scores emphasize individual attainment or whole-school rankings rather than collaboration. The social characteristics of learning do not disappear when national curricula like that of England fail to emphasize it, but social learning is shifted to informal situations and is used only by the most confident schools and teachers.

Social learning has many faces. Of particular interest to teachers are the following groupings outside family, which affect learning and the wider curriculum:

- friendships
- learning groups
- community
- culture.

Friendships

Having good friends is a key component in subjective feelings of happiness (Diener and Seligman, 2002; Layard and Dunn, 2009; Ryff, 1989). Friendship may also be crucial to the development of values (Barnes, 2013b) for both adults and children.

 Friends and teachers are usually the first non-family subjects of attachment behaviour (see Bowlby, 1997; Fisher and Williams, 2004). In adulthood, attachment of this kind may be shown in 'shared life projects' or the union of souls, even the 'union of minds'. Friendships provide a safety net and support system. The risks, disappointments, sadnesses and accidents of life are often softened by friends, who typically sustain with kindness, trust, generosity and care. Whilst childhood friendships may be more fickle and short-lived, they are nonetheless central features of playground and classroom life. Some teachers encourage and use friendships to build comfort, confidence and clarity, whilst others outlaw friendship groupings, fearing disruption and lack of concentration. The evidence of my own research suggests that we should consider supporting the development of friendships between all members of the school community as a high priority (Barnes, 2013b).

Today's interest in friendship reinforces current preoccupations with personality and individuality. Over-emphasis on individuality may weaken determination to improve conditions for communities and neutralize conceptions of equality (see James, 2009), but again my evidence suggests that in helping to buttress fundamental values, friends can strengthen the best in us (see also Noddings, 2003; Pahl, 2000; Sternberg, 2008). Clearly, some friendships are neither constructive nor positive and a balanced approach to the treatment of friendships must be agreed in each school community. Adults and children talking and working together on joint interests and projects often develop and sustain such a balance in school settings.

Learning groups

Traditionally, Western schools have organized children in tightly defined age cohorts, usually with one group per education year. Despite occasional experiments with 'family grouping' in some primary schools in the 1970s, the belief that children should learn with their age-mates has prevailed. Finances and demography may mean that some primary schools have classes of two or three year groups, but this is rarely considered an educational benefit. Regardless of sustained attacks, social learning has consistently been shown by research and teacher experience effectively to promote learning in the majority of children. Rose and Alexander recommended group and paired learning situations in their respective reports, though their earlier writing (Alexander et al., 1992) had been used to argue against group work and for more whole-class teaching. The answer regarding size of learning group, as so often is the case, is a balance between different groupings, each favouring different minds and different situations.

Research in education systems outside Western cultures shows, however, that strict peer group learning is not universal. Rogoff (2003) challenges assumptions that children always learn best in homogenous groups. She shows how in many traditional societies children learn successfully in groups of all sizes and ages, in pairs and singly with adult mentors, relatives and elders.

In critiquing the 'production-line' tendencies of Western education systems, Rogoff stresses the importance of dialogue. She exposes the dangers inherent in age segregation and separating children from family culture, contrasting these unchallenged divisions with the cross-generational learning common in less 'modern' societies.

From a Western perspective, Wenger also favours a stronger intergenerational dialogue. To build successful communities, schools, he suggests, should

> maximise rather than avoid interactions among the generations in ways that interlock their stakes in histories of practice ... teachers, parents and other educators constitute learning resources, not only in their ... roles, but also ... through their own membership in communities of practice ... it is desirable to increase opportunities for relationships with adults just being adults, while down playing the institutional aspects of their role as educators. What students need in developing their own identities is contact with a variety of adults who are willing to invite them into their adulthood. (Wenger, 1998: 276–7)

Adults tend to learn best in groups too. Unfortunately, protected time is rarely given to teachers and school managers to reflect on their work and discuss both personal and professional developments in learning. On a course specifically designed to create space for those conversations, head teachers and the leaders of creative industries met to reflect on learning itself. The results of just six extended conversations between participants with a shared interest in creativity and a shared high level of responsibility, were that each participant significantly changed practice in their institutions towards greater reliance on reflection, conversations and supportive learning groups (Dismore et al., 2008).

The framework document of the current National Curriculum in England (DfE, 2013a) does not mention groupings, neither does it place children's social development as a curricular aim. It speaks of a curriculum which:

> Promotes the spiritual, moral, cultural, mental and physical development of pupils at school and of society and,

> Prepares pupils for the opportunities, responsibilities and experiences of later life. (DfE, 2013a: 4)

This future orientation of education policy is significant. Thinkers and educationalists from Rousseau and Froebel through Steiner, Isaacs, Freire, Neill and Ghandi have expressed the view that an education conscious of the quality of the *present* positive experience of the child is one that most effectively promotes their flourishing in later life. Many of today's teachers agree. The emphasis of the National Curriculum is now on '*essential* knowledge', '*the best* that has been thought and said,' and 'an *appreciation* of human creativity and achievement' (my italics). Whilst such aims sound worthy, they imply a model of society and creativity that is uncontested, un-negotiable and static. Schoolteachers encounter on a daily basis many different models of society, many subdivisions and often strongly contrary views. They meet the so-called 'hard-to-reach' whose world may be far from the imaginations of politicians and policymakers. Teachers are also well aware that each family may understand what is 'the best' or 'essential' differently. A curriculum founded upon the promotion of social learning would perhaps more effectively respond to our increasingly diverse societies, and help build the minds and resources required for a more cohesive, tolerant and happy society.

Case study   Social learning

The London Bubble Theatre Company has for several years pioneered a speech, language and communication (SLC) programme called *'Speech Bubbles'*. Ten children with SLC needs are referred by each participating school. Sessions last for one hour and take place weekly through three terms. One child each week dictates a story to a trained drama practitioner, who writes it down verbatim. The following week the whole group of 10, plus adult helpers and the drama practitioner, rehearse sounds, scenes and characters to capture the story and then act it out within a 'story square' marked on the classroom floor. Weekly sessions begin with the chanting of the group's shared values ('we are kind to each other', 'we do good listening' and 'we take turns'). They then move to structured 'warm up' exercises and rehearsals. After the reading and acting of last week's story, children and adults do 'cool down' and evaluation sessions, where each child tells a cuddly bear what they have liked best about the session. In this structured way and within a very short time, a high percentage (70–80%) of children, initially presenting as very shy, reluctant speakers, become confident, articulate and clear communicators through drama. The gentle atmosphere, rapid build-up of trust and security in the group, its repeated structure, regular sense of personal achievement and informal relationships provide a strong sense of safety for the children. Teachers and theatre practitioners note that children's stories quickly become more adventurous and their dramas more inventive through the first term and develop strongly in the rest of the year. Speech therapists note significant rises in confidence and willingness to engage in conversation and description. The programme currently runs in Key Stage 1 in schools in Wakefield, Manchester and central London (see Barnes, 2014a).

Community

Platitudinous statements, such as 'the school is a community of learners', mask the fact that affirmative communities do not arise automatically. A community can simply be a group of people sharing the same geographical location. For a community to be a personally meaningful support, its members must feel a sense of belonging to it. The linguistically linked words common, communication and commonality help define an effective community.

Examples like case studies 2, 3 and 7 in Chapter 3 remind us that schools may be the places where hopeful futures are constructed. Schools may become cohesive cultures in themselves, offering a model of a sustainable and supportive community. This was certainly Freire's (1994) dream and many schools throughout the country demonstrate that children can lead the way in creating tolerant, cohesive and moral communities from diverse and sometimes even divergent populations. In this way, a community can take on the characteristics of a culture, though a community tends to depend on a geographical (or virtual) link.

The Education Act of 2006 called for schools to be involved in building 'community cohesion' (HMG, 2006: 24). Cohesion in any organization is characterized by the quality and inclusiveness of its contacts and its responses to diversity. Cohesive communities do not ignore tensions and conflicts but use them creatively to enrich and energize. In educational contexts, this involves large measures of trust not always evident in school or ITE hierarchies (Ajegbo, 2007: 34), perhaps because of punitive inspection regimes. The curriculum can provide solutions – if both teachers and pupils are frequently in a position to share what Wenger called 'experiences that allow them to take charge of their own learning' (1998: 272). Such an ideal brings us back to values. Successful communities share values by living them and talking about them (Jeffrey and Woods, 2003). Sharing, conversation, knowledge and understanding may of course be put to dreadful or joyless purposes – communities like schools must therefore decide on their purpose and this process links them to groupings we call cultures.

The Coalition government of 2010 proposed far-reaching plans to make education more community-based. Successful schools were encouraged to consider taking 'academy' status. Communities were encouraged to set up more 'free schools' outside local authority control. Both relatively independent school settings have been expected to develop a curriculum appropriate to the community and to find local sponsors to fund them. Both primary and secondary academies and free schools operate outside local authority control and have considerable freedom to teach and arrange learning in ways felt to be appropriate communally. In many areas of the country half the schools now are outside local authority control and influence. Such a policy shift will leave many schools in a position where they have to make decisions on curriculum that previously were made for them via outside 'advice' via local authority advisers, government circulars and the now disbanded Curriculum and Qualifications Development Agency (QCDA). It is hoped that this book and others like it will provide guidance on how to approach this new-found freedom.

Support in developing community links relevant to a creative and cross-curriculum already mentioned include the *Engaging Places* and *Signature Pedagogies* websites, Creative Partnerships (now privatized under various local names, e.g. *Future Creative* in Kent, *A New Direction* in London (AND, website), *Creative Futures* in Cumbria), English Heritage, Cadw (The Historic Environment Service of the Welsh Government) and Historic Scotland, the National Trust, English Nature, Scottish Natural Heritage, the Northern Ireland Citizenship Resource Directory and countless local museums, galleries, factories, theatres, concert halls and historic houses which combine nationally relevant education programmes with local contacts, sites and communities.

Every community has fascinating places to visit. Teachers planning a relevant programme of experiences for their children might start by visiting their local library with a request for sites and organizations with an education officer. Education visits to English Heritage, Cadw, Northern Ireland Environment Agency or Historic Scotland are free so long as an educational booking is made. It is in the best interests of every organization with an education interest to make a visit to their site as positive as possible and so help with planning, structuring or following up a visit is often available.

Culture

A culture can be defined as the shared patterns of behaviour and thought that hold a group of people together. People can identify with the same culture but live very distant from each other. Culture involves a sense of shared history, shared aesthetic understandings, shared stories, pastimes, tastes, beliefs and traditions. In National Curriculum terms a culture might agree on 'the best that has been thought and said'. Cultures may be big or small and individuals can belong to several at once, for example feeling British, Asian, Muslim, working class, a Liverpool supporter and a keen cyclist.

Cultures literally shape our minds. Working at the boundaries of neuroscience and psychology, Csikszentmihalyi observed that the 'normal state of the mind is chaos' and that we order such chaos by 'inventing' culture (Csikszentmihalyi, 1997). Gardner argued that the culture in which we live begins impacting upon us 'shortly after conception' (1999b). Language and other means of direct communication make the impact of culture far stronger. Sociologist Bernstein demonstrated how language differed between different sub-cultures and went on to show how the type of language used by each sub-culture influenced the life chances, health, aspirations and life span of its members. He showed how different 'codes' of language, at first (1971) divided into 'restricted' and 'elaborated', served to include individuals in certain cultures and exclude them from others. This theory had significant implications for schools seen as usually operating elaborated codes (lots of words, complex linguistic structures, detailed explanations) that conflicted with the restricted codes (few words, short sentences, fewer explanations) dominant in the homes of many 'working class' children. Success at school, according to Bernstein, was defined by the degree to which the language code of the child agreed with the language code of the school. Extending his work on different styles of language use, Bernstein came to believe that all modes of communication influenced the level of the child's achievement in school. He observed:

> different modalities of communication [are] differently valued by the school and differently effective in it because of the school's values, modes of practice and relations with different communities. (Bernstein, 1996: 91)

Outside language, Bernstein's conclusions have been supported from a health perspective by Marmot (2010, website).

If culture significantly alters the life chances and health of its members, then one might expect Initial Teacher Education (ITE) to focus upon it, but it does not. Few newly qualified teachers have studied the sociology of education. Few have the opportunity to consider the relevance of social context in their lesson planning. As a result, few children experience what the Ajegbo report (2007) called an education that seems to them 'contextualised and relevant' (2007: 19).

Adults in education rarely examine their own or others' cultures. They are often unaware of the impact of their own socialization or cultural understandings on their thinking. With Scoffham, I have explored how providing opportunities for initial teacher education (ITE) students to view their culture from outside can impact on their personal and teaching lives (Scoffham and Barnes, 2009). Observing the self from a different perspective, where 'one's own assumptions [are] temporarily suspended to consider others' (Rogoff, 2003: 12), can be a transformational experience. The view from another cultural perspective provides opportunities to learn from other ways of seeing. It seems no coincidence that personal, cultural and creative advances have often occurred where cultures meet. Making a point relevant to addressing the sub-cultures in every classroom, Rogoff argues:

> if judgements of value are necessary, as they often are, they [are] much better informed if they are suspended long enough to gain some understanding of the patterns involved in one's own familiar ways as well as in the sometimes surprising ways of others. (Rogoff, 2003: 12–14)

Observing that 'People who have experienced variation are much more likely to be aware of their own cultural ways' (p. 87), Rogoff reinforces Freire's case that the teacher must be both respectful and open to all cultures and actively involved in building new and shared ones.

Socio-political ideas about learning

Learning is clearly affected by complex interactions outside directly social ones. Psychological, inherited, economic, political and environmental influences all affect learning. Societal and political issues may not feature in formal curriculum discussions yet a range of (often unarticulated) socio-political concepts frame many decisions made in schools. The relative strength of applied social values, such as equality, fairness, trust and inclusion, characterize a school's ethos and often define the degree of success at both individual and academic levels. Whilst social and political considerations inevitably colour judgements made in schools, they are rarely discussed at staff meetings, in-service training or the education of new teachers. Values, explicit or implicit, are central to the character of a school and these often arise from the unexpressed social and political beliefs of head teachers and their senior management team.

Values are social constructions; we do not develop them alone. Sociologists like Bourdieu (1984) argue that every individual carries a measure of social and cultural capital invested in them by the social group(s) to which they belong. If a child's *social capital*, its approach to relationships, authority, disappointment, fun and self, chime with the expectations of the school then they are more likely to succeed. Equally, the child's *cultural capital*, their received attitudes to the arts, design, language, pastimes, curriculum, learning, will steer their route through education. Bourdieu saw that schools and teachers represented a particular, predictable and relatively narrow set of social and cultural standards, and as such were open to challenge. As societies in the UK and USA become increasingly disparate, adherence to one set of narrow social and cultural rules in schools becomes more problematic.

Teachers should be sensitive to the cultures of the children they teach. Such sensitivity has curriculum and pedagogical implications, but as more and more teachers become practitioner researchers, their cultural sensitivity must also be turned in on themselves. In this context, Bourdieu stressed the importance of developing a *reflexive* approach to research. The reflexive teacher examines and exposes their own social and cultural biases before making judgements on the learning and attitudes of children.

Equality

Positive life experience will often spawn optimistic views on friendliness and values like trust and equality. Other lives may generate more sceptical responses. In either case, many societies pay at least 'lip service' to the ideals of fairness and inclusion. The UN's Convention on the Rights of the Child (UNICEF, 1989, website), their Millennium Goals (UN, 2000, website) and national education statements often express egalitarian aims.

Egalitarian ideals do not go unchallenged. Some would see such statements as rhetorical and unrealistic – they are not seen in the everyday lives of millions of the most disadvantaged in society. There are credible suggestions that the UK/US experience of 'selfish capitalism' has made it impossible for schools to change social divisions and suspicious attitudes deeply entrenched in our societies (James, 2008, 2009). There is little doubt that trust between peers in both the UK and USA (WHO, 2012, website, and Chapter 12 in this book) is relatively low and that relationships between adults and children are often strained (UNICEF, 2013, website), but such observations should not smother hope. Schools remain the only institutions set up to change society, but unless teachers and pupils agree on what that society should be like, then the prospects for constructive change are slim.

Other critics of progressive education policy see egalitarian ideals as indicative of a failed social reconstructionist approach to education, and suggest that schools are the wrong places to attempt to right personal wrongs (Furedi, 2009; Hayes and Ecclestone, 2008; Hirsch, 1999). Their criticism extends to the 'social work' and therapeutic roles many schools have taken on as they try to create environments conducive to the motivation and concentration of children suffering from physical, emotional, spiritual, social and interpersonal ill health. Many of these responsibilities have been thrust on schools rather than chosen by teachers, but improving the lot of the underprivileged has been an aim of education for centuries. Cultures claiming values like 'tolerance' might be expected to see economic well-being as a meaningful aspiration only if it makes the culture a wholesome and inclusive thing to belong to.

Fairness

What we see as fair varies according to the way in which we have been socialized. Implicit in the arguments for inclusion is the idea that every human is of equal worth (Booth and Ainscow, 2011). In terms of the organization of schools and their curricula, a belief in equality and inclusion should result in attitudes and practices that treat each child as precious. As teachers become reflective practitioners, many social scientists argue that they should become increasingly aware of the biases and assumptions that lead them, often unintentionally, to value one child over another.

ITE students have become used to detecting obvious unfairness like gender or racially motivated bias, but fewer are aware of their preference towards thinking or intelligence 'styles' (Sternberg, 1997a, 1997b) that match their own. Sternberg has shown how teachers who favour a creative style of showing intelligence often overlook pupils showing it in practical or analytical ways. Analytical teachers similarly can easily miss intelligent solutions shown by creatively minded pupils.

Inclusion

Inclusion in an education context, according to Booth, is 'concerned with reducing all exclusionary pressures' in education cultures (Booth, 2003). In *The Index for Inclusion* Booth and Ainscow offer 'a resource to support the inclusive development of schools' (2011). Used throughout the UK and extensively in 40 other countries, this resource makes values central and requires them to be lived in practice. Its opening section on 'creating inclusive cultures' suggests that schools develop

> shared inclusive values that are conveyed to all new staff, students, governors and parents/carers. The principles and values in inclusive school cultures guide decisions about policies and moment to moment practices in classrooms, so that school development becomes a continuous process. (Booth and Ainscow, 2011: 8)

Illustration 4.1   Children with hearing difficulties learning to communicate with their teacher in a south Indian school (Photo: Cherry Tewfik)

Educators considering establishing inclusive cultures are challenged by 'indicators' of inclusive values:

1. The school develops shared and inclusive values.
2. Inclusion is viewed as increasing participation or all.
3. The school encourages respect for human rights.
4. Expectations are high for all children.
5. Children are valued equally.
6. The school counters all forms of discrimination.
7. The school promotes non-violent interactions and resolutions to disputes.
8. The school encourages adults and children to feel good about themselves.
9. The school contributes to the health of children and adults. (Booth and Ainscow, 2011: 69)

In the *Index for Inclusion*, schools are invited to consider a range of questions under each indicator. These questions offer opportunities for friendly, meaningful and rich conversation, different in every group and community. The discussions, Booth claims, will assist the process of developing improvements in the learning and teaching environment. Progress on the path to inclusion and participation is measured by the degree to which conversations, discussions and opportunities for self-examination are genuine. Bourdieu reminds us that the physical products of our cultures can exclude as well as include. Schools cannot address such huge issues in a vacuum. With up to one in four children in the UK currently living in poverty and nationalism on the rise, Potts (2003) suggests we can only move towards inclusion and participation by addressing the perceptions of difference which exclude.

The products of human cultures

Human creations, whether tangible or conceptual, express our different cultures. Differences between specially prized objects and places characterize our cultures. Philosopher Karl Popper (1978) identified three 'worlds' that humans inhabit. World one is natural and physical and world two is the world of the mind, but his world three consists of the ideas, values, traditions, artefacts and structures that surround us. We cannot avoid influencing and being influenced by the products of human cultures. Those aspects of culture that are most readily accessed by our senses have a particularly strong impact upon children. Our schools: their furniture, technologies, decorations, displays, books, clothes, playgrounds, sports equipment and lunchboxes are filled with expressions of world three – all have their impact on learning.

Learning can be promoted by the objects that surround us. In arguing for the 'active use of knowledge', Perkins (1992, 2009) frequently cites the importance of objects. He coins the term 'mindware' (New Horizons, 1991, website) to describe the things that clutter school life: toys, pencils, calculators, computers, counters, historical artefacts, landscapes or buildings and so on. These artefacts in their various ways extend our minds and help us think more deeply. Concentrating on understanding and metacognition, and acknowledging the distributed/socially constructed nature of intelligence, Perkins champions 'Educational settings where students learn by way of thinking about and with what they are learning, no matter what the subject matter is' (Perkins, 1992: 185). He argues for 'expert-like understanding' (Andrade and Perkins, 1998) describing how in the world beyond school people, places and artefacts interact.

Localities, schools and classrooms

School buildings and neighbourhoods are resources in themselves. They bring together the attitudes, aspirations and skills of a wide range of subject disciplines and form the most familiar backdrop to young learners' lives. Beyond hosting the occasional geography field trip, these free, safe and local resources are rarely well used. A school building is the product of a combination of mathematical, scientific, technological, artistic, geographical, linguistic, historical and social skills and knowledge, yet genuine surveys of the school fabric, forces, functions, materials or plans rarely form part of the primary child's experience of school. The focus exercises in Chapter 3 show some ways in which schools could use these highly accessible and valued resources across the curriculum.

Illustration 4.2   Children working in an artist's studio (Photo: Ian Bottle)

Places can also be the medium through which 'deep learning' (Marton and Saljo, 1976) happens. Deep learning is learning that is transferable and can be applied in different situations. In the UK the *Learning Outside the Classroom* manifesto (DfES, 2006b, website) provided significant 'permission' for shared exploration of places, though primary school teachers argue that external pressures for higher achievement in Mathematics and English cut across time previously devoted to fieldwork. The manifesto and initiatives like Forest Schools pick up Perkins' argument that real problems, real places, real implications, relevant skills and knowledge promote transferable, practical and useful understanding. Part of the reality of these activities is that they are social.

Children respond positively to collaborative work outside the classroom. For many, the process of enquiry begins in settings that children feel are their own. The 'Engaging Places' programme (website) attempts to help teachers support children in experiencing built and open places beyond school as part of their learning environment. Whilst much has been written about learning beyond the classroom by geographers, until recently (Austin, 2007; Catling, 2010) it has been given little attention by other subject practitioners.

Places and objects, when enthusiastically and knowledgeably used, can become the motivation, focus, purpose and product of learning across the curriculum. Because it is probably true that 'no objects that surround us are without their emotional tag' (Damasio, 2003: 55), every child brings a slightly different perspective to learning experiences that use real things and locations. It is possible to counter the excluding properties of certain places and artefacts through education. English Heritage pioneered this approach to learning in the 1990s with its *Teachers' Guide to* ... series of books (English Heritage, 1990, 1999), championing the cross-curricular use of buildings and collections. This approach has been taken up by many museums and great houses across the UK and America (Attingham Trust, 2004). The intention of much work by English Heritage, Cadw, Historic Scotland and the Northern Ireland Environment Agency (NIEA) has been to help all children and adults see great buildings and local architecture as 'their own'. Seeing a place as somewhere that dramatic, intellectual, investigational or personal experiences 'happen' to a child, changes that place from 'theirs' to 'ours'.

Summary

Learning is a social activity. Research and experience suggest that the friendships, learning groups and classes should reflect the social nature of learning. Schools are generated by and exist within communities, cohesive or not, and at their most successful they respond to priorities and values emerging from those communities. Schools often form a social and symbolic hub within their community and as such continue to exemplify and lead on social values. Cultures differ from communities in that by definition they include common ways of thinking and acting that transcend time and place. Schools are entrusted with a significant role in the transmission of culture from one generation to another. Modern nations, being composed of many cultures and sub-cultures each endowed with their own social and cultural capital, present schools with new challenges. In the culturally diverse social context of today, the details of culture championed by schools are open to debate and nego-tiation. Each school must individually examine and agree the social and cultural capital they seek to develop in children – therefore no two schools in the twenty-first century should be alike.

Values are social constructions too. Cultures are defined by the values they hold and display. Values involve fundamental beliefs that power and direct action in the world. Related values like equality, inclusion and fairness are frequently but often rhetorically championed by schools and their success can be judged by the correspondence between rhetoric and deed. Societies also construct the objects and environments that surround their members and these vary in importance and influence between cultures and sub-cultures. Values, environments and artefacts can exclude as well as include and it is up to schools, within an agreed value set, to offer a curriculum that offers the widest range of inclusive environments, resources and cultural activities to support the learning of its children.

Key questions for discussion

- How inclusive are the different social groups in your school?
- How does your curriculum reflect and make use of the social nature of learning?
- What do you think should be the role of friendships (a) between children and (b) between adults, in school?

Further reading

Goleman, D. (2006) *Social Intelligence*. New York: Arrow.
Noddings, N. (2003) *Happiness and Education*. Cambridge: Cambridge University Press.
Rogoff, B. (2003) *The Cultural Nature of Human Development*. New York: Oxford University Press.

CHAPTER 5

WHAT DOES NEUROSCIENCE TELL US ABOUT CROSS-CURRICULAR LEARNING?

Chapter aims

This chapter will suggest that teachers should take account of emerging neuroscientific knowledge. It summarizes recent scientific evidence on changing understandings of intelligence, and particularly on the importance of emotions, that suggest a role for cross-curricular approaches in education. By the end of this chapter you will know of some advances in neuroscientific knowledge that have a bearing on teaching and learning. These include:

- scanning the brain
- neuroscientific views on thinking and learning
- the maturing brain
- emotions and feelings
- stress
- memory and school learning
- neuroscientific views on intelligence
- the influence of environment on the brain.

Neuroscience will increasingly inform education decisions through the twenty-first century. 'Smart pills', brain scans that can observe the workings of aspects of learning in action, new knowledge about neural barriers to learning and pharmacological developments that change brain chemistry and behaviour are a present day reality. Recent developments in educational neuroscience suggest that integrated, meaningful and emotionally engaging approaches are central to learning. If education aims to build human capacity to address the accelerating rates of change outlined in Chapter 1 *and* to ensure individual flourishing then insights from neurology may be of great importance in helping form strategies to improve educational experience.

As we consider the interests, worries and motivations of twenty-first-century children, improved science and technologies may help teachers become more confident about their professional and experiential knowledge regarding thinking and learning. However, applying neuroscientific insights to education raises understandable fears of chemical interference in learning and behaviour reminiscent of Orwell's *1984* (see, for example, *Guardian*, 2006; Theroux, 2006). Some teachers suspect that in the hands of neuroscientists ordinary human differences become pathologized. These and similar worries underline the importance of establishing dialogue and a shared vocabulary between educationalists and neuroscientists. Happily, in both Europe and the USA such interactions have begun (for example, see Bransford et al., 1999; Geake, 2009; Howard-Jones, 2013; Huppert et al., 2005; Perkins, 2009).

Dialogue has shown that each side of the education–neuroscience debate sees a different truth. Neuroscientists and experimental psychologists look for a 'scientific' truth represented by the evidence of numbers, trials and controlled experiments repeatable in the laboratory. Teachers tend to hold to an 'experiential' truth based on qualitative interpretation of their everyday experience in the classroom. Both use experimentation and both have evidence, but the evidence often leads them in different directions. Teachers experiment and get evidence on a minute-by-minute basis with many 'research subjects' in a more-or-less natural setting; neuroscientists work with individuals in a far from everyday context. Teachers can be easily led by so-called 'brain-based' approaches to accept approaches that are dismissed as scientifically baseless by the neuroscientists (Howard-Jones, 2009, 2012). So there is much to talk about!

Until recently, neuroscientists have been involved in thinking about children with various learning difficulties. Teachers have generally been more interested in the implications of neuroscience for learning in all children. Neuroscientists are at pains to remind us that we are only at the beginning of understanding what happens in the brain and how it relates to action in the world. On the other hand, teachers have worked, researched and written about children's learning for millennia and perhaps need to feel confident of the validity of their own observations and experience. The most effective and transferable professional skills of the teacher perhaps more closely resemble an art than a science (Perkins, 2009).

The neuroscientific view on learning

Much current scientific thinking on learning focuses on human ways of learning that appear to have conferred survival advantages on our species (McGilchrist, 2010; Panksepp and Biven, 2012). It is unlikely we would have survived as a species if we were not self-conscious, able to develop complex language systems, make lasting relationships, understand and make signs or symbols, synthesize input via the senses, remember and create. We have seen how our species has achieved through social means (Chapter 4), sharing and building upon specifically human attributes brought together in what philosophers and psychologists have called 'intrinsic values' like: fairness, justice, tolerance, empathy, community, forgiveness, love and sustainability. Some neuroscientists (for example Damasio, 2003), argue that the plasticity of our brains and our ability to form social values has made the successes of the human race possible. Others (for example Robertson, 2012) have stressed neuroscientific evidence of the shape-able and changeable qualities of individual 'mindsets' and how these can be used to raise aspirations and increase the chances of feelings of achievement – an approach taken up also by psychologists like Dweck (2009). Teachers may wish to make use

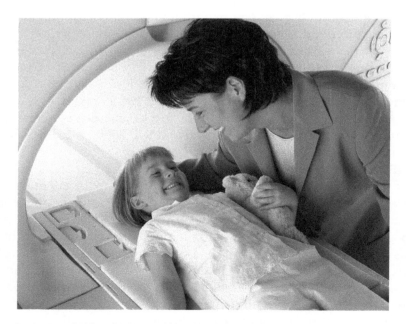

Illustration 5.1   Child entering an fMRI scanner (Courtesy of Siemens)

of such advantages when they make choices relating to the style, means and context of the learning they offer their children.

Through brain scanning, neuroscience offers independent corroboration of what teachers already 'know' about emotional, social and sensory engagement in learning, but it has also revealed new – perhaps even counter-intuitive, knowledge about our learning, such as the observation that joy appears to be the optimal condition for learning (Damasio, 2003). Teachers should know something about how information on the workings of the brain is gathered and seek to be fully informed about the insights neurology brings (Blakemore and Frith, 2006; Goswami and Bryant, 2007).

Brain scans

Brain-imaging technologies such as functional magnetic resonance imaging (fMRI), positron emission tomography (PET) and near infra-red spectroscopy (NIRS) are adding new dimensions to our understanding of the ways in which we learn. Before extending the discussion to the implications for education, it needs to be remembered that fMRI scanners, the machines most often used to measure brain activity in children, are noisy, cumbersome, scary and very expensive. PET scans are not frequently used in education research because they use a radioactive dye to indicate diseased or damaged areas of the brain. These costly scanners are confined to universities, hospitals and neurology departments and, until very recently, their main use has been to research or diagnose abnormalities. Medical beginnings may have resulted in the pathological tendency in neuroscience/education research to concentrate on disability. Dyslexia, attention deficit/hyperactivity disorder (ADHD), dyscalculia and autism and their treatment, rather than learning in general, have preoccupied neuro-researchers. It is still impossible to measure activity in children's brains while they are engaged in everyday learning activities. Neurological research into learning is therefore still very much in its infancy.

Neuroscientists have, however, been able to observe some significant aspects of normal brain activity and development in children. These observations have begun to influence our understanding of thinking, learning, the emotions, the influence of environment and the concept of self. Through findings in these areas, neuroscientific research is poised to make observations that could influence the curriculum our children follow. This is why teachers should be centrally involved in the debate. Since one of our assumptions is that learning is a consequence of thinking, we begin by considering the neuroscience of thought.

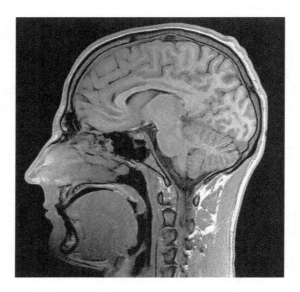

Illustration 5.2   An fMRI scan of the head, showing skull, brain and other soft tissue (Courtesy of Siemens)

Thinking

Thinking is not a simple activity. Our brains and bodies work as an integrated organism with individual parts taking on a variety of functions depending upon which parts are active together. Connections within the 100,000,000,000 neurons that make up the normal brain control what happens in and through our body. We are not conscious of the activation of clusters of neural connections responsible for survival and fundamental physical operations. Such neural activity cannot be called thinking. Even complex and conscious movement, such as playing a piano sonata or driving a car may become almost as automatic as breathing. When consciousness (or sometimes semi-consciousness) is involved in our mental or physical processes, we mark the qualitative difference with the word 'thinking'. The thinking elements of our brain – aspects of memory, planning, monitoring, learning, language, feelings, emotions, spirituality and self-consciousness itself – we call our mind. These faculties depend on even more complex linkages between brain networks, the rest of the body and our environment.

Close your eyes and place the tip of the index finger of your right hand on the base of the underside of the index finger of your left hand. Gently stroke your right index finger up to the tip of your left index finger. Even with your eyes closed, you can probably sense exactly where on your finger the sensation is. Each located sensation you register involves the connection of separate pairs and groups of neurons governing the feeling in that finger. When we think of the implications of this simple exercise, we are involving thousands of other connections: between aspects of memory and feeling, between neurons governing sight and sound, and between the networks which establish the present understanding of self and this book. Almost half the brain is involved in this activity (Blakemore and Frith, 2006).

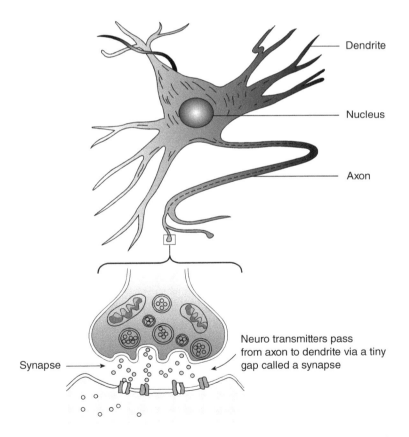

Figure 5.1(a)   A diagrammatic representation of a neuron, showing dendrite, nucleus, axon and synapse

Unlike living skin or bone cells, neurons generally do not replace themselves when they die, and they die when they are not used (see Giedd et al., 1999). Neuroscientists argue that exercising or simply using these neural connections is vital to the survival of individual neurons and our continued learning. Each working cell in our brain carries a minute part of the inherited or learned self. Most neurons are able to connect with others through some 1000 tiny root-like filaments called *dendrites*. Neurons 'connect' via the transmission of a tiny electrical impulse along an *axon* towards receptors on the dendrites of another cell. This pulse results in the emission of chemical neurotransmitters that move across the gap between an axon and a dendrite and are either accepted or rejected by the receiving dendrite. The meeting point between an axon and a dendrite is called a *synapse*. Neurons fail to connect when an electrical or chemical inhibitor is released at the synapse. In making consciousness itself and allowing the conscious act of thinking, these microscopically small synapses become the very stuff of intelligent behaviour (Keverne, 2006; LeDoux, 1999, 2002). Each concept we develop – pain, mother, comfort, tree, god – consists of networks of thousands of such connections, distributed across the entire brain. Individual linkages and wider networks that prove useful become physically conjoined as a *myelin* sheath grows to protect and speed up the connection. Frequent use thus establishes networks of

Structure of a Typical Neuron

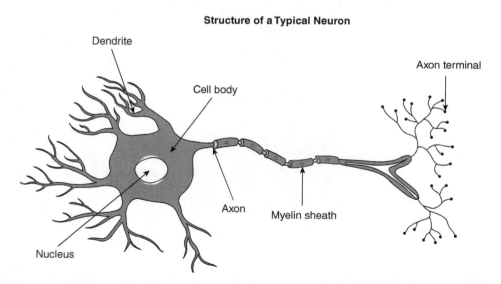

Figure 5.1(b)   A myelin sheath develops to insulate the connection between an axon from one neuron and a dendrite from the next

cells which fire almost simultaneously when required. Each human brain is wired up uniquely and, as Susan Greenfield observes, 'reflects, in its physical form and function, personal experiences with supreme fidelity' (Greenfield, 2003: 148).

An old brain trick illustrates the way these connections work in our mind:

Point to a piece of white paper and ask your audience what colour it is. Point then to a whiteboard or white teacup and ask again what colour it is. Repeat the question for two or three other white things in the room. Then simply ask, 'What does a cow drink?'

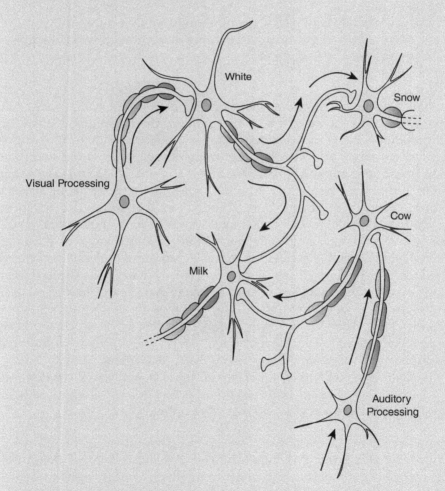

Figure 5.2   Diagrammatic representation of connections between neurons on processing sensory inputs relating to the concept 'white'

The immediate response to this quick-fire question is usually the (wrong) answer 'milk', after which people usually correct themselves and say, ' no, water'.

What has happened in our brain?

When the concept 'white' is visually brought to mind, all previously experienced mental associations with white – summer clouds, milk, snow, drawing paper, the colour of a childhood bedroom or a hated school shirt – will also be brought into or near consciousness. So will the respective associations of each of those concepts. The areas of the brain involved with the concepts milk, paint, shirt and snow, 'glow' and are ready for action if needed. When the aurally introduced stimulus 'cow' is added, our brain circuitry races to fire up all the concepts related to cow. Since the concept milk is already primed by association with white, our reflex answer will be that a cow drinks milk, though we 'know' that only calves drink it. (See Figure 5.2.)

The linkages between certain clusters of neurons via their axons and dendrites and across the synapses in the brain are the beginning of thinking. But thinking is not a purely cerebral activity, neither is it simple. A highly intricate system of two-way links between various parts of the brain and body is activated when we think. We may also think with our body; acting out or physically 'feeling our way' may provoke novel and unexpected mental responses, as many dancers and actors will attest. The advanced and developmentally recent frontal lobes or neo-cortex in the human brain have connections that link with much more primitive areas of the brain controlling the metabolism, senses, muscles, stomach, the immune system, emotions and memory. Neuroscientists have evidence that these unconscious, largely automatic, but primitive systems, which we share evolutionarily with many other vertebrates, are involved in the conscious act of thinking. Thus, scientists are increasingly clear that what affects the body impacts upon thinking and that thinking deeply influences what happens within the body (Goswami and Bryant, 2007; McGilchrist, 2010).

The brain of most higher animals and birds is noticeably divided into two halves. This divided brain seems also to offer evolutionary advantages. McGilchrist observes with regard to animals:

The left hemisphere yields narrow, focused attention, mainly for the purpose of getting and feeding. The right hemisphere yields a broad, vigilant attention, the purpose of which appears to be awareness of signals from the surroundings, especially of other creatures, who are potential predators or potential mates, foes or friends; and it is involved in bonding in social animals. (2010: 27)

In humans these functions seem to have become even more specialized. Whilst both sides of the brain are involved in almost all functions, clear dominances have been observed in recent research. Our brain's right hemisphere seems to control broadly based alertness, sustained attention, divided attention and vigilance, the left is responsible for a narrow focus on things. New and emotionally engaging experiences, new information and new skills tend to be processed mainly on the right side of the brain. Only when they become 'old', well-used knowledge does the left brain become fully involved. The right side of the brain is more associated with creative, emotional, integrating, free, connection-making, metaphorical activity and alternatives whilst the left dominates focused attention, classification, confirmation of what it knows already, precise language, interest in the mechanical. In McGilchrist's words , 'if the left hemisphere is the hemisphere of "what", the right hemisphere … .could be said to be the hemisphere of "how"' (2010: 93).

Recent neuroscientific evidence applied to education might lead teachers to think about the relative importance of a child's:

- sense of personal security
- multi-sensory engagement with the world around them
- perception of what is emotionally significant
- memory
- response to the intellectually challenging.

Such foci in making decisions about learning could be argued to exploit the unique thinking ability of the human. Exercising these and other distinctively human mind/body skills may feel highly satisfying (Panksepp and Biven, 2012) and enhance the sense of achievement in every child and thus positively affect their confidence and other attitudes for future challenges.

The maturing brain

More than a quarter of a century ago, scientists noted periods of especially rapid cell production in the growing brains of very young children. Confirming observations from developmental psychology, neuroscientists established that at 0–3 years, the neurons in the brain multiply at unusually rapid speeds. The volume of the brain does not increase significantly after about 3 years of age (Thompson et al., 2000) but scans show that the *matter* of the brain does undergo very significant reorganization as the density of the brain increases through childhood and early adulthood (see Illustration 5.3).

Between the ages of 8 and 14, we now know there is a second major 'growth spurt' of neurons with copious connection-making dendrites. Neuroscientists have demonstrated that despite this extra capacity the volume of the brain does not increase (Thompson et al., 2000). Unused connections are rapidly 'pruned away' if unused. This finding suggests that the second period of neural growth may be as vital to optimum mental development as that of the early years. Jay Giedd has summarized the significance of this discovery as follows:

> If a teen is doing music or sports or academics, those are the cells and connections that will be hardwired. If they're lying on the couch or playing video games or [watching] MTV, those are the cells and connections that are going to survive. (Frontline, 2002, website)

If the 'use it or lose it' principle applies to the immediately pre-adolescent brain, as other neuroscientists have suggested (Baird and Fugelsang, 2004, website; Keverne, 2006; Tokuhma-Espinosa, 2014), then it is surely incumbent upon schools and teachers to ensure the experience of children is particularly rich, positive and stimulating in the years of puberty. This is especially true for those connections within the young person's brain most susceptible to environmental influence.

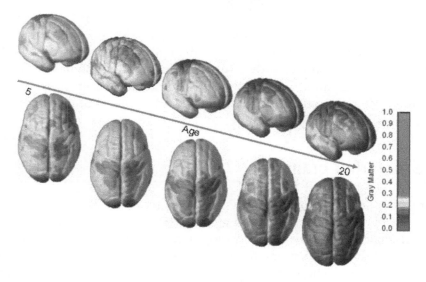

Illustration 5.3   Thompson and Giedd's illustration of the maturing brain 0–21years. Increasing white matter (myelin-sheathed neural connections within the brain) is shown by the darkening colours as the brain matures (Courtesy of Paul Thompson)

Over the period of our education, as more connections within our brain become 'hard wired', a physical change in brain density occurs. As we gain increasing control over physical and mental faculties, the fatty myelin sheath that develops over frequently used connections causes an observable change in colour from grey to white.

This colour change denotes maturity. But not every part of our brain becomes mature at the same time. Research (Gogtay et al., 2004; Thompson et al., 2000) has shown that the pre-frontal areas of the brain are not *fully* matured or 'wired up' until we reach our early twenties (see Illustration 5.3). Physical and sensory areas of the brain mature first, but the much more complex abstract-thinking, decision-making, impulse-controlling networks are among the last to mature. A research example (Luna and Sweeney, 2004) may illustrate this.

Adults and 14-year-olds were asked to perform a similar experiment that tested their ability to control a 'natural' impulse to look at a light. Whilst they were exerting this control, their brains were being scanned using fMRI. It was found that whilst many 14-year-olds showed the same degree of success in avoiding looking at the light, adults and teenagers used different parts of their brains to assert that control. Adults used a range of areas distributed throughout the brain whereas those used by young teenagers were very localized and easily susceptible to emotional 'hijack'.

Maturation involves the reorganization of the brain into more complex networks consisting of numbers of checks and balances. Significantly, these include the ability to envision, or ask, 'what if?' or 'what are the risks?' and to mentally model alternative outcomes. These abilities generally show themselves in the late teens and early twenties and the extensively dispersed neural networks that make such weighing up possible are now known to be amongst the last to mature. Again, these findings may have implications for education. Neuroscientists tell us the mature brain is one where connections and inhibitors are widely distributed and collaborative, and less susceptible to impulse or purely emotional responses. To help 8–14-year-olds' brains reorganize and refine in this direction, perhaps social collaboration and distributing intelligence between various members of a group should be more frequently modelled in educational settings. This social activity in learning would be an external metaphor for what is invisibly happening within the developing brain. Future neuroscientists may well be interested in researching the impact of curricular and class organization attempts at such 'help'.

If the thinking, predicting, reflecting parts of our brain come slowly to maturity and if through education we can make an impact upon which parts of the brain mature more quickly, then this would tend to affect the curricula we plan. Findings from neuroscience might be used to suggest that the school experience of children aged 8–14 should:

- be social
- continue to be physical
- exploit all the senses fully
- not expect too great a degree of abstraction
- be fully aware of the strong impact of emotions.

It is worth noting, however, that currently in England many children between 7 and 14 years old are heavily tested. They have national tests at 11 and 14, and school-based tests at 7, 8, 9, 10, 12, 13 and 15. For significant periods when the brain is growing at its fastest and its higher functions are maturing, children are under the stress of cramming and tests. Large periods of time which should be devoted to new learning, are lost in what has been called the 'never ending cycle of demoralizing, childhood-destroying examinations' (Dawkins, 2003: 70), which summarizes educational experience for many.

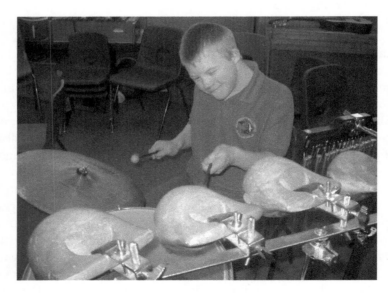

Illustration 5.4 Involvement in practical musical activity, such as rhythm and tune, is primarily fun, but also helps develop skills of coordination, confidence, and an understanding of pattern and structure (Photo: Cherry Tewfik)

Excess stress may cause difficulties for younger children too, establishing negative attitudes to learning and the self as a learner. The neuroscientific research above suggests that there are optimal periods for introducing material into the school curriculum. Both listening to and playing music, for example, has been shown to have a strong impact on the developing brain of young children. Several studies have shown close relationships between musical activity and high scores and improvements, particularly in maths and language (for example Henriksson-Macaulay, 2014; Jensen, 2000). If we know that the progress of brain maturation makes musical, linguistic and physical activities more readily learned in the early years, should we delay the teaching of subjects more likely to be abstract? If we find that good health, positive emotions and feelings of security dispro-portionately affect the thinking of the young, should we angle the cur-riculum more towards activities that promote these things? Focused discussions between neuroscientists and educators are clearly overdue and should consider the following suggestions:

- Introduce physical, practical, sensory, emotional and language learning early.
- Maintain physical, practical, sensory, emotional and language learning throughout years 3–14.
- Do not expect abstract thought too early.
- Do not expect judicial behaviour too early.

Thinking can be good or bad, efficient or inefficient, complex or simple. One condition which apparently *prevents* some otherwise useful thinking connections being made is when we feel under some kind of physical or emotional threat.

Stress

Stress is a vital survival mechanism. We could not learn some things without a considerable degree of stress. The stress of being run over by a car has taught me to be very careful when crossing roads! To support us in stress-ful situations, the parts of the brain that control our secretions of hormones such as adrenalin become active. Our 'fight or flight' reflexes cut in, we think less consciously and react in a more reflexive way (Jensen, 1995; Smith and Call, 2000). This can be very useful in everyday life. Today I was washing up and was, not very sensibly, piling up the wet crockery too high on the draining board. When a cup slipped off the pile and headed for the floor, before I had time to fully register what was happening, my right knee had jerked up to block its fall. The cup then rebounded (unharmed) from knee to cupboard and my left hand was ready to catch it. I could never have achieved this feat of juggling if I had been asked to do it. This balletic response was a simple reflex action triggered at the lowest levels of my nervous system. It did not involve thinking or learning in the terms already discussed, though I have learned that I can trust my reflexes to get me out of trouble … sometimes.

A degree of stress may be important for learning. We should, however, make a distinction between stress that we feel when we have no sense of control or are in danger, and *challenge*, the kind of stress that pushes us towards achieving a goal that may be currently just beyond reach. A *lack* of response to stress hormones, particularly the catecholamines, has been implicated in attention deficit/hyperactivity disorder (Arnsten and Li, 2005). Many of us are very aware of the benefits of stress in meeting deadlines, winning races or provoking creative solutions to problems. But too much stress over too long a period, or stress that threatens our psychological or physical being, may be damaging. The hormone cortisol, produced through stress, has been shown to provoke cell death in the hippocampus area of the brain (Lee et al., 2002: 89) and high levels of stress appear to impact negatively on blood pressure and glucose and cholesterol levels in the blood (Djuric et al., 2008, website; Layard and Clark, 2014).

Illustration 5.5   An upset and angry pupil. Note the position of her shoulders, the configuration of mouth, eyes and cheekbones and the closed body language (This information was provided by Clinical Tools, Inc., and is copyrighted by Clinical Tools)

There is a close relationship between our immune system, nervous system and state of mind. Neuroscientist Francisco Varela goes as far as calling the immune system our 'second brain' (in Goleman, 1997: 50) in that it responds to emotions and external influences in a parallel way to our 'neurological' brain. The feeling of stress, for example, seems to affect the connections between neurons within the brain by restricting blood supply (Kawachi et al., 1994). It also causes the secretion of hormones that weaken the immune system, which of course affects our physical well-being. Physical disease in its turn directly affects the behaviour of the limbic system of the brain which, to complete the vicious circle, makes us feel bad (Goleman, 1997: 58).

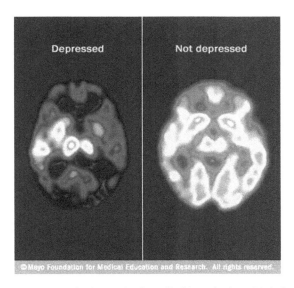

Illustration 5.6   PET scans of a brain before (left) and after (right) treatment for depression. Notice increased blood supply (shown by paler areas) to the recovered brain

Our brain has evolved a tendency to restrict blood supply to parts of the brain inessential to basic physical or psychological survival when under stress. The feeling of being 'unable to think straight' in times of stress can be very inconvenient – think of particularly nerve-racking examinations, angry teachers, unreasonable deadlines or stage fright when you were a child. Stress can restrict activity in the evolutionarily 'younger' parts of the brain – those involved in appraising situations, making fine judgements, analysing consequences, remembering, applying experience and planning (see Tokuhama-Espinoza, 2014).

The pair of PET scan images in Illustration 5.6 above show a depressed patient's brain compared with their brain after treatment. The lighter parts denote areas with a greater supply of oxygenated blood essential to thinking. The frontal parts of the brain (where thinking is most clearly registered) appear relatively dark and therefore poorly supplied with blood. In the image on the right, taken after three months of treatment for depression, a much more general supply of blood is shown; this is especially evident in the frontal and lateral areas associated with high-level thinking.

Recent neuroscientific study therefore suggests that:

- the stress of *unthreatening* challenge may be seen as helpful in some learning
- too much stress may actually reduce brain functioning
- our brains are likely to be less rational under stress
- if a child is feeling worried, embarrassed, sick or scared, they are less likely to be able to think or learn (Greenhalgh, 1994)
- a curriculum that is designed to produce challenge without stress is likely to maximize learning.

Emotions and feelings

The external manifestation of feelings – the smile, the frown or the grimace – we call emotion. These superficial features impact upon our minds and provoke further changes in our bodies. Psychologist Paul Ekman and neuroscientist Richard Davidson, working at the boundary between neuroscience and psychology, found that even pulling the face of happiness had a positive impact upon inner feelings (Ekman, 2004; Goleman, 1997). 'Whistling a happy tune' when we feel worried or upset really *does* seem to make a positive difference to our minds and bodies.

Both our externally shown emotions and our more secret inner feelings appear to be centrally involved in learning (Damasio and Immordino-Yang, 2007). The neurological connections through which body and mind are linked are well illustrated by examining what we call 'feelings'. A feeling is the word we give to our sensing of that exquisite network connecting memory, nervous and immune systems, muscular, visceral and intellectual systems as we respond to a particular event. Feelings, including intuition, serve to help us weigh up the pros and cons of a situation, decide on a course of action and plan our future actions (Claxton, 2003; Damasio, 2010; Goleman, 1996; LeDoux, 1999; Salovey and Sluyter, 1997; Tokuhama-Espinoza, 2014). We are beginning to understand more about the complexity of these interrelated systems. British neuroscientist Hugo

Critchley has shown how EEG, PET and fMRI scans can now be used to measure the impact of events on the living brain so that we are able to say with some confidence, for example, that *negative* non-speech intonations, and sounds like groans, sighs, squeals, shouts and cries, provoke increased activity in the parts of the brain that process threat, just as pictures and words associated with danger do. Numerous other imaging studies have confirmed the link between what is emotionally significant, current attention and long-term memory (Critchley, 2003), and it appears we can also learn to control electrical frequencies within our brain through neuro-feedback (Gruzelier, 2003).

Illustration 5.7   A happy face. Note the crinkles around the eyes, raised forehead, cheeks and eyebrows and the broad smile (This information was provided by Clinical Tools, Inc., and is copyrighted by Clinical Tools)

Neuroscientist Damasio argues that a sense of joy or happiness is the optimum condition of the human organism. He examines biological evidence that supports seventeenth-century philosopher Spinoza's view that the brain/body is constantly seeking ways of promoting its physical and emotional survival. The goal of the human mind, Damasio says, is to 'provide a better than neutral life state … well-ness and well-being' (2003: 35). Translating this into a school context, we could take this to mean that children are likely to be attempting to find aspects of their classroom life that generate those secure, relaxed, fully engaged and exciting feelings we interpret as happiness. Such feelings, whether provided by a stimulating curriculum or peer popularity gained in other ways, will affect body, mind and immune system positively – a condition we generally want to prolong. It is obvious that there is no guarantee that feelings of happiness are always generated by culturally or morally 'good' things. It does seem likely, however, that teachers and all those who work in schools would share the desire to provide in their classes:

- a comfortable and warm place where basic physical needs are supplied
- a place where positive experience for each individual is more likely than negative experience
- a curricular concentration on promoting the conditions of well-being
- a close knowledge of the lives of the children beyond the classroom.

Growing numbers of policy-makers are convinced that 'emotional literacy' programmes, where pupils are helped to 'recognise, understand, handle and appropriately express emotions' (Sharp, 2001: 1; Young Foundation, 2010) have a direct impact not only upon well-being, but on learning and achievement also. Research supporting a curriculum based around 'well-being' has only recently gained general prominence (Antidote, 2003; Frederickson, 2009; Hanko, 1999; Huppert et al., 2005; Warnock, 1996; Weare and Gray, 2003).

Illustration 5.8   This student, linked to a computer that painlessly reveals electrical activity in parts of her brain, is learning, through neuro-feedback, to control aspects of her own thinking

Memory

Memory clearly affects learning. The *working* memory involves present-time operations such as adding numbers in the head, remembering what you just said and following directions. These aspects of memory are controlled in various parts of the pre-frontal cortex and are very susceptible to even mild stress. The *declarative* memory (storage of facts, figures, faces and names, all experiences and conscious memories) is largely controlled by the limbic system including the *hippocampus*. We also have what is sometimes known as 'muscle memory', the memory of *procedures*, actions, habits or skills that are learned simply by repetition. These procedural memories are probably controlled in the *cerebellum* at the back of the brain. Learning is the result of consciously connecting sensory inputs, all three types of memory, language and the emotional charge connected with most aspects of the declarative memory.

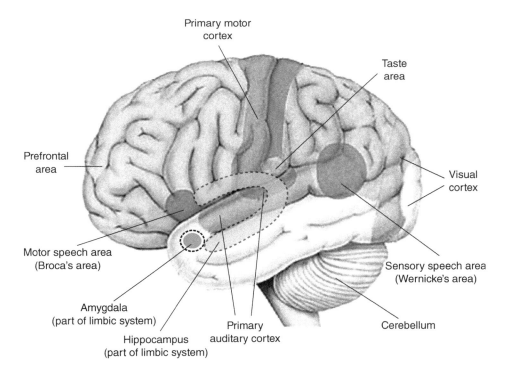

Figure 5.3   The brain marked with some of the major sensory, memory and thinking areas referred to in the text. The amygdala and hippocampus are deep within the brain

It appears that negative memories are stored in different areas of the brain to positive ones. Equally, different organs within the brain have predominance in negative and positive situations. For example, centrally involved in even mildly threatening situations is the *amygdala*. The amygdala and other areas are activated in fearful situations and seem to facilitate rapid but minimally processed responses that evoke alertness and escape behaviour (Garrett et al., 2002; LeDoux, 2002). Even when we 'know' situations are not really threatening, such as watching a boxing scene in a DVD or a violent video, studies have shown that the areas of the brain linked to threat, escape and those that store long-term memory of (real) traumatic events are significantly engaged (Murray, 2007). The concentration of such events in the memory has been argued to affect the degree of aggression, desensitization and generalized fear experienced by individuals.

Positive emotional stimuli tend to arouse quite different and equally complex areas of the brain. Brain areas associated with relaxed, content, secure, 'approach' behaviour are generally distinct from those that provoke 'withdrawal' behaviour typical of feelings of fear, pain and disgust. Even in young babies, the reflex response to their mother's approach activates the areas of the brain that in adulthood process positive emotion. Positive feelings appear to involve larger and more dispersed areas of the brain usually concentrated on the *left* side rather than the right. In emotionally significant situations, the engagement of these areas facilitates more detailed, measured responses and enables analysis, correction or reinforcement.

Neuroscientific research into memory would suggest that schools and teachers:

- provide many situations likely to provide positive memories
- avoid realistic negative scenarios
- cultivate 'approach' atmospheres and relationships in the classroom
- avoid situations where withdrawal is the natural response.

School learning, memory and brain science

Teachers and other adults are understandably interested in how thinking and learning are affirmed, provoked and reorganized. The links between learning and memory are vital and, again, neuroscience has helped us understand them. Learning happens when brain and body combine to make experience part of the conscious memory to be recalled to solve future problems. We have seen how the brain does not mature in a linear fashion, and this is true of the memory in particular. As the connections between senses and amygdala and hippocampus become hard-wired, we can memorize more easily. Between the ages of 3 and 14, memory is more reliable if our already matured senses are involved. Repetition also significantly helps us to memorize (Alexander, 2010; Blakemore and Frith, 2006). Through establishing repeated neural connections, we create permanent or semi-permanent changes in the brain. But context-free memory exercises are not the best way to generate mind change (Gardner, 2004).

Teachers generally aim at what might be called 'quality learning'. Quality learning is the kind of learning that benefits individuals and society and is transferable to many situations. Quality learning may also include the ability to inhibit inappropriate behaviours and thoughts, focus attention and monitor our own actions – each of these abilities, Gogtay and colleagues' (2004) research reminds us, are subject to gradual maturation. Perkins (2009) also draws attention to fMRI studies which show that new knowledge on a particular subject, say the cause of thunder, tends to overlay pre-existing, or 'native' knowledge, rather than replace it, which is why 'backsliding' is so common.

Memory is enhanced by frequently talking about the things we think are important. National or state curricula have helped us by establishing what *politicians* think is most important to remember, but each institution may arrive at other aspects of 'worthwhile' knowledge (see Chapter 8). By establishing and revisiting conversations, by metacognition, making links between present and past class activity and by connecting school learning with the rest of life, teachers can help build useful memory banks in each child's mind. Key, usually subject-based, vocabulary is important here also, and forms part of the proposed lesson plans discussed in Chapter 11.

Adults construct much of the physical and emotional environment within which children learn. Teachers plan progressive sensory and intellectual experience to support the child in building new concepts and reassessing earlier misconceptions. It is therefore of great importance that teachers and other adults involved in education keep abreast of research on the workings and development of the brain.

Parents and teachers are currently targeted with a wealth of 'brain-based' arguments for particular styles of learning (for example, Tokuhama-Espinoza, 2014). These can be very helpful in deciding which new insights are relevant to schooling. Many schools use 'mind mapping', 'brain gym', notions of 'learning styles' or 'brain-based learning' methods that purport to be neuroscientifically founded. This interest in ideas traceable to neuroscience suggests that neurological perspectives have already made significant inroads into education. In the view of most laboratory neuroscientists,

Illustration 5.9   Children engaged with an interactive museum exhibit (Photo: Dorothee Thyssen)

however, many 'brain-based' ideas are over simplified and poorly understood, founded on faulty science and likely to be ineffective in the longer term. Such well-intentioned initiatives have been dismissed by neuroscientists and other academics as 'psycho-babble' (Howard-Jones and Pickering, 2005: 7) and consequently insights of potential worth may be undermined. A teacher's understanding of neuroscientific research is unlikely ever to be as detailed and deep as a neuroscientist's and, in any case, experience, agendas and audiences are very dissimilar. The popularity of brain-based approaches with teachers, however, says much about the contemporary need for 'quick fixes' and external verification from science to justify what might in the past have been called good and intuitive teaching. Neuroscientists already tell us with confidence that the developing brain seeks patterns, holds doggedly on to naive concepts and learns socially and in multi-sensory ways (Goswami and Bryant, 2007). An important challenge for twenty-first-century education is to ensure dialogue between educationalists and neuroscientists for the benefit of children. Schools in the meantime should:

- agree on what 'quality' learning and 'worthwhile' knowledge should be
- continue to use multi-sensory approaches shown to be effective in helping children learn and remember
- talk a lot about important principles, bits of knowledge and skills that have already been introduced
- assess the effectiveness of new brain-based approaches by small-scale research projects within school.

Multiple intelligences

Gardner's theory of multiple intelligences (Gardner, 1993, 1999b) was neuroscientifically founded. Its widening of the concept of intelligence provides academic support for teachers' genuine attempts to be more inclusive and positive. An intelligence, Gardner proposes, can be seen as 'a neural mechanism or computational system ... genetically programmed to be activated or triggered by certain kinds of internally or externally presented information' (Gardner, 1993: 63).

Gardner suggested that the following are each discrete ways of making sense of the world, highly valued in at least one culture and capable of isolation through brain damage (see Gardner, 1999b):

- linguistic
- logical mathematical
- spatial
- bodily kinaesthetic
- musical
- naturalist
- intra-personal
- interpersonal
- existential.

Each of us, he claims, has a mix of all intelligences but every individual has a unique profile of strengths and weaknesses. A related cluster of brain areas distributed across all areas of the brain is involved in processing each mode of mental processing. For example, the way we understand the world *spatially* uses observably different combinations of brain areas than those used to understand it *linguistically*. The same brain area, however, may fulfil a number of different functions and be shared by several different 'intelligences'.

Whilst it seems that in normal situations our brains work as a complex whole, each of Gardner's intelligences is argued to be capable of relatively independent existence. Usually, we use several intelligences to process what is going on around us, but nonetheless we may display positive dispositions towards one or more. So one of us may be more prone to understanding practically through the use of our body and gross and fine motor movements (Gardner's *bodily kinaesthetic* intelligence), whilst another may prefer to understand through reflection and quiet analysis (using his *intra-personal* intelligence).

Illustration 5.10   These fully involved children are using musical intelligence to compose music based around the skin patterns of African animals

Since this neurologically based theory is seen as 'uncontroversial (in scientific terms), unthreatening and simple' (Howard-Jones and Pickering, 2005: 13), it is argued to be 'easily accepted and owned' by education. Whilst it might be owned, it may still not be very deeply understood. My observations in schools suggest that many fail to grasp its founding principles (Barnes, 2005a). Multiple intelligence theory was proposed to help *teachers* and other adults understand that children may learn and show their intelligence in various and contrasting ways. The dangers of encouraging children to label themselves by deciding between nine categories of being 'smart' are obvious – they can easily create an exclusive mindset that refuses to see or try other ways of learning. Such classifications run counter to Gardner's intentions. An understanding of the different ways a child could show intelligence was meant to suggest *to teachers* different ways of mobilizing the brain so that important content can be learned.

Gardner is clear that he does not support the creation of a 'new set of losers' and accepts the strong possibility that the profile of intelligences may change with the situation, maturity or experience (Gardner, 1999a: 98).

Gardner's multiple intelligence theory and other insights into thinking and learning that mirror the many ways in which we can understand the world might suggest the following changes in school:

- Avoid labelling children as having one intelligence or another – this will limit their development.
- Provide as many entry points to learning as possible – this will maximize the chances of engagement.
- Be more inclusive in the use of the term intelligence – look for *how* each child is intelligent, not *if*.
- Value equally all ways of being intelligent.
- Give each curriculum subject equal weight and status.
- Choose a curriculum that provides many powerful and multifaceted experiences to interpret in a wide variety of ways.

School environments

The nature–nurture debate has raged for centuries, but neuroscience helps us see both sides of the argument in more dynamic balance. Robertson and many others have argued that environment has as big an effect on intelligence and our neural circuitry as our genetic inheritance, and that our minds are susceptible to 'sculpture' by our environments. He quotes a number of studies that demonstrate a marked improvement in children's mental processing achieved simply by changing the environment children occupy (Robertson, 1999, 2002, 2012).

Neuroscientists have been able to demonstrate that our brains, particularly the complex pre-frontal cortex (PFC), are shaped by experience (see Goswami and Bryant, 2007; Greenfield, 2003; Marks and Shah, 2006). The PFC is involved in cognitive, social and emotional processes such as the regulation of attention, planning, self-control, flexibility and self-awareness, and seems very sensitive to environment. Studies of children with neurological damage due to accidents have already shown that family and physical environment are key factors in the degree and rate of recovery from such injury (Yates et al., 1997), but the environment consists of much more than family. Neuroscientists have noted that the PFC is also involved in the working memory, mental imagery, audio and visual associations, mental representation of the body in space and the integration of memory with present circumstances.

Illustration 5.11   Working in less familiar environments beyond the classroom can quickly involve children in memorable learning experiences (Canterbury HEARTS project)

It is likely that learners also respond to the values environment that teachers establish. An environment that puts a premium on flexibility, alternative solutions and creativity will use the right brain dominance McGilchrist (2010) has observed. Similarly, an environment that prizes decontextualized facts, tests and highly focused, mainly mechanical activities will serve to develop left-brained approaches. Clearly a balance between both styles is ideal.

The plasticity of the brain is illustrated by an important study on the brain areas concerned with topographical memory. The research use London taxi drivers as its focus (Maguire et al., 2000). Taxi drivers' memory for streets, landmarks, routes and shortcuts is unsurprisingly increased by repetition and practice. This progressive experience results in observable growth in the relevant brain areas, chiefly the hippocampus, which was observed to become more complex, dense and physically enlarged over time. Similarly, experienced musicians have an auditory cortex some 25% larger than control groups of non-musicians (Pantev et al., 1998) and interestingly focused on the left side of the brain. Non-professional and less experienced musicians show activity on the right side. Brain scientists conjecture that other areas of the brain, particularly those involved in our feelings and emotions, may be similarly responsive to the environment (Davidson et al., 2000; Marks and Shah, 2006).

If the plan is changeable by environment perhaps we can control these changes. Some educationalists have taken the concept of the plasticity of

Illustration 5.12   Recording fine detail and personal impressions in a unique and authentic environment

the brain to imply that it ought to be possible to teach ourselves to raise standards via neuro-feedback. Gruzelier (2003) has shown how students can learn (via a monitor screen that shows their own brains in action, see Illustration 5.8) to control the *theta* brainwaves associated with creativity, improved memory, anxiety reduction, self-confidence and a sense of well-being. They were able to improve the creativity and impact of their performance through learning to control the hitherto invisible brain circuits. We have already seen how simple practice makes a great deal of difference to performance, but more complex neurological outcomes can result from particular approaches to learning. Given extra music lessons, for example, children made unexpected and considerable developments in mathematics, emotional literacy and language (Overy, 1998). Other studies have shown the value of music in managing emotion (Justlin and Sloboda, 2009). Each suggestion from neuroscientists has implications for teachers. The general message is that mental activity shapes and organizes itself according to environmental considerations that include atmosphere, unique experience, class, peer group, geographical location, furnishing, objects, temperatures and sounds suggest that schools may need to see intellect and attitude as:

- teachable and able to be changed through experience
- subject to non-maturational influence in particular supportive, stimulating environments
- responsive to learning situations throughout life.

Summary

The implications for education of modern neuroscientific study are only lately being discussed by educationalists (Alexander, 2010; Howard-Jones, 2009; Tokuhama-Espinoza, 2014). The techniques of brain scanning are still in their infancy and we should therefore be tentative about conclusions from neuroscience and wary of unthinkingly adopting 'neuromyths'. However, when neuro-researchers publish findings that match the experienced observations of teachers, it seems inevitable that teachers will take this scientific evidence as corroboration and support for their own professional judgements. When rapidly developing imaging technology makes it possible to see brain connections being made in response to particular stimuli, and when we are able to observe the neural effects of well-being in non-laboratory contexts, then the implications for schools and curricula would be huge. Schools must be prepared for this likelihood. The meeting points between neurology and education are still being forged, but this area is one of the most significant and potentially paradigm-changing developments of the present.

Illustration 5.13   Using emotions, senses, intellect and body in a holistic learning experience

Neuroscientific research supports many of the principles of cross-curricular learning. A curricular approach that maximizes the use of the widest range of mental and physical faculties is likely to be more effective than one that uses only some. The faculties that evolved to ensure human survival and flourishing are those that continue to ensure the most productive learning. The common ground between cross-curricular learning and our current understanding of neuroscience of learning is in the following areas:

- the crucial role of the senses
- the unique human skill of making finely judged discriminations
- the centrality of emotional engagement
- the long-lasting effects of positive experience
- the positive impact of challenge
- the negative impact of threat
- the positive effect of stimulating and supportive environments
- the importance of rich, authentic and multi-layered experiences
- the existence of multiple modes of interpretation.

Key questions for discussion

- Does neuroscience tell us anything new?
- Why do we need evidence from neuroscience?
- What is the difference between stress and challenge?
- What can teachers tell neuroscientists?

Further reading

Damasio, A. (2003) *Looking for Spinoza: Joy, Sorrow and the Feeling Brain*. Orlando, FL: Harcourt.

Huppert, F., Baylis, N. and Keverne, B. (2005) *The Science of Well-being*. Oxford: Oxford University Press.

McGilchrist, I. (2010) *The Master and His Emissary: The Divided Brain and the Making of the Western World*. London: Yale University Press.

Tokuhama-Espinoza, T. (2014) *Making Classrooms Better – 50 Practical Applications of Mind, Brain and Education Science: Lessons from the Cognitive Revolution*. New York: Norton.

CHAPTER 6

PSYCHOLOGY AND CROSS-CURRICULAR LEARNING

Chapter aims

This chapter considers the influence of psychological theory upon cross-curricular teaching and learning. It places knowledge about the development of children's feelings, thinking, play, environments and language at the centre of decision making about curricula in schools. By the end of this chapter you will have considered the following areas where educational psychology provides important insights for the teacher:

- children thinking
- children and play
- environments for thinking and learning
- children and their feelings
- children and language development
- children and flow.

Children often remark that learning seems easier when it makes sense to them. Educational psychologists are interested in how children make sense of experience. They observe children's behaviour and focus on what they *say*, think and do. Amongst many other questions, educational psychologists ask how the curriculum and teachers can improve the learning experience of children. They attempt to make use of experimental findings and test theoretical positions regarding learning and intelligence. Many findings emanating from psychology support the introduction of more cross-curricular practice in schools and this chapter will outline some of them.

Over the last few decades, psychologists have disputed old concepts of intelligence and suggested new ones. To take a few examples: Gardner (1993) and Sternberg (1997b) challenged narrow 'language and logic' definitions of intelligence by introducing wider, more inclusive understandings of what intelligent behaviour could look like. Robertson (1999), on the boundary of psychology and neuroscience, helped establish the concept of the 'plastic' brain, an organism highly responsive to its environment. Psychologists like Jensen (1995), Shayer and Adey (2002) and Perkins (2009) introduced the concept of *learnable intelligence*, which has become a common belief amongst teachers. Perkins' (1995) idea of *distributed intelligence* that sees other people's minds, tools and technologies as playing a significant part in individual problem solving and 'intelligent' behaviour, is widely understood and accepted. Bandura (1994) showed how *self-efficacy*, usually arising from a positive social context, generates the belief that we are able to learn and are empowered to use that learning. John-Steiner (2006) used observations of *creative collaboration* amongst key shapers of the twentieth century, to argue that collaborative groups in educational settings can build more intelligent solutions. Picking up Gardner's ideas, Goleman suggested that *emotional intelligence* (1996) and *social intelligence* (2006) may be more important than Intelligence Quotients. Meanwhile, Rogoff (2003) and Robinson (2008, website) challenged Western assumptions that intelligent behaviour was best nurtured in what they saw as the 'production line' techniques of current Western education where children are taught an economically driven curriculum in large groups of the same age. Teachers recognize McGilchrist's (2010) warning that our education system so greatly favours 'left brain' ways of thinking, that creative, intuitive, imaginative and flexible approaches are under threat.

Methods of instruction have been subject to the ebbs and flows of fashion over the last 80 years. Teaching that focused on whole-class tuition, drilling facts, fixed knowledge, rote learning, texts, formulas and 'the basics' of reading, writing and arithmetic, appropriate to a nineteenth-century industrial, manufacturing society, was not primarily intended to develop understanding. Such pedagogies are seen now by psychologists as engendering only short-term learning (see Gardner, 1999a; Shepard, 1992). Some have offered 'deeper', more transferable, longer-lasting models of learning. Marton and Entwistle pioneered work in this field in Europe (see Chapter 7 for more details of their work). They argue persuasively for active learning concentrating on understanding – transforming 'surface' knowledge by relating ideas to each other, looking for patterns and principles and extracting meaning. They suggest the most effective methods to generate 'deep learning' are within groups and in solving problems which are, or have been made, significant to pupils. The concept of 'teaching for understanding' (Blythe, 1997; Stone-Wiske, 1998) has become common amongst teachers and researchers who want to help students learn *how* to learn (Entwistle, 2000; Lucas et al., 2013). It is the central argument of this book that relevant and meaningful cross-curricular contexts provide some of the most powerful motivators for such learning.

Cognitive psychologists suggest that we can and should learn *how* to learn. Some writers have popularized specific aids to thinking. Ideas like 'Mind Mapping'® (Buzan, 2002), 'Six Thinking Hats'® (De Bono, 1999) and the 'new 4 Rs' of resilience, resourcefulness, reflection and reciprocity (Claxton, 2003) have, like 'brain-based learning', been embraced by teachers because they appear to help children and adults order and deepen their thoughts. Perkins called these tools designed to assist thinking 'Mindware' (New Horizons, 1991, website). Neuroscientists, however, frequently cast doubt on simply expressed models of learning (Geake, 2009; Howard-Jones, 2010).

There are many possible answers to the question 'How do children learn?' locked away in erudite journals and rarely visited websites. Many approaches overlap significantly, however, in highlighting the importance of personal and transformative experience, passion, understanding and cooperation. Teachers wishing to make education exciting and motivating for all children may appreciate the suggestions brought together from current psychological research, under the following headings:

- Children thinking
- The 'thinking classroom'
- Children playing
- Children and their feelings
- Children and 'flow'
- Children and language

Children thinking

Harvard Professor of Education David Perkins famously stated that 'learning is a consequence of thinking' (1992: 34). He continues to argue that rich, stimulating and multi-layered environments, real-world investigations and active participation in discovery and challenging questioning, all promote thinking in both cross-curricular and single discipline contexts (Perkins, 2009). But experience and stimulation alone are not enough to make thinking deep and learning transferable. Most cognitive psychologists argue that there are a range of other influences on the way children think: self-confidence, the ability to be metacognitive, the social and physical environment, the accidents of heredity, the example of peers, and perceived relevance may all play their part. The social aspects of thinking and learning have already been discussed but thought is also influenced by more hidden forces within the individual mind.

Humans' ability to examine and talk about their own thought processes must have provided enormous advantages in the primeval world – psychologists remind us that it is still vital now. Metacognition, or thinking about our thinking, is essential to 'deep learning' (see Chapter 7 and Entwistle, 2000; Fisher, 2008). By calling to mind the *way* in which we think, we rehearse, externalize and buttress that thinking. Even at the age of 5 and probably younger, children can become aware that they think and think differently from others (Fisher, 1999) and they can be lead towards examining their own thought processes. Being asked to consider our own mental process appears to result in measurably positive benefits for young learners in Mathematics, Science and Design/Technology. Grades dramatically improved in national and school tests in a number of London schools in which teachers encouraged children to think, explain and hypothesize about subject-based activities in which they were involved (Shayer and Adey, 2002). Shayer and Adey's research also suggested that the change of teaching and learning style provoked marked improvements in attitude, autonomy and motivation.

Thinking needs preparation time and teachers themselves need to be very aware of what works best. Twenty years ago Adey and Shayer provided five still relevant and simple pointers to generating better thinking:

1. Prepare the child's mind with experience of concrete and practical examples and relevant vocabulary.
2. Arrange some kind of 'cognitive conflict', an apparent contradiction of common sense, a genuine challenge or a problem.
3. Work with others to construct an answer to the problem through speculation and collaboration.
4. Think about your methods of finding an answer to the problem.
5. Transfer the newly formed theory to a new situation. (Adey and Shayer, 1994)

When children explain their thinking, whether in a cross-curricular context like children's philosophy or in a single-subject session, we quickly become aware that not everyone thinks in the same way. A simple musical listening exercise (shared by Fisher), will help demonstrate this:

Music and moving image

Find a section of video where a single slowly changing scene is depicted for about three or four minutes. Several sequences from the documentary film *Powaqqatsi* (1988) directed by Godfrey Reggio are highly suitable, but this will work with the opening sequences from many modern films. Play the same video clip through three times, but each time play it against a different musical soundtrack (perhaps one rock music, one reflective and quiet church music, and one silence). Ask children independently to write down or discuss with a neighbour what they saw in the video clip or what it made them think. A discussion after each clip will reveal that dozens of different connections have been made between the sounds of the music and the details of the image you have chosen. This will remind children of two important messages: that they are (a) all thinkers and (b) all different thinkers.

The suggestion that there may be many different ways of thinking has been developed by a number of psychologists. Robert Sternberg (1997b), a past president of the US Psychological Association, postulates some 13 distinctly different 'thinking styles' (or styles of 'mental self-government') and uses the metaphor of contrasting styles of political government to illustrate them. Within Sternberg's theory, some of us are *monarchic* thinkers who prefer single goals to think about and work towards. Others may be *judicial* thinkers who weigh up the alternatives before deciding on a goal. *Oligarchic* thinkers are motivated by several, sometimes competing, goals of equal importance. Other possible thinking styles are listed in Figure 6.1.

Understanding one's own preferred thinking style and the bias it brings to judgements and choices is clearly useful to teachers. Without this understanding, teachers might expect children to think in same way as they do. Sternberg argues that it is vital for teachers to expect children to think in many different ways and that none of them is intrinsically wrong – if they work. Different thinking styles may be effectively pooled in group discussions and collective activities to produce more satisfying and rounded outcomes than would be possible through one style alone.

Sternberg has also made major contributions to our understanding of intelligence itself. His *triarchic theory* of human intelligence suggests that

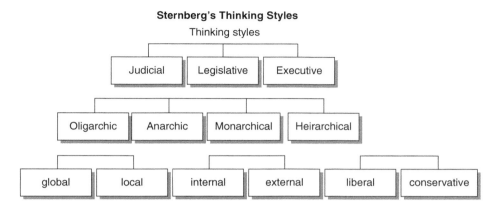

Sternberg's Thinking Styles

Figure 6.1 Sternberg's thinking styles. We may have a preference for thinking in one style in each group shown in the diagram. We don't all think in the same way, yet often assume others think like us

alongside requiring a good memory, intelligence consists of analytical, creative and practical ways of thinking that occur in varying strengths in each of us (Sternberg, 1997b, 2003). He describes research which shows that pupils taught by teachers who share their intelligence strength are much more likely to succeed, but those with a teacher with a different intelligence strength are more likely to fail. For example, a child with a strongly analytical approach taught by a highly 'creative' teacher may receive poorer grades (and perhaps develop a negative attitude to their own ability) than a child who shows more creative approaches. The obvious advice is for teachers to be aware of their own preferred style and plan for many different thinking styles and ways of showing intelligence. These teachers will aim to use a variety of entry points so as to maximize the number of pupils that can be reached.

Whilst some psychologists continue to use IQ tests to measure the quality of children's thinking, many now see both thinking and intelligence as much more complex than simple tests and snap judgements suggest. Research on children's thinking has quite literally changed many teachers' minds as they seek to discover *where* the intelligence strength lies in each individual, rather than *if* it is there. The key suggestions that psychologists bring to teachers are that:

- we all think differently
- there are a wide range of thinking styles/preferences
- each child shows intelligence in different ways
- teachers can help children think better.

Illustration 6.1   Making sense of a view through the window – teacher and pupils thinking and learning together as equals

The thinking classroom

The design, arrangement and resources of the classroom itself can promote thinking (see Barnes, 2014c). The concept of the *setting* of learning or 'situated learning' developed by Lave and Wenger (1991) in a business context, may be of even greater significance for children. Displays, stimulus resources, learning aids, tools, lighting, furniture, window view, corridor space, ICT and access to outside may each be used to help generate thinking. A classroom has social and personal dimensions too. Expensive and excellent physical characteristics are worthless unless the social, personal and spiritual classroom is equally well-resourced and cared for. Teaching experience shows that thinking is generated by an atmosphere where questioning is part of the classroom culture. We know from psychology research that learning growth happens when children are not frightened to make mistakes, where relationships are warm and supportive, and where instructions and goals are clear.

Psychologists argued that environment profoundly impacted on our thinking and learning well before such observations were confirmed by neuroscience. Beliefs about the relationship between environmental and inherited factors affecting learning have always coloured policy and practice in schools. The common view today is that environmental and inherited factors are so intertwined that it is difficult, and possibly

Illustration 6.2   A group discussing a proposed drama. Each brings a different perspective to the discussion

pointless, to untangle them. Psychologist Robert Fisher, for example, identifies three dimensions of the child's intelligence (1999): two of them, *developed intelligence* and *self-developed intelligence*, are clearly affected by environmental conditions. Fisher's third concept, *born-with* intelligence, sounds a biological absolute, but we know that environmental influences such as a mother's diet, lifestyle, poverty or any violence she is subjected to, impact upon her child's developing brain, from shortly after conception (Gardner, 1999a).

The social, emotional and physical environment we occupy is in many ways exclusive to us. Psychologist of language Steven Pinker suggests a roughly 50/50 split in environmental and genetic influences on our learning (Pinker, 2002). Fifty per cent of what we *are* (character, abilities, preferences, intelligence, even habits) is the result, he argues, of our genetic inheritance. The other 40–50% is the result *not* of our generalized, home, family, school or cultural background (or nurture), but what Pinker calls our *unique environment*. The unique environment is what exclusively surrounds us as individuals; exactly what happened to us, where, with whom, what we heard, smelt, touched, saw, felt and thought in the billions of separate incidents that make up our unique lives. Thus, identical twins, physically clones of each other, are not mental clones. Twins are likely to be nearer to 50% alike in character and intelligence than the

100% we might expect, because each of them has inhabited their own special environment from shortly after conception. Pinker's concept of the unique environment could have major implications for schools and teachers. Teachers, as influential adults, consciously and unconsciously control much of the physical and emotional environments that surround the child. Whilst the unique environment experienced by the child could never be directly under a teacher's control, teachers are still likely to influence its general character. Teachers can strive to build the kind of environment most likely to generate meaningful, positive, affirmative and constructive connections within the mind. Teachers can also build environments in their classrooms where the chances of good things happening heavily outweigh the chances of a bad experience.

Illustration 6.3   Meaningful engagement found in a museum. How was each child's 'unique environment' manipulated by the teacher? (Photo: Dorothee Thyssen)

Cognitive psychologists tend to agree on the importance of meaning making in education (Bruner, 1996; Csikszentmihalyi, 1997; David, 2001; Eaude, 2008; Gardner, 1999a; Marton and Booth, 1997). Such writers argue that personal meaning may only be found if an appropriate and personalized language of learning is discovered. The personal often starts with questions of identity. Who am I? Who/what matters to me? What matters to us? How do I like doing things? When a teacher successfully introduces such personally meaningful questions, the experience of children is transformed as passion enters the curriculum.

The provision of multiple aids to understanding does not obviate direct teaching of facts and skills. The human child, and adult for that matter, seems to learn best through inter-personal and intra-personal relationships. Most psychologists involved in education argue for balance between structure and freedom, the didactic and the discovery approach (for example, Alexander, 2010; Hallam and Ireson, 1999). Space in a classroom must be provided for instruction too. Many teachers have therefore taken to choosing furniture for its flexibility. They redesign their classroom term by term, or even daily, to offer a changing palette of opportunities depending upon the term's theme and the most appropriate teaching and learning styles.

Case study   The challenge of working with a conceptual artist

Creative Partnerships UK set up a project about the deliberate marooning of a conceptual artist on a mid-English Channel fort for a month. Local high school children with a wide range of barriers to learning were provided with well-resourced spaces for construction, music and drama activities. Using these spaces, they worked in mixed-age groups to provide comfort, entertainment and food for the mind of the marooned artist. These were delivered to him on the dangerous and isolated fort. In the following term, the same groups of 11–14-year-olds worked in art rooms, comfortable common rooms and ICT suites to produce high-quality brochures and visual presentations on the project. Children reported very positively about their experience. The provision of multiple entry points changed the teacher's view as well. As a result of engagement in the project, their teacher said, 'I think at the start it was subject knowledge I was passionate about … but now I think I'm more passionate about the children's learning and learning something new from each other' (Cremin et al., 2009).

Educational and cognitive psychologists suggest that learning which takes place in a relevant context is learning that sticks and is transferable (for example, Lucas et al., 2013; Perkins, 2009; Shepherd, 1991). Situated learning in school starts within a classroom somehow made relevant for the activities the children will follow, but should quickly move on to more authentic and richer settings beyond the classroom. In such contexts, meaningful learning is easier to construct, but real world settings are also, inevitably, the product of multiple disciplines. Cross-curricular approaches back in the classroom will help provide fuller understanding of real-world experiences.

Illustration 6.4   Positive relationships between teacher, child and resources generate thinking and deeper learning (Photo: Dorothee Thyssen)

The work of cognitive psychologists suggests that classrooms should be arranged, resourced and 'ethos-ed' to generate intrinsic motivation and help the child become aware of their own thought processes. The concept of the unique environment suggests that we construct classrooms and curricula in which the chances of positive experience are high. In summary, recent research suggests that teachers need to:

- make classrooms visually exciting and change the stimuli often
- resource classrooms so that children find it easy to construct mental images of new concepts
- arrange furniture and resources so that stimulus displays, artefacts, other people, tools, machines and technologies are all used to generate, sustain and deepen thinking
- use space flexibly to allow for teachers to move between being instructors, facilitators, observers and coaches
- capture learning in the classroom environment through celebratory and informative displays, exhibitions, gallery walks and collections
- widen the definition of the classroom to include views, corridor, school building, grounds and locality
- ensure that they spend as much time constructing a positive atmosphere as providing a stimulating room.

Children playing

We have known that play is important for learning for a very long time. Psychologists like Piaget saw exploration, intuition and imagination as key sources of all, and especially early, learning (Claxton, 1998; David, 1999, 2001; DfES/QCA, 1999; Goouch, 2010). Guy Claxton argues that to generate more creative attitudes in children, teachers should make less distinction between work and play. Just as unstructured play with sound is an essential foundation for musical development at any age (Swanwick, 1994, 1999), similar playfulness with words, numbers, shapes, colours, objects, time, place and the physical capabilities of our bodies, provides the ground for learning in other disciplines (see Austin, 2007). Research on the 'Forest Schools' of Denmark, Wales, Scotland, Northern Ireland and throughout England has added weight to the suggestion that simply having the opportunity to play in safe, stimulating environments adds significantly to social skills, self-esteem and positive attitude to learning (Knight, 2013; Laevers, 1994b; Maynard, 2007). Playing with language, the voice, body sounds, patterns, objects and social situations are part of the controlled risk-taking and invention that characterizes childhood (David, 2001; Goouch and Powell, 2013).

The humour, abandon and risk of playfulness have serious purposes for learning. James and Pollard (2008) point to the importance of informal learning in the world of the child. Children may play with power relations and the meaning of things, and this activity supports them in establishing social and conceptual boundaries. Laughter often accompanies play and helps children overcome inner anxieties, but its positive effects are frequently observable in the external world of children too. David also highlights how irreverence, challenging and subversive behaviour in young children helps them in discovering personal meaning, creativity and the possibilities of their personality. In play, children learn and practise the rules of their culture or sub-culture. The curricular implications of such observations are many and often cut across traditional subject boundaries, and the Curriculum Guidance for the Foundation Stage (CGFS) recognizes this. There are times when simply to observe and record young children at play is all a good teacher needs to do to: 'Teachers need without intruding into their "tribal culture" or hijacking children's play, to capitalise on children's highly motivated and playful use of language [roles, objects and places] and learn to celebrate it and use it as a tool for learning' (David, 1999: 28).

At other times, the teacher's role may be to make learning take on the character of play. Opportunities to play with movement in Dance, with sound to compose new music, with words to write an original poem or with the concept of roles, symbols or boundaries in History or Geography abound in the National Curriculum. In previous administrations opportunities to play and make links between subjects were overtly encouraged by government advice (DfES/QCA, 1999; Ofsted, 2002; DCSF/QCDA, 2010). Permission to play with ideas on a cross-curricular level was given by Ofsted, for example in the case of drawing:

> Drawing, in a variety of media, is associated with play and playfulness in much early years teaching. Children often tell stories through their drawings, talking about what is happening as they draw. In secondary schools the potential of drawing for releasing and articulating ideas, while an integral part of art and design and design and technology (D&T), was also evident in other subjects such as religious education and geography. In one geography lesson, for example, Year 8 pupils produced annotated drawings of the potential effects of particular planning decisions on a local landscape. (Ofsted, 2003: para. 21, website)

Illustration 6.5   Play in the sand, making an imagined world real by involving all the senses

Such advice rested upon recognition that children may enter an understanding of a particular subject from many contrasting starting points but it also points to the importance of play. Even at the Year 8 level, children are recorded as playing with ideas about the future through drawing. The recent work of psychologists has simply reminded us of the importance of a fundamental human activity.

Playing across the curriculum

Using an example from the classroom, teach children to take a tiny aspect of their world and weave it into a haiku poem (5 + 7 + 5 syllables). Suggest that the ideal haiku might have two lines of description and one (usually final) line which flips the reader onto a higher plane of thought level. After this teaching, take children into the school play area and ask them to identify a small object, a plant or a corner that for a few minutes can be theirs. (They might choose a dandelion clock, a spider's web, a discarded crisp packet – see Illustration 6.6.) Allow them time to reflect and then write and correct their own haikus. On return to class, ask them to gather into groups of five or six and decide on one which might be a good candidate for putting to music. When children have chosen, give them time and resources to construct a piece of music to either accompany or even replace the haiku. It should have the same 'feel' as the poem. They may use the words imaginatively, recite, chant, sing or mumble the words as part of the music, or abandon words entirely and let the sounds speak for themselves.

Illustration 6.6   Here a teacher joins in the haiku-writing exercise with the children

(Continued)

(Continued)

One 12-year-old, reflecting on a single candle viewed on a class visit to a cathedral, wrote:

A lone white candle
Hopeful against dark vastness
Folly or symbol?

Research on the significance of play from Piaget, through Bowlby to Claxton and David suggests that teachers should:

- consider plentiful opportunities for children of all ages to play with ideas, materials and senses
- shift the balance of their teaching towards the playful aspects of their subject
- not fear failure and encourage adventurousness
- observe children's play to get ideas for teaching
- play with the application of the skills in one subject to the understanding of another.

Children and their feelings

Psychological insights point to the importance of what we *feel* to be true about ourselves and our likes and dislikes. Salovey and Sluyter (1997) and Saron and Davidson (1997) pioneered this work, and (Goleman (1996, 1999, 2006) brought together a considerable weight of research by other neuroscientists and psychologists to support his notions of emotional and social intelligence and their importance to human flourishing.

Personal engagement and ownership of the curriculum has been a favourite theme of UK educational writers too. They maintain that positive views of the self as a learner, a belief that mistakes are part of learning and a feeling of personal emotional security are fundamental to transferable learning. The focus on learning rather than teaching has arisen partly in recognition of the stubborn and sizeable 'tail of underachievement', disaffection and feelings of social exclusion which still remain after decades of government education initiatives intended to address them (Abbs, 2003; Arthur and Cremin, 2010; Black and Wiliam, 1998; Gipps and MacGilchrist, 1999; Halpin, 2003; Pollard, 2008; Seltzer and Bentley, 1999). The *Good Childhood* and OECD Reports (Layard and Dunn, 2009; OECD, 2009) showed how the sense of well-being has been compromised for many young people in our post-industrial societies. Whilst the USA and UK have become increasingly rich, there seems no appreciable increase in recorded happiness indicators (Layard, 2005; UNICEF, 2013, website; WHO, 2012, website). One UK government-sponsored report noted that depression and chronic anxiety were the biggest causes of misery and incapacity in Britain amongst 16–60-year-olds (Layard, 2006).

Schools, their staff, children and families are all affected by the realities of mental illness and depression. Encouraging debate on children's and teachers' feelings about themselves, though seen as inappropriate by some (Hayes and Ecclestone, 2008), must be considered in this new social context, and psychology has important contributions to make. Educational psychologists offer some practical answers chiefly through cognitive behavioural therapies, but they also offer teachers corroboration of their intuitive and experiential professional knowledge of children and their learning. Good teachers quickly develop a knowledge and understanding of how to engage children on an emotional level, but if they are unsupported, may lack confidence to fully and adventurously apply it.

The debate regarding children's and teachers' feelings about themselves and their learning hinges on values. How highly do we value individual happiness? What is the importance of individuality? Where

Illustration 6.7   Look for the smiles and other facial signs of involvement in life and learning in classrooms

do we place children in our hierarchy of value? What is the value of a school, a community, a society? Educational psychologists are not above such questions, indeed they are subject to the same pressures and worries as the rest of the population, but they often offer some corroboration for the intuitive and experiential knowledge that teachers and others who work closely with children develop.

The sense of inclusion or exclusion deeply involves feelings. If a child, family or teacher feels excluded in school, it is unlikely they will enter into positive relationships. At its fundamental level, inclusion concerns each individual's emotional response to the people in institutions with which they come into contact. Internationally acclaimed research (Booth and Ainscow, 2011) has contributed centrally to the debate on inclusion in our schools. Their work, initially written against the background of the institutional failures exposed in the Macpherson Report on the murder of Stephen Lawrence (Stephen Lawrence Inquiry, 1999, website), suggests that a forensic examination of the social and structural character of our schools is essential before all adults and children begin to feel included.

Deep learning involves recognizing personal significance in the matter to be learned. Writer Peter Abbs (2003) stresses that education has to be seen by the learner as an *existential* activity for it to be effective. Psychologists from Freud and Jung to Frankl, Seligman and Davidson remind us that the search for meaning is a signature attribute of human being. Sadly, the age-old pupil question 'Why do we have to do this?' is sometime understood by novice teachers as a threat rather than a plea for personal relevance.

We have already seen neurological corroboration of the assumption that we learn better when we are happy. Psychologists confirm this intuition too. Positive psychologists have argued strongly for a renewed focus on aspects of psychology that seek to study enrichment of the human mind rather than just its repair. Psycho-Physiologist Barbara Fredrickson and colleagues (Fredrickson, 2009; Fredrickson and Branigan, 2005; Fredrickson and Tugade, 2004) suggest, for example, that positive events are stored in a metaphorical bank of positive memories that support us in developing resilience in times of difficulty. In her 'Broaden and Build' theory of positive emotions (Fredrickson, 2004), she argues that states of positive emotion ranging from calm, interest, security, to fascination, joy, elation and love enable the mind to broaden its 'thought–action repertoire'. By this she means that when we feel good, we generate within us the resources to make new links, explore new ideas, places or materials and make new and deeper relationships. She also suggests, from a wide research base, that adults in states of positive emotion show a significantly enhanced ability to build new ideas, to be creative and to integrate past knowledge and present circumstances. In states of prevailing negative emotion, she notes that experimental subjects were less able to think of new ideas, build relationships or explore possibilities.

A positive mindset results in a strong sense of 'self-efficacy', the ability to persuade oneself that one is able to reach a particular goal or set of goals (Bandura, 1994; Baron and Byrne, 2004). Numerous psychological studies have suggested links between positive engagement with others and an expressed sense of well-being. Some have shown that negative emotional experiences have a detrimental effect upon health, relationships and longevity (for example, Fraser-Smith et al., 1995). Scientific study now provides evidence that constructive relationships, affirmative experiences and an optimistic mindset can positively affect learning, intellectual activity, physical functioning and enduring personal resources (for example, Fredrickson, 2009; Isen, 2002; Seligman, 2004). But, positivity should never obstruct moral stands against injustice and unkindness – it must be developed within a values framework.

Teachers have little time to read these serious and often tentative scientific studies, and it is left to others to summarize and apply their conclusions to schools and teachers. Inevitably, the work of these scientists is oversimplified and conclusions are over-generalized. Popular books and courses of guidance on 'accelerated learning' (for example, Smith

Illustration 6.8   A positive experience shows itself in the detail and concentration shown by this 5-year-old redesigning his playground

and Call, 2000), whilst sometimes accused of being based only tenuously on psychological evidence, have challenged and in some cases changed the character of teaching towards a more inclusive, engaging and effective/affective curriculum. Half-baked ideas can at times be better than no ideas.

Research in psychology on the importance of emotions in learning suggests that teachers:

- make inclusion a priority
- create a classroom life that seeks to generate the secure, relaxed, fully engaged or exciting feelings we call happiness
- promote positive relationships in the classroom and school as a priority
- seek emotionally relevant starting points – 'speak to the heart'.

Children and language

From our first moments, language forms a key part of our environment. The 6-month-old baby is able to recognize the specific nuances of her mother's language, probably by its dominant tunes and musical tones. Until the child is 2 or 3, they may learn the *exact* tones and tunes of any world language they are exposed to – as Patricia Khul says, they are true citizens of the world. After our infancy, however, it becomes increasingly difficult to speak a foreign language exactly as it is spoken (Khul, 2002). There are possibly windows of opportunity for language development, opened at different times during a child's development that make language acquisition a programmed affair. Understanding seems to develop before spoken language, fluent and grammatical speech; using the home tongue or tongues come next and the detail of 'foreign' languages may come after. If we are deprived of opportunities to develop language until the age of 12, the case of *Genie* suggests that it may be difficult to learn language *at all* (see Jones, 1995).

The language we use and the ways in which we use it are powerful means of constructing the emotional and social setting within which learning might occur. Chomsky's arguments that the growing mind is dependent upon a brain apparently already wired up for language learning seems to match our experience. Regardless of theory, style and philosophy, language is clearly the chief means of most school learning. An understanding of what Pinker (1994) has called the 'language instinct' has been consistently considered by educators to be a prerequisite of good teaching. Our brains seem prepared for ever-more complex, symbolic and abstract uses of language, but they need exercising. The challenge for the teacher is to continually find ways of enhancing the talk of children. Language can be significantly improved by attention to the learning context, as a study by anthropologist Shirley Brice Heath illustrated:

 Case study   Research in the classroom

Language is so much part of what we as humans are, it is hardly surprising to find researchers identifying a pivotal role for language in a project linking art with science. Shirley Brice Heath watched and recorded the interactions between early years children and an artist provided by 'Creative Partnerships' over a year. She observed that whilst using drawing to help them understand aspects of the natural world, children's language developed as strongly as their understanding of science and art. She points out that in concentrating on drawing detail, careful observation of skulls, eyes, the face and fruit, children were subconsciously naming the minutiae of what they were observing, and refining their language accordingly. Their language skills – fluency, use of vocabulary, expression – were all significantly enhanced simply by the act of focusing so strongly on single objects during the act of drawing or painting. Their use of complex language not only improved dramatically through working with a 'real' artist, but Brice Heath notes that the types of language they used in art was remarkably similar to the language needed for science because both disciplines 'testified to the power of curiosity, fascination and mobility of thought'. She noted also that in talking about their art and the art of adult artists, ordinary children aged just 4–6 used complex, multi-syllabic words, and expressed complex and sometimes profound and emotional thoughts (Brice Heath and Wolf, 2005).

Language is inherently creative. We create new sentences moment by moment, and with great ease, to provide commentary on the unique situations we encounter. We cannot assume that this commentary goes on in all households, however, and one of the roles of the school could be described as establishing a minimum base of language experience in a population. Helping children play with language is seen by many as a vital component in developing their creativity. Creativity requires more than simple consciousness of the moment – it requires, as Damasio puts it, 'abundant fact and skill memory, abundant working memory, fine reasoning ability and language' (Damasio, 2000: 315). The more words children can play with, the bigger their world can become (Deutscher, 2010). Language progressively gives children the ability to translate feeling and thoughts into words, and words back into feelings and thoughts. It gives them the ability to classify and to express the imaginary, and to be still more creative.

There is a language of learning too. When teachers and children build a shared vocabulary regarding learning itself, learning is enhanced. The language of metacognition has been vital to children finding success with Guy Claxton's *building learning power* programme, for example (Claxton, 2006, website). In later writing, Claxton, with Bill Lucas (2013), develops the idea of metacognitive learning. Humans appear to be uniquely conscious of themselves and children can learn quickly to identify and expand the detail of their own learning. By using evaluative conversations, reflections, talking about their learning strengths and difficulties, they become conscious of themselves as 'independent learners'. How did I learn that? What difficulties did I find? How could I do it better next time? How did I deal with that distraction? How did I memorize that? Do I need to practise? Whatever the shared language of learning, it can be reinforced by being made visible in wall displays and social with 'talk partners' or a sustained learning dialogue with adult learners. In various commercial or 'home-grown' ways, cognitive psychology suggests that specific language should be used by children to track their own development as learners, thus externalizing and extending their learning.

Role play, 'hot-seating', discussion, 'exploratory talk', problem solving and making sense of authentic situations are time-honoured ways of extending language and the deepened thinking that emanates from a broadened language world. The powerful media and policy emphasis on English and Mathematics have undoubtedly had the effect of narrowing the curriculum (Smith et al., 2004). Dialogue of all kinds has diminished, though for millennia the most successful education systems have depend upon it. Alexander (2008) used research findings from linguists, anthropologists, psychologists and neuroscientists to reaffirm the importance of genuine dialogue, drama, debate and discourse in improving general learning as well as the specific skills of oracy (see Illustration 6.9):

- the language world of children should be extended daily (Khul, 2002)
- art, music and science can very effectively stimulate language development (Brice Heath and Wolf, 2005)
- children should have multiple and contrasting opportunities to play with and extend their language world (David, 1999; Deutscher, 2010)
- using words to explain feelings, problem-solving techniques, new understandings, differences and similarities is an important part of extending learning (Shayer and Adey, 2002)

Illustration 6.9   Children role playing an argument. The class notes down the changes in language they use (Photo: Dorothee Thyssen)

- teachers should strive to use the language of thinking: *hypothesis, hypothesize, believe, predict, guess, think, suggest, understand, compare, contrast, metaphor, analogy, analyse* and so on (see Costa and Kallick, 2014)
- teachers should provide a clear sense of progression in the complexity of language within a real context (Perkins, 2009)
- promote dialogue (Alexander, 2008).

Children and flow

The environment is not simply physical. We have already seen how classroom atmosphere can become the all-pervasive influence on what and how much is learned. There is general consensus that the most productive of learning atmospheres is one in which all participants are fully involved in learning. Ferre Laevers is well known in Europe for the *Leuven involvement and well-being scales* (Laevers, 1994a), which attempt to capture the signs of engagement through which teachers can analyse and improve their practice. Differences occur when psychologists, pedagogues and others argue about the way to construct such an atmosphere. One answer has come from psychologist Mihalyi Csikszentmihalyi, who coined the term *flow* to describe that sense of deep engagement (see Illustration 6.10). We are said to be in a state of 'flow' when we experience: 'that almost automatic, effortless, yet highly focused state of consciousness, which is so enjoyable that we will seek it at considerable risk and expense to ourselves' (Csikszentmihalyi, 2004, website).

Illustration 6.10   Lost in the music. This 5-year-old shows signs of flow as she listens to her favourite music

Moments of flow remain treasured parts of our memory and the flow experience seems recognizable to individuals in all cultures. From asking thousands of people from a wide cross-section of cultures, backgrounds and ages what this state of total involvement feels like, Csikszentmihalyi constructed a list of commonalities. He found that individuals describing any activity they found deeply satisfying and profoundly engaging could agree on the following statements:

- time seems altered
- skills match the challenge presented
- present worries fade
- self-consciousness diminishes
- confidence is strong
- the activity is engaged in for its own sake
- there is a sense of fusion between self and the activity
- there is rapid feedback (usually from the self).

In further questioning, researchers discovered that apart from sex, the most common conditions to provoke the state of flow came during creative or physically challenging activity. Flow was not common when watching television or resting, neither was it recorded as being particularly prevalent in school, although frequently individual teachers were credited with stimulating it. For teachers these findings suggest that a curriculum with plentiful opportunity for physical and creative activity is one most likely to generate flow amongst its pupils. This conclusion is of much more than academic interest, because Csikszentmihalyi goes on to argue that the condition of flow is the optimum condition for learning.

Many teachers will have experienced situations where children are in flow, for example when children are so involved in an activity in class that they do not want to go out to play (or come in *from* play!). Two decades ago Laevers described such total involvement as follows:

> The child is clearly absorbed in his/her activities. His/her eyes are more or less uninterruptedly focussed on the actions and on the material. Surrounding stimuli do not or barely reach him/her. Actions are readily performed and require mental effort. This effort is brought up in a natural way, not so much by will power. There is a certain tension about the action (an intrinsic not an emotional tension) ... the signals of concentration, persistence, energy and complexity abound. (Laevers, 1994a: 39)

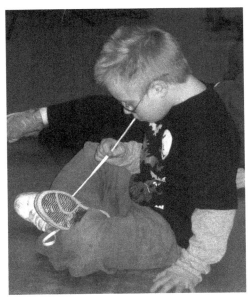

Illustration 6.11   Concentration may show itself in many ways (Photo: Cherry Tewfik)

In the specific context of children and schools, Csikszentmihalyi has controversially recorded that the greatest concentration of flow activities are found in school club activities and practical sessions, in homes with plenty of books, in *poorer* communities, in children with *fewer* technological aids at home, in families where discussion is common and in families where group activities are common (Csikszentmihalyi, 2004, website).

Work on involvement or flow suggests, therefore, that teachers consider:

- providing more opportunities for creative work and physical activity in all subjects
- allowing the timetable to be flexible so that unexpected periods of flow can be sustained
- making more field trips and visits
- encouraging discussion both at home and in school
- encouraging the availability of a wide range of club activities.

Summary

We have made a rapid tour through some of the most exciting work in modern psychology. The conclusions are necessarily oversimplified, perhaps reductionist, but the research of these leaders of the field demands a thoughtful response from teachers. Much of the work discussed was not designed for direct application to the classroom, however many teachers will recognize the congruence between these findings and their own professional judgements.

What educational psychologists write about has to be tentative and provisional (see White, 2002). They know their work is open to debate and contradiction. Teachers, on the other hand, must make daily decisions that affect children's lives. They do not enjoy the luxury of the controlled experiment. Nonetheless, each research finding cited in this chapter has possible implications for schools and their curricula. Each has cross-curricular ramifications too. In summary, current psychological research suggests to teachers that:

- we should not blindly accept IQ, background, current ability, socio-economic status or apparent learning difficulty as a limit on children's aspirations or our aspirations for their learning
- we should see intelligence as learnable and the mind as malleable
- we should make the generation of thinking one of our prime concerns
- we should be concerned about the whole physical, social, spiritual and emotional environment for learning
- we should consider seriously whether a positive, affirmative and happy environment produces better teachers and learners

- we should reflect on and research the effects of multi-faceted, contextualized and relevant learning settings
- we should carefully plan the learning experience of children to include a balance of instruction, coaching, facilitating and challenge
- we should seek to maximize on those learning experiences that promote flow or involvement
- we should take care to enrich understanding and perception by concentrating on new language acquisition.

Key questions for discussion

- How can we construct within our schools shared, social, intellectual and physical environments that optimize the chances of positive experiences for each individual?
- Do we need to change the curriculum to do this, and if so how?
- When have we seen flow in children at school? What curriculum implications does this have?
- How can we promote more talking, more dialogue and more extension of language?
- How can we encourage playfulness at the same time as challenge?
- What do we need to change to get children thinking more?

Further reading

Alexander, R. (2008) *Towards Dialogic Teaching.* York: Dialogos.

Claxton, G. and Lucas, B. (2013) *Expansive Education: Teaching Learners for the Real World.* London: McGraw Hill.

Costa, A. and Kallick, B. (2014) *Dispositions: Reframing Teaching and Learning.* London: Sage.

Csikszentmihalyi, M. (2002) *Flow: The Classic Work on How to Achieve Happiness.* New York: Ebury Press.

Pollard, A. (2008) *Reflective Teaching: Evidence-informed Professional Practice*, 3rd edn. London: Continuum.

CHAPTER 7

THE PEDAGOGY OF CROSS-CURRICULAR LEARNING

Chapter aims

This chapter will highlight pedagogical styles and philosophies that build on cross-curricular approaches. It reminds teachers of the ideas of some radical thoughts and thinkers that continue to challenge traditional attitudes to teaching. By the end of this chapter you will have considered:

- the importance of motivation
- social learning *with* the teacher
- taking account of the child's world
- creativity involving teacher and child
- thinking and barriers to thinking
- values: revisiting old absolutes.

'Start from where the children are.' This exhortation has been given to teacher trainees for generations. It can sound glib, simplistic, even idealistic, and yet as pedagogical advice it has profound implications for teaching philosophy, style and the curriculum itself. Paulo Freire, Brazilian activist, educator and thinker, clarifies the meaning of this big idea:

> The educator needs to know that his or her 'here' and 'now' are nearly always the educands' 'there' and 'then' … The educator must begin with the educands' 'here' and not with his or her own. At the very least, the educator must keep account of the existence of the

educands' here and respect it. You never get *there* by starting from *there*, you get *there* by starting from *here*. This means ultimately that the educator must not be ignorant or underestimate or reject any of the 'knowledge of living experience' with which the educands come to school. (Freire, 1994: 47)

The daily lives of children should be central to curriculum decisions, but the 'here and now' of today's children is not a homogenized whole. Children growing up in certain areas have to add the fear of gangs and gun crime to the 'traditional' fears of childhood. Happily, many still experience an ideal childhood of mindfulness, playful exploration, security and fulfilment, but significant numbers face the additional challenges of parental poverty, joblessness and alcohol, food or drug abuse. Such well-researched aspects of twenty-first-century life, plus the sometimes malign influence of the internet, mass media, celebrity and consumerism, are obvious features of national and state life (see James, 2008) and yet our nationally prescribed curricula almost ignore them. If, in Freire's words, we wish 'to change a wicked world, recreating it in terms of making it less perverse' (Freire, 1994: 55), issues from the daily and weekend life of children must feature in their weekly curriculum.

The coalition government of 2010 reminded us of the flexibility within the existing national curricula, the possibilities for creative interpretation and the need to build more partnerships between the community and schools (*TES*, 2010, website). Such comments may suggest continued support for the well-justified, planned and understood integrated and creative curriculum, but the increased freedoms promised by government were tempered by a prevailing 'back to basics' sympathy encouraged by the Department for Education's reading of Hirsch (1999).

Modern approaches to teaching in the UK and USA are hardly progressive. Few schools have gone far down the wholly child-centred route and most combine a mix of traditional methods, liberal, constructivist ideologies and the economically driven language of competition, targets, objectives and accountability (see Alexander, 2010; Arthur and Cremin, 2010). In the minds of many Western parents, the *delivery model* of teaching and learning is remarkably resilient. The delivery model suggests simply that schools are places where the teacher transmits packages of 'worthwhile' knowledge to children – worthwhile knowledge usually being the knowledge the powerful have deemed useful. The view that in school children learn and teachers teach seems to most lay people the obvious and proper way things should be. 'Traditional' pedagogical methods may, however, be inappropriate in a twenty-first-century society. The growth of the internet and other ICT, the general acceptance of scientific method, secularism, multi-racialism, diverse communities, alternative family groupings, modern psychology and neuroscience, the politics of liberation, global issues of war, climate change and pollution, notions of equality and children's rights have challenged and changed the landscape for schools. Aware of the growing gap between the educational experience of rich and poor children, many now argue for fundamental change rather than a retreat to 'tried and tested' methods (Booth and Ainscow, 2011; McCauley and Rose, 2010; Raffo et al., 2010; Wrigley et al., 2012).

Schools should be offering children a rich and varied palette of experiences. Exposure to the widest curriculum and the most powerful of experiences will be much more likely to help children discover their passions and identify their personal strengths. Yet many observers (for example, Lucas et al., 2013) see schools, mostly primary and even nursery schools narrowing their curricula to accommodate demands for higher and higher SATs results.

Teachers can unlock the doors to an enabling curriculum. It is up to school communities and individual teachers to take the rhetoric of curricular and pedagogical freedom and flexibility seriously. This book provides many leads towards building new and effective curricula more appropriate to the twenty-first century. Such curricula must be research- and experienced-based and founded upon clearly articulated values and aims. Carefully and collegiately, teachers must consider the aims and purposes of education and the values of the community served by the school. When schools are faced by 'no notice' inspections and ever-increasing expectations of accountability, clarity of purpose is vital. Teachers' experience will inform the debate on the aims, values and function but they also need a secure knowledge of research and the experience of others to provide the clear rationale that helps inspectors see the best qualities of a school. These things are probably best done within a teacher education course. It is probably no coincidence that the nations with the best schools and happiest children by PISA, WHO, OECD and UNICEF ratings are those that value their teacher education most highly.

Teachers in the UK and the USA do not enjoy high status. Though they are sometimes consulted in regard to public policy on education, many feel their views are not adequately represented or listened to. Politicians publicly castigate teacher education as too 'progressive' when it tries to apply a critical mind to issues, and pedagogy itself is still uncommon as an academic subject. The word *pedagogy* captures what Pollard (2010) calls the 'art and craft' of teaching. Pedagogy is the fusion of theoretical knowledge, practical experience, environmental management and intuitive response demonstrated minute by minute in the practice of the 'good teacher'. Through daily interaction with large groups of children and their lives, the best teachers quickly become experts on:

- motivation
- social learning
- communication through good pedagogy
- creative solutions
- barriers to thinking and learning
- values.

Illustration 7.1   The teacher physically coming down to the child's level will help equalize the relationship

Motivating children

Children often need to be motivated to learn when in school. Motivation is less of an issue outside school hours, where there are usually more choices and often more freedoms. In school children derive motivation from a range of sources. They might be engaged by *belief* about the relevance of a subject so a teacher may appeal to, or attempt to change, beliefs in order to involve a particular child. Children can be motivated by *fear* or a desire for *acceptance*, by *respect* for a teacher or *love* for a subject. Children may be motivated by the wish to *reach a goal*, to be *involved* in a specific activity or *to please someone* else. Some simply love *learning* itself. The expert teacher will orchestrate these diverse motivations and attempt to involve all in the task ahead. In a culture where the child's voice is heard, the teacher may follow the children's lead, opportunistically combining knowledge meaningful to them with life skills relevant to their community. Alternatively they may construct an atmosphere in which children are led to *believe* they are following their own interests or answering questions to which they really want the answer.

Social learning with the teacher

In the world beyond schools, most people work in teams that contain people with different skills and strengths. Teams in the world of work rarely contain members born in the same year, but have mixtures of ages and genders. The 'economic' justification for group work and shared projects in schools is that they *prepare* children to contribute more fully to an economy where people work in teams. But perhaps a more profound justification lies in the suggestion that working together, sharing experiences and solving problems in groups is beneficial to the social, physical and mental health of the child now. Groups and classes sharing the same age is not the only possible grouping, sometimes mixed age groups are more productive, more focused and more friendly. Sometimes the group can include the teacher as co-learner rather than instructor. Flexibly sized and organized groups where more able students have the opportunity to support the learning of younger or less experienced students (regardless of age) can be used to teach important lessons about community and mutual interdependence.

Social skills like empathy, turn taking, listening to others and patience are not simply caught. They and the personal skills of emotional self-control need to be taught within a whole-school framework. Social, emotional and behavioural (SEB) skills should not be seen as a separate curriculum subject. Opportunities arise naturally from a curriculum designed around children's participation in meaningful, shared experiences and shared responses. Present academic achievement, self-esteem, personal responsibility, tolerance of difference, are all positively affected by a curriculum and ethos that takes SEB seriously. Such personal and social achievements if mastered in a school setting transfer seamlessly to family life, adult friendships and the workplace.

The use of 'thinking partners', group investigations and role play are common features in school. Occasionally teachers themselves take on the role of learner. Both situations allow children to take more control of a project, and as we have seen in earlier chapters the sense of personal autonomy is an important step towards a positive disposition towards learning (Costa and Kallick, 2014). The use of a range of teaching and learning styles takes account of children's different cultural contexts, their preferred styles of thinking and changing emotional needs, and allow for a variety of ways of showing intelligence.

Illustration 7.2   Children and adults learning together while building a real causeway to their Bronze Age settlement reconstruction in Eastbourne (Photo: Michael Fairclough)

Illustration 7.3   Emotional and interpersonal aspects of learning dominate the day for both teacher and child

Case study   The HEARTS project

An experiment in alternative modes of teacher education, the HEARTS project (Barnes and Shirley, 2007) took the idea of 'teacher as learner' still further. Third-year student teachers were given the opportunity to work in small groups of six Year 7/8 children on an open-ended project to 'capture the essence' of an unfamiliar place. They were instructed to avoid the words 'you' or 'I' and to give the role of deputy to any budding child-leader who arose in their group.

Fifteen pairs of students took their groups of four or five children by half-gauge railway to a deserted shingle beach with a nuclear power station at one end, at Dungeness, Kent. They were given a surprise assignment on the 45-minute train ride – they had to compose a short rap by the end of the journey. The children immediately took charge and a series of clever raps were performed in the drizzle at Dungeness railway station.

Neither students nor children knew the beach when they arrived; they knew only they had to prepare a presentation of 'the essence' of their chosen spot for the whole academy on the following day. For this two-day session there were no lesson plans, no clear objectives, no differentiation and no assessment criteria. This contrasted strongly with the student teachers' training!

The only structure the students had was:

1. A list of 15 simple focus exercises to choose from
2. A limit of two hours
3. An injunction on the health and safety of children
4. The need for a 5-minute presentation.

This challenge strongly focused both students and children. The results of the two-day event were 15 powerful, inventive and highly creative presentations. After the afternoon together, students and children brought the collected data from their choice of focus exercises and impressions back to school. They worked on creative ways of bringing several aspects together, presenting them to each other, and performed them to the rest of the year cohort. The 15 presentations could not have been more varied – they included two dramas, an art exhibition, a musical composition accompanying a silent film, a puppet show with characters made from pebbles, a dance where nature battled with humankind, a dramatically presented ghost story with music, a sculpture garden and a 7-minute documentary. These were very well received by the whole academy audience at the end of the two-day project. Students then returned to their university to analyse what had happened. A key finding for researchers monitoring the whole event was that the social nature of the activities resulted in the student teachers feeling that they understood the children for the first time, through facing the same challenges together.

Pedagogues may come to a variety of conclusions from examples like the case study above. A number of issues are worth discussion:

- Are children genuinely working collaboratively when placed in groups?
- Are we as teachers genuinely planning and constructing opportunities to learn alongside children?
- Do our groups promote social, emotional and behavioural skills?
- Have we got the balance right between direct teaching and social learning?

Illustration 7.4   Classroom teachers rediscovering their own creativity on a staff development day

Communication through good pedagogy

Formulaic, one-size-fits-all approaches to teaching are still common. Through government insistence on 'compliance' in matters of curriculum and pedagogy, for example regarding reading, Initial Teacher Education (ITE) has fallen behind the more innovative and adventurous primary schools. The 'Standards' for Qualified Teacher Status (QTS) (DfE, 2013b) have spawned a pragmatic approach to the preparation of teachers in which *training* has become the operative word. QTS standards emphasize the importance of secure subject knowledge on the part of the teacher (the word is used eight times in the 14-page document). The words *creativity, arts, humanities, science, technology, research, reflection, health* do not occur at all in the expectations for teachers. Systematic synthetic phonics and 'appropriate teaching strategies' for Mathematics are the only subject-based requirements in the standards. Such developments risk encouraging a 'training manual' approach to the art of teaching. Some books on how to achieve QTS are dominated by grids and instructions on how to demonstrate the standards but give less help as to *how* to make the curriculum choices that promote learning and thinking. There is a tendency to fall back on bland exhortations such as 'aim for effectiveness through efficiency' and the admission that successful teaching requires a considerable degree of confidence and practice (Hayes, 2003). Perhaps such confidence can only come after many years in the job, but since so many leave teaching in the first five years, maybe ITE and in-service courses need to consider how their own students can themselves become deeper, more creative learners and enjoy the job satisfaction of more creative teaching and learning.

Teachers and teach*ing* shape children's learning, but learning and teaching are not the same. The idea that armed with a basket labelled 'tips for teachers' teachers will effectively teach and children learn, denies the utter complexity of children's (and adults') minds. Ivan Illich reminded us of this in the early 1970s. Most learning, he observed, happens outside schools, casually and as a by-product of some other activity (Illich, 1971). This is still true. The skilful and open-minded teacher recognizes that children arrive at school with a rich understanding of their world, already entrenched and largely sensible. The good teacher knows that they can help the child develop and shape their existing knowledge. They know they can add new knowledge and expose the child to novel and powerful experiences. Understanding and respecting the child's world, their popular culture and 'knowledge of living experience' is very important for the student teacher, but the successful teacher needs more. Illich and

Freire also recognized the importance of the teaching of skills and subject knowledge. The good teacher should look for the deeper meaning of the content being taught, but not shy away from occasional decontextualization and simple direct teaching. The strongly motivated pupil, says Illich, 'may benefit greatly from the discipline now associated with the old fashioned schoolmaster' (Illich, 1971: 20). A disciplined approach to learning was to these progressives as important as respect for the lives of the learners. Freire puts it clearly:

> Teachers who fail to take their teaching practice seriously, who therefore do not study, so that they teach poorly, or who teach something they know poorly, who do not fight to have the material conditions absolutely necessary for their teaching practice, deprive themselves of the wherewithal to cooperate in the formation of the indispensable intellectual discipline of the students. Thus, they disqualify themselves as teachers. (Freire, 1994: 69)

The teacher, in other words, should balance respect for the child's world with a craftsperson's skill at their subject, pedagogy.

Today the child's world is highly technologized. Mobile phones, videos, television, *Xbox*, *Wii*, *Raspberry Pi*, social networking sites and other media are familiar sources of knowledge, but they continue to learn much from the adults around them. Gardner (1993: 34–8) suggested three ways in which children learn from adults: direct or *unmediated* learning, where the child observes an adult engaged in activity; *imitation*, where the child reproduces the actions of an adult who deliberately models them; and *outside the context* learning in which a skill is introduced and practised under adult supervision but in a situation unrelated to the need for the skill. He notes that most formal learning within 'modern technological societies' occurs in specialized institutions far removed from the context in which the knowledge will be applied. The de-contextualized learning that has become dominant in Western schools misses out major opportunities for unmediated and imitation learning.

Watch children play and the physical, interpersonal, practical and creative modes seem dominant. In school often opposite modes such as passive, independent, symbolic, logical and factual are most common. We have seen that both modes are necessary for a holistic education, but much potential is lost if education does not match how children are. Perhaps we should re-examine some old metaphors for teaching and learning, like David Feldman's 'The child as craftsman' (Feldman, 1976). In his analysis, Feldman suggested that teachers looking to an uncertain world future should start by seeing the child as a person who

Illustration 7.5   Roles are reversed as a child leads a 'blind' teacher in investigating an environment

wants to be good at something, take a pride in his or her work and feel an increasing sense of mastery over an area or areas of experience. Feldman argues that:

- the sense of engagement and purpose involved in doing what one feels good at is not possible without developing the related subject knowledge
- mastery cannot be aspired to without a belief that knowledge and understanding within the field can be continually enhanced
- a child's capabilities can only truly be assessed once we have identified an activity that truly engages them
- what might personally engage child craftspeople will be found within 'the full range of activities that enrich and sustain social life … and diverse occupations' (Feldman, 1976: 144).

To work within this idealistic framework, teachers, Feldman suggested, combine four different teaching roles:

- to teach the core skills and knowledge of writing, reading, number, citizenship required by society for all, but to ensure they are taught in meaningful contexts

- to teach bodies of knowledge in a range of other subject areas chosen by community or school and considered necessary for all children
- to discover the 'propensities and proclivities' of each child and then to organize resources progressively to 'further the child's mastery'
- to promote each child's engagement through introduction to and progressive guidance in the principles, key skills and attitudes of discrete areas of knowledge they have chosen.

Subject knowledge is important. As children develop between the ages of 3 and 14 they should have increasing opportunity to refine and deepen their subject knowledge. Learning new knowledge and skills does not happen without the child's agreement Effective teachers gain this agreement by working with the child to identify what is personally engaging to them and by linking it to the new knowledge required by the curriculum. Working in a school community that 'fosters commitment, satisfaction and joy in accomplishment' (Feldman, 1976: 146) will require each child to go beyond the limits of their current understanding. This, I would suggest, is especially likely when groups attempt to solve problems or examine a shared experience. David Perkins has corroborated this analysis. Perkins (2006, 2009) suggests that children need experience of 'playing the whole game', 'undertaking holistic endeavours that make learning meaningful and engaging'. Playing *any* whole game involves receiving coaching, learning the rules, having opportunities to play 'junior versions' of the game, identifying with the experts, having chances to play and be affirmed publicly and, of course, finishing it. In the social settings that involve playing the whole game or being an apprentice craftsperson, children are likely to learn creatively. They will inevitably make unexpected links and connections between areas of knowledge, experience and relationships.

Such observers of teachers teaching suggest that we consider the following advice:

- show respect for the child's background
- give attention to subject knowledge and continually develop it in the self
- learn the arts of pedagogy
- identify the areas of strength in each child
- find what engages each child
- give plentiful opportunities for holistic, contextualized and meaningful learning.

Illustration 7.6   Head teachers rediscovering the child in themselves

Creativity (for teacher and child)

It is strange that creativity is not mentioned in the standards for Qualified Teacher Status. Interestingly, the independent schools, free schools and academies (that do not always require QTS for their teaching staff), often set great store by their creative work and curriculum. Creativity is one of a small group of features that distinguishes humans from other animal species. We know that birds, primates and dolphins may show a degree of creativity in their responses, but in terms of capacity, breadth and expression creativity is a quality that marks out our species. The ability to be creative currently makes us different from machines too. Arthur Koestler's (1964) definition of creativity which involves *bisociation* – the often unexpected coming together of two contrasting planes of thought – is central to understanding the purpose of cross-curricular learning. Creativity, according to Csikszentmihalyi, is 'a central source of meaning in our lives' (1997: 1). The language of *creative teaching*, *creative thinking*, *creative learning* and *teaching for creativity* in schools is a reflection of this preoccupation, but treating it as a temporary fashion would risk losing for many children all that is humanizing and sensitizing in the impulse to be creative.

The creative teacher (Figure 7.1) typically is playful, enthusiastic, flexible, committed and involved. Their teaching style will commonly be personalized to the child, respectful, trusting, diverse and with a clear learning focus. The ethos in which the child is most likely to learn how to respond creatively is safe, secure and supportive of adventurous thinking (Cremin et al., 2009; Thomson et al., 2012).

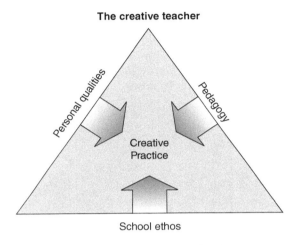

The creative teacher

Personal qualities

Pedagogy

Creative
Practice

School ethos

Figure 7.1 Creative practice depends on the interplay between a teacher's personal qualities of creativity (such as curiosity, humour, adventurousness, flexibility and enthusiasm), a creative pedagogy based upon multiple opportunities to make links and a child-centred supportive ethos established in the class and school

No kinds of learning can be 'conferred' on the child. Throughout time, good teachers have discovered myriad ways of creating relevance and engagement so that children will want to learn. Through force of character, story, anecdote, humour, display, drama, movement, music, games, debate, surprise, visits and visitors (but also by pressure, stress, threats and tests), teachers capture their audience. Research (for example, Brice Heath and Wolf, 2005; Harland et al., 2000; Thomson et al., 2012) confirms the massive motivational and positive affective impact of the arts and artists in education, but the potential for motivation spreads far beyond the arts into every subject of the curriculum. Creative approaches to teaching and encouraging the whole range of creative activity can do far more than motivate, however; they can also engender the new connection-making we earlier described as thinking (Cremin et al., 2009; Grainger et al., 2004).

Teaching is a creative act relying continually on chance meetings of ideas and materials, curiosity, flexibility and adventurous thinking. Although each teaching and learning situation is unique, there are a

Figure 7.2   The creative state of mind recognizes an inherent creativity in itself. Recognizing its own creativity may help it generate more connections, originality, questioning and autonomy

number of characteristics that seem common to most creative teachers. Creative teachers are simply those who adopt and apply a creative state of mind. This mindset on the part of the teacher seems particularly effective in promoting creativity in children (see Fumoto et al., 2012). The core characteristics that appear to recur consistently in creative teachers and that result in creative practice are:

- curiosity and questioning
- connection-making
- originality
- autonomy and ownership.

Thinking and barriers to thinking

Much of what we learn involves thought. Wherever we live and whatever we are doing, a stream of thoughts accompanies most actions. Through

Illustration 7.7   Collaborative creativity: a group of 14-year-olds planning their visual response to a haiku

devoting focused attention to an aspect of our world, we bring together past and present thoughts and, if we do this with others, we also incorporate some of their thoughts as well. In thinking, groups of neurons also make connections. We know that these connections become insulated and 'hard-wired' if they are recalled or reused a number of times. We generally recycle such connections when they are relevant and meaningful to us. Thus, if we think, rethink and think *about* our thinking, we learn. If we agree with Perkins' claim that *learning* is one of the consequences of thinking, the obvious question the teacher must ask is, 'Am I promoting thinking in what I plan to do with these children?'

Children can be helped to think more productively and satisfyingly. Books on improving thinking have become popular with teachers who recognize this important aspect of their role (see, for example, Dweck, 2009; Fisher, 1999). We know, however, that there are myriad barriers to children's thinking too. Good pedagogues are aware that they may be barriers themselves. Through reflection and evaluation, an effective teacher can consider the impact of his or her own differing thinking or learning styles, school or class ethos or interpersonal difficulties before blaming the child for not learning.

The inclusive school will ask itself the question, 'Have we erected barriers to children's thinking that are stopping them learning?' Is the 'hidden curriculum' that Illich referred to in the 1970s stifling personal growth? One way of answering such questions is to use the comprehensive, whole-school approach recommended by the *Index for Inclusion* (Booth and Ainscow, 2011). The Index starts with questions for school self-evaluation, examining fundamental values and the way they influence school policies, practices and cultures. Going through such a procedure quickly reveals the hidden and often unarticulated barriers to inclusive practice in a school.

Children already know many of the barriers that hamper them. One Year 5 teacher in London recently took her children into an empty playground and gave them just such a theme to examine themselves. This is what she observed on her 'Barriers and boundaries' mini topic:

 ### Case study   Barriers and boundaries

It did not take long for the children to realize that the list would consist of more than walls and fences – and they began to become engrossed as they came to realize that nearly everything can be a barrier or boundary – including flower beds, stinging nettles and other people. They began by asking 'Can I put down … ?' and when I asked them what they thought, and explained that there were no right and wrong answers so long as they could explain their reasons, they were unstoppable. We walked the rest of the school the next day, and if anything, the children were even more motivated than the day before – there was no bad behaviour and their lists grew. One child working at level 1 in writing (and who had not produced more than a line or two of writing for me to date) produced a list of 30 items, often correctly spelt and all legible.

In class, we divided the lists into three columns: physical barriers and boundaries, signs (from the children's lists) and invisible barriers. We started the last column with language, which they had already identified, and the further suggestions (attitude, silence, culture, racism, hate, loss of senses, words) were very thought-provoking and although received mainly from children of high ability, were not exclusively so. Had there been time, there was a wealth of opportunities for the children to have more freedom to explore themes in Citizenship, PSHE, Literacy and Drama, Geography, RE, ICT, History and PE/Dance.

Given control of the agenda, children in the above example made multiple and unexpected connections. They were learning and, as the teacher noted, children were linking apparently unrelated areas (like spelling and concentration). Giving children this kind of respect, establishing dialogue between teachers and children, building on the 'social capital' already present in children's lives and their community, and making their 'lived experience' a focus of education are approaches powerfully argued by Freire. He was also one of the first modern pedagogues to stress the importance of learning to learn.

Teachers and all learners gain by thinking about their own learning. Modern developments in psychology and neurology have helped us to learn more about the conditions in which we are likely to learn best, but few teacher education or in-service courses offer advice on *who* to learn from. Of course, the children we teach are rich sources of learning themselves. When trainee teachers passed the locus of control to children in

Illustration 7.8   The open face of learning in an atmosphere of trust (Photo: Cherry Tewfik)

the HEARTS project their teachers noted significant and positive changes in students' respect for children and children's response to them.

As teachers, we should constantly and consistently examine our impact on the ethos of our institution and our classroom. The advice of key pedagogues suggests we consider:

- how we help children think
- where are the barriers to learning
- what are the unseen influences on the wider curriculum and atmosphere of the school
- the range of sources of learning we employ
- how to engage all children in satisfying learning.

Values: revisiting old absolutes

In a postmodern world, conscious of few anchor points, it is interesting to see an academic and educationally focused re-evaluation of 'old-fashioned' concepts such as 'hope' (Freire 1994; Halpin, 2003; Wrigley, 2005), 'good' (Csikszentmihalyi, 2003; Gardner, 2004; Gardner et al., 2000), 'wisdom' (Craft et al., 2008; Sternberg, 2002), 'happiness' (Layard, 2005; Morris, 2004; Seligman, 2004) and 'love' (Bowlby, 1988; Darder, 2002; Gerhardt, 2014; Goldstein, 1997; Goldstein and Lake, 2000). Historic pedagogues such as Comenius, Rousseau, Froebel, Pestalozzi, Rudolf Steiner, Montessori, Dewey, Isaacs, Freire and Malaguzzi were unabashed at using terms like these. The progressive education philosophies of the past were anchored in common understandings of such concepts, which were for them the ultimate purposes of education. These words, holding concepts that most of us feel we understand, remain personally powerful regardless of our religious or political beliefs. Perhaps they should be near the top of our consciousness as we think about the curricula our children follow. Old absolutes still form the basis of the 'here' and 'now' for most of us. Improving the emotional atmosphere of a school may involve using community discussions on hope, wisdom, love and good to help change many entrenched attitudes and practices.

We may need to examine our own institution critically and ask difficult questions. David Halpin, for example, feels that schools often fail to provide a learning environment that leads to a broad sense of security. He reminds us of proto-psychologist Sigmund Freud's use of the German word *sicherheit* (translated as 'security'). Freud regarded *sicherheit* as the chief gift of civilization and, by inference, the prerequisite for education:

This word manages to squeeze into a single term, complex phenomena for which the English language needs at least three terms to convey – security being one, and certainty and safety being the other two. According to Freud, all three ingredients of 'sicherheit' are conditions of self-confidence and self-reliance, on which the ability to think and act creatively depend. The absence or near absence, of any of the three ingredients has much the same effect – the dissipation of self-assurance and the loss of trust in one's own ability, followed in quick succession by anxiety and growing incapacitation. (Halpin, 2003: 110–11)

For Halpin, no child should leave school feeling a loser. Equally, no teacher should end a school day feeling depressed. The cross-curriculum is well placed to turn the dream of a *liberating curriculum* into reality. Through it, children can be freed to be children. Teachers are in a persuasive position to work with communities towards achieving this utopia. They need only to agree on the meaning of the four exhortations at the end of Terry Wrigley's (2005) book, *Schools of Hope*:

- We need commitment to a better future.
- We have to be visionary.
- We must dare to dream.
- We will have to rethink education and not simply improve schools.

Summary

Even in today's largely secular, increasingly diverse and global culture, we cannot escape the fact that education is value-laden and attitude-rich. The values we display either consciously or in the equally powerful 'hidden curriculum' will not always match the official values of the school. Neither will the values of today be the same as those that sustained very different societies of the past. If we do not address values, then the learning experience of the child has no coherent context and perhaps the majority will find little meaning in it. We should therefore not dodge questions such as:

- Who decides on what 'worthwhile knowledge' is?
- What is *good* behaviour?
- Who chooses the topic under discussion?
- How can we agree?

A suggested way forward is to focus on children's well-being and that of parents, teachers and others working with children (Young Foundation, 2010). This means discussing the questions above in the light of agreed concepts of well-being and designing a curriculum based around achievement, enjoyment, experience and personalized ways of making sense of the world. I would suggest that this is most possible through teachers and children working within a flexible, responsive and relevant curriculum.

Illustration 7.9   Fourteen-year-old pupils performing their own musical composition about a garden in the garden that generated it

---

Key questions for discussion

We should keep the debate open and free from extremes, and be aware of the provisional nature of any of our decisions on what worthwhile knowledge and good pedagogy is. In the light of previous chapters, key questions a school might ask before rethinking its curriculum might be as follows:

- Do we (adults in school) feel fulfilled and secure as people *ourselves*?
- Are we modelling lifelong learning?
- Is the teaching and learning in our classrooms promoting each child's well-being?

- Is the social, spiritual and physical environment we control helping to develop positive attitudes to learning and the self?
- What is the role of popular knowledge?
- Does each child have an opportunity to find and develop an area of expertise?
- Is the physical, emotional and intellectual environment we control keeping them safe?
- What content *should* we teach and learn? Who selects it and how do we decide how it is to be taught?
- What is the role of the teacher?
- Are schools able to change the world?
- Is our curriculum giving hope?
- Are we teaching wisdom?
- Is this school preparing all to make a positive contribution to future society?

Such questions are not very far from those posed by Plato, Comenius, Rousseau, Pestalozzi, Froebel, Dewey, Plowden or Alexander. As professionals, we are in a strong position to use the daily experience of today's successful primary teachers to help us judge which are the most appropriate attitudes, what is the most useful knowledge, the most helpful skills for children's lives *now*. Because we also serve society, we also need to seriously consider what kind of people we want to shape this increasingly fragile world in the coming years.

Further reading

Craft, A. (2005) *Creativity in Schools: Tensions and Dilemmas*. London: Routledge.

Freire, P. (1994) *The Pedagogy of Hope: Reliving the Pedagogy of the Oppressed*. New York: Continuum.

Fumoto, H., Robson, S., Greenfield, S. and Hargreaves, D. (2012) *Young Children's Creative Thinking*. London: Sage.

Richhart, R. (2002) *Intellectual Character: What It Is, Why It Matters and How to Get It*. New York: Jossey–Bass.

Wrigley, T., Thomson, P. and Lingard, B. (eds.) (2012) *Changing Schools: Alternative Ways to Make a World of Difference.* London: Routledge.

CHAPTER 8

WHAT VALUES SHOULD WE APPLY?

Chapter aims

This chapter explains the idea that thinking, talking about and living shared values are vital activities for a successful school. Values and the curriculum are addressed in relation to a range of fundamental beliefs about education, understandings about knowledge and attitudes to teaching and learning. By the end of this chapter you will have thought about:

- beliefs about learning
- understandings about knowledge
- attitudes to teaching
- attitudes towards children
- an informed adult view of the world.

We are driven by values, whether or not we are conscious of them. If we want to be effective teachers, we should be clear about why we want to teach and what we hope for children to learn in our classes. Teachers and children need opportunities to develop, consolidate and apply their values and to have numerous chances to discuss them. A thriving school is a place where debate about principles and big questions is alive and well. David Perkins once remarked: 'the quality of an organization can be measured by the quality of its conversations' (Perkins, 2002). The conversations he was referring to were the ordinary daily chats in staffrooms, by the water cooler, in the playground and on the way to or from school. Overheard snatches of dialogue in happy schools are often sensitive, caring and concern the deepest purposes of education. Such conversations feed and inspire novice teachers as they refine their values and arrive at the dispositions that in many cases serve them throughout a life in education (see Barnes, 2013a, 2013b; Gardner et al., 2000).

To become collegiate institutions or communities of practice, schools must subscribe to agreed values. It is difficult for any organization to move far forward without the sense of direction that values provide. For some time, schools have published in their compulsory prospectuses, 'mission statements', 'key aims' or 'overarching goals' outlining the values that underpin intentions for pupils' spiritual, moral, cultural and social development. These statements can succinctly represent the character of the school and be the vital (and often revisited) core of everything it does. However, sometimes such statements are far from the reality of the lives lived in the school. The CPR and other recent reports have highlighted clarity about values and recommended early discussions and decisions as part of any curricular revision.

Schools keep their values alive by talking about them (Jeffrey and Woods, 2003). In Figure 8.1 values are represented as existing within an

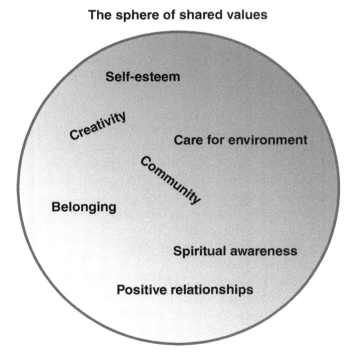

Figure 8.1   The sphere of shared values: discussing core values should be the school's first, most frequent and most important conversation

all-embracing sphere because, like the earth's atmosphere, they encompass everything a community – in this case the school – does. If the values are shared the sphere is perfect, stable, sustaining and protective. If values conflict the sphere is pulled out of shape and loses its shielding, wholesome and life-giving functions. The values a school shares will differ according to place, time, culture, personalities and current issues and therefore before a school embarks on any other discussion, the community – teachers, children, leaders, support staff, parents and governors – should together decide on their individual and collective answers to some of the following questions:

- What is education for?
- What is our attitude to children?
- How should adults behave towards children?
- What kind of children do we want our children to be?
- What kind of adults do we want our children to become?
- What kind of education do we want our children to have?
- What kind of education do *children* want to have?
- What are the most important issues for this community?
- What negative or unhelpful mindsets should we try to shift?
- What sustains, motivates and generates optimism in the school's adults?
- How can we build hope into children's lives through the curriculum?
- What things do we treasure most?

Taking the last two points first, it is arguably the teacher's prime professional responsibility to be optimistic (Booth, quoted in Dismore et al., 2008). Optimism might stem from religious, political or philosophical beliefs, from a shared but non-religious spiritual understanding or from deeply felt beliefs about humanity, children and the environment. There will inevitably be a variety of answers, but even embarking on the values discussion is valuable. Debating the meaning of education exposes many of our core dispositions and friendly dialogue can consolidate or encourage us towards positive change.

We mostly learn what is truly and personally relevant to us. In a postmodern, Western, educational context, Peter Abbs argues that without existential engagement there is no deep learning:

education cannot take place against the intentions of the student or without his or her active participation … Learning may be released by the teacher but it can never be conferred – for it is not an object so much as a particular cast of mind, a creative and critical orientation towards experience. The student has to learn to be the protagonist of his or her own learning. (Abbs, 2003: 14–15)

The concept of education itself lies outside any single morality or world view. Education takes place in *any* and every cultural setting but only becomes really effective when it is meaningful. Meaning may be generated by fear, economic, cultural, political or religious obligation, duty, ambition, pleasure, self-fulfilment, self-actualization or a desire for the loss of self. In secular societies, the challenge is to find a commonly acceptable formula that can bring shared meaning to all. The outcome of such discussions should profoundly affect the content and organization of the curriculum.

Illustration 8.1   A typical primary school classroom in action

There are a number of starting points for values discussions. In 1999 the UK government provided a 'statement of values' by the National Forum for Values in Education and the Community (DfEE/QCA, 1999: 147–9). There are frequent debates in press and parliament about the meaning of 'British' values. Forty governments throughout the world lent support to the *Index for Inclusion* (Booth and Ainscow, 2011) which, through its sections on curriculum and creating inclusive cultures, establishes a firm link between values, what is taught in a school and how teaching happens. Japan's Soka schools, inspired by education philosopher Makiguchi, and the Ghandi-inspired schools of India, are inspiring attempts to link values, pedagogy and curriculum. More generally, the UNESCO-supported Association of Living Values (ALIVE website) is an example of an international organization offering support to schools wishing to think about their values.

Appropriately, half of the discussion questions above contain the word *children* and representing the child's voice in making curriculum decisions is now commonplace (see Burke and Grosvenor, 2003; Catling, 2005; Cheminais, 2012). Valuing the views of children alongside the experience and (hoped for) wisdom of adults ensures lively interchanges and broad-based support for school policy. From an adult perspective, we might want education to promote creativity, make the world a kinder place, address democracy or make children aware of the key issues of the day. Teenagers, however, may take a much more pragmatic view of education, seeing it as the provider of qualifications, the route to a better job or irrelevant to their aspirations (Popenici, 2006). Some adults may feel

Illustration 8.2 Peace Art: school children in Uganda have worked with schools in British Columbia to turn their war toys into a whitened peace sculpture (Anthropological Museum, British Columbia, Canada)

that education should make our children more obedient, less challenging or more aware of 'high culture', others that it should hardly influence children all. Either way, the curriculum will be the route through which we attempt to achieve our aims. One suspects the school curriculum would look very different if the views of 3–14-year-olds were truly taken seriously and represented.

As an example, let us take several commonly cited but general aims of education, gleaned from school websites:

1. To promote a feeling of well-being for all children.
2. To ensure that the beliefs and values of the Christian/Jewish/Muslim/ Sikh/Hindu/Buddhist faith underlie all we do.
3. To support the development of self-esteem and personal responsibility.
4. To promote lifelong learning.
5. To develop high standards across the school, striving to reach and go beyond national standards in all subjects and key stages.

These aims clearly imply a specific ethos requiring specific approaches to the curriculum. Perhaps a progressive, creative and child-centred curriculum is suggested by the first aim. If we want to ensure that a particular religious belief system 'underlies all we do', our assemblies, playground expectations, lunches, our Science, Languages, History, PE, Geography and English curricula will be affected as much as the RE curriculum. If we aim to support the development of self-esteem, this should show itself in

Illustration 8.3   Walking the talk: children from the Scottish Children's Parliament leading adults on their 'health and happiness' march (Courtesy of Scottish Children's Parliament)

the behaviour policy, but also the ways in which adults relate to each other and how they teach. The fourth aim focuses on developing positive attitudes to learning, whilst the last aim might be said to promote competition and continuous challenge. None of these aims is likely to have arisen from consultation with children, though all can be readily understood and acted upon by them. They will most likely have been decided upon in good faith, by adults who feel they know what is best for children. It is surprising, however, that few school aims directly mention identity, the environment, sustainability, relationships, new technologies or the global dimension.

The following examples of more detailed aims may have even more precise implications for their schools' curricula:

- To provide a community of creativity, challenge, curiosity, wonder, love and joy, where we shape our learning, life and spirituality; growing together within a framework of Christian values, enriched by worship and celebration. (Wingrave C of E Combined School, Buckinghamshire, website, accessed 21 July 2014)
- As a School of Creativity, we ensure every child has the opportunity to develop through a wide range of creative activities including art, drama, music, dance and philosophy for children. We believe that encouraging our children to think and to question, helps them to develop essential life skills. (Priory School, Slough, website, accessed 21 July 2014)
- To help pupils and staff realize their own self worth. To thereby develop self-esteem and independence. To encourage mutual respect and an appreciation of the worth of others within a multicultural community. (Castlebar School, Ealing, prospectus, accessed 21 July 2014)
- Our school recognizes each child as an individual with different needs, different abilities and different learning patterns. We aim to help each child fulfil his or her potential in all areas of development, regardless of background, ability or gender. (St Peter's Junior School, Marlborough, website, accessed 21 July 2014)
- Our ethos is based upon four principles: Care for each others and the school, courtesy towards everyone in the school, consideration of others in the things we do and say, cooperation, the success of our school is based upon the learning community working together. (Highlees Academy, Peterborough, prospectus, accessed 21 July 2014)
- We inspire and empower independent and creative learners, who will continue to enrich their lives and those of others within a culture of high achievement and mutual respect. (West Rise Junior School, Eastbourne, website, accessed 21 July 2014)

- The important freedom the right to play. All lessons are optional. There is no pressure to conform to adult ideas of growing up, though the community itself has expectations of reasonable conduct from all individuals. Bullying, vandalism or other anti-social behaviour is dealt with on-the-spot by specially elected ombudsmen, or can be brought to the whole community in its regular meetings. (Summerhill School, website, accessed 21 July 2014)
- The provision of philosophical and moral discipline and training through the visual arts and to maintain a state of intellectual and artistic development across all ages … a belief in the importance of each individual's integrity, and the importance of the expression of that individuality. (Room 13 International, website)

Words may not have come directly from children, but there is a sense that the realities of the children's world may have influenced these aims. There is perhaps a greater emphasis on enhancing and explaining the lives of children here and now, not simply preparing children for a future (adult-envisaged) world.

What, then, are the beliefs and values that might underpin the establishment of a curriculum that promotes cross-curricular links and activities? Common school values may be linked under the five main categories:

1. Learning
2. Knowledge
3. Teaching
4. Children
5. The world.

The values listed under these headings do not form a comprehensive list, but capture a personal ideology based upon 40 years in teaching. Each teacher would doubtless construct a different list. Readers are encouraged to consider the suggested values and discuss those *they* would wish to see active in their settings. The discussion itself can also be used to clarify personal beliefs and attitudes towards education.

Beliefs about learning

As outlined in Chapters 4, 5, 6 and 7, current work in social science, neuroscience, pedagogy and psychology has added much to our understanding of learning. However, the word 'beliefs' in the sub-heading is

Illustration 8.4 Deep learning comes from deep thinking – these Year 2 children show signs of both

intentional. Ultimately, as professionals in education, we have to decide what we *believe* to be right and true about learning. These beliefs will arise from our own history and particular personal or professional experiences. Hopefully, teachers' beliefs will not be narrow, uncritical or closed, but influenced by practice, research, reflection, conversation and the theoretical perspectives of others. Beliefs about education should always be open to discussion because life – technologies, social mores and situations continually change. Some current beliefs might be summarized for discussion as in the following list, list A.

- There are many different ways of thinking and understanding ... each child has their own way of being bright.
- Generative topics and challenging experiences provide motivation to question, problem-solve and find answers.
- Learning is a consequence of thinking.
- Emotional, practical and personal engagement are essential to learning.
- Group work, particularly in promoting conversation and other means of communication, is an effective way to promote learning.

- Modern technologies are powerful ways of promoting, sustaining and deepening learning.
- The resources that support intelligent behaviour do not lie only within the mind and brain, but are distributed throughout the environment and social system in which we operate.
- Learning happens in quiet, reflective and solitary moments too.
- Deep transferable learning is best facilitated in conditions of 'positive emotion'.
- Applying the skills and knowledge of the subject disciplines is an effective way of making sense of experience.
- Children can learn how to learn through an introduction to metacognition and aids to thinking – intelligence is learnable.
- Enjoyment is an important part of the development of positive attitudes towards learning, self and community.
- Education should be democratic.

Such beliefs about teaching and learning are related and can be placed into four categories: beliefs about *individual* learners; beliefs about learning *collaboratively*; beliefs about the importance of *environment*; and beliefs about subjects or *the disciplines*. These four aspects of pedagogy might be seen as a professional framework of beliefs aimed at the liberation of the individual within a cohesive and supportive community.

Illustration 8.5   Each individual expressing their own response to freedom (Courtesy of Scottish Children's Parliament)

Other beliefs may have different sources and different aims. Consider the following list, list B:

- Society is 'broken' and schooling should be used to mend it.
- Children should primarily be taught to appreciate and participate in the dominant culture.
- There is a canon of core knowledge that all children should be familiar with.
- Schools should not concern themselves with social, health or political issues.
- Adults should decide what is right and wrong.
- Children should be taught to respect adults and established adult systems.
- Child-centred approaches are responsible for low standards in basic skills.
- Children cannot be truly creative.
- Creativity only arises after a wide body of knowledge has been assimilated.
- There are absolutes and our religion/philosophy/political system knows them.
- The rules of the market place should be applied to education.
- Learning is more secure when teachers simply teach.
- 'Traditional' methods/subjects/classroom arrangements are best.

Beliefs like those above contrast markedly with list A. They represent some views expressed and evidence collected by a range of commentators, including Furedi (2009), Hayes and Ecclestone (2008), Hirsch (2007), Palmer (2007), Peal (2014). Some of these thinkers support the view that 'progressive' educational approaches, perhaps represented by list A, are responsible for US and UK relatively poor PISA ratings. They often ignore or discount their high ratings in such things as creativity, innovation, scholarship and philanthropy. Critics of the views expressed in this book also commonly overlook the child-centred and liberal beliefs of 'successful' education systems like those of Finland. Those calling for the return of 'traditional' or nineteenth-century approaches, perhaps believe that what was good for them will inevitably be good for all others.

List A and list B beliefs are not necessarily opposed. Child-centred methods used without understanding or in settings where values are unclear, can be destructive and unprogressive. Belief in certain absolutes is found in all educational approaches and a mix of traditional and progressive educational methods is more inclusive than either on its own.

Beliefs do not become values until they direct action. So after discussing individual beliefs and attitudes, it is necessary to decide if they can be turned into a fixed statement about teaching, upon which all stakeholders can agree. These statements turn values, for example equality, into a set of principles that guide action. Thus, a belief that each child has their own way of being intelligent might be turned into the principle: 'We will act on the understanding that all children have different ways of showing intelligence'. Beliefs about the importance of enjoyment in learning may be expressed in the principle: 'We will seek daily opportunities to promote enjoyment of learning'. In their briefest form, beliefs about education arising from list A above might be expressed as the following principles.

We will:

- help each child discover their strengths and interests
- use relevant, powerful and challenging experiences to motivate learning
- attempt to promote high-level thinking in all learning situations
- ensure learning is practical and physical
- seek out emotional/personal links between desired learning and learner
- make frequent use of genuine group work
- find opportunities for solitary and reflective activity
- use modern technologies to support and encourage learning
- endeavour to create a sense of security and well-being in all
- help children learn to learn
- promote enjoyment of the learning process
- ensure all children have opportunities to achieve
- establish democratic structures to include children in decisions on all aspects of schooling.

Understandings about knowledge

For most teachers, the only opportunity to think at length about their knowledge comes during their Initial Teacher Education (ITE). However, ITE is so dominated by 'school experience', assessments against standards and preparations for the 'correct' way to teach reading and Mathematics that little time is devoted to understanding knowledge itself. Knowledge is different from information. A library or the internet is full of information but this inert mass of data cannot become knowledge unless it is internalized, organized and able to be used by the individual. Knowledge

Illustration 8.6   Drawing focuses the eyes and also the mind so that both visual and linguistic skills improve (Brice Heath and Wolf, 2005; Creative Partnerships Kent, 2005)

is not absolute but involves choice and degree; we never have 'the knowledge', rather we move towards what our culture says it is. It helps, however, if a teacher feels they are more knowledgeable, in at least one area, than most people (Cremin et al., 2009). The following list of statements about knowledge is arbitrary and personal, but might form the basis of a discussion on 'What is knowledge?':

- Knowledge outside the classroom is cross-curricular and organic in nature. It is not confined to single-subject disciplines.
- Knowledge is not absolute, but a matter of degree.
- Knowledge may be constructed through education.
- What constitutes worthwhile knowledge should be agreed upon by those involved in it.
- Progressive understanding of subject disciplines is essential to effective learning.
- All subject disciplines are equally valuable in understanding the world and no group of subjects should have special status.

If we agree with these statements of belief, then making them imperatives would turn them into whole-school principles to underlie planning and teaching behaviour. The list might therefore start as follows.

We will:

- look at the world in cross-curricular ways
- get to know the school locality very well
- be open to change
- involve all in deciding what we should know
- use subject disciplines as useful ways of 'chunking' knowledge
- treat all subject disciplines as of equal value.

Attitudes to teaching

'Everyone remembers a teacher', said the Teacher Training Agency (TTA) advertisement in the 1990s. Today many of the celebrities attending the annual National Teaching Awards remember enthusiastic, encouraging, inspiring, caring, fascinated individuals who clearly enjoyed teaching. Much research confirms the powerful impact specific teachers had on the development of individual interests and careers (see, for example, Csikszentmihalyi, 1997: 174–6). Little research has been carried out in the

Illustration 8.7   Teacher and pupil working together to display ceramic tile prototypes generated from looking very closely at a medieval building

sensitive area of the damage teachers and schools have done to the confidence and self-image of pupils. Anecdotal evidence and emerging empirical research (see, for example, Riley, 2006, 2009) suggest that many teachers are fully aware that at times they feel driven to humiliate and emotionally harm children.

Teaching style is influenced by attitude. Research has suggested that simply ascribing words such as 'creative', 'original', 'expert' or 'caring' to novice teachers can make a significant difference to their feeling of worth and their confidence in the classroom (Barnes and Shirley, 2005; Cremin et al., 2009). The need to feel we are 'making a contribution' is as important for the teacher as it is for the child. School leaders should be fully aware not just that their staff is the crucial resource, but that each individual's personal sense of well-being is essential to the flourishing of both the school and the individuals within it (Barnes, 2001, 2013b).

A greater focus upon teacher well-being would transform staff development programmes. Currently, most staff development time is taken up by addressing externally driven initiatives, revising administrative requirements, preparing for or following up inspections, or making school self-evaluations or pupil assessments. Necessary though these are, staff development time exclusively devoted to these things does little to develop staff as people. In contrast, the implementation of a planned and focused progression of personally engaging learning activities for staff is likely to transform atmosphere and achievement in a school by positively changing adult attitudes. Supporting teachers in finding and celebrating

Illustration 8.8 Teachers planning creative activity for themselves in a staff meeting

their personal creative and professional strengths builds their capacity and benefits the children in their classes (Barnes, 2013b). Many academies, free schools and teaching schools now devote a much more time to staff development. If five or ten days per year were assigned to building up the intellectual, cultural, spiritual, physical and social lives of each staff member, current poor rates of teacher retention and recruitment are likely to improve along with the standard of teaching.

My own research has strongly suggested that staff development should provide frequent opportunities for teachers and other adults working in school to develop the following:

- confidence in 'safe risk taking', playing with ideas and using imagination
- belief in the importance of making time and opportunity to reflect on successful and not so successful lessons
- determination to avoid restrictive formulas with regard to teaching and learning
- enthusiasm for developing creative teaching
- expectations that they will plan opportunities for creative thinking and action
- their own areas of creativity and interests
- understanding of the importance of formative assessment in adding to challenge and ensuring progress
- awareness that their own subject knowledge can and should be constantly improved
- freedom to work together with staff with other areas of expertise to enrich teaching and the experience of children
- encouragement to build supportive relationships. (Barnes, 2013b)

A staff development programme with such aims could result in a set of principles that capture what the individual teacher is 'signing up to' by being part of the team. For example, the aims above might result in the following teaching principles:

In this school, teachers will:

- expect children to have fun
- plan activities aimed to interest children
- work with children to make the school a better place socially

(Continued)

(Continued)

- work with children to improve life in the community and local environment
- help children risk new ideas/uncertain answers
- give children time to think and dream
- make space for unique answers
- strive to be creative themselves
- help children achieve their plans and dreams
- try to include all children
- constantly be adding to their own knowledge
- work with each other to make lessons more engaging
- be friendly and supportive to each other.

Illustration 8.9   A teacher dances a sea shanty with a group of children, enjoying their world with them

Attitudes towards children

If teachers' positive attitudes to themselves are an important feature of strong cross-curricular planning, then positive, even idealistic, attitudes towards children are also necessary. Idealism does not have to deny the everyday realities of working in real, overcrowded, under-resourced classes and communities, it simply attempts to look beyond and above present realities to a positive and possible future. As well as being optimistic, maybe it is also the teacher's job to nurture the kind of idealism that many of them expressed during their job interviews. This idealism may be essential to maintaining the positive frame of mind that so often characterizes good teachers. Such optimism can be summarized in the following attitudes:

- a belief in providing frequent and multiple opportunities for children to discover what interests them as individuals – to develop passions
- a belief in the importance of education as meaning making in a social setting
- an understanding that the child's world is different from the adult's and that this needs to be taken into account when planning activities, curricula and environments.

Put clearly as guiding principles for a whole school, these attitudes might read as follows:

We will:

- provide the basic knowledge and skills children need to make a positive contribution to their world now and in the future
- help children see themselves as budding experts in a chosen area of knowledge
- help children see themselves as creative beings with original thoughts
- help children find personal meaning in school activities
- help children understand love and caring as central attributes of being human
- support children in feeling good about themselves
- understand that the world of our children may be different from that of adults.

An informed adult view of the world of the twenty-first century

The emphasis on children in the preceding paragraphs is an attempt to help redress the adult-centred balance of primary education. It would be wrong to assume, however, that adult views, beliefs and knowledge should be ignored or sidelined. We have seen (Chapter 1) that, through the internet and television, today's children are much more in touch with (adult-related) global issues than in the past. Thompson and Giedd's research (Thompson et al., 2000; see also Chapter 5) into the maturing brain has reminded us that adult minds are in some ways very different to those of children. Adults may more easily see consequences, look into the future and plan strategies. Adults are also responsible for the wars, environmental catastrophes, unsustainable practices and evils children see in today's world. At our best, we adults can offer the wisdom of experience, a wider perspective and a more balanced and broad-based approach to knowledge and experience. However, there are as many adult viewpoints as there are adults – reality TV and the news remind us of this daily. Teachers work daily with classes of children from families whose views range from permissive and liberal to fundamentalist and conservative. They are charged with representing and understanding all perspectives.

Illustration 8.10   Neuroscience confirms the human tendency to seek, use and create patterns from the earliest ages

Regardless of the importance of education for the present, teachers are expected to prepare children for life in the world of the future. We have seen (Chapter 1) how international, economic, environmental, values and cultural conflicts will colour children's lives and already do. It is probably essential that today's teachers have a view on these issues and address them at some level within the ITE curriculum and the curriculum children follow when in school.

A values-based case study

Children from an Eco-School in Brent designed an eco-garden with a landscape gardener from the local authority. The professional gardener used the Design/Technology curriculum to teach the skills of garden design and the principles of sustainability were discussed and learned during Geography lessons. There is a weekly gardening club that grows vegetables and fruit for sale and consumption in school, and children recycle food waste via a wormery. After attending a 'Climate Change Challenge' competition, Year 7 pupils instituted paper and bottle recycling and led an eco day through the school. The school itself sees human 'responsibility for the stewardship of the environment' as a core aim of education and designs its curriculum to 'empower members of the school to improve the environment' and to 'witness the positive impact on the school'. The PSHE and RE leaders in the school coordinate the curriculum focus on water, energy and litter. These cross-curricular themes centrally involve teaching and learning in Geography, Science and Design/Technology, but the whole school ethos is coloured by the heightened consciousness of our responsibility for a fragile environment.

As a starting point for discussion all teachers should know about the UN Development Goals. The United Nations agreed its Millennium Development Goals in 2000 (UN, 2000, website). They are:

- Eradicate extreme poverty and hunger.
- Achieve universal primary education.
- Promote gender equality and empower women.
- Reduce child mortality.
- Improve maternal health.
- Combat HIV/AIDS, malaria and other diseases.
- Ensure environmental sustainability.
- Global partnership for development.

Every one of these eight goals requires a principled response; each raises an issue upon which children in our classes can consider and form a view. Perhaps one or two aims could prompt discussion leading towards whole-school agreement on the big ideas behind school conversations, curriculum and culture.

Summary: what have principles got to do with cross-curricular learning?

Every age has its major challenges. Today's challenges cannot be kept local. Our global economy, instant communications and global pollution have meant that whatever happens in one place quickly affects every other. If they want it, ordinary adults, and particularly teachers, are now in a position to exert some influence over the interrelated future of this world. To do so effectively, teachers and children need to be very clear about (a) what they value most and (b) what parts of our society, environment and the wider world they can effectively influence. The answers to these questions and the challenges inherent in the UN's Development Goals could and should underpin all our education decisions.

This book suggests that a cross-curricular approach is the approach most suitable to addressing core values in the learning context of children's own lived experience. I have selected and examined four key areas where the formulation of shared values in a school is a pressing need: learning, knowledge, teaching and children.

Each of these areas is subject to a number of often contrasting beliefs and attitudes. A school's first priority is to work towards turning its combined beliefs and attitudes into a set of agreed principles, which will inform all decisions about staffing, resources, curriculum, time management and classroom organization. Such principles will also guide school self-evaluation and parents' and children's views on the achievements and qualities of the school. A school's statement of principles, or its fundamental aims, should be the result of an in-depth and frequently revisited conversation between all stakeholders. In many ways, this conversation is the most important policy decision that the school can make. The discussion on school principles should:

- involve parents, governors, children, volunteers and other adults working in the school, as well as teachers and the head teacher
- be regularly discussed and often revised
- be used to make internal evaluations of the success of the school
- be expected to be used by both stakeholders and external bodies to judge the quality of the school.

Teachers are amongst the key individuals who can help our populations face the unprecedented challenges of the twenty-first century. They must therefore have a clear understanding of global issues and a principled view on how to help tackle them. Teachers must start by becoming growing, learning, positive and interesting people themselves.

Key questions for discussion

- What do we stand for as school teachers and a school?
- What do we believe is important in framing our teaching?
- What has all this to do with the UN's Millennium Goals?

Further reading

Gardner, H., Csikszentmihalyi, M. and Damon, W. (2000) *Good Work: When Excellence and Ethics Meet*. New York: Basic Books.
Halpin, D. (2003) *Hope and Education*. London: Routledge.
Robinson, K. and Aronica, L. (2010) *The Element: How Finding Your Passion Changes Everything*. London: Allen Lane.

CHAPTER 9

WHAT THEMES ARE SUITABLE FOR CROSS-CURRICULAR LEARNING?

Chapter aims

This chapter offers practical examples of themes suitable for cross-curricular learning. It begins by discussing the importance of meaningful projects and the role of children's views. The chapter develops the idea of meaningful schooling where learning results from deep engagement and full participation in educational experiences. It offers sample themes suitable for cross-curricular investigation using two subject perspectives. By the end of this chapter you will have been introduced to thoughts about how to choose themes and been offered a range of examples:

- planning a shared experience
- choosing only subjects that add understanding
- planning the skills, subject knowledge and progression required
- aiming at a state of flow in children
- finishing with a performance of understanding
- some subject-based themes.

The brain learns best and retains most when the organism is actively involved in exploring physical sites and materials and asking questions to which it actually craves the answers. Merely passive experiences tend to attenuate and have little lasting impact. (Gardner, 1999a: 83)

Any subject can be suitable for cross-curricular learning. We have seen with the *Single Transferable Subject* mode of cross-curricular learning

(Chapter 2) that any subject can offer a perspective on knowledge and/ or experience, but schools have found themes, projects, topics or generative experiences a useful means of integrating the curriculum. Experiences as disparate as a well-read story, a visit from the community police officer, a child's holiday with relatives in Tyneside or Tobago, the death of a beloved hamster, the discovery of a spider's web in the playground or a birthday trip to the adventure playground, can all generate learning across a number of subject disciplines. Similarly, a generic project or theme such as *water* or *people who help us*, might be enlightened by any curriculum subjects. If we aim for a learning curriculum (Lave and Wenger, 1991), then any topic presented with enthusiasm, careful planning *and flexibility* can be approached using the skills and knowledge of any of the disciplines developed over the past two millennia. I have argued that personal significance and limited subject focus are important features of successful projects, but so too is the learner's own sense that they are learning.

External features such as postural, facial and attentional characteristics are probably the most accessible indicator that a child might be learning. Laevers (1994a) argues that signs of *involvement* are the first we should look for. Laever's work with children in their early years suggested that for most (but not all) children signs of genuine involvement in learning include:

- facial expressions of enjoyment, concentration and motivation
- a bodily posture of positive tension
- relaxed relationships with peers and other co-workers
- a performance that matches or exceeds the known capabilities of the child
- a reluctance to be distracted.

In addition, and in the light of the emphasis I have placed on principles (Chapter 8), we should also consider whether the kind of learning happening could be described as:

- worthwhile
- reflexive
- meaningful
- good
- right
- helping develop values like beauty, truth, justice, etc.

Research into deep learning suggests that those who strive or who are helped to make *meaningful* connections between themselves and new knowledge, retain and are able to transfer their understanding more effectively. As children grow older they are often able to discern their own influence on a subject and the subject's influence on them. This *reflexive* and personal aspect of learning was implicit in the Plowden Report (DES, 1967) and was picked up explicitly by researchers contributing to the Cambridge Primary Review (Alexander, 2010) (see Chapter 2). A combined interest in fostering knowledge for its own sake, establishing a broad and balanced education and enhancing thinking skills are common features of schools attempting to create a curriculum accessible to all (CPR, 2014; Ofsted, 2009a, 2009b).

Meaningful projects

In the 1970s and 1980s heyday of topic or project work, teachers (often independently) chose cross-curricular topics for their classes. They felt they knew children would be interested in 'pirates' or 'buried treasure', dinosaurs, Egyptians and Romans. The effect was that some children followed topics on the Romans or made 'Treasure Island' maps three times during their primary school career! Whilst there were stunning examples of very motivating, memorable and successful 'topics', I believe we were mistaken in many of our choices. Certainly, in my classes, children quickly saw through the pirate maths and pirate RE, pirate poems and pirate geography. They tired easily of measuring planks to walk upon and adding 57 doubloons to 25 doubloons – both activities were still 'sums'. Whilst the complex 'Topic Webs' we constructed were often impressive and should have won prizes for ingenuity, they shoe-horned subjects into spurious themes and the deepest thinking was the teacher's. Indeed, provoking *thought* in children was possibly the last thing on the teacher's mind and any sense of relevance came more by luck than judgement. Children were indeed more engaged than in the days of simple 'chalk and talk' but teachers often failed to ask whether such work led to significantly raised standards. When teachers today say that current cross-curricular approaches are 'going back' to the topics of the 1970s and 1980s, I worry, because there was a great deal wrong with them. How then do we arrive at relevant and contemporary themes or projects that make connections across the curriculum and also raise standards in the subjects?

The following guidelines should be considered:

1. Consult the children about the theme and key questions.
2. Plan a shared and authentic experience closely related to the theme, but also capable of provoking strong engagement and sustained interest.

3. Plan in a degree of flexibility to follow relevant interests of the children.
4. Choose only curriculum subjects that clearly add understanding to the experience.
5. See language as a subject that runs across the whole curriculum.
6. Ensure all subjects are treated as of equal importance.
7. Plan the subject skills, knowledge (including special vocabulary) and progression required for each focus subject.
8. Aim at generating a state of *flow* in children.
9. Finish with some means of demonstrating the new understandings generated by the topic/project.
10. Use the whole-school and wider community as a resource.

Chapter 3 demonstrated how some schools used community links to develop speedy and more deeply rooted learning in children. The case studies also showed how working with adults who are *not* teachers can help some children develop a greater sense of the everyday relevance in their school activity. But a teacher's growing professional and personal understanding of the daily lives of children will increasingly reveal relevant and meaningful themes. The aim is to elicit the kind of responses expressed by children in terms like these:

> It's just like I have discovered a new world of music that I never knew existed. (Alisha, Key Stage 3 pupil talking about a sound composition project)

> We were sitting there actually enjoying learning. (Year 7 pupil talking about a history project enlivened by an artist)

> I'm going to spend my birthday money on getting the equipment to set things up at home. (Year 8 pupil talking about a pinhole camera project)
>
> (Robert Jarvis, personal communication)

Consulting the children

> My dream school would be a school which would let me explore the world and tell me human knowledge … At the start of every year the children will choose the topics they are most interested in. There are no compulsory time-tables. Five professors will help the children in each place. (Gautier, Key Stage 2, quoted in Burke and Grosvenor, 2003: 62)

Subjects like Citizenship and initiatives like the United Nation Convention on the Rights of the Child (UNCRC) draw attention to the importance of pupil participation (see, for example, Cheminais, 2012; Ruddock and MacIntyre, 2007). The UNCRC Article 12 makes it clear that children should be consulted on *all* decisions affecting their lives (UNICEF, 1989, website). The establishment in the UK of the Children and Young Persons Unit (CYPU), Children's Commissioners in England, Northern Ireland, Scotland and Wales (e.g. Children's Commissioner, website). A preliminary research document to the Children Act of 2004 made the following points in its summary:

- 'Taking account of what children say is what makes their involvement meaningful …'
- 'Acting on children and young people's views brings positive outcomes in … increasing young people's sense of citizenship and social inclusion and enhancing their personal development.' (Kirby et al., 2003)

Whilst the preliminary documents for the Children Act have been archived and are no longer public policy, they helped establish in children's services and society at large the expectation that the child's voice should be heard. The child's opinion on what matters to them about the world often reveals interest in highly relevant and contemporary issues. A sample of children's views from Year 6 in three primary schools in Kent showed the following interests:

- conservation issues related to their local environment or wider world locations like the rain forest
- natural disasters like earthquakes, volcanoes, tsunamis
- human-caused disasters including wars, accidents and pollution
- travel pros and cons
- global warming
- fair trade
- health and fitness (including healthy food)
- poverty
- cleaning up ugly places
- links with other places, for example their school connections with a school in another country.

Commercial companies have taken up such moral and politically aware themes amongst our young people. The International Primary Curriculum (IPC, website), for example, offers popular units like:

- Earthquakes and volcanoes.
- Roots, shoots and fruits.
- Footprints from the past.
- Saving the world.
- What's on the menu?
- From Bronze to Bioplastic.
- Explorers and adventurers.
- Black Gold.

National developments that will inevitably influence curricular choices in academies, frees schools as well as local authority include:

- the adoption of 'Circle Time' (Moseley, 1996), aimed at developing empathy, relationship skills and personal values
- the social and emotional aspects of learning (SEAL) (DfE, 2011)
- school councils where elected representatives have a meaningful role in school decision making (for example, the Department of Education for Northern Ireland (DENI, website)
- pupil representatives on some governing bodies
- children's commissioners and children's parliaments.

Some schools like Summerhill (website) have always included children centrally in decisions about the curriculum. In Steiner schools for almost 90 years, parents of each class have regularly met as a body to discuss the curriculum their children follow and general concerns about their children's physical, spiritual, moral and intellectual development. Whilst the curriculum follows a prescribed and adult-led route, the realization of the themes is strongly tailored to the holistic needs of the growing child and the personality of the class. Thus, for example, children study *volcanoes* and *revolutions* at the same time as their bodies and relationships are in the upheavals of puberty. When I asked the head of a case study primary school (Barnes, 2005c) what their curriculum themes would be next term, she answered that staff did not know because they had not asked the children yet.

Some schools decide upon themes well in advance to ensure curriculum balance or guarantee consideration of issues relevant to school context, policies, aims or philosophy. Others use published schemes as starting points. Each source of ideas for projects has its strengths. It is also legitimate for adults to make decisions about what it is important to learn because schools are seen as society's way of inducting the child into itself. However, children can be helped to feel centrally involved in the choice of theme and that the choice is meaningful to them. In a culture that increasingly raises children's awareness of rights, the school that denies children's participation at the curriculum level is in danger of adding to the atmosphere of disaffection outlined in Chapter 1.

Other schools may follow a whole school approach to the curriculum. Norfolk schools following the *Index for Inclusion* often change their curriculum in the light of their desire to become more inclusive. The headings for curricular activity may have a strong cross-curricular character. Those considering what the Index calls, *A global rights-based curriculum* throughout the school, for example, may use the following headings through which to apply the traditional subject curriculum (examples shown in brackets):

- **Food** (Chemistry, Geography, Design/Technology)
- **Water** (Chemistry, Geography, Art, Mathematics)
- **Clothing** (Design/Technology, Art, PSHE)
- **Housing/Building** (History, Design/Technology, Physics, Geography)
- **The environment** (Geography, Chemistry, Biology, Music)
- **Energy** (Science, Mathematics, PE, Music)
- **Transport** (History, Geography, Physics)
- **Communication and Communications** (Language and literature, MFL, Art, Music, Dance)
- **Technology** (ICT, Physics, Art)
- **Health/Relationships** (PSHE, Religion, Science)
- **Literature/Arts/Music** (Religion, PSHE and Arts subjects)
- **Work/Activity** (Mathematics, PE, Science)
- **Ethics, Power and Government** (PSHE, Citizenship, Geography, History Language)

(Booth and Ainscow, 2011)

The subjects bracketed above are the more obvious links to the headings but other subjects could with equal relevance be applied to them. As always language, speaking, listening, writing and reading applies to all.

Planning a shared experience

Trends towards individualized learning run the risk of divorcing children from their physical, social and sensory selves. Some schools and academies boast of the high numbers of independent workstations instead of classrooms, primary schools often have tablets or *iPads* for whole classes. It is possible to access the whole curriculum without personally experiencing the real world or getting hands dirty. Having the technology to ensure an education based almost wholly in cyberspace is possible, but it may not be good. The values discussion, held frequently, helps in clarifying what a school is for.

Personal, social and physical experiences are great teachers. The strength of active, real-world and interpersonal learning is that it is interpreted in many different ways and means something different to each individual. Active, communal and physical experiences are more often preferred by children because their sensory, physical and social faculties develop first (see Chapter 5). Indeed the exquisite combination of empathy, language, touch, smell, taste, feeling, movement and hearing that gave the human animal advantages over other animals in the past are just as important today. The evolutionary reward for these preferences shows itself in the pleasure creative, physical, exploratory activity gives us (Panksepp and Biven, 2012).

If we add our range of sensory accomplishments to the huge species advantages of self-conscious thought and culture, then arguments for learning together, in real life and relevant contexts, become difficult to refute. Yet much of our curriculum can seem directed at children working alone, hardly using their highly refined senses of touch, hearing, visual discrimination, taste, empathy.

Our personal histories are important too. Most objects and sounds that surround us generate personal memories and associations. These 'objects' (including categories of place and people) form part of the memory bank we unconsciously 'call up' whenever appropriate (Damasio, 2003). This appears to be true whether the experience is major or minor. The teacher can construct major experiences with a view to using these personal insights productively. If your class shares time at the circus, lakeside, theatre, car park or supermarket, each member will bring a different mind to the experience. Shared experiences might include:

- a public event (such as a carnival, charity fair, parade, Olympics, festival, political or state visit)
- any fieldwork within the school grounds or building
- fieldwork in the school locality, the forest or in some contrasting locality (such as on a school activity holiday)
- a visit (to a museum, supermarket, theatre or nature reserve)
- a special visitor (such as a grandparent, local nurse, poet, builder or gardener)
- a themed week (such as a 'Science week', 'Technology week' or 'Africa week') or day (e.g. 'Red Nose Day')
- a performance (such as a play, opera, dance, gymnastics, a musical or concert)

- a collection of objects (from a school collection, museum, school dig or visiting expert)
- a school event (such as sports day, open day, Victorian day or anniversary)
- a combined construction project (such as building an adventure playground, sculpture garden or 'robot wars' vehicle)
- a reflective activity (such as meditation, a quiet day, a church/temple or mosque visit)
- the writing of a class story, set of poems or book based upon aspects of the local environment or using detailed knowledge of a local place as the setting.

Some schools start their cross-curricular theme with a shared activity, whilst others choose to aim for such an event at the end of a term's interdisciplinary work. The teacher's professional skill is shown in their ability to make something useful from diverse responses. They may link individual responses and craft them into meaningful expressions of community and cultural values. They might use the variety of responses to illustrate a philosophical proposition, or to help children learn about working in teams and valuing individual insights. Finally the experienced teacher can pass the issue to the children – *'We have five different opinions/responses/answers from this experience, what do you think we should do?'*

Choosing only subjects that add understanding

The cross-curriculum models of the 1970s and 1980s often foundered on the contrived inclusion of *all* subjects on every Topic Web. Often in best cross-curricular practice only two or three subjects (plus always English) are necessary to bring a balanced understanding to a theme. A serious danger of interdisciplinary work is that the boundaries between the subject disciplines become less distinct and progression within subjects is weakened.

 Case study   Research into a cross-curricular project

A school in the USA chose the year 1492 (when 'Columbus sailed the ocean blue') as its theme for a term. Apart from the obvious history focus (What was it like then? What happened? Why? How do we know?), pupils studied from the perspective of science (What is true? How have living things changed over the last 500 years? How do plants adapt to change?), and using a geographical lens, children looked at diverse eco-systems that represented contrasting parts of the country in 1492 (they made a series of maps, discussed human–environment interactions and specifically the impact of humans since 1492). Using storybooks, the internet, non-fiction publications, practical experimentation, fieldwork, the application of mapping and diagrammatic skills, the different perspectives of scientist, historian and geographer were explored. The linking theme of a single year drew children into much wider debates and understandings of the ways in which historians develop interpretations, scientists develop explanations and geographers develop descriptions. The researcher (Roth, 2000) reflecting upon this project noted, however, that science learning within the theme was not as deep as social studies learning.

My own research (Barnes and Shirley, 2007) suggests that in delivering cross-curricular themes, teachers should:

- identify and focus on clear, appropriate, subject-based learning objectives
- continually monitor the depth of understanding by informal assessment during the activities
- avoid compromising subjects in efforts to 'fit them' to a theme
- be prepared to drop the theme for a period in order to teach subject-specific skills and knowledge
- give children early opportunities to *apply* newly learned skills and knowledge when returning to the theme
- strive to generate a genuine questioning stance in the children
- be prepared to intervene in any group activity in order to help raise standards and meet challenging objectives.

Planning the skills, subject knowledge and progression required

The National Curricula of England, Wales, Northern Ireland and the Curriculum for Excellence in Scotland are permissive and flexible documents. There is little content in the non-core subjects, rather directions on what sort of topics should be covered at what ages and what children should know by the end of their key stage. Decisions on content are largely left to schools. English, Mathematics and Science are significantly heavier in knowledge and skills content and provide useful guidance and frameworks to work within. If you are planning learning within a theme, then a clear idea of progression within the subjects is essential. This is given in the Mathematics, English and Science documents but a progression of skills and knowledge is not so evident in the non-core. Table 9.1 offers a simple guide to progression that can apply across all subjects and may support teachers in planning. For example, in history a child might move from *describing* what they see in a piece of evidence (for example, an object or a picture), to *organizing* and *categorizing* what they see, to *asking questions* about it and *coming to simple conclusions* about its value. If these abilities are demonstrated the child might be challenged to make *informed guesses* about its function, or *make links* between it and another piece of evidence and finally coming to well-balanced and well-evidenced *conclusions and statements* as to its significance.

Working with the generic concepts the teacher can devise clear, measurable objectives for each lesson. Through constant interaction, concentrated feedback, open-ended (and occasionally closed) questioning, the teacher can ensure aspiration and achievement is raised. With clear objectives, either directly stated to the children or elicited after the activities ('*What do you think I wanted you to learn from this?*'), the teacher can ensure that subject skills and knowledge are not lost in a 'bland broth' of interdisciplinary study (Wineburg and Grossman, 2000). Using the generic concepts in Table 9.1, the teacher may plan for differentiated support and appropriate progression within each subject. The individual child's stage of development becomes the determinate of expectations rather than their age.

Table 9.1 Generic progression for national curriculum subjects

Attainment level	Generic concepts	Typical generic activities
Level 1	Literal	See, experience, respond, describe
Level 2	Organization	Arrange, compare, contrast, classify, put into own words
Level 3	Evaluation	Make choices, give reasons, ask questions, find and use, present
Level 4	Inference	Work out, explain, select, combine, make educated guesses
Level 5	Appreciation	Justify, generalize, look for qualities, modify, establish own conclusions

The author is grateful to Jane Heyes and Brompton Westbrook Primary School, Gillingham for this analysis.

Aiming at a state of flow in children

The school I'd like … could slow down a little. Hugh, age 6 (Burke and Grosvenor, 2003: 74)

Csikszentmihalyi's concept of flow summarizes that sense of complete involvement we teachers often see when children are fully engaged in an activity over which they feel they have some control. The state of flow has been described as the sensation we feel when ideas, thoughts and life itself seem to run freely and well. Csikszentmihalyi's research (see Chapter 6) suggests that when we are in that state of flow we feel at our most alive, and have a great sense of meaning. We become intrinsically motivated.

Intrinsic motivation is often observed in the school playground, in school plays or concerts, or in engagement in practical, sporting and creative sessions. Flow occurs when play, physical activity, exploration, challenge, connection-making, creativity or friendly relationships are connected with new challenges or a degree of difficulty. These observations are powerful arguments for a curriculum that operates outside the limits of the normal classroom in the real and multi-disciplinary world outside.

 Case study   Flow in action

In a school serving a deprived, 'raw, rough and unsociable' area of the bankrupted city of Berlin, a group of 250 young people were asked to join a project to learn and perform a ballet to Stravinsky's *Rite of Spring.* Sir Simon Rattle, a famous conductor, and choreographer Royston Maldoom led this social project, expressly designed to change minds and counter disaffection through involvement in a cross-arts project. These young people had never had contact with Western classical music, had never danced and many were battling severe social, emotional and health problems of their own, with some very reluctant to participate. The story of their transformation from low aspirations and negativity towards a more hopeful, positive, confident and sensitized life is told in the film *Rhythm Is It* (Sanchez and Gruber, 2005, website). At one point in the film, choreographer Maldoom says 'Don't think you are just doing dancing. You can change your life in a dance class!' The film ends with extracts from the final rehearsal and performance in which one can observe flow in action in the faces and bodies of the children. The film portrays the combination of real, hard and painfully earned skill and a high challenge that two months previously had seemed insurmountable, and that clearly had resulted in some transformed lives.

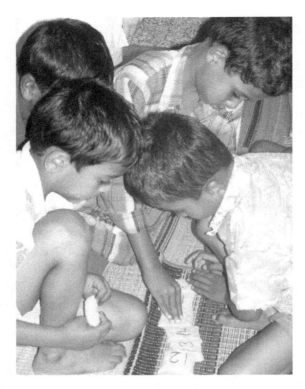

Illustration 9.1   Flow in action

Finishing with a performance of understanding

Perhaps the most effective means of monitoring and formatively appraising work done across several curricula is the *performance of understanding* (Perkins in Blythe, 1997). In this kind of assessment procedure, children create some kind of demonstration of the degree of their understanding. Assessment generally and specific attention to the performance of understanding will be the subject of Chapter 10.

Themes

It is clear that there are as many relevant and fascinating themes as there are objects, places, feelings, ideas and living things in the universe. There can be no definitive list. The essence of a theme that will generate learning is one that both teacher and children can feel enthusiastic about and committed to. For cross-curricular work to be successful in raising standards it must be well planned, assessed formatively and continued attention should be paid to specific objectives within focus subjects. The short lists below are some themes that have successfully been used in schools. I have chosen below to single out themes that suggest one major focus subject. The second subject applied to the theme (in brackets) is a suggestion but could be any curriculum subject made relevant. The choice may come from teacher or class preference or may seem an obvious second subject link. English will always be present. Key learning objectives within the subjects need to be restricted within each theme so that subject learning is not 'watered down'. A Foundation Stage or Key Stage 1 theme with a Science focus like 'Why won't my seed grow?' (de Boo, 2004) will lay the foundations for Science later on in school by helping children handle, tend and think about seeds and growth, but true to good early years practice, children will also sort and classify, count, draw, construct, make musical instruments and listen to and invent stories. The Knowledge and Understanding of the World or Key Stage 1 science objectives may be 'to identify the features of living things', 'to be able to relate the life process of a plant' or 'to identify similarities and differences in natural things'. The class teacher will know the expected range of levels of understanding and be able to differentiate and encourage children to higher levels of achievement.

Some themes with a Science focus

Systems (Music)

Models (Design/Technology)

Turn on the light (Geography)

Patterns of change (PE)

Interactions (Art and Design)

Colour (Art and Design)

Bubbles (Music)

Why won't my seed grow? (Geography)

Why is water important? (RE)

How many legs? (Mathematics)

Some themes with a Geography focus

Our street/our neighbours (RE)

Improving a derelict site/school playground (Design/Technology)

Weather (Science)

A building site (History)

A basket of fruit from …(Arts)

A day out in the town/country/seaside/India (PSHE)

A linked school in a distant locality (RE)

Finding our way/maps and mapping (Mathematics)

A local river, lake, dam or coast/geographical processes (Science or Music)

Getting there/transport systems (PSHE)

My footprint/sustainability and me (Science or History)

My home/systems that serve us (Science or History or Citizenship)

A sustainable school/community/garden/building (Science or Art)

What's in the news and where is it? (PSHE or Citizenship)

Some themes with an RE focus

People (Science)

Journeys (Geography)

Celebrations/Festivals (Art or Music)

Stories (History)

Special places (Geography or Art)

Symbols and signs (Art or Geography)

Judaism, Sikhism, Buddhism, Islam, Christianity, Hinduism, Shamanism, Animism (Geography or Art)

What's in the news? (Geography or PSHE or Citizenship)

What is beauty? (Art, Music, Dance)

What is truth? (Mathematics or Science)

What is good? (History or Geography)

What is bad? (History or Geography)

Some themes with a history focus

Change (Science)

My birthday (SEAL or PSHE)

My family (RE)

Medicine/transport/houses/kitchens through the ages (Science)

A particular building (Geography or RE or Design/technology)

Grandma Brown's visit (PSHE)

Florence Nightingale and Mary Seacole (Science)

The Olympic Games (Geography)

The Gunpowder Plot (RE)

The excavation (Geography)

In an artist's/engineer's/scientist's shoes (Design/Technology or Science)

Our school (Geography or Mathematics)

The 1851 Great Exhibition (Art or Design/Technology or Science)

A visit to the museum (Design/Technology or Science)

A mystery object (any)

Summary and key questions

Perhaps you might consider the following questions before coming to a firm decision on a theme:

1. Consulting the children

- Does this theme fit with the school's wider aims?
- How will I make it relevant and meaningful to the children?
- How can I involve children in decisions?

2. Planning a shared experience

- How can I involve and enhance community links though this project?
- What are my overarching goals for this theme? In what big ways do I want the children to be different at the end of this topic?
- What shared experiences can we plan?

3. Choosing only subjects that add understanding

- What two or three (maximum four) curriculum subjects best throw light on this theme?
- What are the curriculum needs this term/year/week?

4. Planning the subject skills, knowledge and progression required

- What level of skills and knowledge in each subject do I need to help children demonstrate?
- What experts from the community can I call on to help me?

5. Aiming at a state of flow in children

- What can I do to generate a state of flow in the children during aspects of this theme?
- How can I make this project personally meaningful to the maximum number of children?

6. Finishing with a performance of understanding

- In what ways can the children demonstrate the depth of their learning?
- How can I help children show that their learning is transferable to other situations and settings?

Further reading

Faultley, M. and Savage, J. (2012) *Cross Curricular Teaching and Learning in the Secondary School: The Arts.* London: Routledge.

Kerry, T. (ed.) (2010) *Cross-Curricular Teaching in the Primary School.* London: Routledge.

Rowley, C. and Cooper, H. (2009) *Cross-Curricular Teaching and Learning.* London: Sage.

Wyse, D. and Rowson, P. (2008) *The Really Useful Creativity Book.* London: Routledge.

CHAPTER 10

HOW CAN WE ASSESS CROSS-CURRICULAR AND CREATIVE LEARNING?

Chapter aims

This chapter will consider how and what to assess in cross-curricular learning contexts. Using examples from a cross-section of schools it offers examples of child-led, sensitive, cross-curricular and innovative assessment. It introduces the idea of 'Performances of Understanding' trailed at Harvard University's School of Education. By the end of this chapter you will know about:

- what to assess
- formative assessment
- 'performances of understanding'
- presentations and peer assessments
- self-assessments
- assessing engagement.

Learning is difficult to assess if subject aims are unclear. Cross-curricular and personalized learning methods present particular challenges because school assessments tend to involve generalized, 'broad brush', 'box-ticking' approaches. In opportunistic, multi- or inter-disciplinary contexts, learning occurs on too many levels and in too many domains to be susceptible to summative assessment. This book has attempted to make the case that cross-curricular learning is a powerful way to generate creative thinking on a personal and collaborative level and creativity is also notoriously difficult to assess. *Formative* and individualized assessment aimed at deepening learning, however, can and should form part of all creative and cross-curricular activity (see, for example, Assessment Reform Group, 2002, website). Assessment that promotes further learning allows for a range of different assessors of equal value: self, peer group, audience, expert practitioner, interested observer or teacher. Constructive approaches to evaluation should empower the learner both to appreciate their own progress and hunger after new and richer understandings.

The most significant and lasting of assessments are those we make on ourselves. In periods of deep and positive engagement, concentration is sustained, even deepened, by the feedback we give ourselves. In children, self-assessment often comes in the form of 'self talk', the spoken commentary that commonly accompanies play (see Barnes, 2010). Self-talk is generally internalized as we grow older but forms an ever-present critical appraisal as we act out our lives. This personal feedback is added to by the often wordless reactions of others close by, who by body language and the occasional comment tell us how we are doing. These often subtle and unconscious sources of feedback are vital components of the flow state described earlier (Chapter 6). Teachers observe this kind of self and peer assessment when school work takes on the nature of play and exploration – a desirable characteristic of cross-curricular learning. Pupils should be involved in the preparation of tests and be should be used to making sensitive and discriminating assessments on each other's work.

What to assess

Teachers continually assess. We quickly sense the 'atmosphere' of a room full of pupils, we judge the verity of an explanation after a playground spat, we evaluate the amount of work going on even before we crouch beside a table of working children. As we listen to the questions, comments and chatter of children engaged in activity throughout the school day and beyond, we cannot help making value judgements, comparing and checking. Assessment has not always been made against progressive, planned, articulated and monitored learning objectives. In the past, rather than being linked with future learning, assessments were often more to do with capturing the quantity of correctness. From the earliest days of formal education, teachers kept detailed mark books and made annual reports: summative assessments of individual progress in reading, writing, tables, arithmetic, Latin, general knowledge. From surviving school assessment records, we can see, for example, that Isaac Newton, Albert Einstein, Winston Churchill and John Lennon were clearly destined for lives of failure!

More frequent, stringent, statutory, uniform and formalized assessment has become a noticeable feature of teaching since the 1980s. With the advent of SATs, voluntary SATs, booster classes in English and Mathematics and published league tables of school results, children in England are amongst the most assessed in the world. These assessments have a number of functions. They provide regular updates on a child's progress for parents and carers. For school governors they give confidence that the school is fulfilling its legal responsibilities. Assessments also serve to inform of a school's progress (usually in the core subjects only) against other similar schools or its own previous record. For school principals, heads or subject coordinators, they may serve to monitor the success of a particular teacher in delivering a subject. An Ofsted inspector may use records of assessments to judge curriculum coverage and age-appropriate expectations and to ensure an adequate degree of accountability on the part of the teacher. Whilst assessments are expected in all foundation subjects and RE, the assessments most consulted during inspections are the core subjects of English, Mathematics, Science and, increasingly, ICT. None of the official functions of assessment matter very much to most children, and yet assessment intended to promote *further learning* can be a most productive and positive part of a teacher's interaction with the child.

Since the publication of the English National Curriculum for 2014 the subject associations have worked hard to produce materials to support teachers in formative assessment. Teachers and student teachers should consult subject association websites and publications, alongside the wealth of advice offered by the subject expert panels (see CPR, 2014 for a digest of the assessment advice for each curriculum subject). But subject advice alone is not enough to ensure assessment is truly helpful to children and their teachers. The Scottish Curriculum for Excellence, the RSA *Opening Minds* curriculum, the *International Primary Curriculum*, *Cambridge Primary Review*, *Index for Inclusion* and this book offer overarching frameworks within which the subjects make coherent and linked-up sense.

The kind of curriculum promoted by this book aims at the personal growth and fulfilment of children. Illich (1971), and many since his day, remind us that personal growth is ultimately immeasurable. But if teachers are to feel confident that they are supporting children in their journey, some means of capturing progress may need to be developed. If creativity is to be promoted through our school system, then we have to evolve some ways of finding out if and to what degree it is happening in our classes. The following sections are intended to inform discussion on how assessment can be both integrated in the learning process and inform teachers of the effectiveness of their teaching. In cross-curricular work intended to take learning at all levels forward, we should therefore assess attitudes towards and progress in: self-understanding, understanding of others, collaboration, understanding of issues significant to the community and understanding of global issues as well as disciplinary understanding.

Assessing well-being

The importance of well-being as a precondition of learning and effective teaching has been stressed throughout this book. Well-being can be assessed (Diener, 2009; Laevers, 1994a) and it is good for teachers to be aware of some simple ways of gauging whether they are placing individuals in the right condition for learning. Laevers developed the Leuven Well-Being Scale (LW-BS) describing typical features of well-being at five levels in early years children. Common and basic emotions like joy, love, fear, sadness and anger and their related emotions are thought to be universally 'readable' in most people's faces and body language (see Ekman, 2004). However, work with children with a range of communication and social barriers to learning shows that many accepted signs of engagement and happiness are not necessarily displayed outwardly. Teachers quickly, and often unconsciously, become adept at recognizing subtle changes in the faces and body language of their children. It may be instructive to use a list of emotions like that in Table 10.1 and make a mental tally of the kinds of emotions shown in an observed class. For some children, however, these feelings may be hidden or the facial expressions showing them may be absent. Not all children smile when they are happy, not all smiles mean happiness. Teachers should therefore always be cautious when making judgements and seek other evidence before acting on first impressions. Additionally some positive characteristics, like empathy, wisdom, creativity and fulfilment are less physically obvious and may be better ascertained through simply asking children about themselves and each other.

Table 10.1 Assessing well-being

joy	love	fear	sadness	anger
relaxation	interest	worry	loneliness	disgust
happiness	affection	anxiety	shame	rage
contentment	caring	nervousness	regret	jealousy
pride	fondness	terror	unhappiness	disappointment

Formative assessment

Formative assessment is assessment intended to carry the child forward in learning. British schools paid lip-service to formative assessment throughout the 1990s, when the first National Curriculum was being launched. However, the NACCCE report in 1999 (paras 200–11) noted its relatively minor importance in school procedures and argued for a more privileged place for formative assessment (Recommendation 5). In the same year as the NACCCE investigations were being conducted, researchers Black and Wiliam (1998) found that, at its best, formative assessment could achieve the following:

- raising children's attainment
- increasing their self-esteem
- giving them a greater stake in their learning
- enabling a greater prospect of 'lifelong learning'.

In a subsequent project on formative assessment, led by educationalist Shirley Clarke, teachers were introduced to now familiar terms such as 'learning intentions', 'success criteria' and 'pupil self-evaluation' (Clarke, website). Even after only a term of serious application, teachers felt able to credit the *assessment for learning* techniques she had introduced with the following benefits:

- Children liked knowing the learning intentions and success criteria.
- Most teachers saw benefit in sharing the learning intentions and success criteria.
- Seventy-five per cent of teachers said that children understood tasks better.
- Almost all teachers said that sharing learning intentions and success criteria had had a positive effect on their teaching.
- Just under half of lessons involved successful use of self-evaluation questions.
- Most teachers said children were no longer afraid to make mistakes and were more able to admit to difficulties.
- Half of the teachers said that children of all abilities are able to access self-evaluation questions.
- Two-thirds of children had some perception of the true point of self-evaluation.
- Of the teachers who tried pupil self-evaluation, almost all said it had a positive effect on their teaching.

Findings like these remain relevant to assessing cross-curricular activities in the classroom. The personally meaningful, less formal and open-ended nature of much cross-curricular learning, lends itself to pupil self-evaluation. Many primary schools since the publication of the 2014 curriculum have said that they will continue to use a topic or project based cross-curriculum because they find it the best way to motivate and engage children. They find that thematic work that makes links across the curriculum and to children's lives generates an atmosphere conducive to joyful learning and that this includes critical and evaluative think on the part of the children.

 An assessment case study

A student teacher in the Schools Direct scheme was observed by a music specialist. The student had arranged his class into a circle each with a Djembe (west African drum) and children were learning to combine several different drum rhythms and composing their own rhythms using rhythmic word phrases The student teacher sat in the circle with the children and led the lesson from there. The children were learning fast and enjoying their learning. The tutor commented on the students' observation report:

> Modelling was a consistent feature of your lesson. The children could always refer to your playing/singing to support their learning. You also encouraged a two-way process – encouraging and picking up on children's suggestions – such as rhythm phrases (TS1.3; TS3.1; TS4.2).

> You have high expectations for behaviour, through an engaging lesson where children wanted to learn, and strategies which are both clear and fair.

In this session the student was continually assessing by making positive individual comments, *'can you just copy what I'm doing?'*, *'listen to Gemma she's really got a good one'*, *'try and make your rhythm fit with Gemma's'* or *'listen carefully to the pulse'*. The student firstly worked with the whole class and then split the children into groups of four and circulated around the groups. Most of the time, however, assessment was being done by listening carefully to when the rhythms fitted each other. The student occasionally asked a quartet of children to play their combination to the others and children were able to self-assess without the teacher's intervention.

> The student then continued with a geography lesson developing children's understanding of a village in Ghana. Here similar assessment methods predominated. Children worked in groups combining four themes – water, links, change and patterns – to discuss the evidence of a wide range of photographs and artefacts. In groups they were asked to make presentations on their understanding of daily life in the village. These were presented as a performance with interludes of drumming music. (With thanks to David Wheway)

Difficulty and sometimes failure should not be avoided. In successful schools operating cross-curricular approaches challenges are embraced. A positive atmosphere that accepts mistakes as a vital part of learning allows for more general engagement within a class. One school in Eastbourne planned and built a wooden causeway across the marshes from near its school site to an island where they kept sheep and water buffalo and are creating a reconstructed Bronze Age settlement (see case study 2, Chapter 3). There were many mistakes and difficulties along the way, but the authenticity, social learning, physical and sensory activity and strong purpose of the project kept them learning at high levels and *wanting* to add to their skills and understanding. Taught, book or computer-led approaches could not possibly compete with real experience to promote engagement. The head teacher reports:

> Within our Bronze Age habitat we worked alongside Eastbourne Museum to teach our students (8–11-year-olds) prehistoric crafts. Using fleeces from our flock of sheep the children spun and dyed wool. They dug clay from the marsh and made replica Bronze Age pots, firing them in an open fire. We have taught the children a range of traditional open fire cooking techniques and have even had them skinning rabbits and plucking pigeons. (Mike Fairclough)

Formative assessment is of course a vital ingredient in keeping the children safe in such contexts, but also in ensuring that their various products were authentic. There are many ways of managing formative assessment: the informal feedback of the teacher as he or she moves around the class offering help, posing questions and listening to observations; the supportive marking of class work; or the informal testing of certain factual knowledge in order to identify barriers to learning. Each approach, however, runs the risk of becoming a 'bolt-on' assessment, not truly integrated with the vital activity of the topic of study. The concept of the 'performance of understanding' (PoU) (Blythe, 1997) was devised to address this issue and create a structure within which planning teaching and assessment were integrated. David Perkins, Tina Blythe and their associates at Project Zero (Project Zero, website) have developed this

Table 10.2 Asking the right assessment questions

Assessing	Examples of key assessment questions
Self-understanding	In what ways has this person added to their understanding of their own character, likes and dislikes, talents, weaknesses, strengths and influences? What are their attitudes to their own work and learning? What are the next steps they could take?
Understanding others	In what ways has this individual added to their understanding of the feelings and strengths of others? In what ways do they demonstrate understanding of the minds of others? What social skills do they need to develop or nurture?
Working with others	In what ways does this person work and play with others? How do they use their knowledge of others (a) to influence (b) to empathize (c) to collaborate? What do they need to learn, celebrate or control?
Creativity	In what ways and in which areas does this individual show originality, the ability to link ideas or to make valuable new contributions? In what ways have they been able to make connections between the skills/ knowledge of one subject and those of another? How can these things be cherished, fostered and developed?
Community issues	To what degree is this individual aware of the dominant values of their community? What do they understand of the important issues for their community? How are these things shown? Where do they need to go from here?
Global issues	To what degree is this person aware of the major issues facing our world? In what ways are they aware of their role in addressing these issues in their everyday lives?
Disciplinary understandings in two or three subject disciplines	At what level is this individual's understanding of the skills, knowledge, attitudes and values of each of the subjects combined in this cross-curricular study? How have they built on past understandings? How have they shown their new understandings? What are the next steps in each subject?

approach through work with the 'satellite' elementary and high schools associated with Harvard University School of Education.

Performances of understanding

Children grow in understanding through their own presentations. Their presentations can also form a pleasant and efficient vehicle for peer or teacher assessment. The performance of understanding (PoU) as a form of formative assessment was mentioned briefly in Chapter 9. It is a curriculum opportunity for a child or a group of children to demonstrate the depth and degree of their learning by applying it in an authentic context. The 'performance' is not necessarily at the end of a unit and neither is it necessarily a dramatic or musical performance, but an opportunity publicly at the beginning, middle or end of a unit of work, to show learning in a wide variety of ways. A PoU may be:

- a collection
- a construction
- a dance
- a debate
- a demonstration
- a diagram
- a led discussion
- a map or plan
- a meal
- a mime
- a newspaper article
- a piece of music
- a thought shower
- a poem
- a poster
- a reading
- a recital
- a song
- a talk
- a walk or guided tour
- an annotated drawing
- an essay
- an exhibition
- an experiment
- an exposition
- a play or a film

or any combination of these and other ways of communicating understanding. The essence of the PoU is that the performers have not previously expressed their understanding of the topic in this way (see Illustration 10.1).

A PoU is a formative event – it presents current understanding but through presentations suggests its own improvement. The preparing and sharing of such presentations is potentially a key growth point in any medium-term scheme of work (see Chapter 11). Through applying and demonstrating their current level of understanding children can become more aware of the gaps in their own understanding. They are also more likely to receive the advice of their peers with whom they have shared the

Illustration 10.1   A performance of understanding. Children explain their responses to a 'health and happiness' workshop in Scotland (Courtesy of Scottish Children's Parliament)

challenges and problems. As groups and individuals grow in confidence about their learning towards the end of a unit of work they may plan a final PoU that will (still formatively) be assessed in closer detail against the subject targets for the unit.

A class in a performing arts school in Kent carried out cross-curricular learning related to a recent major earthquake. The theme was planned to cover six weeks (see Table 10.3). Using skills and learning the relevant knowledge in geography, they were introduced through maps, videos, newspaper reports, diagrams and photographs to the landscape, weather and economic conditions in the area. They were also given a direct teaching session on what causes earthquakes. They studied the normal daily lives and religion of a community living there through both RE and geographical perspectives. Their PSHE lesson with newspapers told them a great deal about conditions there directly after the earthquake and about different ways of reporting such news. A friend of the school who was born near the area of the earthquake spoke to the class about his life there and answered questions during another PSHE/Citizenship lesson. In another geography lesson, they considered in detail what conditions must be like in the community they studied and used an email link with a charity to get up-to-date information on the aid effort. They have learned about the cooking and culture of the earthquake area from a local cultural group and some parents.

Table 10.3 An earthquake: a six-week plan leading to a fund-raising event

Week 1 theme	Week 2 theme	Week 3 theme	Week 4 theme	Week 5 theme	Week 6 theme
Introduction With video/ newspapers Children's comments and questions	Physical geography Maps Diagrams	What happened to the villages? What life is like now for the survivors	What religion tells us about natural disasters/helping our neighbour	Caribbean culture: food, clothing, music, dance	Fund-raising week for the victims of the earthquake
Demonstrating subject understanding	*Demonstrating subject understanding*	*Demonstrating subject understanding*	*Demonstrating subject understanding*	*Demonstrating subject understanding*	*Performance of understanding*
Geog. cit. Asking geographical/ citizenship questions	**Geog.** Constructing maps Understanding diagrams and photographs	**Geog.** Making intelligent guesses based upon geographical understanding. Suggesting possible improvements and solutions	**RE** Asking spiritual questions Understanding the spiritual dimension **Cit.** Our role in disaster relief The role of aid agencies	**D/T** Cooking, designing a menu **Music** Recognizing pattern, pitch and applying knowledge to own compositions	**Geog.** PowerPoint presentations on geog of Haiti **RE** Replay on caring for hungry and homeless. **Cit.** Haiti – in the news; the facts D/T Caribbean menu, planned and served.

Since the school was based in an area of open countryside with large grounds, rural science and gardening formed a significant part of the curriculum. The children decided to use their work and talents to grow food for sale to friends and parents in order to raise money for their identified project connected with the disaster. This was to extend aspects of the theme and the associated learning through the next term.

The final taught week of this relevant and emotive theme consisted of children planning and mounting a charity collection for the victims of the natural disaster. The teacher in this final week acted as adviser, responding to the lead of children as they chose their presentations to parents. The planned charity event included elaborate visual and arts-based presentations on a village in the earthquake area. One group of four children researched maps, images, sounds, artefacts, photographs and information from aid agencies to produce their piece. Another prepared local food and drink, and presented and served it wearing appropriate clothes from the region. A group of six chose to perform a short play about helping the hungry and homeless. Three other children created a detailed and accurate backdrop of palm trees and other local vegetation from the coastal area that had suffered. Finally, a group of five children decided to write and duplicate a newspaper-style fact sheet for parents and guests to take home with them. This was extended in subsequent terms to bring news of the money-raising fruit and vegetable sales.

During the preparation week before the final day of performances, each group was asked a number of times to rehearse what they were going to do/say/show to the rest of the class, and the class was encouraged to offer advice or ask questions, which resulted in improvements. This process of refinement significantly raised the stakes and markedly improved standards through peer assessment. On the last day, each activity refocused attention on the main theme (and in the process generated a great deal of money for the cause) but throughout the week, teachers were able to use the various demonstrations of subject understanding to help them assess the level of learning.

These assessments were fully formative. They were integrated with day-to-day activity and intended to have a positive effect on future learning. The assessment involved the children, who knew what subject expectations they were being supported with. In the last week of the project, teachers were able to act less like instructors and more like coaches. In this role, they were able actively to point to possible improvements or ask formative questions during the mounting of exhibitions, painting of scenery or cooking of food. During and after the event, they were able to involve the children themselves in their own self-assessment.

Children's peer assessment questions

- What went well? Why do you think it went so well?
- What did you enjoy most? Why?
- Whose work do you think communicated best? Why?
- What did you like about [N's] presentation?
- What would you do to improve your presentation, if you had another chance?
- What still puzzles you about what [N] said/showed?
- Has the project as a whole left you with any questions?

Throughout this project, teachers had multiple opportunities to record the level of subject understanding displayed by individuals. Through effective questioning and careful observation, teachers noted children's responses to the suggestions of others, the kinds of questions children used, individual application within their own group and the level of subject understanding shown in rehearsals and performance. On average, one teacher assessed six children a day, and on some days subject coordinators were invited to make subject-specific assessments. The organizing teacher made a further 15 assessments during the final performances. The collected observations and records during this themed term honoured a host of individual achievements which coloured end-of-year reports. In the following term, children were in a strong position to build

Illustration 10.2   Peer assessment in action. Children pass focused and positive comments to other participating groups after a practical workshop (Courtesy of Scottish Children's Parliament)

upon past learning and had new strategies with which to acquire new skills and further knowledge in other subject areas.

Presentations and peer assessment

In learning through the arts, a cycle of activities known as the *Processes of the Arts* (Robinson, 2001; Robinson and Aronica, 2010) provides a useful model. The cycle of activities may start at any point, but includes activities generic to the arts, such as exploring, forming, presenting, evaluating and performing. The concept of *presenting* is considered quite distinct from performing and I believe this distinction may usefully be applied across the curriculum, well beyond the arts. Presenting in Robinson's model consists of taking time out of a creative process to show colleagues what has been formed, learned, understood *so far.* There is no pretence that this is a performance; it is 'work in progress' and has an important peer assessment function. When a group or individual has the chance to demonstrate subject understanding in a provisional setting, where everyone knows it is 'not finished yet', a real opportunity to 'raise the bar' presents itself (see Illustration 10.3).

In cross-curricular settings like that outlined above (and in Chapter 3), it is common for work to be done in collaborative groups engaged in related activities. Hopefully, the class ethos is one of mutual support, confidence and a positive attitude to mistakes; each group will understand

Illustration 10.3   Student teachers present their understanding of place for their peers to comment upon

the issues confronting the others. When groups present their work in progress for comment, feedback from others who have trodden a similar path quickly becomes personally engaging, relevant and formative in character. Children report that it is in these situations that they learn the most – their peers have become their teachers (Barnes and Shirley, 2007; Dismore et al., 2008). Perkins makes 'distributed cognition', that is, thinking shared across the group, the central theme of his views on learnable intelligence (Sternberg and Williams, 1998).

Table 10.4   A simple format for (individual or group) peer assessment

Assessment focus	Examples
Say two things you really liked about the presentation.	• I really liked the way you started that piece off with a very simple tune and then changed it in little ways each time we heard it. • I especially liked the way you told us how you thought about a castle servant's life.
Ask about two things which puzzle you.	• Why did you decide to paint on the frame as well? • What made you think of using water for power instead of air? • Did you think of using any other instruments? • Why did you finish in that way?
Offer one point of advice.	• Next time you present this, I think you should ... • Have you thought of ...? • Do you think you could ... ?

Self-assessment

Figures 10.1 and 10.2 show two haikus on the subject of barriers, which started with observations in the school playground. They were composed by 8-year-olds. How would you formatively assess them? What would you pick out as particularly good? What would you want to ask? Do you have any advice?

(Continued)

(Continued)

Joshua   Wednesday 20th
July 2005.

Soft Silky cobwebs
attached apon the great wall,
Silk - carpenter's lodge

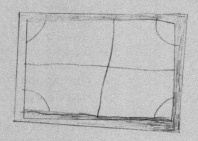

Figure 10.1   An 8-year-old responds to the tiny detail of his immediate environment

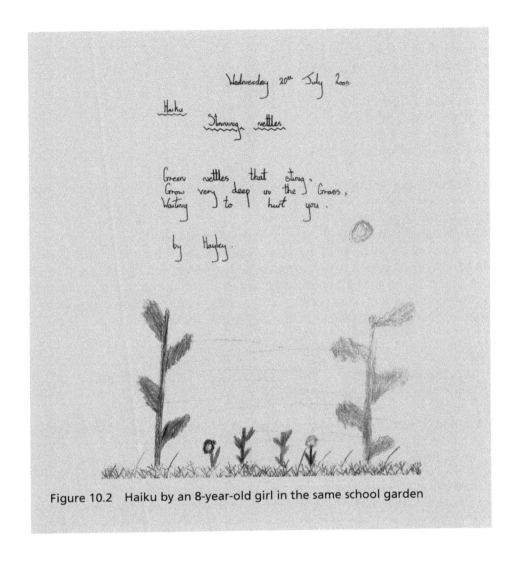

Figure 10.2   Haiku by an 8-year-old girl in the same school garden

The benefits of presentation do not end with peer appraisal. Presentation can be a non-threatening way of provoking self-criticism. In publicly presenting their understanding so far, the presenters are more likely to become aware of the gaps in their own understanding. Presenting can become a route towards deeper learning. This links back to Csikszentmihalyi's concept of flow, one of its universal characteristics being the 'rapid feedback' associated with a self wholly engaged in an activity. Ask individuals in a class involved in a successful cross-curricular activity and compare their attitude and engagement to typical descriptions of the flow experience:

- time seems different
- skills match the challenge given
- personal worries diminish
- lack of self-consciousness
- increased confidence
- at ease with 'mistakes'
- enjoyment of the activity for its own sake
- feeling 'lost' in the activity.

Cross-curricular learning can only generate flow within supportive and secure environments. It flourishes when curriculum challenges are carefully planned and individualized so as to put newly learned skills and knowledge into action. Full engagement happens when a theme or activity takes on some kind of *existential significance* for the child. Under these circumstances, cross-curricular activity itself may generate formative assessment of a highly personal and meaningful kind. Such reflexive self-assessment will also prepare the child's mind to receive supportive assessments and additional challenges from others.

Written reflections of a Year 6 child after a cross-curricular project in the school environmental area

I felt really calm in the environment area, although I have been there loads of times before I hadn't really paid so much attention to everything ... My favourite activities were the object focus and when we laid [*sic*] down and looked up at the sky through the eyes of our object. I felt really quiet as I studied my chosen object, and we all know that doesn't happen very often! It felt kind of nice and relaxed and peaceful, but the time went really quickly and I could have spent longer out here ... I feel that we are working so well together ...

Assessing engagement

Looking for the outward signs of flow is a good way of assessing the degree of engagement, and learning, in a child. Important assessment information can be missed if teachers fail to look at the faces and postures of their children at work (Barnes, 2005d). Teachers should be aware of and responsive to the non-verbal signs children give us. Ferre Laevers has been influential in formulating a usable five-point scale to measure the physical signs of such involvement, though as with all formal assessments, care should be taken to apply personal knowledge of the child before arriving at decisions. The Leuven Involvement Scale (LIS) (Laevers, 1994a) attempts to help teachers recognize children's degree of participation during a specific activity and a summary is shown in Table 10.5.

Illustration 10.4   The detail and care taken by this 5-year-old as he planned additions to his playground is an indication of high levels of engagement. Describing his choices, he reveals the level of his understanding of design/technology principles and his views about improving the quality of his environment

Table 10.5   Measure of a child's degree of participation

Level 1	No activity, the child is mentally absent and there is stereotypic repetition of elementary movements.
Level 2	Actions with many interruptions.
Level 3	Actions more concerted, but concentration seems lacking and motivation and pleasure are lacking.
Level 4	Moments of intense mental activity shown by times of concentration beyond the routine.
Level 5	Total involvement expressed by full concentration, signs of enjoyment and absorption. Any disturbance or interruption is experienced as frustrating.

Source: adapted from Laevers (1994a)

As with the LW-BS, teachers should be cautious with such scales. No apparent activity does not always mean no engagement and some children may *have* to interrupt their work frequently in order to keep involved. Linking this work with the research of Ekman (2004) and others into facial expression, teachers and others working with children quickly come to recognize the quizzical and intense facial expressions of engagement. Responding unconsciously to such facial and bodily nuances is probably part of our biological inheritance, but bringing that understanding into consciousness and attempting to generate particular expressions of engagement or enjoyment could significantly add to the effectiveness of teaching.

Summary

Whilst summative assessment may be helpful at the end of a key stage formative assessment, using it as part and parcel of daily learning activities makes it a more effective learning tool. Assessment should be a social and collaborative process involving children as well as adults, and should be linked to the wider aims and values of the school as well as subject learning. Assessments can be performed more usefully and accurately through giving children opportunities to apply new knowledge to real situations. The concept of 'performances of understanding' is a helpful model of meaningful assessment for both child and teacher.

Illustration 10.5   Look for the signs of enjoyment and absorption

Key questions for discussion

- How can we make assessment meaningful and a useful learning tool?
- How can we make marking more formative?
- Should we always share learning objectives?
- How can we promote distributed cognition as part of the daily experience of children in school?
- What should be the balance of flow experiences and more mundane activities in class?
- Should subject skills and knowledge be assessed in a different way from their cross-curricular application?

Further reading

Clark, S. (2008) *Active Learning through Formative Assessment.* London: Hodder.

Glazzard, J., Chadwick, D., Webster, A. and Percival, J. (2010) *Assessment for Learning in the Early Years Foundation Stage.* London: Sage.

Laevers, F. (1994) *Defining and Assessing Quality in Early Childhood Education.* Leuven: Leuven University Press.

Wiliam, D. (2011) *Embedded Formative Assessment.* Bloomington, IN: Solution Tree.

CHAPTER 11

HOW SHOULD WE PLAN FOR CROSS-CURRICULAR ACTIVITY?

Chapter aims

This chapter focuses on planning large and small cross-curricular projects. It begins by re-asserting the importance of values conversations, inclusion, flexibility, opportunities to develop creativity and good teacher knowledge. Using the evidence of research and experience the chapter then offers planning advice and examples. By the end of this chapter you will have new thoughts about:

- planning before the paperwork
- planning for democracy in school
- planning for inclusion and participation
- planning for creativity
- planning for safe and stimulating places
- planning subject knowledge and skills
- planning for progression
- planning powerful, personal learning experiences
- long-, medium- and short-term planning
- balancing experience, skills and knowledge.

Planning before the paperwork

Planning is essential if teaching is to result in learning. Planning cross-curricular activity requires paperwork, just as any other curriculum planning, but arguably its most important features come before anything is written. Thoughtful conversations should come first. We have seen (Chapter 4) how learning is a social activity and so teaching should be too. Dialogue between all involved in teaching needs time, structure and direction, and should first be used to establish the coherent and consistent values discussed in Chapter 8. The values conversation is probably the most important conversation to hold before formal planning starts. Values discussions should be a regular and dynamic part of school life and include all involved. Values conversations will and *should* arrive at different conclusions in different schools. Each school community has different priorities and those priorities will change over time. Whilst no single set of values is applicable to all schools and communities, there may be significant overlaps as the on-going political debate about 'British values' suggests. The values underpinning this book suggest that planning should be founded on:

- democratic structures, including regular attention to children's views
- inclusion and participation
- recognizing, allowing and nurturing creativity
- flexibility to allow for children to take the lead at times
- subject-based knowledge and skills
- a sense of progression in learning
- meaningful and shared experiences
- strong and positive relations with the community and locality
- safe and stimulating spaces for learning, including outdoors.

Each item above rests on a belief, and needs thinking and talking about. Other underpinning values will arise from dialogue. Curriculum conversations should be thoughtful too, considering how the application of values will affect individuals young and old and ensuring the proper inclusion of all stakeholders. Each decision has a planning implication. Finally, and still before the paperwork, thoughts about planning must address the balance between generating motivation and fulfilling the demands of national requirements. This chapter shows how National Curriculum expectations can be used to construct meaningful, lively and even satisfying planning. It emphasizes the planning of powerful shared experiences that generate both motivation and creativity, and supports its conclusions with reference to current research and practice.

Planning for school democracy

The United Nations Convention on the Rights of the Child (UNCRC) (UNICEF, 1989, website) challenged traditional hierarchies in schools.

Children's voices should be heard. They should be consulted on how best they learn, allowed to play, participate in arts and culture, and propose relevant changes wherever they are in the world and in whatever kind of school (see Chapter 2 and Barnes in Clift and Camic, 2015). This is an ideal of course and currently far from the truth in many places. The UK, as one of the first signatories of the UNCRC, could be argued to have a moral obligation to be among the first to ensure that curriculum planning acknowledges children's right to make choices and for their social and psychological well-being to be at the top of the priority list.

Democracy does not apply to children only. Staff and other adults in school should also feel their voice is heard and impacts on policy and practice. Staff development policies are important in this context. Planning for democracy in a staffroom should include time for true collaborations, honest values discussions, the voicing of the hopes and insights of individuals and the sharing of strengths and affirmations.

A curriculum for democracy might well use Citizenship and PSHE studies to discuss and develop ideas like fairness, equality, tolerance, respect and free speech central to democracy. Citizenship is a cross-curricular concept drawing from History, RE, PSHE, philosophy and Geography but also affecting actions in the domains of Science, PE, Mathematics, English, Design/Technology and the Arts. Democracy itself can therefore be seen as a single transferable subject itself with cross-curricular applications. Establishing a democratic ethos must involve planning opportunities to examine tolerance and respect as well as responsibilities and rights. Such concepts colour decisions about the nature of the curriculum – is it rigid or flexible, does it allow for other views to be represented? The subject content of Geography, History, PE, Science or Languages can be used to place democracy in an authentic context. A fundamental belief that the life of each individual is of equal importance (Booth and Ainscow, 2011) could be argued to underpin the ideal of democracy and is perhaps best shown in schools by their attitude to inclusion.

Planning for inclusion and participation

Cross-curricular approaches provide inclusive and participatory learning opportunities. Participation needs to be planned, however, and the principles of inclusion must be fully discussed, understood and agreed upon. Booth and Ainscow (2011) provide one example of a principled resource to support schools in developing this conversation, but cross-curricular pedagogies themselves provide a context to express and extend pivotal values and aims.

Whether teaching and learning use hierarchical, thematic, multi-disciplinary, inter-disciplinary or opportunistic approaches, I have suggested that the prime motivators for school learning should be shared, relevant, meaningful experiences. Shared experience is by definition inclusive; meaningful and relevant experience motivates participation, but such experiences need careful planning. If experiences are truly shared and genuinely meaningful, then they are likely to reach all children at a level appropriate for them.

There is no need for a 'special educational needs' category. In a broad and balanced curriculum where each subject has parity of prestige, children should be encouraged to work from their strengths. Indeed one of the key findings of the *Signature Pedagogies* project (Thomson et al., 2012) was that the successful creatives (not usually teachers) working for Creative Partnerships adopted highly inclusive methods, expecting high standards from all and not providing differentiated work. In the first case study in Chapter 3, the singer/songwriter supported one child with difficulties in speaking and other aspects of communication. She used rhythmic song to provoke a dancing response in the child and used the child's recognition of repeated musical structure to allow her to lead her mother and the rest of the 3-year-olds in responding to her lullaby. She had little difficulty in communicating in this practical and musical setting and her teacher was able to build on this to develop her speaking.

Teachers plan for inclusion by knowing each child's strengths. They predict or discover the most appropriate entry point for learning for each child in their care. The inclusion statements of the national curricula of each country of the UK make it abundantly clear that progressive learning of skills and knowledge in all subjects is the birthright of every child. Despite changes in policy, 'broad and balanced' and inclusive applies to the school curriculum, not just the National Curriculum. This means that language, ethnicity, lifestyle, immigration status, intellectual, income or physical ability should make no difference to a child's opportunity to experience the whole curriculum. It also means that to engage all learners, all should experience a curriculum that provides children with creative and imaginative opportunities across the curriculum (Ofsted, 2012, website).

For some, learning will be more easily provoked and extended by the use of modified equipment, extra staffing or specific practical aids, but an experience-led curriculum may be the best way of involving all children, regardless of barriers to their learning. Narrowing the curriculum to one dominated by tests in the core subjects will inevitably limit the potential of large percentages of children. Ofsted recognizes this challenge and asks schools to ensure that 'preparation for national tests and examinations is appropriate' and that it does not 'limit the range of the curriculum or pupils' opportunities for creativity in English' (2012: 7).

Thankfully, concepts of literacy and numeracy constantly widen. 'Literacy' includes non-verbal, visual, tactile and aural means of understanding the world. Indeed, the abolition of the Key Stage 2 (11-year-old) tests in writing mean that teacher assessment can now be made on a rage of writing across the whole of Year 6. Numeracy has for many become an opportunity for meaningful and progressive play and exploration with numbers, measurements and shapes. The wordless, sensory and practical aspects of any subjects introduced to make sense of a cross-curricular experience are often noted as a transformative entry point to wider learning and social communication for those who find verbal or written expression difficult (see Roberts, 2006, for example).

Planning to recognize, allow and nurture creativity

The fact that creativity can be developed is a continuing theme in this book. Chapter 7 discussed definitions and implications of creative pedagogy, but creativity needs thoughtful planning for. Creativity does not simply happen when planned. Creativity thrives on the unexpected and is founded upon human ability to be imaginative and original, but sensitive planning can *promote* creativity by:

- teaching creatively
- teaching for creativity
- creative thinking and learning.

Teaching creatively

Every teacher needs to understand that they are a creative being. The individual's unique inheritance, history, social milieu, personal environment and neural connections ensure that originality and imagination are possible in all. What varies is firstly our ability to recognize our inherent creative strengths, our motivation to use them and the formal structures we work within. When teachers are asked to identify creative colleagues, the tendency is to look to the artistic or rather theatrical member of staff. Some teachers may deny any sense that they are creative. However, research (Cremin et al., 2009) has shown that working alongside non-teacher creative practitioners from any field – town planners, website designers, film-makers, landscape gardeners, architects, research scientists, photographers, lighting designers, electronic engineers, as well as musicians, sculptors and artists – has awoken dormant creative skills in teachers. Working alongside 'creative outsiders' some teachers in the above research recognized their own creativity for the fist time. The first planning suggestion is therefore to plan inputs from other experts from the community beyond the classroom.

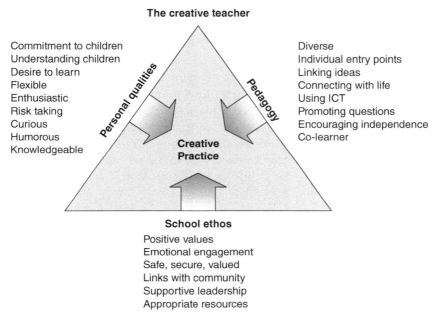

Figure 11.1   The three dimensions of creative teaching, based on literature review

(Source: Cremin et al., 2009; copyright Cremin, Barnes and Scoffham, 2009)

Conversation helps in developing creativity too. Two teachers discussing how to approach a particular topic or shared experience will inevitably bring different mindsets to bear on the same problem. Such differences open the door to creative teaching. The synthesis of ideas, the recognition that other solutions exist, the unexpected viewpoint or different starting point can each generate new ideas for presentation/support or assessment. Plan, therefore, with someone else.

Creative teaching requires a blend of personal and institutional characteristics. Managerial decisions, such as planning-in flexibility, are important but so too are personal decisions. Preferences in and within subjects, newly learned skills and strengths and the perceived 'character' of the class are all taken into account by the creative teacher. Literature review (Cremin et al., 2009) suggested that a range of personal characteristics such as curiosity, flexibility, enthusiasm, humour and a thirst for knowledge are usually displayed in creative teaching. A particular set of pedagogical skills is also frequently evident: these include liking children and knowing the entry points for learning in each individual, using diverse approaches, a tendency to make links, adopting a questioning stance and encouraging questioning, independence and responsibility (see Figure 11.1). Plan, therefore, opportunities for humour and curiosity, and leave room for surprises.

Research in eight primary and secondary classrooms showed that even if all creative characteristics were in place, creative teaching was not sustainable unless practised within wider ethos of support and encouragement. Such an ethos cannot usually be generated by lone teachers, but depends upon a supportive management team and community. Rather than three equal dimensions of creative teaching, we suggest that there may be a hierarchy – the ethos permitting the expression of personal qualities and a pedagogy of creativity (see Figure 11.2). One cannot plan to have a senior management team sympathetic to creativity, but it may be a feature to look for when choosing a workplace!

Teaching for creativity

Unlocking the innate creativity in every teacher and pupil is a suitable aim of education. If we agree with this, our planning and teaching should

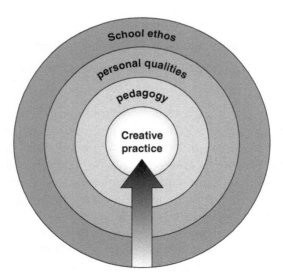

Figure 11.2   A revised model of the dimensions of creative teaching

(Source: Cremin et al., 2009; copyright Cremin, Barnes and Scoffham, 2009)

make it possible. Teaching for creativity means teaching so that confidence, connections, speculation, imagination, originality, questioning and safe risk-taking are encouraged and part of the day-to-day experience of the child. Early years practice has for many years successfully developed a pedagogy that depends upon such characteristics in the context of play and exploration. The statutory framework for the Early Years Foundation Stage (EYFS) was seen as cross-curricular from its inception in 1999 and this emphasis has been reaffirmed by recent review (DfE, 2011, website; DfE, 2012). The language of EYFS documents avoids reference to separated subjects and speaks instead of 'areas of learning'. The promotion of a strong self-image and high self-esteem are specifically mentioned as aims for the curriculum. The EYFS framework accepts that real, relevant and personally engaging experience interpreted through several areas of learning is most likely to promote both confidence and creativity. Political emphasis on 'school readiness' and the idea that nurseries should send children out 'properly prepared for school' (DfE, 2014a, website) cuts across the original aims of the framework and play, exploration and experience are subsequently under threat of being downgraded.

Practitioners and researchers have for centuries recognized that play stimulates learning in 3–5-year-olds (Rogers, 2010). Play is usually creative and clearly motivates and sustains older children and adults. Speculative, imaginative, even playful attitudes are equally commonplace at the cutting edge of university research in every subject/discipline. If creativity enlivens both ends of the learning continuum, perhaps it is time that the 5–14-year-olds in the middle experienced teaching styles that promote more unexpected, playful, original thinking and connection-making across the curriculum. We should plan therefore for playful opportunities in our units of work.

Creative thinking and learning

We cannot make children think or learn creatively. As teachers, however, we can provide the conditions where both are more likely. Although creativity is unpredictable and does not always result from plans, a creative atmosphere in a classroom can be planned and resourced. A creativity-friendly classroom includes decisions on everything from the timetable and type, arrangement and flexibility of furniture, to classroom light levels, temperature and the smile on the teacher's face.

Creativity-friendly classrooms are flexible. One day the classroom may be a lecture theatre, the next a theatre. One week children might arrive to find it turned to a jungle, library or spaceship. Equipment too may be a major provocation towards creativity. Objects, machines, computers, images and tools can become part of our distributed intelligence – the subject of drawing, interrogation, imagination or comparison. The language and stance of the teacher, the morning greeting and the other daily rituals can all promote creativity and creative thinking, but each source is enhanced by teacher knowledge and the development of new knowledge in children. When learning in two or three subjects is used to interpret an experience, topic, problem or question, overlaps between them are inevitable. We have seen how creative advances happen at the boundaries between subjects or cultures and at a classroom level well-planned cross-curricular approaches have a high chance of generating creative ideas and exchanges too.

Planning safe and stimulating spaces for learning

All learning is influenced by the spaces where it happens. The spaces where children learn therefore need careful attention. This, for example, has been a preoccupation of those who plan learning spaces for the children of Reggio Emilia in northern Italy. In Reggio pre-schools great attention and considerable resources are devoted to the fine detail of the children's environment. The fabrics, the design and materials of coat hooks, the colour of furniture, the lighting, the placing of services such as the school kitchen, or the views from windows are all carefully considered. There is a distinct child-centredness to every decision, immediately evident in the child-friendly levels of window sills, door handles and taps, as well as the powerful use of light, colour, fabrics and soft edges.

Jerome Bruner has worked with Reggio's pre-schools and isolated three essentials for planning pre-school learning spaces. These principles could be profitably applied throughout education. For Bruner, a learning space must be:

- *mine, thine, and ours* (it 'needs to provide places for each individual who occupies it ... but must be communal as well')
- *in and of the broader community* (it should be in the physical community and its activities should arise from the community)
- *a learning community* ('a place to learn together about the real world, and about possible worlds of imagination ... where the young discover the uses of mind, of imagination, of materials, and learn the power of doing these things together'). (Bruner, 2003: 137)

The exquisite learning outcomes of such attention to detail are well known and provide ample evidence of the ease of generating high levels of achievement in child-centred conditions (see Reggio Emilia, website).

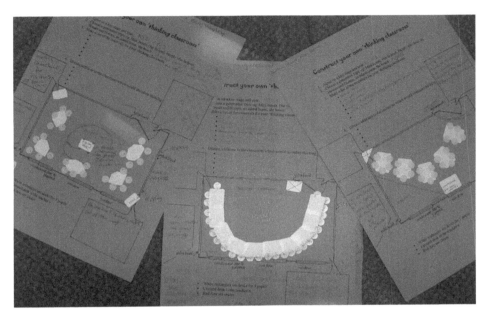

Illustration 11.1   Student teachers' plans for a 'thinking classroom'

In Reggio, generous local funding and the economic profits of fame have worked together to construct exciting places and learning tools for the children. Reggio Emilia 'principles', however, are applicable in any setting. Here are just a few 'Reggio principles':

- *put the child at the heart of the decision-making process*
- *give the child a real problem to solve*
- *teach children the skills they need to solve the problem*
- *let adults and children work together.*

The implications of such principles were explored in an English context by Shirley Brice Heath in a community school in Hythe, Kent. Nursery, Reception, Year 1 and Year 2 children worked on a project to redesign and oversee the building of a new reception area for their school. The 3–7-year-olds regularly met architects, an artist and interior designers to plan and follow through plans for a truly child-centred entrance and route-way through their school (Brice Heath and Wolf, 2004). Through planning and orientation meetings, questionnaires and a major exhibition of their plans and ideas, the children and architects arrived at a brief for the rebuilding and redesign of large areas of the school. The official brief to the architects and designers was to explore 'how good design can improve the quality of life in schools by listening to the voices of the consumers. It inspires pupils by putting them in the driving seat, giving them control and responsibility as clients' (Brice Heath and Wolf, 2004: 9). But the children's brief to the architects was in the form of a mighty exhibition. Designer Ben Kelly, who worked with the children, recounted:

> We posed questions to them and their response was this exhibition; that's how they overcame the practical problems of communication. They communicated in the way that young children do best, by chucking a load of stuff out from within themselves; drawings, paintings, models, collages, written stuff, tons and tons of it – all over the walls! Their brief/exhibition was incredible. It had such vigour, life and enthusiasm. It really was stimulating. It was the key that unlocked the process. (Brice Heath and Wolf, 2004: 14)

Children's decisions about space for learning and celebrating their learning were taken seriously by adults and the results were far in excess of expectations. Profound discussions about morality, security, culture, beauty, life and death were common in this context. Children decided, for example, that they did not want their reception area to be boring, 'just about sitting', they wanted to move people around and they wanted to showcase the art they were so proud of. They planned a display system and 'Barbie pink' carpeted route-way around their displayed work that was in many ways to be the heart of the school. Interestingly, adults took on the playfulness of children in their design and the children took on some aspects of the seriousness of adults. The deep implications of these genuine and meaningful interactions between adults and children may be summarized in a single comment from Jack: 'We learned to make things. My favourite was the bucket lights (yellow ceiling lights made to look like sand castle buckets from the nearby beach) – they looked cool. When I walk into this reception area after it's built, I think I'll feel famous' (Brice Heath and Wolf, 2004: 19). Such a sense of specialness, accomplishment and meaning which results from involvement in creative acts, could be argued to be every child's birthright.

The Hythe project was clearly cross-curricular. Children were involved in this project for a whole year before the building was complete. They richly developed their language at both its most practical and most symbolic levels.

Illustration 11.2   Children proudly introduce their display in the entrance they designed with architects (Courtesy of Creative Partnerships, Kent)

Illustration 11.3   Infants school entrance designed with 'big art' and buckets as light shades by the 5–7-year-old pupils (Courtesy of Creative Partnerships Kent)

Most curricula can be flexible enough to support cross-curricular planning and creative thinking. A lively and relevant curriculum must also be flexible, constantly revised, sensitively tuned to contemporary lives and communities.

Many children say they find outdoor learning more enjoyable and memorable. Curriculum advice has reflected this preference (for example, Austin, 2007; DfES, 2006b, website; Hopwood-Stephens, 2013). Forest Schools (Knight, 2013), which have developed all over Europe, offer stimulating, safe, flexible spaces and well-trained leaders for play-based learning out of doors, for all age groups. Increasing numbers of schools use these sites and practitioners in planning their curriculum. Schools often repeat their visits to the woodland or beach sites a number of times in a term to observe seasonal changes, consolidate community links and ensure a progression of learning in a wide range of subjects. Activities on site include: construction, way-finding, plant and animal identification/classification, traditional crafts, estimation, physical, personal and group challenges. The learning arising from such activities is inevitably cross-curricular. Experiences in a Forest School are held together by the overarching values of sustainability and care for the environment and a belief in child-led, exploratory, active learning. But effective learning depends on new knowledge too.

Illustration 11.4   Year 8 children using physical responses to a Haiku to make links between creative writing and movement

Planning to teach subject-based knowledge and skills

Creative teachers have considerable subject knowledge (Cremin et al., 2009). There is no escape from the conclusion that a good teacher *knows* stuff, is enthusiastic to learn more and is good at communicating knowledge and enthusiasm. *Subject knowledge is not an optional extra in cross-curricular teaching and learning – without a clear understanding of subject progression, neither appropriate challenge nor appropriate skill development are possible.* In early years, primary or secondary contexts, the need for subject expertise in cross-curricular learning reaffirms the importance of teachers talking to each other and planning together.

Knowledge and skills can be taught before, during or after a powerful motivating experience. There is, of course, also a time for simple observation and less teaching – in the early years children often learn most effectively when there is *less* adult intervention (Goouch, 2010; Rogoff, 2003). The HEARTS project on the other hand (see Case study in Chapter 7) found that children, highly motivated by their explorations on a beach, *wanted* to learn new skills and extra facts to enhance their presentations when they returned to school. Where their teachers only observed, or accepted contributions without raising the level of challenge, little new subject learning occurred.

A school in Eastbourne taught a wide range of new historical, geographical and design/technology skills related to Bronze Age settlements *before* actually making an exciting visit to a real Bronze Age site via their fleet of coracles. The teaching ensured that children understood what they experienced at a deeper level and this was shown in questioning, recording and follow-up activities during and after the visit. In the term after the visit the class returned to memories of their powerful experience and decided to build a real wooden causeway like the one their Bronze Age forbears had built 3000 years ago. After making detailed drawings and on-the-spot instruction, they subsequently built a full-sized Bronze Age house based upon archaeological evidence of dimensions, materials and styles.

The use of outside, (usually non-teacher) experts to boost subject knowledge and skills and the development of community links is championed in all approaches to education. Expert partners do not take on teacherly responsibilities or compromise their skills but add significantly to the teacher's enjoyment and their fund of knowledge. Research (for example Brice Heath and Wolf, 2005; Roberts, 2006; Thomson et al., 2012) has found that creative, knowledgeable outsiders with the support of freshly motivated teachers can persuade children to attempt greater challenges and achieve higher standards and improve the quality and range of skills.

Planning for progression

Progression in learning comes from attention to suitable challenges for children. Csikszentmihalyi showed that if we wish children to enter the flow state, teachers need either to raise the challenge for children who are bored, or raise the level of skills for those who are anxious about learning.

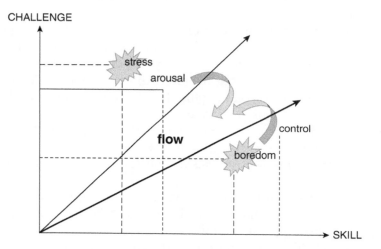

Figure 11.3 The impact of differing levels of skill and challenge (Source: adapted from Csikszentmihalyi, 2004, website)

Subject levels have been removed from the English National Curriculum. Subject specialist teachers, however, should be able to identify progressions of skills and knowledge and support colleagues in planning. Progression does not simply involve the learning of new facts and skills – growth should be evident in attitudes and the ability of pupils to apply new learning. Planning the successful development of learning starts with thinking about *involvement*, moves on to considering how to sustain *engagement* and then, using individually crafted challenges, decides on how to help the learner feel a sense of *progress*. Finally, it is the role of a teacher to help each individual recognize the *achievement* of their goals. The progression from involvement to achievement is one that needs as much planning time and conversation as the details of knowledge and skills.

Case study

Children in a nursery class had seen a hedgehog in their garden. The teacher involved everyone in looking carefully as the hedgehog moved towards the hedge, but she wanted the children to have an opportunity to take something lasting from the experience. The teacher decided on leading the children to make a clay model of the hedgehog. Engagement was ensured by giving the children the experience of feeling the cold damp clay in their hands and shaping it into an ovoid, and it was deepened by the suggestion that they stuck multiple matchsticks into the clay to make the spines. Children moved from engagement to a sense of progression as they noticed their featureless ovoids looking more and more like hedgehogs. Finally, the children felt a real sense of achievement as they presented the carers with their finished models.

Planning powerful, personal experiences for your class

We have already seen how strong, emotionally engaging experiences are often a catalyst for effective learning. Choices of topic, of experience, must *feel* meaningful to learners before they agree to enter into a learning contract with the teacher. Experienced teachers are used to this kind of negotiation. I call the motivating and engaging events that generate learning *powerful, personal experiences* and I gathered the following set of short examples during a single week of lesson observations:

- A teacher in east Kent made *longshore drift* relevant to her Year 8 Geography fieldwork class, by getting part of the class to dance the zigzag movement of the pebbles on the beach as she described their movement.
- A class teacher in Rotherham used his class's ringside seat at the demolition of the old school building as an excuse to bring elder members of the community into the new school building to be interviewed.
- A Year 3 teacher made the Science theme of transparency and opacity relevant by asking groups of children to make cool sunglasses for the class teddy bear.
- A teacher in Whitby significantly improved the creative writing of all her pupils by asking them to include their detailed observations of her precise movements as she wandered furtively between the ruins of an old monastery the day before.

- Year 6 imaginative writing was weak. Their class teacher gave each child 7 minutes to wander separately around the school and write random words on an A4 sheet folded into 16 rectangles. On return to class the words were then torn out and each child had to reassemble them into a meaningful sentence by adding or subtracting 8 words.

The learning motivated by such activities was not simply a product of good teaching, it relied on detailed planning of the personal/emotional setting of learning. Relevance was created by starting from a child's view, giving choices and sustained by an emotional and intellectual content that seemed meaningful. In each example the teacher structured the learning experience by making links from the child's world to the school learning required by the curriculum.

The Foundation Stage curriculum – a model of cross-curricular planning

The Statutory Framework for the Early Years Foundation Stage expects teachers and other adults to plan for real experiences from which children learn. Essentially, such learning experiences should feel like play. Planning for generative play is a key and wholly natural way for all children to learn (Rogers, 2010). To make learning likely, however, adults need to consider structures to plan within. In teams, teachers of preschool and Reception class children should consider how to:

1. provide the physical and emotional security that allows for safe risk-taking and encourages a positive view of mistakes
2. introduce the element of challenge into the planned play activity
3. support the play without intervening too much
4. extend the activity and the learning
5. ensure that spontaneous play is likely
6. add to the child's language world (see Illustration 11.5).

The most effective spaces and situations for challenging and generative play are often outside the classroom. The kindergartens of Germany, Switzerland and Scandinavia, Forest Schools, Beach Schools and the playgrounds of the Reggio Emilia pre-schools, each use the semi-natural world of woodland, fields, nature trails and parks as major resources. Rain or shine, within these outdoor environments, children may be asked

Illustration 11.5   Six-year-olds effectively linking art, language and science by working with an artist on careful looking and drawing (Courtesy of Future Creative, Kent)

to find their way, travel, imagine, collect, classify, build, record or express themselves within wider themes such as:

- Getting bigger
- Going on a bear hunt
- Life around us
- People who help us
- Shelters
- Journeys
- Feeling happy; feeling sad
- Finding the way home.

Within the classroom, the world of the imagination may take children much further away. Questions can extend the thinking, socialization and motor skills of every child. With its 3–7-year-olds Reggio Emilia has used questions like:

- What do angels look like?
- What do I look like when I'm peaceful?
- How do we think the internet works?
- How do television pictures get to us?
- What would the world look like if I was a bird/germ/giant/ant?

Getting down to the paperwork

The thinking, talking, deciding, reflecting and space preparation having been done, the paperwork aspects of planning should be more straightforward. Schools must have long-term plans to address particular issues identified in school self-reviews, inspections or development plans. They are likely to have medium-term plans covering a six-week unit and each teacher will have a series of daily lesson plans, often called short-term plans.

Long-term planning

Long-term planning must take account of:

1. National/local curriculum subjects – designed to help children understand their world *now*.
2. Cross-curricular or other approaches the school has chosen for its own contribution to curriculum.
3. Teachers' own or others' development and research.

National Curriculum subjects

Each country of the UK has differing groupings of subjects, as indicated in Chapter 2. Chapter 3 showed how some schools have used time in cross-curricular contexts. The timing allocations between subjects are not mandatory and core subjects may, with thorough planning, be incorporated into cross-curricular study. As non-fee-paying independent schools begin to outnumber local authority schools and become more autonomous, no doubt many inventive curricula will emerge. An engaging curriculum for all requires a balance between 'academic' and practical, foundation and core, traditional and modern subjects. If we aim to take account of individual differences in learning, offer a broad palette of subject starting points and help each child become a self-regulated learner, then thematic, technology-supported, real-world projects are the way forward.

Cross-curricular approaches

We have used the term cross-curricular learning to cover thematic, project-based and real-world learning of all kinds. Regardless of the differing priorities of United Kingdom countries, skills that apply across the curriculum are common to all administrations. These should be planned for and include skills identified in the English National Curriculum of 1999:

- Communication.
- Application of number.
- Information and communications technology (ICT).
- Working with others.
- Improving own learning and performance.
- Problem solving.

Communication

English is a truly cross-curricular subject. Reading, writing, speaking and listening should be used in meaningful and sometimes extended contexts across all school experience. In this sense English is the most cross-curricular of all subjects and is central to all topic or thematic work. Other powerful forms of communication exist however. Children (and adults) communicate effectively through pretend play, pictures and symbols, through music, numbers, dance and mime, and in facial expressions and body language. Schools should honour alternative modes of communication, including signing, by offering a wide range of methods through which children can present their learning. Understanding in PE might be better communicated in movement or a game, geographical understanding might be clarified by a plan, annotated GPS map, table, graph, drawing or journey. Historical learning could be expressed in an exhibition, a role play or dance; new musical knowledge may more appropriately be shown in an improvisation, composition or digital recording.

Application of number

Number is another language through which children can understand a more general curriculum theme. The school itself can become the subject of a cross-curricular project. One school in South Australia has numbers, measurements, distances and number questions printed all over its architectural surfaces. Topics centred on Design/Technology, Art and PE might practically apply concepts of weight, angles, measurement, symmetry and balance. In Geography or History projects, distance, graphs, statistics, scale and time are key to understanding the wider world. A theme illuminated by the perspectives of Music, RE, Languages, English or Science may plan for numerical perspectives to help children understand sonic, spiritual, linguistic and natural patterns around them. Again, in contexts like these Mathematics becomes cross-curricular subject transferable to any learning topic.

Information and communications technology (ICT)

The world of children is dominated by new technologies. Drone, Raspberry Pi, social networking, 3D photocopiers, digital and internet-based technologies are understood rapidly by young people, who can often take the lead in devising inventive uses for them. The challenge to teachers is not simply to use ICT, but to ensure it supports the progressive development of subject skills, knowledge and understanding. For example, a Year 1 class might use their mobile phones to record still and moving images of significant aspects of their locality and then classify them into four categories: 'natural life', 'our historic environment', 'working in our village' and 'what's changing?' These images can now be easily shared with the rest of the class via interactive wall, floor or desk projections. School buildings and furnishings can be redesigned using the range of designing software and built using laser and other technologies.

Working with others

School is the only place where most children regularly relate to a range of age mates. In many societies, however, children are not restricted to *only* those of their age. Mixed age groups may seem a more natural setting in which to engage and challenge children. Group work on real-life challenges provides opportunities to build new relationships and develop emotional literacy, especially if older children are leading the learning of those a little younger than themselves. Empathy, the capacity to relate, turn-taking, leadership or 'followership', and coping with disagreements and disappointments, are all part of the experience of working on combined projects. In terms of planning, choose problems that require group investigations, games, murals, model-building, the construction of classroom or other environments, the design of posters, machines or furniture, background music for plays, animations, musical improvisations and compositions for public performances (see Illustration 11.5).

Improving own learning and performance

When children focus on their own learning, great things happen. We have seen (Chapter 6) how metacognition helps consolidate and grow learning. Five- and six-year-old children in a Cognitive Acceleration study (Shayer and Adey, 2002) were asked questions that provoked thinking at a level not usually associated with their age. In a practical science session on materials, teachers asked questions such as:

- How do you think you learn best?
- What could I do to help you learn more/better/more deeply?
- What do you think we are going to have to think about?
- What could you do if you have problems?
- How do you know that?
- What might make this easier?

Plan frequent opportunities for children to ask and answer such questions – and it is the duty of teachers to respond to the answers to such vital questions and requests.

Research in teaching and learning

Increasingly, teachers are encouraged to formalize the analysis and data collection they do as a normal part of their work (Alexander, 2010). Children too can be expert researchers into what makes for effective learning. Otherwise routine observations, records and reflections of teachers can easily become research. The development of teachers as action researchers is particularly relevant to curriculum planning (Wilson et al., 2010). Throughout this book, the research of neuroscientists, psychologists, sociologists or educationalists has been cited to support the suggestion that cross-curricular activities are appropriate, motivating and educationally beneficial to children. Summarized, the research already cited in this book suggests that teachers can plan to:

1. Create a positive, secure and comfortable atmosphere.
2. Ensure a range of practical, creative and analytical activities for each child.
3. Have clear goals, challenges and individualized targets pitched a little above current ability.
4. Use a manageable number of relevant subjects to throw light on the topic.
5. Build emotionally significant links to the life of each child, engaging all the senses and using tools and objects to support and promote thinking.

(Continued)

(Continued)

6. Involve developmentally appropriate progression in skills, knowledge and understanding.
7. Work within structures and a wider framework that includes concepts, subject skills, knowledge and attitudes.
8. Emphasize individual and cooperative thinking and learning throughout.
9. Provide supportive assessment procedures that build security and include time and tools for reflection.
10. Offer a wide range of opportunities to discover engagement, enjoyment and other positive emotions.

Education research also suggests that the best schools aim at personalized learning and effectively address emotional health and well-being for all. These schools develop philosophies that value and aim to develop resilience, problem solving, emotional intelligence, differences and cooperation between individuals and groups (DfES, 2003b; Ofsted, 2009a, 2009b). So the philosophy and values of the school should be clear before they are applied to the big blocks of curriculum. Long-term planning asks questions like:

What is the wider context of this theme/issue/skill?

Why is this theme/issue/skill important for the lives of the children?

How can we deepen the thinking and experience of children through this theme/issue/skill?

Medium-term planning

In applying the principles suggested elsewhere in this book, it is clear that planning cross-curricular modules will involve decisions on:

- *limiting* subjects
- planning powerful personal experiences
- maintaining a balance between freedom and structure.

Limiting subjects

It is possible to bend any subject to fit a chosen theme, but this can be confusing and counterproductive. Limiting the subjects to two or three

Illustration 11.6   A team of two Year 7 children discuss their Design and Technology solution with a creative practitioner (Courtesy of Future Creative)

has been discussed in previous chapters, but in medium-term planning, specific detail of the programme of study and specific learning targets for each subject should be included.

The naming of a subject in a cross-curricular module is not enough. The specific contribution of that subject and the progression of skills and knowledge within it must be itemized in plans. A useful way of planning progression and deeper thinking is to formulate key questions within the theme/issue/skill under study.

Key questions

Key questions should address the issues within a subject perspective that preoccupy people at any intellectual level. Both the university professor and the young child are interested in the big questions of life: Who are we? Where are we going? What's the meaning of it all? Peter Abbs (2003) would suggest that any questions that touch upon the existential would be likely to draw the child into active participation in his or her learning, for example:

- What is my responsibility to the environment? (a Geography key question)
- What are my dreams for the future? (a PSHE key question)

- What is beauty? (an Art/Music/Dance/Mathematics/English/Science question)
- Who is my neighbour? (an RE or PSHE key question)
- What does it mean to be alive? (a Science key question)
- What is war like? (a History key question)
- How does learning about other cultures help me understand about myself? (an RE key question)
- What is beauty? (an Art/Music/PE/English/Mathematics key question)
- What does fit for purpose mean? (a Design/Technology key question)
- How can I express emotion without words? (a Music/Art/PE key question)
- What is good/evil? (a History/RE/PSHE key question)

Subject progression

The easiest route towards planning for subject progression is to ask each subject coordinator/specialist/team to advise on the next steps for their subject. The 1999 National Curriculum offered a progression of sorts called attainment targets and these consisted of a series of statements summarizing steps along the route towards a mature understanding of the subject in question. From these lists it is still possible to build up a progression of skills, knowledge or attitudes without the need to grade or 'level' each child. The subject 'expert panels' working with the DoE and the subject associations for each curriculum subject have issued very helpful advice on progression since the publication of the National Curriculum for 2014 (see, for example, Historical Association and Geographical Association websites and CPR, 2014).

Planning powerful personal experiences

Children (and probably most of us) learn most easily through being *physically* involved in exploring sites, materials and ideas. It is incumbent upon schools to create and control a range of those experiences so as to stimulate involvement and learning for all children. This can be done by carefully planning not just for the physical and social environment the children work in, but the experiences they will learn through. Perkins (1992) calls such experiences powerful because they generate learning. These 'generative experiences' can become the motor driving a lively and meaningful curriculum. Generative experiences also need to be *personal*, involving the emotions and feelings of personal relevance. Planning powerful, personal experiences should be done by a team if possible, *and better still with a team of children*. The teacher's role is to decide what specific learning will arise from the experience and what teaching needs to be done to maximize and progress learning.

The progression of experiences in a curriculum needs careful mapping. Some experiences will be revisited. A second, third or weekly workshop with a theatre group or repeated contacts with the local church, nature trail, museum or mosque will almost inevitably deepen understanding. Using different foci, different leaders (including child leaders) and different subject lenses, repeat experiences can become cross-curricular events in themselves. A curriculum based around shared and powerful personal experiences is best constructed by taking a whole-school approach and planners should audit the valuable curriculum resources they have (often for free) on their doorsteps:

- What local buildings/institutions/places can be used as a focus for curriculum?
- What local contacts in the world beyond the school can be brought in to enliven the curriculum?
- What personal skills/interests/experience of staff and governors can be used to enrich curriculum?
- What subjects best throw light on the activities, places and people we centre our curriculum upon?

Not all learning arises from specially planned experiences however. Some knowledge is handed down from past generations, some is gathered from the internet, films, pictures and books, some is passed on by peers, friends or family. These more everyday and sometimes personal sources can also provide a powerful means of kick-starting and deepening learning. The essence of a motivating or generative experience is that it is meaningful to the participants. Experiences can be big or small, mental, physical, social, creative, cerebral, emotional or practical, but their common feature is that they bring us into the present.

Experiences do not have to be fancy. A well-read story, water play, a science practical, a new song, painting, or measuring how high we are will each become memorable to someone in our class. More major experiences, of course, need more planning. Big experiences capable of sustaining interest and engagement over several weeks should be planned for at least six occasions through every school year, one per six-week term. It is inevitable that a host of literacy skills will be developed as a result of every experience. Case study 1 (Chapter 3) showed a year's generative experiences for pre-school children. The vignette below records contrasting responses to generative experiences for a Year 8 class.

Illustration 11.7   A First World War 'sound mirror', designed to detect the presence of approaching enemy aircraft, captures the attention of a pupil (Courtesy of Creative Partnerships Kent)

 Case study

One Year 8 class in Birmingham was taken to the top of the nearby Malvern Hills for what was intended to be an enriching and inspiring Geography field trip. Their teacher reported on her return that the children seemed totally unmoved, uninterested and unfocused. When the next week the same group was taken to their own shopping street for well-prepared and detailed fieldwork on the shops and services there, the class reported that it had been their best day's work ever. When asked to explain, a female student said, 'We thought it was nice you had taken the trouble to find out stuff about our place, and we could tell you stuff about it too.'

Balancing experience, skills and knowledge

The skills and subject knowledge of the disciplines help us to translate experience into learning. The disciplines provide a specialized

Illustration 11.8 An impromptu classroom display after a Reception class walk in the playground (Photo: Cherry Tewfik)

vocabulary and structure to understanding, and any engaging, sustainable and relevant curriculum should balance subject craft skills and knowledge, on one hand, and opportunities for the application of that knowledge/those skills on the other. The six- or seven-week timetable suggested in Figure 11.4 uses half the week for cross-curricular experience using two subjects and the other half for ongoing units covering the remaining National Curriculum subjects. Through a year a curriculum structure like this would allow for both coverage of each subject and rich opportunities to put subject learning into practice.

Such a timetable is flexible enough to allow for the essential visit, visitor or responses to specific issues arising from the visit. In the example in Figure 11.4, Science, Geography and English are the focus subjects, but other curriculum subjects continue to be taught every week. In the following term, substantially more time may be given to Mathematics,

Monday	Core Literacy/ English	Core Numeracy/ Maths	RE (Core learning)	Geography (C-C theme)
Tuesday	Core History	Literacy/ English (C-C theme)	Cross-curricular (C-C-theme, geog. and sci. focus)	Cross-curricular (C-C theme)
Wednesday	Core Numeracy/ Maths	Core Design and Technology	Core PE	Core Art
Thursday	Science (C-C theme)	Science (C-C theme)	Creative Literacy/ English (C-C theme)	Core Music
Friday	Core Literacy/ English/MFL	Ongoing Investigative Numeracy/ Maths	Cross-curricular (C-C theme, geog. and sci. focus)	Cross-curricular (C-C theme, geog. and Sci. focus)

Figure 11.4   A primary school curriculum for a six-week term where English, Geography and Science were focus subjects

History and PE. In the subsequent term Art, Design/Technology and MFL may have the floor. A timetable like this is not very radical and fits easily within established approaches. More adventurous schools may wish to devote more time to the theme, but half a week each week for six weeks is sufficient to build successfully upon the generative experience for each child.

Alternatively, a school may wish to plan a unit of work based on Blythe and Perkins' (Blythe, 1997) concept of 'performances of understanding' (PoU), introduced in Chapter 10. Performances in this context are opportunities for children to demonstrate the degree and complexity of their learning by applying their new learning to an authentic problem. The teacher uses several PoU throughout the unit to gauge the progress of the class and of individuals. The first performance (in the first week of a unit of work) may be a 'thought shower' – a chance for children to show what they know already and what they can gather from collections, internet or library searches, focus exercises or questioning *without* formal teaching. The second performance (perhaps in week three or four) gives groups or individuals the space to articulate what they have learned from a period of focused teaching relevant to the foci identified. The final or 'culminating performance' (at the end of a unit) results from an open-ended opportunity for children to put their new knowledge into action by applying it to a new challenge. The 'performances' theme therefore combines an assessment strategy integral to the learning and a structure to the unit.

A cross-curricular unit using the PoU method requires the planning of particular 'Understanding Goals' for each subject and further goals for creative expression. In the example below, Music and History learning combine in an inter-disciplinary unit for Year 7 based on an aspect of the Tudors. The idea of the Tudors was introduced in an activity fun day run by a group of travelling actors/craftspeople/musicians who bring the 'Tudor experience' to schools. Because the unit is *inter*-disciplinary, the teacher will expect a degree of creative fusion between the knowledge and skills learned from two disparate subjects by the end. The culminating performance will involve the children being asked, in groups of five, to make a two-minute video on a Tudor theme with an appropriate soundtrack.

A Year 7 inter-disciplinary unit based on the Tudors

Creative expression might be graded as follows:

1. Awareness of links between ideas/materials/skills (e.g. the child knows that Tudors had different popular music from us).
2. Working with others on links between ideas/materials/skills (e.g. the child participates in a group talking about making some music for a Tudor video drama or animation).
3. Independently suggesting links between ideas/materials/skills (e.g. the child suggests that the musicians wear Tudor clothes as well as the actors).
4. Making original links between ideas/materials/skills (e.g. the child bases an improvised tune and structure on an example of Dowland's lute music).
5. Successfully accomplishing a finished and original idea/product/process (e.g. the child directs the refinement and final performance of their original composition as background to their Tudor video/animation).

The relevant Music subject skills and knowledge might be to:

- know that much Tudor music was modal and be able to know and use the Dorian mode when writing a tune
- know that Tudor music often used simple 'troubadour' drum rhythms as accompaniment and be able to use them in a composition

(Continued)

(Continued)

- be able to describe the intended emotional impact of Tudor examples using appropriate music vocabulary
- recognize and apply dominant and tonic chords and troubadour drum rhythms to accompany their Tudor style compositions.

The relevant knowledge and skills for History might be to:

- know key dates from the Tudor period and the names and contribution of some key musical and historical characters
- know of and understand three different sources of evidence of the distinctive features of church and state during Henry VIII's reign
- describe some distinctive features of church and state life in the time of Henry VIII
- understand and be able to describe some reasons for major religious changes between the reigns of Henry VIII and Elizabeth I.

A medium-term pro-forma for a Year 7 cross-curricular module of three weeks. The module is intended to develop History and Music skills and knowledge in a cross-curricular context and be assessed through performances of understanding

Generative experience: *The visit of 'History Alive' theatre group for a Tudor activity day*

Subject 1: *History*
Understanding Goals

-
-

Subject 2: *Music*
Understanding Goals

-
-

Resources (what you will need to make this unit a success)

-
-
-

SEQUENCE OF EVENTS	PERFORMANCES OF UNDERSTANDING (Plan how children will show the level of their understanding by applying their newly learned skills/knowledge to a new challenge)	ASSESSMENT (How will you know that children have (a) engaged, (b) sustained interest and (c) achieved new learning?)
Day or week 1 Introductory performance(s)	What do we know already? What do we want to know? What is the focus going to be? Using brainstorm, mind maps, Venn diagrams, lists, debates, internet, experts, collections, etc. e.g. 'everyone find twelve surprising facts about Tudor London'. What do you hear in this recorded music from the Tudor period?	Feedback: Informal and oral, by peers and teachers, written or drawn reflections by students Criteria: Developed collaboratively by students and teacher
Day or week 2 Performance(s) resulting from the teaching of relevant new skills and knowledge	What skills and knowledge do you need to teach as a result of interest generated by the experience? In what ways can children show the new subject knowledge they have gained in each of two subjects? e.g. musical improvisations and compositions in Tudor style. Three different interpretations of burning of Martyrs outside the city wall	Feedback: Informal and oral, by peers, visitors, parents and teachers Criteria: Students complete a summary sheet about their learning
Day or week 3 Culminating performance(s)	How can children creatively combine the new subject skills in answering a new and independent problem or challenge which uses them? e.g. make a two-minute Tudor video based on a true story and with appropriate soundtrack	Feedback: Informal and oral, by peers and teachers, formal written evaluation by student groups and teacher. Criteria: Matched against relevant levels in national curriculum

Short-term planning

Many schools and most ITE institutions provide standard formats to ensure coverage of the complex demands of National Curriculum strategies, cross-curricular strands and school policies. I do not intend to offer a lesson plan format. Aside from the strictures of legislation and policy, daily or single lesson plan research and cross-curricular experience suggests just four reminders. Every lesson should have:

- small-scale experiences and challenges
- small achievable steps and noticeable progress
- small opportunities for performance
- opportunities for a sense of achievement.

Small-scale experiences and challenges

Focus exercises have been explained and exemplified in Chapter 3. Such exercises are intended to provide small-scale personal/sensory experience and engagement. Some will involve, some will seem boring or nonsensical, but experience in using them over a number of years shows that they are remarkably resilient means of capturing attention and generating thinking (Dismore et al., 2008). Because the focus exercises listed are primarily sensory and open-ended, they are cross-curricular in themselves and can be interpreted and extended in many directions. Their openness provides its own challenge.

Throughout every good lesson, a series of planned and unplanned challenges come from the teacher or arise from children's responses – these add to pace and surprise but also help to refocus attention. Questioning is important and can be as subtle as a quizzical look or clearly articulated; either way it stimulates mirror neuron responses in most children.

Small achievable steps and noticeable progress

The active teaching of knowledge and skills is a required part of cross-curricular learning. If cross-curricular activity is poorly planned and not founded upon teaching, there is little chance that deep learning will occur for all. Opportunistic approaches to cross-curricular learning depend upon significant stores of teacher knowledge and the ability to marshal it when appropriate. Children should feel that they have learned something new: new knowledge learned, new skills applied, new attitudes considered. Such feelings of achievement need to be planned for and Ofsted argues it makes the difference between good and failed creative teaching (Ofsted, 2010a).

A simple way of including small achievable steps is through vocabulary. For every lesson, plan three or four key words that 'hold' or represent the new concepts/skills/knowledge to be learned. These words should be displayed on the whiteboard, around the room, on the desks, the glass of the windows – anywhere they will catch attention. They can form the skeleton of the lesson. Within the lesson the teacher should refer to those words continually, physically pointing them out in the room and persuading children to use them in their responses and to take them home to 'test' their parents! Similarly, an object that expresses the new learning to be made can be brought in – '... *at the end of this lesson we will all understand and be able say why and how this object is important'*.

Cross-curricular approaches do not need to mean that assessment is more difficult. If for two subjects the small, achievable steps of progression are planned and articulated then progress can be tracked by the teacher and felt by the student.

Small opportunities for performance

One of the unintended outcomes of the literacy and numeracy strategies is that children often feel they have not finished their work. Greater rigour, increased expectations on schools to provide test evidence of progress, means that children rarely get the chance to revisit and finish this incomplete work. Yet personal and high aspirations and meaningful challenges are the drivers of raised standards – so children of all ages need to see their work completed and their aims achieved on a regular basis. Bringing together new learning at the end of each session clarifies what subject has been extended and specifically whether the understanding goals for that subject have been achieved. Even 40-minute lessons can have a structure of warm-up–subject development–concluding performance, which provides the completed feel of the 'whole game' (Perkins, 2009).

Opportunities for a sense of achievement

A sense of achievement motivates and sustains. If achievement becomes a regular expectation in a school context then children should find it easier to have aspirations. Teachers should therefore plan and publicly recognize the achievements of each child on a regular basis.

Summary

The research cited throughout this book is highly relevant to planning cross-curricular activity. Long-, medium- and short-term plans must take account of the observations and experience of teachers and researchers thinking about learning if *all* children are to be enriched by education. The values stressed in Chapters 1, 2, 4, 7 and 8 should underpin planning at all levels before, during and after the paperwork. Some values inspire particular planning preoccupations: fairness, justice and democracy result in planning for inclusion and participation; individuality, to the nurturing of creativity and progression; knowledge, to a respect for the subject discipline; hope and faith, to a desire to engender meaningful and shared experiences; community, to the desire to foster good relationships; health, to the espousal of outdoor, active learning; and care and kindness, to an abiding interest in safe and stimulating environments for learning.

Key questions for discussion

- How can we help generate an atmosphere where conversations about children's learning are common?
- How can we minimize on the paperwork whilst maximizing the quality learning experience for the children?
- How can we ensure that understanding is expressed in visual, graphical, movement, artistic, creative, aural, numeric and interpersonal as well as linguistic ways?
- What is the advantage in planning in teams?

Further reading

Driscoll, P., Lambirth, A. and Roden, J. (2015) *The Primary Curriculum: A Creative Approach*. London: Sage.

Jeffrey, B. and Woods, P. (2003) *The Creative School*. London: Routledge.

Perkins, D. (2009) *Making Learning Whole: How Seven Principles of Teaching Can Transform Education*. New York: Jossey–Bass.

Wineburg, S. and Grossman, P. (2000) *Interdisciplinary Curriculum: Challenges to Implementation*. New York: Teachers College Press.

CHAPTER 12

KEY ISSUES FOR DEBATE

Chapter aims

This chapter introduces a range of issues for discussion and debate. It aims to stimulate animated conversation amongst students of education, novice and experienced teachers, governors and politicians that will help clarify the shared values and approaches that underpin good cross-curricular learning.

Use this chapter to inform curriculum planning or professional/personal development meetings. The issues and related questions are also useful starting points for ITE seminars and discussions. The subjects are intended to provoke debate that will impact upon ethos, management, planning, delivery, learning and personal experience in school.

Teachers do not have to choose between *either* subject disciplines *or* thematic methods, *both* are essential (Alexander, 2010; Ofsted, 2009a, 2009b, 2010a; Rose, 2009). At times, de-contextualized, didactic approaches are the best way to maintain challenge, introduce and develop subject skills, teach important facts and measure progression. Alongside cross-curricular modes of teaching and learning, equally creative instruction and coaching in skills and knowledge within the separated disciplines allow breadth and depth of learning experience. Sometimes a wholly cross-curricular approach is the only way to address a theme. A sense of balance should prevail in all discussions aimed at finding an appropriate curriculum and pedagogy for today's children.

In this book cross-curricular methods have been argued to provide high degrees of motivation in children. However, motivation arises from many sources and children are inspired by different and unpredictable inputs. We should allow for cultural and personal differences and avoid seeking one-size-fits-all solutions. Chapter 1 discussed children's responses to rapid and apparently inexorable change but, as Chapter 8 suggested, school learning should also offer the continuity and security of agreed values, aims and purposes.

Power and who holds it is a live issue for schools. The UN Convention on the Rights of the Child (UNICEF, 1989, website) issues a challenge to schools to share power with children. As children's voices are more frequently heard, schools are changing, but positive developments may be hampered by unclear values. Teachers may also be subject to lack of confidence, their own poor education, over-centralized education policies, the 'litigation and surveillance culture' (Furedi, 2009), news media, 'selfish capitalism' (James, 2009) or a range of other negative-sounding influences. Young people are rarely out of the news and rarely portrayed positively, yet the future depends upon how they are educated and their relationship to concepts like: self, creativity, culture, society, the environment and globalization. What follows is a personal response to some of these issues; deliberately provocative, obviously open to question, but an attempt to mark out areas for productive debate in staffrooms, seminar groups, school councils and planning meetings.

Motivation

The motivation to learn must come first. As I visit classes in widely contrasting parts of the UK and the world, I feel increasingly confident to suggest that motivation is key to efficient, satisfying and lifelong learning. Indeed, research for the Organization for Economic Cooperation and Development (OECD) pinpointed motivation as the main factor in learning (OECD, 2003). Although devised in the first half of the last century, Maslow's notion of a hierarchy of needs remains an interesting model to describe various sources of motivation (Maslow, 1943).

The motivation of physical and economic well-being

To flourish, we need to feel physically and mentally secure. Observing classes of 7–16-year-olds in rapidly developing regions such as southern India, Indonesia or East Africa, I hear from children that they are motivated by a desire for a life economically more secure than that of their

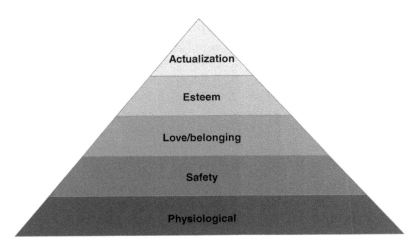

Figure 12.1   Maslow's hierarchy of needs. Does this apply today or is the picture more complex? (Source: Maslow, 1943)

parents. In the developing countries of the world and the poorer sections of developed economies, physical and economic security needs dominate. School learning for many is an instrumental activity providing the basic skills, knowledge and certificates to successfully compete for jobs in an increasingly tough and global jobs market. Schools in economically insecure areas may place more emphasis on the authority of the teacher, a didactic and subject-based approach to teaching, and learning that is generally more reliant upon memory and repetition. Education in the developing world is usually seen as a means of liberation from poverty. Whilst love, belonging, self-esteem and self-actualization appear abundantly present in the lives of the vast majority of those I observe, these attributes come largely from wider cultural and family contexts. In cultures that typically value community, spiritual interpretations, respect for elders and hard work, schools might appear to be places where peers are trusted, there is little bullying and children's sense of belonging is high.

Globalization, via the internet, satellite and cable TV, mobile phones and World Bank-sponsored curriculum revision, is now changing attitudes, educational practice and philosophy in many developing countries (James, 2009; Sharma, 2008). Education practice has become less polarized as global needs for creative solutions to economic and social problems have become more apparent (Craft et al., 2008). The powerful belief that education provides the way out of poverty and disadvantage remains, but schools in India and Malaysia for example (see Dorman and Scoffham, 2007; Scoffham, 2010), are increasingly considering environment, individuality, sustainability and globalization – issues that also concern their Western counterparts.

Motivation and psychological well-being

Rich countries continue to face significant degrees of child poverty (UNICEF, 2013, website) but in addition face problems of relative affluence. Every four years since the 1940s children between 11 and 15 throughout Europe and in the USA have been asked about their general well-being by researchers from the World Health Organization. The *Health Behaviour in School Aged Children* (HBSC) study reveals attitudes that will clearly affect education as well as general health. Some recent figures should be particularly concerning for UK and US schools:

- 24% of Welsh 13-year-olds rate their health as 'fair or poor' (compared to 23% in the USA and only 8% in Switzerland and 7% in Spain), and both 11- and 13-year-old girls in each of 40 developed countries considered their health to be poorer than that of boys.
- 87% of English and 86% of US children at 11 report 'high life satisfaction', but 95% of the children in Armenia, Netherlands and Greece say their satisfaction with life is high.
- 15% of both English and Scottish children report having been drunk at least twice by the age of 13 (compared to 3% of Italians and 5% of French 13-year-olds).
- Only 64% of US 11-year-olds (72% in England) agree that their peers are 'kind and helpful' (compared with 88% in Scotland and 90% in Macedonia).
- 32% of 11-year-olds in England (33% in the USA) say they feel 'pressured by schoolwork' (compared with 8% in the Netherlands). This figure rises to 39% in England and 40% in the USA by the time children are 13.
- Only 25% of English 13-year-olds (27% in the USA) could say they 'liked school a lot' (compared with 58% in Armenia and Macedonia).

(WHO, 2012, website)

The attitudes of children in a class make a significant difference to their application. The statistics above suggest that large numbers of children in the UK and USA are unlikely to be motivated by school. Whilst the physiological, physical and security needs of children in rich countries may generally be more fulfilled than those in poor ones, the HBSC report suggests that children in richer countries may have greater deficits in feelings of purpose, relationships, self-esteem, positive experience of school and safety. Psychologist Viktor Frankl (1992) noted half a century ago that the feeling of meaninglessness had become rife since the 1950s and was responsible for much psychological illness. Bringing Frankl's fears up to date, in 2010 The Prince's Trust reported that 15% of young people in the UK between 16 and 22 (representing the older brothers and sisters of the 11–15-year-olds surveyed by the HBSC) felt 'down', 'depressed' and 'isolated'; this percentage rose to 32% if the youngsters were out of work or education (Prince's Trust, 2010).

If relatively high percentages of children in our schools are unhappy, stressed, untrusting, engaging in risky behaviour or don't like school and a significant number also share a home with a depressed elder sibling, the educational implications are obvious. Every teacher knows how the presence of one class member suffering from a profound lack of well-being affects its atmosphere and learning. The figures above suggest that two or three members of our classes could be suffering in this way. Perhaps government, and others decision makers directly impacting upon the curriculum, should do significantly more to develop opportunities for team building, enjoyment, self-actualization, meaning making and social responsibility.

The construction of self-esteem, the re-establishment of community, support for family and an understanding of what it is to love, trust, hope and belong may be fundamental to effective learning itself.

Questions for discussion

- Do you think motivation is an important feature in learning? Give examples from your experience.
- Are there any specific kinds of activity that you have noticed motivate most children in your class/Year 7/Year R?
- What can we learn about motivation from observing children's play?
- How do we go about motivating the unmotivated child?
- What should government do to promote life satisfaction in children?
- What can teachers do to promote flourishing in children?

Managing change

Schools in the UK have been subjected to 40 years of continual curriculum change. One year they are asked to make their curricula and teaching styles more creative and cross-curricular, the next to maintain a relentless focus on the basics. Some teachers feel comfortable with literacy and numeracy filling every morning and didactic approaches to the other subjects in the afternoons – for these teachers, creative approaches may seem too demanding. But many have become unchallenged and bored by formulaic teaching methods. Teacher retention rates demonstrate this (House of Commons Education Committee, 2012, website). In both the USA and UK about half of teacher leave within their first five years in the profession. Teachers and student teachers may have been professionally deskilled by being encouraged to depend too heavily on de-contextualized and externally prepared formulae and contemplating more creative responses to the curriculum may seem a daunting prospect. Teachers need professional and personal support if they are to help steer children successfully through a life of change.

Subjects have suffered from the changes too. The first National Curriculum was quickly seen as too demanding, and shortened. Later the QCA produced schemes of work intended to support teachers. Just before the schemes were published, the ironically titled *Maintaining Breadth and Balance* told primary schools that they 'no longer had to teach the full programmes of study in the six foundation subjects' (QCA, 1998b: 3). The result was a loss of breadth, an upsetting of balance and a steady decline in time, thought and energy devoted to foundation subjects in primary schools. Inevitably, foundation subject standards suffered and training teachers noted significantly diminishing opportunities to observe practice in them (see Barnes, 2001; Rogers, 1999, 2003). The foundation subjects increasingly suffer from lack of well-trained champions (for example, Ofsted, 2008 on Geography in schools). Various official attempts have been made to address a situation where literacy and numeracy dominate school time and the foundation subjects – Science, RE, ICT, PSHE and Citizenship – are squeezed into the remaining space. *Designing and Timetabling the Primary Curriculum* (QCA, 2002b) offered case study examples of how schools with differing aims fulfilled them though creative and sometimes cross-curricular approaches to the timetable. Ofsted in its turn showed how primary and secondary schools achieved excellence 'against the odds' (Ofsted, 2009a, 2009b) through new curriculum and organizational approaches or through creativity (Ofsted, 2010a).

Current education policy emphasizes core skills and knowledge in the National Curriculum and offers schools greater freedoms to decide upon their own curriculum if they become 'free schools' or academies. In schools still bound by the National Curriculum, about 30% of curriculum time can theoretically be used for non-National Curriculum educational activity. These freedoms present problems for schools and teachers. Where do they find guidance and support for establishing more creative or connected curricula? Opportunities to invent their own lessons and schemes of work, or respond opportunistically to children's unplanned-for interests, can only be embraced if teachers feel confident in their own creativity and knowledge base (Cremin et al., 2009).

A climate of change presents new perspectives on transitions too. One such example in the UK is the difficult jump between Key Stages 2 and 3. Some imaginative schools in both key stages are developing a 'bridging curriculum', where primary and secondary school staff and children work together on a theme shared by Years 6 and 7 pupils (see Davies and McMahon, 2004, and case study 5 in Chapter 3). Shared themes, often focused around Science (probably because of a secondary school's superior science resources), cushion the sometimes worrying shift between schools at 11 years but also serve to raise teaching and learning standards, ensure progression and enhance the status of learning over teaching.

Empowering and meaningful curricula can be constructed to suit community and specific subject strengths in the context of increasing school independence and social change. In Chapters 3, 4, 5 and 6, we read how writers across several disciplines addressed the issues of twenty-first-century change, but few looked to the curriculum for an answer. Yet a well-designed curriculum delivered by committed and community-conscious adults is a powerful force. The curriculum can

Illustration 12.1   How do we assess the confidence of this 12-year-old?

become more effective in promoting positive social change when the child's voice is taken into account in forming it. Good relationships, good planning, a strong sense of personal/emotional relevance, authentic challenge and a recognition of the child's world will help children understand and engage with an otherwise bewildering world. As both back-up and guide in a caring society, such a curriculum can help children cope with multifarious categories of change now and in the future. To help children develop the skills, tenacity and self-motivation they will need to face unimaginable change, we need a curriculum to develop:

- personal, family and community meaning and belonging
- sensitivity and care for the self, others and environment
- an understanding of emotions and how to handle, harness and read them in the self and others
- their ability to learn new things
- a positive view of others, valuing diversity and uniqueness
- an appreciation of what is beautiful, good, true and right
- methods of working that are cooperative, patient, fair and fulfilling
- a knowledge of the distinctive contributions of the subject disciplines to understanding the world
- holistic views of experience, emotion, place, things, patterns, processes and ideas
- the understanding that humans are creative beings, able to produce inventive, unique solutions to problems
- confidence and accuracy with technologies and in handling information from other sources.

These could be argued to be required skills, regardless of what the future holds. They constitute a series of competencies that are markers towards the (re?) establishment of communally accepted values that transcend change.

Questions for discussion

- How can we adapt the curriculum in our school to take account of changing technologies?
- How can we support children in thinking about their role in the future?
- What kind of changes can we see happening around us, in our own area at the moment? How do they relate to more global issues?
- How can we counter the feeling that individuals are powerless in the face of change?

Power

Power relationships are changing in Western societies. The deference with which in former times we treated royalty, church, police, judiciary, the famous and the wealthy is constantly challenged. Celebrities wield massive influence. Detailed awareness of rights and the possibility of litigation have come to characterize many aspects of daily life. Whilst power remains vested in politicians, newspaper magnates, senior civil servants, captains of industry, and even health and safety executives, power is also increasingly placed in the hands of the less powerful through social networking sites like *Twitter*, *Facebook* and various petition sites. Transferring power to local, community levels has been central to Coalition government education policy and also touched upon in discussions concerning schools councils and children's participation. When pupils took control of information-gathering activities in the HEARTS project (see Chapter 7) their motivation, application and concentration increased. There are many arguments for the frequent shifting of power within a school setting (for example, Barnes, 2013b; Cheminais, 2008, 2012; Ruddock and MacIntyre, 2007; Wrigley et al., 2012). Clearly, in many circumstances and for safety's sake, ultimate power has to reside with adults, but there are plentiful opportunities in a school day where

Illustration 12.2 Power reinterpreted from a different camera angle (Photo: Robert Jarvis)

children can feel they have the power to influence things (see Summerhill School, website). In this regard, one teacher education student likened the effective teacher to 'a cunning dictator' who contrives to make a population feel they have freedom and power whilst actually retaining most for themselves. But power sharing can be more genuine than this.

Cross-curricular practice often depends upon group work and times of self-directed activity. In both cases children may need to be taught how to handle power. Role-playing sessions in which children practise making decisions, taking a lead or dealing with disputes are invaluable just before the onset of genuine group problem solving. A class debate about the responsibilities of power need not be theoretical if this PSHE and Citizenship theme is followed by a democratic class meeting to decide on the class theme or how to meet a particular challenge.

Illustration 12.3   Children's response to the question 'What can adults and children do together?' (Courtesy of Scottish Children's Parliament)

Questions for discussion

- How do we shift the locus of control whilst retaining responsibility for the health and safety of children?
- What are the health and safety implications of shifting power towards children?
- How do we give children the impression of choice whilst we continue to make decisions about curriculum content?
- What differences have new technologies made to children's sense of power and control?

Creativity

Cross-curricular learning and creativity go hand in hand; this has been consistently recognized by UK education advisers (for example QCA, 2002a, 2003, website; Ofsted, 2010a) and in the practice of thousands of teachers. Applying children's minds and two subject perspectives to a single event, theme or object results in unusual insights, original questions, unique perspectives and valued products. As we have seen, children bring their own unique mind to any situation. The teaching of distinct bodies of subject knowledge and skills remains irreplaceable. The robustness and rigidity of a disciplined understanding of any subject can provoke creativity in many directions. 'Structure ignites spontaneity,' says Nachmanovitch, who continues in a musical context:

> In ragas, or solo jazz play, sounds are limited to a restricted sphere, within which a gigantic range of inventiveness opens up. If you have all the colours available, you are sometimes almost too free. With one dimension constrained, play becomes freer in other dimensions. (Nachmanovitch, 1990: 85)

Creativity in education should not be a matter of blindly 'letting go' or weakly allowing 'free expression'. The NACCCE report made it very clear that sustained creative achievement 'involves knowledge of the field in question and skills in the media concerned … [and] recognise[s] the interdependence of freedom and control at the heart of the creative process' (NACCCE, 1999:para. 49). Ofsted guidance continually stresses good planning, high degrees of teacher knowledge and frequent evaluation in successful creative learning (for example Ofsted, 2010a).

Creative responses are controlled by a single brain area or generated by a particular pattern of behaviour. It can be planned or be stimulated by the accidental coming together of thoughts, materials or people. Cross-curricular approaches make such accidents more likely. As Boden suggests:

> Creativity is best construed not as a single power which you either have or do not, but as multidimensional. Creative processes involve different mental functions, combinations of skills and personality attributes … they involve special purposes for familiar mental operations and the more efficient use of our ordinary abilities, not something profoundly different. (Boden, 1990: 250)

Creative acts are judged so by acceptance by a particular field of judges, and this applies, as Pope says, 'at every level from considering Nobel Prize nominations to the scribbles of four year olds' (Pope, 2005: 68). Whilst Csikszentmihalyi (1997) generally speaks of creativity within one domain of understanding, Pope reminds us that much of the most startling and influential creativity goes on in the margins *between* domains, in interdisciplinary or cross-cultural exchanges that result in hybrid forms. Such exchanges happen in nature too. In human cultures some of the most creative advances and ideas have come at the overlap of cultures; think of medieval Venice, ninth-century Spain, Moghul India, jazz in the southern states of the USA, or the fusions of classical cultures in first-century Egypt.

Thematic work provides opportunities for the overlap of ideas in a school setting too. Creative solutions to a well-defined brief from the teacher might involve a mathematical sequence applied to a music composition, a geographical process described in a dance, scientific understandings like the movement of water created through painting or a design/technology problem solved through reference to historical solutions.

My own research has consistently suggested the importance of teachers recognizing and naming creative acts amongst children as they work on such projects.

 Case study

One class of eight-year-olds was designing and constructing a handbag, which was to be filled with objects that showed what their head teacher, Ms Masters, was interested in. Throughout a lesson the teacher highlighted original responses from individual children (Barnes, 2005b):

Teacher: Talking to other people helped Linda have more ideas didn't it?
Sarah: Jordan has just written what *he* likes [to put in his model of Ms Masters' bag].
Teacher: Is that what you think he thinks? I think he's got very good reasons for drawing a Dalek *as well* as liking them himself ... What is that telling us about Ms Masters? ...
That's a really good idea, Taylor, combining two ideas in one ... Who would like to come up and share just a little bit of what they are doing?
Raise your hand if you have thought of anything new or different today.

My co-researchers and I showed that establishing a creative frame of mind both in teachers and children, is a key aspect of promoting creative thinking and creative activity. A background atmosphere where creativity is frequently (and discriminatingly) honoured has distinct and positive effects on the children's view of their own and others' creativity. The children observed had little problem in naming aspects of their teacher's creativity and spoke confidently of their own. Being aware of one's own creativity may be good for confidence but also seems to be related to a sense of well-being, prolongs concentration and promotes warm, positive relationships and is associated with an enhanced sense of meaning (Barnes, 2013a; Barnes et al., 2008; Cremin et al., 2009; Pope, 2005).

Questions for discussion

- How can we identify and promote creativity in the adults in our school?
- How can we sustain the sense of growth in our own learning?
- How could we gain more job satisfaction?
- How can we create the conditions in which these things are likely to be the experience of children too?

Behaviour

Controlling behaviour is important for teachers. Some are concerned that group work, increased autonomy, 'pupil voice' and activity outside the classroom will provoke poor conduct. It is difficult to counter this perception unless teaching teachers do it. In the HEARTS project (Chapter 7) most ITE students expected behaviour challenges amongst their 12-year-olds, but after two full days of the project over 80% remarked upon the good conduct of the children in this child-led setting. Additionally, almost 50% of the student teachers used the words 'enthusiastic', 'collaborative', 'relaxed' and 'new ideas' to describe their feelings about the behaviour of the children. More than 70% used the words 'enjoyed' or 'engaged' to describe children's attitude to learning in this context. Planning and helping children find personal relevance was crucial to the success of this cross-curricular activity, just as it is for *any* school activity. Furthermore, involvement in cross-curricular and creative activities appears to have been responsible many times for *producing* good behaviour. In the case of the HEARTS project, finding relevance did not involve identifying direct links with children's everyday lives, but discovering tiny aspects of an unfamiliar environment that connected in one way or another to the lives of every individual. For one it was fossils, another a fairy story, another an angry friend and yet another a film, but for each, that link had a kind of personal existential significance – a recognizable part of their autobiographical self.

Illustration 12.4   After finding out about wind direction and air pressure, these 13- and 14-year-olds send messages to a 'marooned' artist in the middle of the English channel as part of a Creative Partnerships initiative (Courtesy of Creative Partnerships Kent)

Just as productive group work needs teaching, so does behaviour. Careful, considerate, respectful behaviour is not always 'caught' as we might hope. Neither do specific subjects like Music (see Gov.UK, 2010b, website) necessarily improve behaviour, but high expectations and clear ground rules for safe, caring responses do work for many children. Identifying, describing and praising specific examples of 'good' behaviour as it occurs keeps children aware of these expectations.

Added to general subject planning and specific learning objectives, one of the most powerful motivators to increased self-control is success at something perceived as challenging. The teacher or team should therefore plan and work to generate enthusiasm through authentic challenge targeted just a little *beyond* the current grasp of individuals.

Illustration 12.5   These six-year-olds are discovering personal links to a medieval castle by meaning making their own descriptive and atmospheric music whilst on their visit

---

Questions for discussion

- Is behaviour best improved by rules or a stimulating curriculum?
- How can we help children become aware of and responsible for their own behaviour?
- How can we positively involve family, community and child in discussions about behaviour?

The global dimension

We have become very aware of the global dimension in our lives. The global financial crisis of 2008/9, the travel disruption caused by an

Icelandic volcano in 2010, the environmental damage from an oil spill, the damage to a nuclear power station caused by a tsunami in Fukushima, Japan, in 2011, wars in Afghanistan and Iraq and tensions between the West and Iran, North Korea, Israel and Palestine remind us daily of global interdependence. The curriculum cannot ignore pandemics, the World Wide Web, global terrorism, the global economy, global climate change and global pollution. Yet despite guidance from the Development Education Association (for example, DEA, 2001), the global plays only a small a role in our programmes of study, schemes of work or school prospectuses. Government periodically reminds us of the importance of the global dimension in an attempt to broker partnerships between schools across the globe, but such centralized advice often comes with economic 'strings' attached – notice the UK government's three economy-driven aims:

1. Equipping children for life in a global society and work in a global economy.
2. Engaging international partners to achieve their goals and ours.
3. Maximizing the contribution of education to overseas trade and inward investment. (DfES, 2004)

UK schools partnerships with schools across the world need to be conscious of the dangers of unequal and neo-colonialist outcomes. The global can play a big part in the kind of thematic activity already outlined in this book, but partnerships should strive to be equal. The global dimension does not have to be as overtly British-economy serving as the government's three aims. Neither do they need to involve charitable giving, which can reinforce unhelpful power relationships (Martin, 2012). Global connections between schools can be used to develop a more sensitive and informed understanding of cultural differences and common issues facing all people.

 Case study

One school on the Kent coast established a link with a primary school in Tanzania and their link forms the core of thematic work for several weeks of combined Geography, PSHE/Citizenship and English work. Children write letters with real questions they know will be answered, and they research and present comprehensive details about the actual locality of their partner school: its weather statistics, its population, maps of the village, plans of the farms and detail about daily life of a few actual families. This year they worked with a teacher who had visited the area. In groups of five, they took on family roles and used the plans of six fragmented and steeply sited farms to discuss what the family could do with £50 given by the local church organization for improvements. They were able to check out what actually happened in subsequent letters, but this activity gave the children a remarkably deep and lasting insight into the issues facing four-fifths of the world's population. (Glen Sharp)

Illustration 12.6   This village child in south India has access to the rest of the world through the internet

Questions for discussion

- What global links do we already have?
- How can we make the global significant to the children in our school?
- How can the global be made an integrator in our curriculum?

Litigation and 'the surveillance culture'

Advice on school policy and legislation regarding safety on school visits (DfE, 2014b, website) reflects the increasing concern for children's safety after a number of well-publicized and very tragic accidents involving children on school visits. The fear of such accidents, litigation and the extra paperwork involved in detailed 'risk assessments' along with the requirement of particular ratios of adults to children, costs of transport and the need for individual parental permission, has resulted in a reduction of school visits. *None of the requirements is unnecessary – all are the result of carefully considered and responsible practice and none should be disregarded*. Schools that continue to make fieldwork a major priority have found that establishing such procedures as:

- clear and uniform school-based guidelines
- adequate and school-provided preparation time
- accessible and easily understood paperwork
- the advice of experienced practitioners
- the preparation of individual 'class visit packs' containing essential medication, mobile phone, first aid kit and permission slips etc.

significantly lessens the load on teachers.

In the past, Parliamentary education committees appeared to be in full agreement that education outside the classroom is a valuable and motivating thing in itself:

> Outdoor learning supports academic achievement … as well as development of 'soft skills' and social skills particularly in hard to reach children … neither the DfES nor Local Authorities have done enough to publicize the benefits of education outside the classroom …'
> (House of Commons Education and Skills Committee, 2005: 3)

The same committee agreed that the bureaucracy associated with school visits is a major problem but found no evidence that school visits are inherently risky. The committee recommended a 'Manifesto for Outdoor Learning' (House of Commons Education and Skills Committee, 2005: section 7, Conclusions and recommendations), with structures and a personality to champion outdoor learning across all curriculum areas. It also recommended that unions currently advising their members not to go on school trips reconsider their position.

The gradual rise of surveillance activities in our schools as well as our high streets is an additional indication of the fear and mistrust felt by many. Many schools now use closed-circuit television (CCTV) to reduce perceptions of increased risk to children. Stringent curriculum surveillance, unannounced inspections, forced resignations and judgements of 'non-compliance' add to a climate of fear in some schools. Increasing use of observation by heads, curriculum coordinators, parents, governors and inspectors is likely to lead teachers to choose the 'safest' and least disruptive options for their teaching.

Safe educational risks have been explored throughout this book. Cross-curricular teaching *is* risky; sometimes a well-prepared topic does not catch the hoped-for imagination. Group work, open-ended questions and situations, or creative lessons will often be nosier and appear less controlled than a highly structured and inflexible 'off-the-shelf lesson'. But I have argued that this risky, noisy, exciting and unpredictable education is vital to the healthy present and flourishing future of children and our society.

Questions for discussion

- What kind of curriculum/lessons best build positive attitudes to life-long learning?
- What kind of curriculum/lessons help children develop transferable skills for use in a variety of future circumstances?
- What kind of curriculum/lessons assist children in forming positive views of themselves?
- What kind of curriculum/lessons teach social and emotionally intelligent skills necessary for work in teams in later life?
- What kind of curriculum/lessons help children learn independence, understand how to use initiative, cultivate flexibility, rehearse prioritizing and discover their own creativity?
- What kind of curriculum/lessons can prepare children for an uncertain future of inevitable and yet unimaginable change?

The changing role of the school

The nature of schools is fast changing. Independent academies and free schools, Children's Centres or Community Learning Centres, and closer relationships between children's medical, social and educational services are established throughout the UK and the USA. Many schools effectively operate variations of the 8.00 a.m. to 6.00 p.m. day with breakfast clubs, after-school clubs and the like. Primary and secondary academies and academy chains make community and other links a priority. In the UK, Directors of Children's Services and coordinated local authority responsibility for all aspects of childhood mean that each school has to consider a widening of its role in the community.

Alongside these changes, contradictory and economically driven developments threaten the very communities governments wish to sustain.

School closures continue because of falling or low rolls, removing schools from the heart of small and fragile communities who have already lost their post offices and village shop. The administration of primary health care and social services suffer from the inexorable pressures to economize, sometimes by being organized in bigger, less locally accountable units, sometimes with local GPs with little background in administration. Increasing poverty and an increasing gap between the haves and the have-nots in the developed world especially affects the lives of young people in the UK, adding to the list of social, health and educational problems confronting them (Marmot, 2010, website).

Information and communication technologies make it possible for each child to have a separate and isolated education. Education can conceivably be totally individualized. The BBC attempted to deliver 50 per cent of the National Curriculum to 5–16-year-olds over the heads of teachers in an 'interactive dialogue directly with learners', but this project failed partly because of competition laws. Wholesale digital education is possible, but is it right? Are children already too much subject to a screen

Illustration 12.7   Infant children's plans for their school entrance realized by a team of architects who worked with them (Courtesy of Creative Partnerships Kent)

culture (Greenfield, 2010)? Against the burgeoning communications, technological and political background, schools will inevitably become more complex organizations with multiple functions beyond the simple passing on of knowledge. Schools will be increasingly charged with developing independence as well as community, self-direction and moral behaviour. With so many demands, an old-fashioned timetable or traditional curriculum may be totally unfit for purpose, which is why organizations like the Curriculum Foundation (website) and the RSA (see Chapter 3, case study 6) and academy chains offer alternatives.

Teachers will bear the brunt of many of these new initiatives. To ensure that children continue to get the best from their teachers, teachers themselves need to be more fully aware of the unique, precious and professional knowledge they possess. The knowledge teachers gain is not possessed by any other professionals, and it should not be underestimated, neglected or dismissed. Neither should teachers feel trapped into propping up systems and approaches they know from experience do not work. Human beings are social and cultured animals – we only consider ourselves mentally well when we are generally happy with the relationships we form with others. Whilst society continues to see education as a social, communal, culture-driven affair, teachers will be the key adults in children's lives after their primary carers. At their best, teachers are made distinctive by the insights they accumulate about young people's learning. At its best, teachers' contribution to the well-being of each individual and of society can be expressed in the following statements:

1. Teachers are the only professionals who serve their clients daily and *en masse.*
2. Teachers understand and use many different methods of presenting information so as to match different styles of learning within a single class. They know simultaneously how to engage children from a wide range of backgrounds.
3. Teachers know how to organize activities in groups so as to ensure social, emotional and personal development at the same time as intellectual development.
4. Teachers know how to control large groups of young people without fear, how to motivate them without bribery, how to excite them without losing control, how to take risks without danger and how to praise without lying.
5. Teachers understand the importance of motivation in learning and the variety of ways of persuading children that they want to learn.

6. Teachers understand about simultaneously stretching the most and the least able child in the same class *and know that those two children may be interchangeable in different learning situations.*
7. Teachers are unique in knowing, understanding and in many ways representing the range of sub-cultures within the communities they serve. They know how to arrange educational experiences so that they generate meaningful learning *and* avoid offence to both the most liberal and most conservative members of society. They know and understand how different extremes of society feel about things that matter to them.
8. Teachers experience daily the close relationship between physical and mental well-being and learning. They see the multitude of ways family break-up, a house move, the loss of a friend, pet or an eraser can affect a child's learning. They also regularly witness the impact of deprivation or wealth.
9. Teachers are at the front line of applying government policy to generate change in society and the economy through the curriculum, yet they are rarely directly consulted.

Teachers rapidly become experts in children's learning and the kind of curriculum that motivates them. They need to be carefully listened to in building the new approach to the curriculum required for a world of new types of school, new technologies, new definitions of family, globalization, new challenges and very old moral dilemmas. No other professional has the teacher's wealth of research knowledge of how to make connections between the disciplines, manage children in groups, how to fire an individual's imagination, how to rebuild a child's self-esteem and how to construct an environment that awakens the desire to learn. Both the child's and the teacher's well-being depend on balance of attention to the disciplines, the group, the individual and the environment for learning. Good teachers have always balanced these factors. With these and many more unique qualities, it is amazing that teachers continue to be so maligned in the press or by ministers of state, threatened by inspection, replaced by under-qualified assistants or under-prepared peers and put upon by politicians. In the changing world of the school, teachers' unique and professional skills and knowledge must be fully and sensitively utilized. Ask teachers about the curriculum that will best serve today's children for now and their future, and I believe the majority will respond with a variant of the creative and cross-curriculum.

REFERENCES

Abbs, P. (2003) *Against the Flow*. London: Routledge.

Adey, P. and Shayer, M. (1994) *Really Raising Standards*. London: Routledge.

Ajegbo, K. (2007) *Diversity and Citizenship*. Nottingham: DfES.

Alexander, R. (2008) *Towards Dialogic Teaching*. York: Dialogos.

Alexander, R. (2010) *Children, Their World, Their Education: The Report of the Cambridge Primary Review*. London: Routledge.

Alexander, R., Rose, A. and Woodhead, C. (1992) *Curriculum Organisation and Classroom Practice in Primary Schools: A Discussion Paper*. London: DES.

Alexander, T. (2001) *Citizenship Schools: A Practical Guide to Education for Citizenship and Personal Development*. London: Campaign for Learning/ UNICEF.

Alexander, T. and Potter, J. (eds) (2005) *Education for a Change: Transforming the Way We Teach Our Children*. London: RoutledgeFalmer.

Andrade, H. and Perkins, D. (1998) Learnable intelligence and intelligent learning, in R. Sternberg and W. Williams (eds), *Intelligence Instruction and Assessment: Theory into Practice*. Mahwah, NJ: Erlbaum.

Antidote (2003) *The Emotional Literacy Handbook*. London: David Fulton.

Arnsten, A. and Li, B. (2005) Neurobiology of executive functions: catecholamine influences in prefrontal cortical functions, *Biological Psychiatry*, 57 (11): 1377–84.

Arthur, J. and Cremin, T. (2010) *Learning to Teach in the Primary School*, 2nd edn. London: Routledge.

Attingham Trust (2004) *Opening Doors: Learning in the Historic Environment*. London: Attingham Trust.

Austin, R. (2007) *Letting the Outside In: Developing Teaching and Learning Beyond the Early Years Classroom*. Stoke-on-Trent: Trentham Books.

Bandura, A. (1994) Self-efficacy, in V.S. Ramachaudran (ed.), *Encyclopedia of Human Behaviour*, vol. 4. New York: Academic Press. pp. 71–81.

Barnes, J. (1994) The city planners of St Peters, *Remnants, Journal of English Heritage Education Service*, 24 (Autumn): 1–4.

Barnes, J. (2001) Creativity and composition in music, in C. Philpott and C. Plummeridge (eds), *Issues in Music Education*. London: Routledge.

Barnes, J. (2005a) On your mind, *Nursery World*, 105 (3965): 12–13.

Barnes, J. (2005b) Case study notes, 28 November.

Barnes, J. (2005c) Case study notes, 14 December.

Barnes, J. (2005d) You could see it on their faces: the importance of provoking smiles in schools, *Health Education*, 105 (5): 392–400.

Barnes, J. (2010) The Generate Project: curricular and pedagogical inspiration from parents working with their children, *Improving Schools*, 13 (2): 143–57.

Barnes, J. (2013a) What sustains a fulfilling life in education? *Journal of Education and Training Studies*, 1 (2): 74–88.

Barnes, J. (2013b) What Sustains a Life in Education? Unpublished PhD thesis, Canterbury Christ Church University.

Barnes, J. (2014a) Drama to promote social and personal well-being in six and seven year olds with communications difficulties: The Speech Bubbles Project, *Perspectives in Public Health*, 134 (2): 101–9.

Barnes, J. (2014b) The Haringey Lullabies Project; Music Enhancing Education and Health Outcomes in an Early Years Setting. Canterbury: Canterbury Christ Church University.

Barnes, J. (2014c) 'Can teachers build a successful learning environment for children?', in M. Sangster (ed.), *Challenging Perceptions*. London: Bloomsbury.

Barnes, J. and Hancox, G. (2004) Young, gifted and human: a report from the National Gifted and Talented Summer Academy, *Improving Schools*, 7 (1): 11–21.

Barnes, J. and Shirley, I. (2005) Strangely familiar: Promoting Creativity in Initial Teacher Education, paper presented at British Educational Research Association (BERA) conference, 16 September.

Barnes, J. and Shirley, I. (2007) Strangely familiar: cross-curricular and creative thinking in teacher education, *Improving Schools*, 10 (2): 289–306.

Barnes, J., Hope, G. and Scoffham, S. (2008) A conversation about creative teaching and learning, in A. Craft, T. Cremin and P. Burnard (eds), *Creative Learning 3–11 and How We Document It*. Stoke-on-Trent: Trentham Books.

Baron, R. and Byrne, D. (2004) *Social Psychology*, 10th edn. London: Allyn and Bacon.

Beetham, H. and Sharpe, R. (2013) *Rethinking Pedagogy for a Digital Age*. London: Routledge.

Bell, D. (2004) The value and importance of geography, *Primary Geographer*, 56: 4–5.

Bentley, T. (2006) Towards a self creating society, presentation at 'This Learning Life' conference, Bristol, 21 April.

Bernstein, B. (1971) *Class, Codes and Control*, vol. 1. London: Paladin.

Bernstein, B. (1996) *Pedagogy, Symbolic Control and Identity*. Lanham, MD: Rowman and Littlefield.

Black, P. and Wiliam, D. (1998) *Inside the Black Box*. Slough: NFER/Nelson.

Blacking, J. (1974) *How Musical is Man?* Washington: University of Washington Press.

Blake, W. (1789 [1967]) *Songs of Innocence and Experience*. London: Oxford University Press.

Blakemore, S. and Frith, U. (2006) *The Learning Brain: Lessons for Education*. Oxford: Blackwell.

Blythe, T. (ed.) (1997) *The Teaching for Understanding Guide*. New York: Jossey-Bass.

Boden, M. (1990) *The Creative Mind: Myths and Mechanisms*. London: Abacus.

Boix-Mansilla, V., Gardner, H. and Miller, W. (2000) On disciplinary lenses and interdisciplinary work, in S. Wineburg and P. Grossman (eds), *Interdisciplinary Curriculum: Challenges to Implementation*. New York: Teachers College Press.

Booth, T. (2003) Inclusion and exclusion in the city, concepts and contexts, in P. Potts (ed.), *Inclusion in the City: Selection, Schooling and Community*. London: Routledge.

Booth, T and Ainscow, M. (2011) *Index for Inclusion*. Bristol: Centre for Research in Inclusive Education.

Bourdieu, P. (1984) *Distinction: A Social Critique of the Judgment of Taste*, trans. Richard Nice. Harvard, MA: Harvard University Press.

Bowlby, J. (1988) *A Secure Base: Clinical Applications of Attachment Theory*. London: Routledge.

Bowlby, J. (1997) *Attachment and Loss: Vol. 1: Attachment*, revised edn. London: Pimlico.

Bragg, S. (2010) *Consulting Young People: A Literature Review*. London: Creativity, Culture and Education.

Bransford, J., Brown, A. and Cooking, R. (1999) *How People Learn: Brain, Mind, Experience and School*. Stanford, CA: National Research Council.

Brice Heath, S. and Wolf, S. (2004) *Visual Learning in the Community School*. London: Arts Council.

Brice Heath, S. and Wolf, S. (2005) Focus in creative learning: drawing on art for language development, *Literacy*, 39 (1): 38–45.

Bruner, J. (1960) *The Process of Education*. Cambridge, MA: Harvard University Press.

Bruner, J. (1968) *Towards a Theory of Instruction*. New York: Norton.

Bruner, J. (1996) *The Culture of Education*. Cambridge, MA: Harvard University Press.

Bruner, J. (2003) Some specifications for a space to house a Reggio preschool, in G. Ceppi and M. Zini (eds), *Children, Spaces, Relation: Metaproject for an Environment for Young Children*. Milan: Reggio Children and Domus Academy Research Center.

Bruner, J. and Haste, H. (1987) *Making Sense: The Child's Construction of the World*. New York: Methuen.

Burke, C. and Grosvenor, I. (2003) *The School I'd Like: Children and Young People's Reflections on an Education for the 21 Century*. London: Routledge.

Buzan, T. (2002) *How to Mind Map*. London: Thorsons.

CPR (Cambridge Primary Review/Pearson) (2014) *Primary Curriculum: Developing an Outstanding Curriculum in Your School (conference materials)*. Cambridge: CPR Press.

Catling, S. (2004) Primary student teachers' world map knowledge, in S. Catling and F. Martin (eds), *Researching Primary Geography*. London: Register of Research in Primary Geography.

Catling, S. (2005) Children's personal geographies and the English primary school geography curriculum, *Children's Geographies*, 3 (3): 325–44.

Catling, S. (2010) Organising and managing learning outside the classroom, in J. Arthur and T. Cremin (eds), *Learning to Teach in the Primary School*, 2nd edn. London: Routledge.

Catling, S. and Willey, T. (2009) *Teaching Primary Geography*. Exeter: Learning Matters.

Cheminais, R. (2008) *Engaging Pupil Voice to Ensure that Every Child Matters: A Practical Guide*. London: David Fulton.

Cheminais, R. (2012) *Children and Young People as Action Researchers: A Practical Guide to Supporting Pupil Voice in Schools*. Maidenhead: Open University.

Claxton, G. (1998) *Hare Brain, Tortoise Mind*. London: Fourth Estate.

Claxton, G. (2003) *Building Learning Power*. London: TLO.

Claxton, G. and Lucas, B. (2013) *Expansive Education: Teaching Learners for the Real World*. London: McGraw Hill.

Clift, S. and Camic, P. (eds) (2015) *The Oxford Textbook of Arts and Health*. Oxford: Oxford University Press.

Collishaw, S., Maughan, B., Goodman, R. and Pickles, A. (2004) Time trends in adolescent mental health, *Journal of Child Psychology and Psychiatry*, 45 (8): 1350.

Comenius, J. (1967) *The Great Didactic*. London: Russell and Russell.

Costa, A. and Kallick, B. (2014) *Dispositions: Reframing Teaching and Learning*. London: Sage.

Craft, A. (2000) *Creativity across the Primary Curriculum*. London: Routledge.

Craft, A. (2005) *Creativity in Schools: Tensions and Dilemmas*. London: Routledge.

Craft, A., Gardner, H. and Claxton, G. (2008) *Creativity, Wisdom and Trusteeship: Exploring the Role of Education*. Thousand Oaks, CA: Corwin Press.

Creative Partnerships Kent (2005) *Footnotes to an Idea*. London: Creative Partnerships/Arts Council.

Cremin, T. (2009) *Teaching English Creatively*. London: Routledge.

Cremin, T., Barnes, J. and Scoffham, S. (2009) *Creative Teaching for Tomorrow: Fostering a Creative State of Mind*. Margate: Future Creative.

Critchley, H. (2003) Emotion and its disorders, *British Medical Bulletin*, 65: 35–47.

Csikszentmihalyi, M. (1997) *Creativity: Flow and the Psychology of Discovery and Invention*. New York: HarperCollins.

Csikszentmihalyi, M. (2002) *Flow: The Classic Work on How to Achieve Happiness*. New York: Ebury Press.

Csikszentmihalyi, M. (2003) *Good Business*. New York: Hodder and Stoughton.

Damasio, A. (2000) *The Feeling of What Happens: Body, Emotion and the Making of Consciousness*. London: Heinemann.

Damasio, A. (2003) *Looking for Spinoza: Joy, Sorrow and the Feeling Brain*. Orlando, FL: Harcourt.

Damasio, A. (2010) *Self Comes to Mind: Constructing the Conscious Brain*. New York: Vintage.

Damasio, A. and Immordino-Yang, M. (2007) We feel therefore we learn: the relevance of affective and social neuroscience to education, *Brain, Mind and Education*, 1 (1): 3–10.

Darder, A. (2002) *Reinventing Paulo Freire: A Pedagogy of Love*. Oxford: Westview.

Davey, C., Burke, T. and Shaw, C. (2010) *Children's Participation in Decision-making: A Children's Views Report*. London: National Children's Bureau.

David, T. (1999) *Teaching Young Children*. London: Paul Chapman Publishing.

David, T. (2001) Curriculum in the early years, in G. Pugh (ed.), *Contemporary Issues in the Early Years*, 3rd edn. London: Paul Chapman Publishing.

Davidson, R., Daren, C. and Kalin, N. (2000) Emotion, plasticity, context and regulation: perspectives from affective neuroscience, *Psychological Bulletin*, 126 (6): 890–906.

Davies, D. and McMahon, K. (2004) A smooth trajectory: developing continuity and progression between primary and secondary science education through a jointly planned projectiles project, *International Journal of Science Education*, 26: 1009–21.

Dawkins, R. (2003) *A Devil's Chaplin: Selected Essays*. London: Phoenix.

De Bono, E. (1999) *Six Thinking Hats*. New York: Black Bay.

De Boo, M. (ed.) (2004) *The Early Years Handbook: Support for Practitioners in the Foundation Stage*. Sheffield: Geographical Association.

DCSF (Department for Children, Schools and Families)/QCDA (Qualifications and Curriculum Development Agency) (2010) *The National Curriculum Primary Handbook*. Coventry: Qualifications and Curriculum Development Agency.

DEA (Development Education Association) (2001) *Global Perspectives in Education*. London: DEA.

DES (Department of Education and Science) (1967) *Children and their Primary Schools: A Report of the Central Advisory Council for Education (England)* (Plowden Report). London: HMSO.

DES (Department of Education and Science) (1989) *The National Curriculum for England and Wales*. London: HMSO.

Deutscher, G. (2006) *The Unfolding of Language: An Evolutionary Tour of Mankind's Greatest Invention*. New York: Owl Books.

Deutscher, G. (2010) *Through the Language Glass: How Words Colour Your World*. London: Arrow Books.

Dewey, J. (1897) My pedagogic creed, *The School Journal*, 54 (3): 77–80.

DfE (Department for Education) (2011) *The Social and Emotional Aspects of Education in Secondary Schools*. London: DfE.

DfE (Department for Education) (2012) *Statutory Framework for the Early Years Foundation Stage*. London: DfE.

DfE (Department for Education) (2013a) *The National Curriculum*. London: DfE.

DfE (Department for Education) (2013b) *Teachers Standards: Guidance for Headteachers, School Staff and Governing Bodies*. London: DfE.

DfEE (Department for Education and Employment) (1999) *The National Numeracy Strategy*. London: DfEE.

DfEE/QCA (Department for Education and Employment/Qualifications and Curriculum Authority) (1999) *The National Curriculum Handbook for Primary Teachers in England*. London: DfEE.

DfES (Department for Education and Skills) (2003a) *Excellence and Enjoyment: A Strategy for Primary Schools.* Nottingham: DfES Publications.

DfES (Department for Education and Skills) (2003b) *Developing Children's Social, Emotional and Behavioural Skills: Guidance.* London: DfES.

DfES (Department for Education and Skills) (2004) *Putting the World into World Class Education: An International Strategy for Educations, Skills and Children's Services.* London: DfES.

DfES/QCA (Department for Education and Skills/Qualifications and Curriculum Authority) (1999) *Curriculum Guidance for the Foundation Stage.* London: HMSO.

Diener, E. (2009) *Assessing Well-Being.* Milton Keynes: Springer.

Diener, E. and Seligman, M. (2002) Very happy people, *Psychological Science,* 13: 81–4.

Dismore, H., Barnes, J. and Scoffham, S. (2008) *Space to Reflect.* London: Creative Partnerships.

DoH/DfES (Department of Health/Department for Education and Skills) (2005) *National Healthy Schools Status: Guide for Schools.* London: DoH/DfES.

Dorman, P. and Scoffham, S. (2007) Multiple perspectives, profound understandings, *Primary Geographer,* 64: 31–3.

Dunbar, R. (1998) The Social Brain Hypothesis, *Evolutionary Anthropology,* pp. 178–90.

Dunbar, R. (2003) The Social Brain, mind, language and society in evolutionary perspective, *Annual Review of Anthropology,* 32: 163–81.

Dweck, C. (2009) *Mindset: How You Can Fulfil Your Potential.* New York: Ballentine.

Eaude, T. (2008) *Children's Spiritual, Moral, Social and Cultural Development,* 2nd edn. Exeter: Learning Matters.

Ekman, P. (2004) *Emotions Revealed: Understanding Faces and Feelings.* London: Phoenix.

English Heritage/Barnes, J. (1999) *A Teachers' Guide to Design/Technology and the Historic Environment.* London: English Heritage.

English Heritage/Durbin, G., Morris, S. and Wilkinson, S. (1990) *Learning from Objects.* London: English Heritage.

Entwistle, N. (2000) Promoting Deep Learning through Teaching and Assessment: Conceptual Frameworks and Educational Contexts, paper presented at Teaching and Learning Research Programme (TLRP) conference, Leicester, 11 November.

Evans, J. and Philpott, C. (2009) *A Practical Guide to Music and the Secondary School.* London: Routledge.

Faultley, M. and Savage, J. (2012) *Cross-Curricular Teaching and Learning in the Secondary School: The Arts.* London: Routledge.

Feldman, D. (1976) The child as craftsman, *Phi Delta Kappan,* 58 (1): 143–9.

Fisher, R. (1999) *Head Start: How to Develop your Child's Mind.* London: Souvenir Press.

Fisher, R. (2008) *Teaching Thinking: Philosophical Enquiry in the Classroom.* London: Continuum.

Fisher, R. and Williams, M. (2004) *Unlocking Creativity: A Teacher's Guide to Creativity Across the Curriculum*. London: David Fulton.

Frankl, V. (1992) *Man's Search for Meaning*. London: Rider.

Fraser-Smith, N., Lesperance, F. and Talajic, M. (1995) The impact of negative emotions on prognosis following myocardial infarction: is it more than depression? *Health Psychology*, 14: 388–98.

Frederickson, B. (2003) The value of positive emotions, *American Scientist*, 91: 300–5.

Fredrickson, B. (2004) The broaden and build theory of positive emotions, *Philosophical Transactions of the Royal Society: Biological Sciences*, 359 (1449): 1367–77.

Fredrickson, B. (2009) *Positivity*. New York: Crown.

Fredrickson, B. and Branigan, C. (2005) Positive emotions broaden the scope of attention and thought–action repertoires, *Cognition and Emotion*, 19 (3): 313–32.

Fredrickson, B. and Tugade, M. (2004) Resilient individuals use positive emotions to bounce back from negative experiences, *Journal of Personality and Social Psychology*, 80 (2): 326–33.

Freire, P. (1994) *The Pedagogy of Hope: Reliving the Pedagogy of the Oppressed*. New York: Continuum.

Froebel, F. (1826) *Die Menschenerziehung (On the Education of Man)*. Leipzig: Weinbrach.

Fumoto, H., Robson, S., Greenfiedl, S. and Hargreaves, D. (2012) *Young Children's Creative Thinking*. London: Sage.

Furedi, F. (2009) *Wasted: Why Education Isn't Educating*. London: Continuum.

Gardner, H. (1993) *Frames of Mind: The Theory of Multiple Intelligences*, 2nd edn. London: Fontana.

Gardner, H. (1999a) *The Disciplined Mind: What All Students Should Understand*. New York: Simon and Schuster.

Gardner, H. (1999b) *Intelligence Reframed: Multiple Intelligence for the 21 Century*. New York: Basic Books.

Gardner, H. (2004) *Changing Minds: The Art and Science of Changing our Own and Other People's Minds*. Boston, MA: Harvard Business School.

Gardner, H., Csikszentmihalyi, M. and Damon, W. (2000) *Good Work: When Ethics and Excellence Meet*. New York: Basic Books.

Garrett, A., Carrion, V., Pageler, N., Menon, V., Mackenzie, K., Saltzman, K. and Reiss, A. (2002) fMRI Response to Facial Expression in Adolescent PTSD, paper presented at the 49th Annual Meeting of the American Academy of Child and Adolescent Psychiatry, San Francisco, CA, 22–27 October.

Geake, J. (2009) *The Brain at School: Educational Neuroscience in the Classroom*. Maidenhead: Open University Press.

Gerhardt, S. (2014) *Why Love Matters: How Affection Shapes a Baby's Brain*. London: Routledge.

Giedd, J., Blumenthal, J., Jeffries, N., Castellanos, F., Liu, H., Zijdenbos, A., Paus, T., Evans, A. and Rapoport, J. (1999) Brain development during childhood and adolescence: a longitudinal MRI study, *Nature Neuroscience*, 10: 861–3.

Gipps, C. and MacGilchrist, B. (1999) Primary school learners, in P. Mortimore (ed.), *Understanding Pedagogy and Its Impact on Learning*. London: Paul Chapman Publishing.

Gogtay, N., Giedd, J., Hayaski, K., Greenstein, D., Vaituzis, C., Hugent, T., Herman, D., Clasen, L., Toga, A., Rapoport, J. and Thompson, P. (2004) Dynamic mapping of human cortical development during childhood through early adulthood, *Proceedings of the National Academy of Sciences of the USA*, 101 (21): 8174–9.

Goldstein, L. (1997) *Teaching with Love: A Feminist Approach to Early Childhood Education*. New York: Peter Lang.

Goldstein, L. and Lake, V. (2000) Love, love, and more love for children: exploring pre-service teachers' understandings of caring, *Teaching and Teacher Education*, 16 (7): 861–72.

Goleman, D. (1996) *Emotional Intelligence*. London: Bloomsbury.

Goleman, D. (ed.) (1997) *Healing Emotions*. Boston, MA: Shambhala.

Goleman, D. (1999) *Working with Emotional Intelligence*. London: Bloomsbury.

Goleman, D. (2006) *Social Intelligence: The New Science of Human Relationships*. New York: Arrow.

Goouch, K. (2010) *Towards Excellence in Early Years Education: Exploring Narratives of Experience*. London: Routledge.

Goouch, K. and Powell, S. (2013) *The Baby Room*. London: Routledge.

Goswami, U. and Bryant, P. (2007) Children's Cognitive Development and Learning, *Primary Review Research Briefings 2/1*. Cambridge: University of Cambridge Faculty of Education.

Gove, M. (2009) 'First year education priorities for a new government', speech to the Centre for Policy Studies by Michael Gove, 5 November 2009.

Grainger, T., Barnes, J. and Scoffham, S. (2004) A creative cocktail: creative teaching in ITE, *Journal of Education in Teaching (JET)*, 30 (3): 243–53.

Greenfield, S. (2003) *Tomorrow's People*. Harmondsworth: Penguin.

Greenfield, S. (2009) *ID: The Quest for Meaning in the 21st Century*. London: Sceptre.

Greenfield, S. (2010) *You and Me: The Neuroscience of Identity*. London: Notting Hill.

Greenhalgh, P. (1994) *Emotional Growth and Learning*. London: Routledge.

Gruzelier, J. (2003) Enhancing music performance through brain rhythm training, *Music Forum* (Journal of the Music Council of Australia), October, pp. 34–5.

Guardian, The (2006) Alzheimer's drug could be widely sold to make everyone brainier, 27 January, p. 11.

Hallam, S. and Ireson, J. (1999) Pedagogy in the secondary school, in P. Mortimore (ed.), *Understanding Pedagogy and Its Impact on Learning*. London: Paul Chapman Publishing.

Halpin, P. (2003) *Hope and Education*. London: Routledge.

Hanko, G. (1999) *Increasing Competence through Collaborative Problem Solving*. London: David Fulton.

Harland, J., Kinder, K., Lord, P., Stott, A., Schagen, I. and Haynes, J. (2000) *Arts Education in Secondary Schools: Effects and Effectiveness*. Slough: NFER.

Hayes, D. (2003) *Planning Teaching and Class Management in Primary Schools.* London: David Fulton.

Hayes, D. and Ecclestone, C. (2008) *The Dangerous Rise of Therapeutic Education.* London: Routledge.

Henriksson-Macaulay, L. (2014) *The Music Maracle: The Scientific Secret to Unlocking Your Child's Full Potential.* London: Earnest House.

Hicks, D. (2006) *Lessons for the Future: The Missing Dimension in Education.* London: Routledge.

Hicks, D. (2014) *Educating for Hope in Troubled Times: Climate Change and the Transition to a Post Carbon Future.* Stoke-on-Trent: Trentham Books.

Higgins, S., Baumfield, V. and Leat, D. (2003) *Thinking Through Primary Teaching.* Cambridge: Kington.

Hirsch, E. (1999) *The Schools We Need: And Why We Don't Have Them.* New York: Anchor.

Hirsch, E. (2007) *The Knowledge Deficit: Closing the Shocking Education Gap for American Children.* New York: Houghton Mifflin Harcourt.

HMG (Her Majesty's Government) (2004) *Children Act 2004.* London: TSO.

HMG (Her Majesty's Government) (2006) *Education and Inspections Act.* London: TSO.

Hopwood-Stephens, I. (2013) *Learning on Your Doorstep.* London: Routledge.

House of Commons Education and Skills Committee (2005) *Education Outside the Classroom: Second Report of Session 2004–2005.* London: TSO.

House of Commons Education and Skills Committee (2007) *Creative Partnerships and the Curriculum.* London: TSO.

Howard-Jones, P. (2009) *Introducing Neuroeducational Research: Neuroscience, Education and the Brain, from Contexts to Practice.* London: Routledge.

Howard-Jones, P. (2012) *Education and Neuroscience: Evidence, Theory and Practical Application.* London: Routledge.

Howard-Jones, P. and Pickering, S. (2005) *Collaborative Frameworks for Neuroscience and Education: Scoping Paper.* Bristol: TLRP-ESRC.

Huppert, F., Baylis, N. and Keverne, B. (2005) *The Science of Well-being.* Oxford: Oxford University Press.

Illich, I. (1971) *Deschooling Society.* London: Calder and Boyars.

Isen, A. (2002) A role for neuropsychology in understanding the facilitating influence of positive affect on social behaviour and cognitive processes, in C. Snyder and S. Lopez (eds), *Handbook of Positive Psychology.* New York: Oxford University Press.

Jacobs, H. (2004) *Interdisciplinary Curriculum, Design and Implementation.* Heatherton, Victoria: Hawker Brownlow Education.

James, M. and Pollard, A. (2008) Learning and teaching in primary schools: insights from TLRP, *Primary Review Research Briefings 2/4.* Cambridge: University of Cambridge, Faculty of Education.

James, O. (2008) *The Selfish Capitalist: Origins of Affluenza.* London: Vermilion.

James, O. (2009) *Britain on the Couch: How Keeping Up with the Joneses Has Depressed Us Since 1950.* London: Vermilion.

Jeffrey, B. and Woods, P. (2003) *The Creative School*. London: Routledge.

Jensen, E. (1995) *Brain Based Learning*. Del Mar, CA: Eric Jensen.

Jensen, E. (2000*) Music with Brain in Mind*. San Diego, CA: The Brain Store.

John-Steiner, V. (2006) *Creative Collaboration*. Oxford: Oxford University Press.

John-Steiner, V., Panovsky, C. and Smith, L. (eds) (2008) *Sociocultural Approaches to Language and Literacy: An Interactionist Perspective*. Cambridge: Cambridge University Press.

Jones, P. (1995) Contradictions and unanswered questions in the Genie case: a fresh look at the linguistic evidence, *Language and Communication*, 15 (3): 261–80.

Justlin, P. and Sloboda, J. (2009) *Music and Emotion*. Cambridge: Cambridge University Press.

Kawachi, I., Sparrow, D., Vokonas, P. and Weiss, S. (1994) Symptoms of anxiety and risk of coronary heart disease, *Circulation*, 89: 1992–7.

Keverne, B. (2006) Understanding well-being in the evolutionary context of brain development, in F. Huppert, N. Baylis and B. Keverne, *The Science of Well-Being*. Oxford: Oxford University Press.

Khul, P. (2002) *Born to Learn: Language, Reading and the Brain of the Child*. North West Region, USA, Idaho, Early Learning Summit, 9–10 June.

Kirby, P., Lanyon, F. and Synelaw, R. (2003) *Building a Culture of Participation*. London: DfES.

Knight, S. (2013) *Forest School and Outdoor Learning in the Early Years*. London: Sage.

Koestler, A. (1964) *The Act of Creation*. London: Penguin Arkana.

Laevers, F. (1994a) *The Leuven Involvement Scale for Young Children, LIS-YC, Manual*. Leuven: Centre for Experiential Education.

Laevers, F. (ed.) (1994b) *Defining and Assessing Quality in Early Childhood Education*. Leuven: Leuven University Press.

Lave, J. and Wenger, E. (1991) *Situated Learning: Legitimate Peripheral Participation*. Cambridge: Cambridge University Press.

Layard, R. (2005) *Happiness*. London: Penguin.

Layard, R. (2006) *The Depression Report: A New Deal for Depression and Anxiety Disorders*. London: Centre for Economic Performance.

Layard, R. and Clark, D. (2014) *Thrive: The Power of Evidence-Based Psychological Therapies*. London: Penguin.

Layard, R. and Dunn, C. (2009) *A Good Childhood*. London: Penguin.

LeDoux, J. (1999) *The Emotional Brain*. London: Phoenix.

LeDoux, J. (2002) *The Synaptic Self*. New York: Viking.

Lee, A., Ogle, W. and Sapolsky, R. (2002) Stress and depression: possible links to neuron death in the hippocampus, *Bipolar Disorders*, 4 (2): 117.

Lucas, B., Claxton, G. and Spencer, E. (2013) *Expansive Education: Teaching Learners or the Real World*. London: McGraw Hill.

Luna, B. and Sweeney, J. (2004) The emergence of collaborative brain function: fMRI studies of the development of response inhibition, *Annals of the New York Academy of Science*, 1021 (1): 296–309.

McGilchrist, I. (2010) *The Master and His Emissary: The Divided Brain and the Making of the Western World*. London: Yale University Press.

Maguire, E., Gadian, D., Johnsrude, I., Good, C., Ashburner, J., Frackowiak, R. and Frith, C. (2000) Navigation-related structural change in the hippocampi of taxi drivers, *Proceedings of the National Academy of Sciences USA*, 97 (8): 4398–403.

Marks, M. and Shah, H. (2006) A well-being manifesto for a flourishing society, in F. Huppert, N. Baylis and B. Keverne, *The Science of Well-being*. Oxford: Oxford University Press.

Martin, F. (2012) 'The geographies of difference', *Geography,* 97 (3): 116-22.

Marton, F. and Booth, S. (1997) *Learning and Awareness*. Mahwah, NJ: Lawrence Erlbaum Associates.

Marton, F. and Saljo, R. (1976) On qualitative differences in learning: I – outcome and process, *British Journal of Educational Technology*, 46: 115–27.

Maslow, A. (1943) A theory of human motivation, *Psychological Review*, 50: 370–96.

Maynard, T. (2007) Forest schools in Great Britain: an initial exploration, *Contemporary Issues in Early Childhood*, 8 (4): 320–31.

Mithen, S. (1996) *The Prehistory of the Mind: A Search for the Origins of Art, Religion and Science*. London: Thames and Hudson.

Mithen, S. (2005) *The Singing Neanderthals: The Origins of Music, Language, Mind and Body*. London: Phoenix.

McCauley, C. and Rose, W. (2010) *Child Well-being: Understanding Children's Lives*. London: Kingsley.

McCrea, R. (2005) Personal email communication 25/10/2005.

Morris, D. (2004) *The Nature of Happiness*. London: Little Books.

Morris, E. and Scott, C. (2002) *Whole School Emotional Literacy Indicator*. Frampton on Severn: School of Emotional Literacy Press.

Moseley, J. (1996) *Quality Circle Time in the Primary School*. Wisbech: LDA.

Murray, J. (2007) TV violence: research and controversy, in N. Pecora, J. Murray and E. Wartella (eds) *Children and Television: Fifty Years of Research*. Mahwah, NJ: Erlbaum.

Nachmanovitch, S. (1990) *Free Play: Improvisation in Life and Art*. New York: Penguin Putnam.

NACCCE (National Advisory Council on Creative and Cultural Education) (1999) *All Our Futures: Creativity, Culture and Education*. London: DfEE.

Noddings, N. (2003) *Happiness and Education*. Cambridge: Cambridge University Press.

OECD (Organization for Economic Cooperation and Development) (2003) *Learners for Life: Student Approaches to Learning*. Paris: OECD Publications.

OECD (Organization for Economic Cooperation and Development) (2009) *Doing Better for Children*. Paris: OECD.

Ofsted (Office for Standards in Education) (1998) *Maintaining Breadth and Balance*. London: Ofsted.

Ofsted (Office for Standards in Education) (2002) *The Curriculum in Successful Primary Schools*. London: Ofsted.

Ofsted (Office for Standards in Education) (2008) *Geography in Schools: Changing Practice*. London: TSO.

Ofsted (Office for Standards in Education) (2009a) *12 Outstanding Secondary Schools – Excelling Against the Odds*. London: Ofsted.

Ofsted (Office for Standards in Education) (2009b) *20 Outstanding Primary Schools – Excelling Against the Odds*. London: Ofsted.

Ofsted (Office for Standards in Education) (2010a) *Learning: Creative Approaches that Raise Standards*. London: Ofsted.

Ofsted (Office for Standards in Education) (2010b) *Personal, Social, Health and Economic Education in Schools*. Manchester: Ofsted.

Ofsted (Office for Standards in Education) (2012) *Moving English Forward: Action to Raise Standards in English*. London: Ofsted.

Overy, K. (1998) Can music really improve the mind? *Psychology of Music*, 26: 97–9.

Pahl, R. (2000) *On Friendship*. Cambridge: Polity Press.

Palmer, S. (2007) *Toxic Childhood: How the Modern World Is Damaging Our Children and What We Can Do About It*. London: Orion.

Panksepp, J. and Biven, L. (2012) *The Archaeology of the Mind: The Neuroevolutionary Origins of Human Emotion*. New York: Norton.

Pantev, C., Oostenveld, R., Engelien, A., Ross, B., Roberts, L. and Hoke, M. (1998) Increased auditory cortical representation in musicians, *Nature*, 392: 811–14.

Peal, R. (2014) *Progressively Worse: The Burden of Bad Ideas in British Schools*. Civitas: London.

Perkins, D. (1992) *Smart Schools*. New York: Free Press.

Perkins, D. (1995) *Outsmarting IQ: The Emerging Science of Learnable Intelligence*. New York: Free Press.

Perkins, D. (2002) *The Eureka Effect: The Art and Logic of Breakthrough Thinking*. New York: Norton.

Perkins, D. (2006) Whole game learning, presentation at 'This Learning Life' conference, University of Bristol, 20 April.

Perkins, D. (2009) *Making Learning Whole: How Seven Principles of Teaching Can Transform Education*. San Francisco, CA: Jossey–Bass.

Piaget, J. (1954) *The Construction of Reality in the Child*, trans. M. Cook. New York: Basic Books.

Pinker, S. (1994) *The Language Instinct: The New Science of Language and Mind*. New York: Penguin Science.

Pinker, S. (2002) *The Blank Slate*. London: Penguin.

Plato (1955) *The Republic*, trans. D. Lee. London: Penguin Classics.

Plato (1970) *The Laws*, trans. T. Saunders. London: Penguin Classics.

Pollard, A. (1996) *The Social World of Children's Learning*. London: Cassell.

Pollard, A. (2008) *Reflective Teaching: Evidence-informed Professional Practice*, 3rd edn. London: Continuum.

Pollard, A. (ed.) (2010) *Professionalism and Pedagogy: A Contemporary Opportunity: A Commentary by TLRP and GTCE*. London: TLRP.

Pope, R. (2005) *Creativity: History, Theory, Practice*. London: Routledge.

Popenici, S. (2006) Imagine the Future: Role Models and Schools' Captured Imagination, paper presented at the International Conference on Imagination and Education, Vancouver, July.

Popper, K. (1978) Three Worlds, paper presented at the Tanner Lecture on Human Values, University of Michigan, 7 April.

Potts, P. (ed.) (2003) *Inclusion in the City: Selection, Schooling and Community*. London: Routledge.

Powell, S. and Barnes, J. (2008) *Evaluation of the TRACK Project*. Report to Future Creative (formerly Creative Partnerships). Margate: Future Creative.

Prince's Trust (2010) *YouGov Youth Index: Tune In*. London: The Prince's Trust.

QCA (Qualifications and Curriculum Authority) (1998a) *A Scheme of Work for Key Stages 1 and 2: Geography, History, Design Technology, Physical Education*. London: QCA.

QCA (Qualifications and Curriculum Authority) (1998b) *Maintaining Breadth and Balance*. London: QCA.

QCA (2002a) *Citizenship at Key Stages 1–4*, 1 January QCA/02/944. London: QCA.

QCA (2002b) *Designing and Timetabling the Primary Curriculum*. London: QCA.

Raffo, C., Dyson, A., Gunter, H., Hall, D., Jones, L. and Kalambouka, A. (eds) (2010) *Education and Poverty in Affluent Countries*. Abingdon: Routledge.

Rees, G., Haridhan, G., Pople, L., Bradshaw, J., Keung, A. and Main, G. (2012) *Measuring National Well-Being – Children's Well-being*. London: National Office of Statistics.

Riddle, J. (2009) *Engaging the Eye Generation: Visual Literacy Strategies for the K-5 Classroom*. Portland, OR: Stenhouse.

Riley, P. (2006) To Stir with Love: Imagination, Attachment and Teacher Behaviour, paper delivered at the International Conference on Imagination in Education, Vancouver, July.

Riley, P. (2009) An adult attachment perspective on student–teacher relationship and classroom management difficulties, in Teaching and Teacher Education, 25 (5): 626–35.

Roberts, P. (2006) *Nurturing Creativity in Young People: A Report to Government to Inform Future Policy*. London: DCMS.

Robertson, I. (1999) *Mind Sculpture*. London: Bantam.

Robertson, I. (2002) *The Mind's Eye*. London: Bantam.

Robertson, I. (2012) *The Winner Effect: The Neuroscience of Success and Failure*. New York: Thomas Dunne.

Robinson, K. (2001) *Out of Our Minds*. London: Capstone.

Robinson, K. and Aronica, L. (2010) *The Element: How Finding Your Passion Changes Everything*. London: Penguin.

Rogers, R. (1999) *The Disappearing Arts*. London: RSA/Gulbenkian.

Rogers, R. (2003) *Time for the Arts?* London: RSA.

Rogers, S. (2010) Play and pedagogy: A conflict of interests?, in S. Rogers (ed.), *Rethinking Play and Pedagogy: Contexts, Concepts and Cultures*. London: Routledge.

Rogoff, B. (2003) *The Cultural Nature of Human Development*. New York: Oxford University Press.

Rose, J. (2008) *Independent Review of the Primary Curriculum: Interim Report*. London: DCSF.

Rose, J. (2009) *Independent Review of the Primary Curriculum*. London: DCSF.

Roth, M. (2000) The metamorphosis of Columbus, in S. Wineburg and P. Grossman (eds), *Interdisciplinary Curriculum: Challenges to Implementation*. New York: Teachers College Press.

RSA (Royal Society of Arts) (2003) *Opening Minds: Project Handbook*. London: RSA.

Ruddock, J. and MacIntyre, D. (2007) *Improving Learning through Consulting Pupils*. London: Routledge.

Ryff, C. (1989) Happiness is everything, or is it? Explorations on the meaning of psychological well-being, *Journal of Personality and Social Psychology*, 57 (6): 1081–9.

Salovey, P. and Sluyter, D. (1997) *Emotional Development and Emotional Intelligence*. New York: Basic Books.

Saron, C. and Davidson, R.J. (1997) The brain and emotions, in D. Goleman (ed.), *Healing Emotions*. Boston, MA: Shambhala.

SCAA (School Curriculum and Assessment Authority) (1997) *The Arts and the Curriculum*. London: SCAA.

Scoffham, S. (ed.) (2010) *Primary Geography Handbook*. Sheffield: Geographical Association.

Scoffham, S. and Barnes, J. (2009) Transformational experiences and deep learning: the impact of an intercultural study visit to India on UK Initial Teacher Education students, *Journal of Education for Teaching*, 35 (3): 257–70.

Scottish Executive (2004) *A Curriculum for Excellence*. Edinburgh: Scottish Executive.

Seligman, M. (2004) *Authentic Happiness*. New York: Basic Books.

Seltzer, K. and Bentley, T. (1999) *The Creative Age: Knowledge and Skills for the New Economy*. London: Demos.

Sharma, N. (2008) *Makiguchi and Ghandi: Their Educational Relevance for the Twenty-first Century*. Plymouth: University Press of America.

Sharp, P. (2001) *Nurturing Emotional Literacy*. London: David Fulton.

Shayer, M. and Adey, P. (2002) *Learning Intelligence: Cognitive Acceleration Across the Curriculum from 5 to 15 years*. Buckingham: Open University Press.

Shepherd, L. (1991) Psychometricians' beliefs about learning, *Education Researcher*, 20 (8): 2–16.

Shepard, L. (1992) What policy makers who mandate tests should know about the new psychology of intellectual ability and learning, in B. Gifford and M. O'Conner (eds), *Changing Assessments: Alternative Views of Aptitude, Achievement and Instruction*. London: Kluwer.

Shirley, I. (2007) Exploring the great outdoors, in R. Austin (ed.), *Letting the Outside In: Developing Teaching and Learning Beyond the Early Years Classroom*. Stoke-on-Trent: Trentham Books.

Silber, K. (1965) *Pestalozzi: The Man and His Work*. London: Routledge.

Smith, A. and Call, N. (2000) *The Alps Approach: Accelerated Learning in Primary Schools*. Stafford: Network Educational Press.

Smith, F., Hardman, F., Wall, K. and Mroz, M. (2004) Interactive whole class teaching in the national literacy and numeracy strategies, *British Educational Research Journal*, 30 (3): 395–411.

SOED (Scottish Office of Education) (1993) *National Guidelines 5–14: Environmental Studies*. Edinburgh: SOED.

Steiner, R. (1919) *Education: An Introductory Reader*. London: Rudolf Steiner Press.

Sternberg, R. (1997a) *Thinking Styles*. Cambridge: Cambridge University Press.

Sternberg, R. (1997b) *Successful Intelligence*. New York: Plume.

Sternberg, R. (2002) Teaching Students to Be Wise and Not Just Smart, keynote lecture delivered at the 10th International Conference on Thinking, Harrogate, 16 June.

Sternberg, R. (2003) *Wisdom, Intelligence and Creativity Synthesised*. Cambridge: Cambridge University Press.

Sternberg, R. (2008) *The New Psychology of Love*. New York: Yale University Press.

Sternberg, R. and Williams, W. (eds) (1998) *Intelligence, Instruction and Assessment*. Mahwah, NJ: Lawrence Erlbaum Associates.

Stone-Wiske, M. (ed.) (1998) *Teaching for Understanding*. San Francisco, CA: Jossey-Bass.

Swanwick, K. (1994) *Musical Knowledge: Intuition, Analysis and Music Education*. London: Routledge.

Swanwick, K. (1999) *Teaching Music Musically*. London: Routledge.

Teacher Training Agency (TTA) (2003) *Qualifying to Teach: Handbook of Guidance*. London: TTA.

Theroux, L. (2006) *The Call of the Weird*. London: Pan.

Thomson, P., Hall, C., Jones, K. and Sefton Green, J. (2012) *Signature Pedagogies*. London: Creativity, Culture and Education.

Thompson, P.M., Giedd, J.N., Woods, R.P., MacDonald, D., Evans, A.C. and Toga, A.W. (2000) Growth patterns in the developing brain detected by using continuum mechanical tensor maps, *Nature*, 404: 190–3.

Tokuhama-Espinoza, T. (2014) *Making Classrooms Better – 50 Practical Applications of Mind, Brain and Education Science: Lessons from the Cognitive Revolution*. New York: Norton.

Twigg, S. (2012) *Policy Review, Devolving Power in Education: School Freedom and Accountability*. London: Labour Party.

UK Board of Education (1931) *The Primary School* (Hadow Report). London: HMSO.

Vygotsky, L. (1962) *Thought and Language*. New York: Wiley.

Vygotsky, L. (1978) *Mind in Society: The Development of Higher Psychological Processes*, Cambridge, MA: Harvard University Press.

Warnock, M. (1996) Foreword, in M. Bennathan and M. Boxall, *Effective Intervention in Primary Schools*. London: David Fulton.

Weare, K. and Gray, G. (2003) *What Works in Developing Children's Emotional and Social Competence and Well Being?* Norwich: TSO.

Wenger, E. (1998) *Communities of Practice: Learning, Meaning and Identity*. Cambridge: Cambridge University Press.

White, J. (2002) *The Child's Mind*. London: Routledge.

Willingham, D (2013) *Why Students Don't Like School: A Cognitive Scientist Answers Questions About How the Mind Works*. San Francisco, CA: Jossey-Bass.

Wilson, V., Durrant, J., Stow, W., Barnes, J. and Gershon, J. (2010) Virtuous Triangles for Curriculum Innovation and Pupil Participation: Supporting School-based Action Research Through Local Authority and HEI Collaboration, BERA conference, University of Warwick, 3 September.

Wineburg, S. and Grossman, P. (eds) (2000) *Interdisciplinary Curriculum: Challenges to Implementation*. New York: Teachers College Press.

Wood, D. (2001) Scaffolding, contingent tutoring and computer supported learning, *International Journal of Artificial Intelligence in Education*, 12: 280–92.

Wrigley, T. (2005) *Schools of Hope: A New Agenda for School Improvement*, reprinted edn. Stoke-on-Trent: Trentham Books.

Wrigley, T., Thomson, P. and Lingard, B. (2012) *Changing Schools: Alternative Ways to Make a World of Difference*. London: Routledge.

Yates, K., Taylor, H., Drotar, D., Wade, S., Klein, S., Stancin, T. and Schatschneider, C. (1997) Pre-injury family environment as a determinate of recovery from traumatic brain injuries in school aged children, *Journal of the International Neurophysiological Society*, 3: 617–30.

Young Foundation (2010) *The State of Happiness*. London: Young Foundation.

WEBSITES

A New Direction (AND): www.anewdirection.org.uk/ (accessed 21 July 2014)

Ashley Primary School website: www.ashleyschool.org.uk/ (accessed 21 July 2014)

Assessment Reform Group: www.aaia.org.uk/afl/assessment-reform-group/ (accessed 25 June 2014)

Australian Curriculum Assessment and Reporting Authority (2013): www.aus traliancurriculum.edu.au/CrossCurriculumPriorities (accessed 21 July 2014)

Baird, A. and Fugelsang, J. (2004) The emergence of consequential thought: evidence from neuroscience, *Philosophical Transactions of the Royal Society*, published online November, available at: http://royalsocietypublishing.org/journals (accessed 21 July 2014)

Bawden, A. (2006) On social cohesion, *Guardian* article, available at: www.guardian.co.uk/society/2006/oct/05/comment.politics (accessed 21 July 2014)

BBC News (2010) Facebook is a major influence on girls, says survey. http://news.bbc.co.uk/1/hi/education/10121931.stm (accessed 21 July 2014)

British Columbia Ministry of Education (2013) *Rethinking Curriculum*, available at: https://curriculum.gov.bc.ca/node/2311#rethinking_core (accessed 21 July, 2014)

Callaghan, J. (1976) Towards a national debate (The full text of the speech by Prime Minister James Callaghan, at a foundation stone-laying ceremony at Ruskin College, Oxford, on 18 October 1976), available at www.educationeng land.org.uk/documents/speeches/1976ruskin.html (accessed 30 August 2014)

Campaign for Learning: www.campaign-for-learning.org.uk/cfl/index.asp (accessed 7 September 2014)

CBBC Newsround, Mobile phones. http://news.bbc.co.uk/cbbcnews/hi/find_out/guides/tech/mobiles/newsid_1608000/1608701.stm (accessed 21 July 2014)

Childnet International: www.childnet-int.org (accessed 21 July 2014)

Children's Commissioner for England: www.childrenscommissioner.gov.uk/ (accessed 22 June 2014)

Children's Society (2014) The Good Childhood Report. www.childrenssociety.org.uk/ (accessed 7 September 2014)

Clarke, S.: www.shirleyclarke-education.org (accessed July 21 2014)

Claxton, G. (2006) Building Learning Power, available at: www.buildinglearning power.co.uk (accessed July 21 2014)

Creativity, Culture and Education (2012) *Changing Young Lives*, available at: www.creativitycultureeducation.org/changing-young-lives-2012 (accessed 21 July 2014)

Csikszentmihalyi, M. (2004) Lecture on flow theory, available at: www.ted.com/talks/mihaly_csikszentmihalyi_on_flow.html (accessed 21 July 2014)

Curriculum Foundation, available at: www.curriculumfoundation.org/ (accessed 21 July 2014)

DfE (Department for Education) (2011) *The Early Years Foundation Stage (Tickell review): report on the evidence*, available at: www.gov.uk/government/publications/the-early-years-foundation-stage-review-report-on-the-evidence (accessed 22 June 2014)

DfE (Department for Education) (2013) Primary National Curriculum in England, available at https://www.gov.uk/government/uploads/system/uploads/attachment_data/file/335133/PRIMARY_national_curriculum_220714.pdf (accessed 18 December 2014)

DfE (Department for Education) (2014a) *Sure Start Children's Centres: Local Authorities' Duties*, available at: www.gov.uk/sure-start-childrens-centres-local-authorities-duties (accessed 21 July 2014)

DfE (Department for Education) (2014b) Health and safety: advice for schools, available at: www.gov.uk/government/publications/health-and-safety-advice-for-schools (accessed 21 July 2014)

DfE (Department for Education) (2014c) www.education.gov.uk/get-into-teaching/teacher-training-options/school-based-training (accessed 12 September 2014)

DfES (Department for Education and Skills) (2004) Every Child Matters, available at: http://webarchive.nationalarchives.gov.uk/20130401151715/https://www.education.gov.uk/publications/standard/publicationDetail/Page1/DfES/1081/2004 (accessed 21 July 2014)

DfES (Department for Education and Skills) (2005) Social, emotional and behavioural skills, available at: www.teachernet.gov.uk/wholeschool/sen/datatypes/Behaviour_emotionaldevelopment/ (accessed August 2010)

DfES (Department for Education and Skills) (2006a) The Creative Learning Journey, available at www.creativelearningjourney.org.uk/ (accessed July 2010)

DfES (Department for Education and Skills) (2006b) Learning Outside the Classroom Manifesto, available at: www.lotc.org.uk/getmedia/fe5e8f73-a53c4310-84af-c5e8c3b32435/Manifesto.aspx (accessed 21 July 2014)

DENI (Department of Education for Northern Ireland) School Councils website, available at: www.deni.gov.uk/index/support-and-development-2/school councils-2.htm (accessed 22 June, 2014)

Djuric, Z., Bird, C., Furumoto-Dawson, A., Raucher, G., Ruffin, M., Stowe, R., Tucker, K. and Masi, C. (2008) Biomarkers of psychological stress in Health Disparities Research, available at: www. ncbi.nlm.nih.gov/pmc/articles/PMC2841407/ (accessed 21 July 2014)

Dunbar, R. (1998) The Social Brain Hypothesis, *Evolutionary Anthropology*, pp. 178–190, available at: http://psych.colorado.edu/~tito/sp03/7536/Dunbar_1998.pdf (accessed 22 June 2014)

Eco-Schools: www.eco-schools.org.uk (accessed 21 July 2014)

Educationscotland: www.educationscotland.gov.uk/schoolsglobalfootprint/videos/index.asp (accessed 21 July 2014)

Engaging Places (2009) www.engagingplaces.org.uk/network/art68390 (accessed July 2010)

Forest Schools: www.forestschools.com/ (accessed 21 July 2014)

Frontline (2002) Article/video on the teenage brain, available at: www.pbs.org/wgbh/pages/frontline/shows/teenbrain/view/ (accessed 21 July 2014)

Geographical Association: www.geography.org.uk (accessed 29 August 2014)

Gov.UK (2010a) Government announces changes to qualifications and the curriculum, available at: www.gov.uk/government/news/government-announces-changes-to-qualifications-and-the-curriculum (accessed 7 September 2014)

Gov.UK (2010b) Education Secretary Michael Gove announces review of music education. www.gov.uk/government/news/education-secretary-michael-gove-announces-review-of-music-education (accessed 8 September 2014)

Guardian (2014) Pupil premium struggling to close GCSE attainment gap, available at: www.theguardian.com/education/2014/jan/28/pupil-premium-gcse-attainment-gap (accessed 21 July 2014)

Historical Association: www.history.org.uk (accessed 29 August 2014)

Hoffer, E. (2006) www.en.wikipedia.org/wiki/Eric_Hoffer (accessed 21 July 2014)

House of Commons Education Committee (2012) *Great Teachers: Attracting, training and retaining the best teachers*, available at: www.publications.parliament.uk/pa/cm201012/cmselect/cmeduc/1515/151508.htm (accessed 21 July 2014)

IPC (International Primary Curriculum): www.greatlearning.com/ipc/ (accessed 22 June 2014)

MACOS (2010) *Man: A Course of Study.* www.macosonline.org (accessed 21 July 2014)

Marmot, M. (2010) *Fair Society Healthy Lives*, The Marmot Review, available at: www.ucl.ac.uk/whitehallII/pdf/FairSocietyHealthyLives.pdf (accessed 21 July 2014)

New Horizons (1991) Perkins article on Mindware, available at: http://education.jhu.edu/PD/newhorizons/future/creating_the_future/crfut_perkins.cfm (accessed 21 July 2014)

Northern Ireland Curriculum: www.nicurriculum.org.uk

NSPCC, Annual review, available at: www.nspccannualreview.org.uk/ (accessed 21 July 2014)

Office for National Statistics (2012) *Measuring National Well-Being – Children's Well-being*, available at: www.ons.gov.uk/ons/dcp171766_283988.pdf (accessed 21 July 2014)

Ofsted (Office for Standards in Education) (2003) *Expecting the Unexpected*, available at: www.ofsted.gov.uk/resources/expecting-unexpected-0 (accessed 21 July 2014)

Ofsted (Office for Standards in Education) (2012) *Moving English Forward*, available at: www.slideshare.net/Ofstednews/moving-english-forward (accessed 21 July 2014)

Ofsted (2013) Inspection Report: West Rise Junior School. www.ofsted.gov.uk/inspection-reports/find-inspection-report/provider/ELS/114467 (accessed 8 September 2014)

Pew Internet and American Life project: www.pewinternet.org/Reports/2001/Teenage-Life-Online/Part-2/1-Family.aspx?r=1 (accessed 21 July 2014)

P4C (Philosophy for Children): www.philosophyforchildren.co.uk/ (accessed 21 July 2014)

Project Zero: http://pzweb.harvard.edu/ (accessed July 21 2014)

Public Health England (2013) *How Healthy Behaviour Supports Children's Well-Being*, available at: www.gov.uk/government/uploads/system/uploads/attachment_data/file/232978/Smart_Restart_280813_web.pdf (accessed 21 July 2014)

Puttnam, D. (2009) *We Are The People We've Been Waiting For.* www.wearethepeoplemovie.com/ (accessed 21 July 2014)

QCA (2003) Respect for all: reflecting cultural diversity through the curriculum, available at: http://webarchive.nationalarchives.gov.uk/20090902230247/qcda.gov.uk/6753.aspx (accessed 21 July 2014)

Reggio Emilia (2006) http://zerosei.comune.re.it/inter/index.htm (accessed 21 July 2014)

Robinson, K. (2008) Changing Education Paradigms, RSA lecture, available at: http://comment.rsablogs.org.uk/2010/10/14/rsa-animate-changing-education-paradigms/ (21 July 2014)

Room 13 International: http://room13international.org/ (accessed 21 July 2014)

Rousseau, J-J. (1762) Emile: http://oll.libertyfund.org/titles/2256 (accessed 7 September 2014)

RSA Opening Minds Curriculum: www.rsaopeningminds.org.uk/ (accessed 21 July 2014)

RSA Peterborough Project: www.thersa.org/action-research-centre/learning,cognition-and-creativity/education/practical-projects/area-based-curriculum/reports-and-case-studies/peterborough-curriculum-case-study-bishop-creighton-academy-and-peterborough-cathedral (accessed 21 July 2014)

Sanchez, E. and Gruber, H. (2005) *Rhythm Is It* [film], available at: www.rhythmisit.com/en/php/index_noflash.php (accessed 21 July 2014)

School Councils UK: www.schoolcouncils.org/ (accessed 21 July 2014)

Scottish Curriculum for Excellence: www.educationscotland.gov.uk/thecurriculum/whatiscurriculumforexcellence/thepurposeofthecurriculum/index.asp (accessed 22nd June 2014)

SEAL (Social and Emotional Aspects of Learning) (2006) www.gov.uk/government/publications/social-and-emotional-aspects-of-learning-seal programme-in-secondary-schools-national-evaluation (accessed 21 July 2014)

Signature Pedagogies: www.signaturepedagogies.org.uk/ (accessed 21 July 2014)

Sing up: www.singup.org (accessed 21 July 2014)

Stephen Lawrence Inquiry (1999) Macpherson Report, available at: www.gov.uk/government/publications/the-stephen-lawrence-inquiry (accessed 21 July 2014)

Storyline (2010) www.storyline-scotland.com/what-is-storyline-2/ (accessed 21 July 2014)

Summerhill School website: www.summerhillschool.co.uk/an-overview.php (accessed 21 July 2014)

Teachers Assurance (2013) *Stress Levels Affecting Performance*, available at: www.teachersassurance.co.uk/money-news/teachers-stress-levels-affecting-performance (accessed 25 July 2014)

Techeye (2010) www.techeye.net/internet/children-find-social-networking-more-important-than-family (accessed 21 July 2014)

TES (Times Educational Supplement) (2010) Gove on education, 28 May, available at: www.tes.co.uk/article.aspx?storycode=6045168 (accessed 21 July 2014)

UN (2000) United Nation's Millennium Goals, available at: www.un.org/millenniumgoals/ (accessed 21 July 2014)

UNICEF (1989) *The United Nations Convention on the Rights of the Child*, available at: www.unicef.org.uk/Documents/Publication-pdfs/UNCRC_PRESS200910web.pdf (accessed 21 July 2014)

UNICEF (2010) *The State of the World's Children*, available at: www.unicef.org/rightsite/sowc/pdfs/SOWC_Spec%20Ed_CRC_Main%20Report_EN_090409.pdf (accessed 21 July 2014)

UNICEF (2013) *Innocenti Report Card 11: Child Well-Being in Rich Countries*. UNICEF Office of Research, available at: www.unicef.org.uk/Images/Campaigns/FINAL_RC11-ENG-LORES-fnl2.pdf (accessed 21 July 2014)

University of Michigan health website: www.med.umich.edu/yourchild/topics/tv.htm (accessed 21 July 2014)

West Rise Juniors, *The Brian Stent Story*, YouTube: www.youtube.com/watch?v=2KH_wG9YGHo (accessed 21 July 2014)

WHO (World Health Organization) (2012) *Social Determinates of Health and Well-Being Among Young People: Health Behaviour in School Aged Children: International Report from the 2009/10 Study*. Copenhagen: World Health Organization Regional Office for Europe, available at: www.euro.who.int/__data/assets/pdf_file/0003/163857/Social-determinants-of-health-and-well-being-among-young-people.pdf (accessed 29 August 2014)

Youth Music: www.youthmusic.org.uk/musicispower/index.html (accessed 21 July 2014)

INDEX

Added to a page number 'f' denotes a figure or illustration and 't' denotes a table.

Abbs, P. 174, 208, 289
abstract thinking 139
academies 21, 61, 117, 196, 221, 233, 306, 319
accelerated learning 175
acceptance 187
accommodation 16
accomplishment 195
achievement 2, 79, 116, 119, 125, 130, 146, 188, 275, 280, 298, 299
action researchers 287
active learning 52, 159
activity 16, 51, 60, 112, 181
Adey, P. 159, 161
adult-dominated curriculum 2, 15
adults
   informed view of twenty-first century 223–5
   learning from 193
   relationships with 115
   views on education 210–11
Advanced Skills Teachers 55
Ainscow, M. 122, 268
Ajegbo report (2007) 119
alcoholism 43
Alexander, R. 51, 111, 114, 178
   see also Cambridge Primary Review
amygdala 147f, 148, 149
analytical teachers 122
analytical thinking 163
appreciation 116
Area Based Curriculum 104
areas of learning 59, 60
art(s)
   as a curriculum subject 53, 55, 59, 67, 69, 268, 285, 294
   impact on education 197
   language in 177
   working with local organizations/bodies 22
Art/Design 55, 170
artefacts 124

Article 12 (UNCRC) 232
assessment 245–65
   of child's capability 194
   early forms of 246
   of engagement 262–4
   formalized 247
   functions 247
   performances of understanding 240, 253–8, 294–5
   significant and long-lasting 246
   of well-being 248
   see also formative assessment; peer assessment; self-assessments; summative assessment
assessment for learning 249
Assessment Reform Group 58
assimilation 16
Association of Living Values 210
assumptions 12–13, 122
attachments 34, 113
attainment targets 290
attention deficit/hyperactivity disorder 131, 142
attention regulation 152
attitudes
   of children in class 304
   cross-curricular pedagogies and 14
   playful 273
   school perception of 155
   to teaching 219–22
   towards children 222–3
   see also creative attitudes; negative attitudes; positive attitudes
auditory cortex 154
Australia 61
authentic challenge 2
autobiographical self 36, 314
autoethnography 3, 4–5
autonomy 34, 188, 313
axons 134, 136

backsliding 149
Bandura, A. 111, 159
Barriers and boundaries (case study) 200
Beach Schools 282–3
behaviour 313–15
behavioural and emotional difficulties 43
beliefs 213–17
belonging 67, 303
Bentley, T. 22–3
Bernstein, B. 111, 119
best work 58
biases 122
bisociation 87, 196
Black, P. 249
Blythe, T. 294
Boden, M. 311
body language 248, 285
body-mind 39, 132, 136, 144, 145
Booth, T. 122, 123, 268
born-with intelligence 165
Bourdieu, P. 111, 120–1, 124
Bowlby, J. 172
brain
    effects of stress on 142, 143
    left and right hemispheres 136–7
    maturing 137–41, 224
    response to positive states 39
    see also neuroscience
brain development 141, 165
brain scans 131–2, 137, 143f, 145, 149, 156
brain-based approaches 129, 149, 150, 151, 160
Brice Heath, S. 177, 275–6
bridging curriculum 307
British Columbia 61–2
British values 267
'Broaden and Build' theory 39, 174
Bruner, J. 17, 31, 52, 111, 112–13, 274
Building Learning Power 178
Burke, C. 43

Cadw 118, 126
Callaghan, James 52
Cambridge Primary Review (Alexander) 7, 21,
    58–60, 63, 207, 230, 247
Campaign for Learning 17
catecholamines 142
Catling, S. 13
cerebellum 147
challenge 2, 65, 142, 298, 314
challenging behaviour 169
change
    experience of 20–1
    managing 305–8
    and teacher health 61

chaos (mental) 118
child as craftsman 193–4
child development 52
child well-being
    assessment 248
    curriculum based around 146
    government interest in 18
    importance of 38
    in post-industrial societies 172
    relationships and 35
    school reports and self-assessments 45, 55
child-centred education 16–17, 50, 51, 216
childhood 41–5, 185
ChildLine 34
children
    assumption of creative potential 12
    attitudes towards 222–3
    consulting 231–4
    marginalization of 13
    as partners in relationships 111–12
    pessimism about the future 22
    see also pupil voice
Children Act (2004) 232
Children learning in schools (DES) 51–2
Children and Young Persons Unit (CYPU) 232
Children's British Broadcasting Corporation
    (CBBC) 31
children's centres 34
Children's Commissioners 232, 233
children's interests
    cross-curricular themes 47
    in global themes, supporting 30–3
    in ICT, harnessing 23–30
    in relationships 33–5
children's parliaments 233
children's rights *see* United Nations Convention
    on the Rights of the Child
children's services 45
Children's Society 34
child's world 13, 63
choice 233
Chomsky, N. 176
chronic anxiety 173
Circle Time 233
citizenship 13, 22, 35, 53, 55, 59, 62, 68, 69, 87,
    232, 268, 306, 310
Clarke, S. 249
classroom culture 164
classrooms
    creative-friendly 273–4
    education outside 318
    see also thinking classrooms
Claxton, G. 169, 172, 178
co-learners 188

Coalition government 21, 58, 60, 61, 117, 185, 309
'codes' of language 119
Cognitive Acceleration study 287
cognitive psychology 160, 166, 167, 168, 178
cohesive communities 117
collaborative groups 112, 159
collaborative learning 215
collaborative work 125–6
collegiate institutions 207
Collishaw, S. 43
Comenius, J. 14, 15, 202
commitment 195
Common Curriculum (1991) 54
communication 67, 110, 119
    planning 285
    through good pedagogy 192–6
    see also conversations; dialogue; language;
        mobile phones; self-talk; social
        networking
communities of practice 207
community(ies)
    and effective learning 305
    issues, assessment questions 252t
    and social learning 117–18
    see also cross-community understanding;
        school-community partnerships
community cohesion 117
community curriculum 59
confidence 23, 273
connections 273
    creative 111
    deep learning and meaningful 229–30
    making
        between curriculum and children's lives 2
        between subjects 72–3, 75, 87
    with the wider world 32
    see also neural connections
consciousness 51, 132, 134, 180
consulting children 231–4
control
    through ICT 26, 29
    see also impulse control; locus of control;
        self-control; sense of control
conversations
    about values and curriculum 267
    development of creativity 271
    within schools 206–7
core self 36
core subjects 53, 54, 67, 79, 247
    see also English; mathematics; science
cortisol 142
Craft, A. 87
creations/products 124

creative attitudes 169
creative collaboration 159
creative colleagues 270
creative curriculum 87–96
Creative Futures 118
creative outsiders 271
Creative Partnerships 3, 55, 73, 76, 118, 167, 177, 269
creative schools 74–5
creative teachers 197, 198, 279
creative teaching 11, 270–2, 298
Creative Teaching for Tomorrow (CTFT) 3
creative thinking 55, 65, 72, 86, 273–4, 313
creativity 59, 111, 196–8
    as an issue for debate 311–12
    appreciation of 116
    assessment questions 252t
    assumptions about 12
    authentic contexts 12
    behaviour and 169
    bisociation 87
    control of brainwaves 155
    defined 11
    depression and 38
    happiness and 39
    in language 177
    planning 270–4
    possibility thinking 87
    and security 203
    teaching for 11, 272–3
    Waldorf curriculum 51
Critchley, H. 144–5
cross-community understanding 35
cross-curricular experience 1–2
cross-curricular learning
    arguments for 46–7
    assessment 245–65
    assumptions 12–13
    change, uncertainty and 21
    definitions 8–11
    key issues for debate 301–3
    opportunities (case studies) 85–7
    principles 226–7
    psychology and 158–83
    research
        autoethnography 4–5
        interviews 3–4
        observations 4
        projects 2–3
    and teaching
        disappearance between
            1997-2003 53
        double-focus 78–81, 94–5

cross-curricular learning *cont.*
    effective 62–5
    hierarchical 66–8
    historical background 13–14, 49–50
    interdisciplinary 72–5, 88–9, 245, 295–7
    multi-disciplinary 70–2, 104, 245
    opportunistic 75–8, 245, 298
    single transferable subject approaches
        68–9, 228–9
    taxonomy 65–6
    theme-based 69–70, 89–94
  themes suitable for 228–44
  tokenistic 66
cross-curricular pedagogies 14, 60, 63, 184–205
cross-curricular planning 266–300
  for creativity 270–4
  inclusion and participation 268–70
  long-term 284–8
  medium-term 288–97
  model of 282–3
  powerful, personal experiences 281–2
  safe and stimulating spaces for learning
    274–8
  school democracy 267–8
  shared experiences 234–6, 269
  short-term 298–300
  subject knowledge and progression 77,
    237–8, 279–80, 281, 290
cross-curricular policy 49–83
  National Curriculum (1998-2010) 53–6
  reviews of education 56–62
  twentieth-century thinking 50–2
cross-generational learning 115
Csikszentmihalyi, M. 9, 39, 41, 118, 180, 181,
    182, 196, 239, 280, 312
cultural capital 120, 127
cultural contexts 189
culturally exclusive curriculum 17
culture(s)
  communities and 117
  creativity and overlapping of 312
  delegated to the monitor screens 27
  inclusive 122–4
  play and practice of 169
  products of human 124
  relationships between 35
  and self 36
  sensitivity to 121
  and social learning 118–20
  of surveillance 317–19
  and values 127
  see also classroom culture; intercultural
    understanding; sub-cultures
curiosity 271, 272

curriculum
  adult-dominated 2, 15
  child-centred 50
  children's lives and 2, 13
  choice 233
  competencies-based 6
  complexity of current 18
  conversations 267
  creative 87–96
  definitions 9, 17, 19
  engagement/ownership of 172
  experience orientation 6
  flexibility 56, 185, 237, 278
  narrowing of 56–7, 186
  of Plato 13
  and social change 307–8
  topic-based, project or thematic 11
  virtual 29
  Waldorf schools 51
  see also bridging curriculum; Common
    Curriculum; community curriculum;
    Curriculum for Excellence; hidden
    curriculum; International Primary
    Curriculum; National Curriculum; spiral
    curriculum
Curriculum for Excellence 54, 59, 70, 237, 247
Curriculum Guidance for the Foundation Stage
    (CGFS) 54, 169
Curriculum and Qualifications Development
    Agency (QCDA) 118
Cyberworld Fairy Story (case study) 26

Damasio, A. 36, 39, 145, 177
dance 67, 169
dangers, of new technologies 27
David, T. 169, 172
Davidson, R. 144, 172, 174
de-contextualized approaches 193, 301, 306
debate 178, 206
decision-making 139, 233, 276
declarative memory 147
deep learning 75, 86, 125, 159–60, 161, 174,
    229–30
democracy (school) 267–8
democratic approach 50
dendrites 133f, 134, 136, 138
Denmark 169
depression 18, 38, 43, 173, 305
deprivation 34
design/technology 53, 55, 67, 69, 161, 170, 268,
    285, 294
Designing and Timetabling the Primary
    Curriculum (QCA) 306
deskilling 306

Deutscher, G. 36
developed intelligence 165
developing countries 32, 303
Dewey, J. 50, 51, 202
dialogue 114, 115, 129, 150, 178, 201, 267
didactic teaching 10, 52, 58, 75, 167, 301, 303
difference(s) 124, 129, 188
digital education 320–1
direct teaching 76
disciplinary rigour 65
discipline
    defined 9–10
    see also subject disciplines
discourse 178
discovery 23
discovery days 68–9
discovery learning 52, 167
discussion 178
distributed cognition 259
distributed intelligence 159, 274
doing 51
domains of learning 9, 58, 59, 60, 312
double-focus methods 78–81, 94–5
Downsbrook Middle School 105–6
drama/performing arts 55, 59, 67, 178
drawing 170, 177
Dunbar, R. 111
Dweck, C. 130

Early Years Foundation Stage (EYFS) 60, 273
Ecclestone, C. 216
Eco-Schools programme 32, 33, 104–7, 225
economic well-being 122, 302–3
education
    in the 21st century 19–48
    assumptions about 12, 13
    commonly cited aims 211–13
    digital 320–1
    economy-driven 185, 188, 316
    and health 18
    nineteenth-century pedagogues 15–16
    relevance of current 17
    reviews of 56–62
    seventeenth- and eighteenth-century
        pioneers 14–15
    see also child-centred education; digital
        education; progressive education;
        teacher education
Education Act (2006) 117
Education Outside the Classroom 113, 125, 318
education policy 115, 121, 306, 309
Education Reform Act (1988) 52
educational psychologists 158, 167, 173, 174, 182

Ekman, P. 144, 264
elaborated codes (language) 119
electroencephalography (EEG) 145
Émile ou de l'éducation 15
emotional health 59
emotional intelligence 35, 159, 172
emotional literacy 47, 67, 155
emotional literacy programmes 35, 146
emotional security 172
emotional well-being 2
emotions
    in learning 176
    music and management of 155
    neuroscience 144–6
    readability of 248
    see also negative emotions; positive
        emotions
emotive subjects/issues 31
empowerment 18, 76, 159, 246
engagement 12–13, 44f, 55, 63, 90, 103, 107,
        172, 179, 194, 197, 248, 251, 280
    assessment of 262–4
    see also existential engagement
Engaging Places 78, 118, 126
England 43, 53, 54, 55, 61, 169, 232, 247, 304
English 53, 54, 68, 69, 75, 125, 178, 238, 285
English Heritage 118, 126
enjoyment 2, 39, 40f, 54, 67, 217, 305
Enlightenment 14
enquiry 125–6
enthusiasm 112, 272, 314
Entwistle, N. 159
environment
    beliefs about importance of 215
    influence on thinking and learning 161,
        164–6
    interest in 32, 33
    see also school environments
environmental knowledge 32
equality 114, 121–2
equipment 274
ethics 63
ethos 197, 268, 272
Europe 79, 129, 304
Every Child Matters 45
examinations 140
Excellence and Enjoyment (DfES) 54
exclusion 111, 172, 174
existential engagement 208–9
existential significance 174, 262, 314
experience(s)
    brain shaped by 153
    of childhood in twenty-first century 41–5

experience(s) *cont.*
    and learning 14–15, 52, 54, 115, 117
    planning small-scale 298
    polarization between knowledge and 51
    of rapid and global change 20–1
    see also cross-curricular experience; life
        experiences; meaningful experiences;
        powerful experiences; shared
        experiences
experiential truth 129
experimental psychologists 129
experiment(ation) 50, 129
expert partners 279
expert visitors 86–7
exploration 60, 69, 125, 169, 270, 273
exploratory talk 178

Facebook 24, 27, 31, 33, 309
facial expression 28, 264, 285
fairness 122
family relationships 34, 39
fear 187
feedback 246, 251, 259, 261
feelings 144–6, 172–6
Feldman, D. 193–4
the field 8
fieldwork 318
'fight or flight' reflexes 141–2
Fisher, R. 165
flexibility 272
    of classrooms 167, 273–4
    curricular 56, 185, 237, 278
    of good teachers 12
    pre-frontal cortex and 153
flow 179–82, 239, 261, 262
focus exercises 76, 97–101, 125, 298
following up 103–8
Forest Schools 113, 125, 169, 278, 282–3
formal learning 193
formative assessment 245–6, 247, 249–53
    see also performances of understanding
foundation subjects 53, 55, 247, 306
    see also individual subjects
Frankl, V. 174, 304
Fredrickson, B. 39, 174
Free Schools 21, 61, 117, 196, 221, 233, 306,
    319
Freire, P. 115, 117, 184–5, 193, 202
Freud, S. 174, 202–3
friendships 113–14
Froebel, F. 16, 115, 202
frontal lobes 136
    see also pre-frontal cortex

fulfilment 23, 209
functional magnetic resonance imaging (fMRI)
    131, 145, 149
Furedi, F. 216
furniture (classroom) 167
Future Creative 3, 118
futures education 22
the future
    preparing for an uncertain 21–3
    security about 46–7

Gardner, H. 6, 118–19, 151–3, 159, 193
gender 22, 24
genetic influences 165
geographical knowledge 32
geography 53, 54, 55, 59, 66, 67, 69, 75, 170,
    241–2, 268, 285
Giedd, J. 138
global issues 315–17
    assessment questions 252t
    supporting children's interest in 30–3
    teacher understanding of 226–7
global rights-based curriculum 234
global-school partnerships 316
globalization 303
Gogtay, N. 149
Goleman, D. 35, 111, 159
A Good Childhood 172
Goswami, U. 111
Great Debate 52
The Great Didactic 14
Greenfield, S. 27, 36, 135
Grosvenor, I. 43
group, importance of 50
group work 52, 114, 159, 188, 310, 319
Gruzelier, J. 155

Hadow Report (1931) 51
Halpin, D. 202, 203
happiness 2, 38, 39, 42f, 55, 145, 146, 248
hard-to-reach 116, 318
'hard-wired' neural connections 139, 149, 199
Haringey Lullabies Project 88–9
Hayes, D. 216
Head, shoulders, knees and toes (case study) 68
health 304
    and education 18
    effect of change on teachers' 61
    emotional 59
    inequalities 41
    negative emotions and 175
Health Behaviour in School Aged Children
    (HBSC) 304

Healthy Schools campaign 55
here and now 2, 36, 63, 185, 202
heredity 161, 164–5
Hicks, D. 22
hidden curriculum 9, 200
hierarchical cross-curricular methods 66–8
hierarchy of needs (Maslow's) 302, 303
Higher Education Arts and Schools (HEARTS)
    projects 3, 190–1, 202, 279, 313–14
hippocampus 142, 147, 149, 154
Hirsch, E. 6, 216
Historic Scotland 118, 126
history 53, 54, 55, 59, 69, 75, 170, 238, 242–3,
    268, 285, 294
Hoffer, E. 17
home computers 23–4
hot seating 178
human rights policy 56
humour 272
Hythe project 275–6

idealism 222–3
identity 36, 115, 166
Illich, I. 192–3, 200, 247
imagination 51, 169, 273
imitation 193
immune system 143
impulse control 139
inclusion 35, 111, 122–4, 174, 268–70
inclusive schools 200
independence 26, 272
independent learners 178
independent schools 21, 196, 284, 319
The Index for Inclusion 122–4, 200, 210, 234, 247
individuality 23, 114
individualized assessment 245–6
informal learning 169
information and communications
    technology (ICT)
  cross-curricular presentations 80
  as curriculum subject 53, 62, 67, 247, 306
  harnessing children's interest in 23–30
  individualized education 320–1
  planning 286
Initial Teacher Education (ITE) 117, 119,
    192, 217
innate wisdom 51
inspection 21, 53, 55, 57, 90, 117
Instagram 25
integration 87
intellect 155
intelligence
  assumption/view of 12
  dimensions of children's 165

intelligence *cont.*
  environment and 153
  psychology and new concepts of 159
  triarchic theory of 162–3
  see also distributed intelligence; emotional
      intelligence; multiple intelligences;
      social intelligence
intelligence quotient (IQ) tests 163
intelligence styles 122
intelligent behaviour 134
intelligent toys 28
interactionism 111
interactive cyber toys 28
intercultural understanding 35
interdisciplinary approaches 72–5, 88–9, 245,
    295–7
intergenerational dialogue 115
International Primary Curriculum (IPC) 87,
    232–3, 247
internet campaigns 31, 32
internet use 24–5, 27, 29f
interpersonal learning 235
intrinsic motivation 168, 239
intrinsic values 130
intuition 144, 169
invention 36, 169
involvement 63, 181, 182, 187,
    229, 280
iPlayer 27
irreverence 169
Isaacs, S. 52, 115, 202
isolation 305

James, M. 169
Japan 23
Jensen, E. 159
John-Steiner, V. 111, 159
Journey in dance (case study) 71–2
joy 39, 40, 145, 195
    see also enjoyment
judicial thinkers 162
Jung, C. 174

Kelly, B. 276
key questions (planning) 289–90
Khul, P. 176
kindergartens 16, 282–3
knowing 51
knowledge
  creation 50
  emphasis on essential 115–16
  geographical and environmental 32
  objects and active use of 124
  polarization between experience and 51

knowledge *cont.*
  thirst for 272
  understandings about 217–19
  see also professional knowledge; subject
      knowledge; teacher knowledge;
      worthwhile knowledge
knowledgeable outsiders 279–80
Koestler, A. 87, 196

Labour government 56
Laevers, F. 103, 179, 181, 229, 248, 262–4
language
  cross-curricular work and 80
  impact of culture 119
  inclusion/exclusion through 111
  music and 141, 155
  psychology, children and 176–9
  and self 36
  see also body language; modern foreign
      languages; vocabulary
language development 176, 177
language instinct 176
language of learning 166, 178
laughter 169
Lave, J. 111, 164
Lawthorn Primary School 106–7
league tables 21, 53, 54, 113
learnable intelligence 159
learners
  beliefs about individual 215
  see also co-learners; independent learners
learning
  application of new 80
  assessment promoting 246
  assumptions about 12
  beliefs about 213–17
  defined 10–11
  disciplinary 9
  experience-led 14–15, 52, 54, 115, 117
  language of 178
  memory and neuroscience 148–51
  neuroscientific view 130–1
  planning improvement in 286–7
  planning research in 287–8
  positive emotion and 39
  social perspectives on 110–27
  stage theory 16–17
  support 34
  see also cross-curricular learning; deep
      learning; lifelong learning; transferable
      learning
learning difficulties 131
learning groups 114–16, 159
learning intentions 249

learning spaces, planning for safe 274–8
learning styles 189
left hemisphere 136, 137
left-brain dominance 154
lesson objectives 238
Leuven Involvement Scale 103, 179, 263
Leuven Well-Being Scale 248
liberating curriculum 203
life expectancy 41
life experiences 38, 121
life satisfaction 38, 43
lifelong learning 17, 38
limbic system 143, 147
literacy 59, 67, 270, 306
litigation 317–19
localities 124–5
Locke, J. 15
locus of control 45, 201
lone scientist 52
long-term planning 284–8
longevity 175
love of learning 187
Lucas, B. 178

McGilchrist, I. 136–7, 154, 159
Macmillan, R. 52
Macpherson Report 174
Maintaining Breadth and Balance
    (QCA) 306
Makiguchi 23, 210
Malaguzzi, L. 202
Man: a Course of Study 112
marginalization 13
Marmot Review 38, 119
Marton, F. 159
Marxism 111
Maslow, A. 302, 303f
mastery 194
mathematics 53, 54, 66, 67, 68, 69, 75, 125, 141,
    155, 161, 178, 192, 238
maturing brain 137–41, 224
meaning-making 166, 209, 305
meaningful connections 229–30
meaningful experiences 10, 79–80, 97, 188
meaningful learning 167
meaningful projects 230–1
meaninglessness 304
medium-term planning 288–97
memory 145, 147–51, 153, 154, 177, 180, 235
mental activity, environment and 155
mental illness 173
metacognition 161, 178, 286
metacognitive learning 178
Millennium Goals (UN) 32, 225, 226

mind 132
 see also body-mind
Mind Mapping® 160
mindsets 130, 175
Mindware 124, 160
mission statements 207
mistakes 172, 251
mobile phones 26, 27, 29, 30, 32
modern foreign languages (MFL) 53, 66, 69, 75, 185, 294
modern studies 54
monarchic thinkers 162
monitor screens 27
Montessori, M. 52, 202
moral choices 37
more knowledgeable others 17
Morris, D. 39
motivation 2, 67, 168, 187–8, 239, 302–5
Movement Haikus (case study) 75
multi-disciplinary approaches 70–2, 104, 245
multi-sensory approaches 151
multiple intelligences 151–3
muscle memory 147
music 13
 as curriculum subject 53, 59, 67, 285
 fusion of knowledge and skills 73
 interdisciplinary approach (case study) 88–9
 relationship between mathematics, language and 141, 155
musicians 154
myelin sheath 134, 139

Nachmanovitch, S. 311
National Advisory Council on Creative and Cultural Education (NACCCE) 54–5, 249, 311
National Curriculum 52, 60, 118 (1989-2010) 53–6
 attainment targets 290
 changes 306
 emphasis on essential knowledge 115–16
 flexibility 185, 237
 planning 284–5
 revised primary, for England 61
National Curriculum Primary Handbook 58
National Forum for Values in Education and the Community 209
National Literacy Strategy (NLS) 53
National Numeracy Strategy (NNS) 53
National Society for the Prevention of Cruelty to Children (NSPCC) 34
National Strategies 57
nature 14, 15
nature-nurture debate 153
near infra-red spectroscopy (NIRS) 131

negative attitudes 141, 163
negative emotions 175
negative experiences 38, 175
negative influences 40
negative memories 148
neo-cortex *see* frontal lobes
neural connections 132, 134, 135–6, 137, 138, 139, 143, 144, 149, 199, 201
neural networks 134–5, 139
neural plasticity 130, 154–5, 159
neuro-feedback 145, 146f, 155
neurons 132, 133f, 134, 138
neuroscience 128–57
 brain scans 131–2
 emotions and feelings 144–6
 maturing brain 137–41
 memory 147–8
 multiple intelligences 151–3
 school environments 153–5
 school learning, memory and 148–51
 social nature of learning 111
 stress 141–4
 thinking 132–7
 view on learning 130–1
neurotransmitters 39, 134
New Curriculum (BC) 61–2
new technologies 27, 29, 32, 46f, 286
A New Direction 118
Newsround 31
nineteenth-century pedagogues 15–16
noble savage 14, 45
Noddings, N. 111, 112
non-core subjects 55
non-specialist primary teachers 77
Northern Ireland 21, 54, 61, 169, 232
Northern Ireland Environment Agency (NIEA) 118, 126
novice teachers 71, 77, 112, 207
number, application of 285–6
numeracy 67, 270, 306

objects 124, 126, 235
OECD Report (2009) 172
Ofsted 54, 55, 57, 74, 90, 170, 247, 269–70, 298, 306, 311
oligarchic thinkers 162
Opening Minds (RSA) 6, 87, 247
opportunistic approaches 75–8, 245, 298
optimism 208, 223
oracy 59
originality 273
others
 assessing understanding of 252t
 role of, in learning 111

others *cont.*
    see also more knowledgeable others;
        working with others
outcomes (ECM) 45
outdoor learning 278, 318
'outside the context' learning 193
outside-school focus exercises 97–101

paired learning 114
Palmer, S. 216
parental empowerment 18
participation 63, 67, 123–4, 188, 232, 234, 263,
    268–70
partnerships *see* Creative Partnerships; global-
    school partnerships; school-community
    partnerships
pathologization 129, 131
Peal, R. 216
pedagogical skills 64–5, 272
pedagogies
    pupil voice 56
    see also cross-curricular pedagogies;
        Signature Pedagogies
pedagogues, nineteenth-century 15–16
peer assessment 246, 257, 258–9
peer group 112
peer relationships 34
Penair School 105
performance
    planning improvement in 286–7
    planning opportunities for 299
    see also drama/performing arts
performances of understanding 240, 253–8,
    294–5
Perkins, D. 12, 124, 125, 149, 159, 160, 195,
    199, 206, 259, 294
personal histories 235
Personal Learning and Thinking Skills (PLTS) 61
personal significance 229
personal, social and health education
    (PSHE) 13, 22, 35, 53, 55, 68, 69, 268,
    306, 310
personalized language of learning 166
Pestalozzi, J. 16, 202
Peterborough Project (RSA) 104
Philosophy for Children (P4C) 36
physical education (PE) 13, 14, 40, 53, 55, 67,
    69, 285, 294
physical experiences 235
physical play 40
physical wellbeing 143, 302–3
Piaget, J. 15, 16–17, 52, 169, 172
Pinker, S. 111, 165, 166, 176
Pintrest 25

places 32, 125–6
planning *see* cross-curricular planning
Plato 13, 14
play 60, 270, 273
    importance of 16
    psychology 169–72
    sense of self 40
    see also role play
'playing the whole game' 195
Plowden Report (1967) 51–2, 230
political demands 41
Pollard, A. 63–4, 111, 169, 186
Pope, R. 311–12
Popenici, S. 35
Popper, K. 124
positive attitudes 169, 222
positive emotional stimuli 148
positive emotions 38, 39, 141, 174–5
positive experiences 121, 168
positive learning dispositions 188–9
positive mindset 175
positive psychologists 39, 174
positive self-image 47
positive sense of self 35–41
positron emission tomography (PET) 131, 143f,
    144, 145
possibility thinking 87
Potts, P. 124
poverty 34, 38, 41, 304
power relationships 169, 309–10, 316
powerful experience(s), planning 281–2,
    290–2
powers (Secretary of State) 61
pre-frontal cortex 139, 147, 153
preferred thinking styles 162, 163, 189
presentations 80, 258–9, 261
Primary National Strategy 53
primary teachers, non-specialist 77
Prince's Trust 305
privacy 26
problem-solving 50, 159–60, 178
Processes of the Arts 258
'production line' techniques 114, 159
professional knowledge 173
progression, planning 77, 237–8, 280–1, 290
progressive education 51, 121, 202, 216
project work 230–1
project-based curriculum 11, 250
psycho-babble 150
psychological well-being, motivation and
    304–5
psychology 158–83
    children and flow 179–82
    children and language 176–9

psychology *cont.*
  children's feelings 172–6
  and learning 201
  play 169–72
  thinking 160–4
  thinking classrooms 164–8
pupil representatives 233
pupil voice 43, 56, 77, 112, 188, 210, 313
purposeful activity 51
Putnam, D. 32

Qualifications and Curriculum Agency (QCA)
    54, 306
Qualified Teacher Status (QTS) 55, 192, 196
quality learning 149, 151
questioning 272, 273

raising standards 57, 155
reciprocity 160
reflection 115, 160, 199
reflexivity 121, 230, 262
Reggio Emilia schools 274–5, 282–3
Regional Schools Commissioners 61
relationships
  with adults 115
  between creativity and happiness/
      enjoyment 39
  children as partners in 111–12
  cross-curricular learning and 47
  fostering of social and global 23
  and learning 167
  negative emotions and 175
  recognizing the importance of 33–5
  see also power relationships
relevance 2, 17, 22, 63, 67, 112, 187, 197
religious education (RE) 53, 69, 242, 247, 268,
    285, 306
religious justification, for education 16
repetition 149
research, planning 287–8
research-informed approaches 63
resilience 38, 160
resourcefulness 160
respect 187, 268
responsibility 51, 188, 268, 272, 305
restricted codes (language) 119
right hemisphere 136, 137
right-brain dominance 154
risk assessments 318
risk-taking 169, 273
risky behaviour 43
Robertson, I. 153, 159
Robinson, K. 159
RoboSapien 28

Rogoff, B. 111, 114, 120, 159
role models 27–8, 34
role play 178, 188, 310
Romania 35
Room 13 (case study) 80–1
Rose review 7, 21, 56–8, 114
Rousseau, J.-J. 14–15, 115, 202
'Ruskin College' speech 52

safety 317–18
Salovey, P. 172
Saron, C. 172
satisfaction 38, 39, 40, 43, 67, 195
scaffolding 17, 111
schemes of work 54, 306
school buildings 124–5
school councils 233
school curriculum 21
school democracy 267–8
school environments 153–5
school readiness 273
school self-assessments/evaluation 55, 200
school visits 55, 63, 118, 318
School-centred initial teacher training
    (SKITT) 61
school-community partnerships 21, 63, 87, 185
schooling *see* education
schools
  changing role of 319–21
  competition between 113
  creative 74–5
  social work/therapeutic roles 121
  statement of principles 226
  use of ICT in 28–9
  see also academies; Forest Schools; free
      schools; inclusive schools; independent
      schools; Reggio Emilia schools; *Soka*
      schools; Steiner/Waldorf schools;
      Teaching Schools
Schools Direct 21, 61, 77
Schools of Hope 203
  The School I'd Like 43
science 53, 67, 69, 75, 161, 238, 241, 268, 285,
    306, 307
  language in 177
Scoffham, S. 119
Scotland 21, 54, 59, 61, 70, 106–7, 169, 232,
    247, 304
Secretary of State for Education 61
security 38, 39, 46–7, 141, 172, 202
self, observation from a different perspective
    119–20
self-actualization 23, 209, 303, 305
self-assessments 55, 246, 259–62

self-awareness 153
self-confidence 161, 203
self-consciousness 35–6, 132
self-control 153, 188, 314
self-developed intelligence 165
self-directed activity 310
self-efficacy 23, 38, 159, 175
self-esteem 2, 169, 188, 273, 303, 305
self-harm 43
self-image 47, 273
self-reliance 203
self-talk 36, 246
self-understanding 252t
selfhood 51
selfish capitalism 121
Seligman, M. 39, 174
sense of control 2, 47
sense making 178
sense of self 35–41
sex education 53
shared experiences, planning 234–6, 269
shared meaning 209
shared values 117, 122, 207–8, 323f
Shayer, M. 159, 161
short-term planning 298–300
sicherheit 202–3
Signature Pedagogies 74, 118, 269
Sing Up 113
single transferable subject approaches 68–9,
    228–9
situated learning 164, 167
Six Thinking Hats® 160
Sluyter, D. 172
smoking 43
sociability 110
social capital 120, 126–7, 201
social change 308
social context 52
Social, Emotional Aspects of Learning
    (SEAL) 55, 233
social, emotional and behavioural (SEB)
    skills 188
social intelligence 23, 159, 172
social learning 112–20
    with the teacher 188–91
    values and understanding of 111
social learning theory 111
social networking 24, 25, 27, 33, 309
social polarization 34, 35
social reconstruction 111, 121
social skills 169, 188
social subjects 54
social values 112, 120, 130
socialization 119, 122

socio-political ideas, about learning
    120–1
Soka schools 23, 210
special educational needs 79
speculation 273
Speech Bubbles (case study) 116
Spinoza 145
spiral curriculum 112
sports 40
staff development 2, 61, 220–2, 268
stage theory (Piaget) 16–17, 52
standards 55, 57, 155, 192, 196, 306
statement of principles 226
statement of values 209
Statutory Framework for the Early Years
    Foundation Stage 60, 282–3
Steiner, R. 50, 51, 115, 202
Steiner/Waldorf schools 51, 233
Sternberg, R. 12, 87, 122, 159, 162–3
Storyline® 54
stress 38, 61, 140, 141–4
Strong, R. 17
sub-cultures 35, 119, 120, 169
subject boundaries 6, 54, 63, 236, 274
subject disciplines 6
    assessment questions 252t
    beliefs about 215
subject divisions 51, 54
subject knowledge 6, 63, 67, 75, 76, 90, 193,
    194, 195
    fusion of skills and 73, 295
    planning 237–8, 279–80, 292–3
subject parity 54, 55, 269
subject skills 6, 90, 193
    fusion of knowledge and 73, 295
    planning 237–8, 279–80, 292–3
subject-based curriculum 51, 56
subject-based teaching 58, 303
subject-specific weeks 68–9
subjects
    choosing for understanding 236–7
    focus on traditional 58
    limiting 229, 288–9
    making connections between 72–3, 75, 87
    timing allocations between 284
    see also individual subjects
subversive behaviour 169
suicide 43
summative assessment 264
Sure Start 34
surveillance culture 317–19
suspicion 34–5
sustainability 33
synapses 134, 136

Teach First 21, 61
teacher education 2, 21, 36, 55, 61, 77
    see also Initial Teacher Education
teacher knowledge 71, 86, 173, 321
    see also subject knowledge
teacher as learner 190–1
teacher well-being 61, 220
teachers
    as action researchers 287
    analytical 122
    assumption of creative potential 12
    effective/good 79, 192–3, 195, 199–200,
        310, 322
    retention rates 306
    as role models 27–8
    sensitivity to cultures 121
    social learning with 188–91
    speed of change and health of 61
    status 186
    understanding
        of child's world 192
        of global issues 226–7
        of neuroscience 150
        of preferred thinking styles 162
    see also Advanced Skills Teachers; creative
        teachers; novice teachers; primary
        teachers; trainee teachers
Teachers' Guide to ... series 126
teaching
    attitudes to 219–22
    for creativity 11, 272–3
    defined 10
    delivery model 185
    fashions in 159
    flexible 12
    planning research in 287–8
    roles 194–5
    styles 12, 189, 197, 220
    see also creative teaching; cross-curricular
        learning, and teaching
Teaching Schools 21, 77, 221
teaching for understanding 160
technology *see* design/technology; information
    and communications technology; new
    technologies
teenagers 43, 210
television 27, 29, 31, 32
theme-based approaches 11, 51, 69–70, 89–94,
    228–44, 250, 312
theta brainwaves 155
thinking
    barriers to 198–202
    defined 10
    education and generation of 12

thinking *cont.*
    language of 179
    neuroscience 132–7
    psychology 160–4
    see also abstract thinking; creative thinking
thinking classrooms 164–8
thinking partners 188
thinking skills 54, 55
thinking styles 162, 163, 189
Thomson, P. 74
thought-action repertoire 174
Tickell Review (2011) 60
time 2
timetables 30–1
tokenistic approaches 66
tolerance 268
tolerance of difference 188
topic work *see* project work
topographical memory 154
toys 28
TRACK project 3
trainee teachers 55, 122, 201–2, 313
transferable learning 38, 39, 75, 86, 125, 159,
    160, 172, 230
transitions 307
triarchic theory of intelligence 162–3
Troops to Teachers 61
trust 117
truth(s) 129
Twitter 31, 33, 309

underachievement 172
understanding(s)
    about knowledge 217–19
    application of new learning 80
    assessment questions 252t
    choosing subjects that add 236–7
    disciplinary 9
    expert-like 124
    intercultural 35
    see also performances of understanding;
        teaching for understanding
UNICEF 34, 43
unique environment 165–6, 168
United Kingdom 22, 38, 41–3, 56, 121, 173,
    185, 306
    see also England; Northern Ireland; Scotland;
        Wales
United Nations Convention on the Rights of the
    Child (UNCRC) 45, 56, 76–7, 121, 232, 267–8
United Nations Development Goals 32, 225, 226
United States 22, 24, 27, 29f, 38, 43, 46f, 79,
    121, 129, 173, 185, 304, 306
unmediated learning 193

value judgements 120
values 206–27
    cross-curricular pedagogies 14
    culture and 127
    discussion of 267
    ICT use and 30
    and planning 300
    political demands and 41
    re-evaluation of old-fashioned 202–3
    schooling and 19
    shared 323f
    social polarization and gulf between 35
    squeezed out of the curriculum 23
    and understanding of social learning 111
    see also British values; intrinsic values;
        shared values; social values
values environment 154
Varela, Francisco 143
virtual curricula 29
vocabulary 149, 299
voice *see* pupil voice
Vygotsky, L. 17, 52, 111

Waldorf curriculum 51
Wales 53, 61, 169, 232, 304
wealth 43
Web 2.0 technologies 29

well-being
    creativity and 313
    motivation and 302–5
    positive engagement and 175
    stress and 143
    teacher's contribution to other's 321–2
    see also child well-being; economic well-
        being; emotional well-being; teacher
        well-being
Wenger, E. 111, 115, 117, 164
West Rise Junior School's marsh project 89–92
Western education, 'production line'
    techniques 114, 159
Wii technology 29
Wiliam, D. 249
working memory 147, 153, 177
working with others 252t, 286
World Health Organization (WHO) 24, 43
worlds (human) 124
worthwhile knowledge 149, 185
wow experiences *see* meaningful experiences
Wrigley, T. 203

Youth Music 88–9, 113
YouTube 25

Zone of Proximal Development 111